PROMISE AND FULFILMENT PALESTINE
1917-1949

PROMISE AND FULFILMENT

Palestine 1917-1949

Books by Arthur Koestler

PROMISE AND FULFILMENT

Palestine 1917–1949

BY

ARTHUR KOESTLER

NEW YORK

THE MACMILLAN COMPANY

1949

TO
ABRAM AND JASHA WEINSHALL
CITIZENS OF ISRAEL
AS A TOKEN OF A QUARTER-CENTURY
OF FRIENDSHIP

ACKNOWLEDGMENTS

MY sincere thanks are due to : R. H. S. Crossman,
M.P., and Messrs. Hamish Hamilton, for permission
to use the long extract (pp. 102-7) from Crossman's
Palestine Mission ; to a member of the Israeli Foreign
Office, who wishes to remain anonymous, for permission to print his " Report from Jerusalem "
(pp. 234-8) ; to Mr. George Pape, Librarian of the
Public Information Office in Tel Aviv, and Dr.
G. Pollack of the Israeli Ministry of Finance, for
valuable research work ; and to Miss Daphne Wood-
ward, for helping with the proofs.

A. K.

PREFACE

I

THIS book consists of three parts, " Background ", " Close-up " and " Perspective ". The first part is a survey of the developments which led to the foundation of the State of Israel. It lays no claim to historical completeness, and is written from a specific angle which stresses the part played by irrational forces and emotive bias in history. I am not sure whether this emphasis has not occasionally resulted in over-emphasis — as is almost inevitable when one tries to redress a balance by spot-lighting aspects which are currently neglected. But it was certainly not my intention, by underlining the psychological factor, to deny or minimize the importance of the politico-economic forces. My aim was rather to present, if I may borrow a current medical term, a " psycho-somatic " view of one of the most curious episodes in modern history.

The second part, " Close-up ", is meant to give the reader a close and coloured, but not I hope technicoloured, view of the Jewish war and of everyday life in the new State. It opens and ends with extracts from the diary of my last sojourn as a war correspondent in Israel. The emphasis here is on life in the towns, with only occasional glimpses of the collective settlements, since I have given a detailed description of these in an earlier book.

The third part, " Perspective ", is an attempt to present to the reader a comprehensive survey of the social and political structure, the cultural trends and future prospects of the Jewish State.

2

I have tried to show elsewhere that the creative processes of the artist and the scientist follow the same mental pattern, and that the sciences may legitimately be called " neutral arts ", separated from the " emotive arts " not by any distinct barrier but merely by the quality of our emotive reactions. In this sense history, too, is a " neutral art " — with mythology and bardic folklore as connecting links to the " emotive arts " of drama and fiction. But the emotive neutrality which should characterize the chronicler is not the same thing as indifference, and his object-ivity can only be the result of a subjective passion for the pursuit of truth. It is a poor sort of impartiality which stands outside the parties, untouched by their emotions ; the good judge, like the playwright and historian, absorbs the subjective truth con-tained in each of the conflicting pleas, and his verdict is a syn-thesis of their part-truths, not their denial. In other words, " objectivity " is a state of balanced emotions, not an emotive vacuum.

This book, then, should be regarded as a subjective pursuit of the objective truth. I lived in Palestine from my twentieth to my twenty-third year, as a farmer, tramp, and on various odd jobs ; finally as a foreign correspondent. I have since revisited the country at fairly regular intervals, and each of these visits provided an occasion not only to study developments in the country, but also my personal attitude to it. The last phase of this pilgrim's progress through a thicket of emotive and ideo-logical entanglements is summed up in the Epilogue. It may also be read as a prologue, and serve as an indication of the point of view from which certain controversial problems are treated in this book.

3

Leaving controversial issues aside, the first and main purpose of this book may be summed up by a phrase of Laplace : " If we were able to make an exact catalogue of all particles and forces which are active in a speck of dust, the laws of the universe at large would hold no more mysteries for us ".

On a medium-sized school globe the State of Israel occupies not much more space than a speck of dust ; and yet there is hardly a political, social or cultural problem whose prototype cannot be found in it, and found in a rare concentration and intensity. The very smallness of this country of about three-quarters of a million souls makes it easy to survey trends which in other nations appear confused and diluted by size. The fact that it so often was in the past, and is again in the present, in the focus of global conflicts and passions, makes the speck of dust glow in a phosphorescent light. The fact that it is a State of Jews, and of Jews of the most conscious and intense type, makes the microscopic processes in this microscopic country reflect laws of universal validity : for Jewry is not a question of race — " it is the human condition carried to its extreme ".

Israel's rebirth as a nation after two thousand years is a freak phenomenon of history. But in all the branches of science the observation of freak phenomena yields important clues to general laws. Dwarf stars and human giants, radioactivity and partheno-genesis, prophets, maniacs and saints are all freaks which carry the conditions of normality to a pointed and profiled extreme. So does this race of eternal victims with its flayed skin and exposed nerves, which demonstrates, with the horrible precision of an anatomic atlas, a condition of man otherwise mercifully hidden from us.

This book, then, is not about the Jewish race and the country of Israel as such, but that country and its people are regarded here as a specimen of humanity to be examined under the social microscope. Some of the reasons why this specimen is so par-ticularly fit to yield to the observer results of general interest have just been explained. Whatever else the State of Israel may be, it has come to signify to me a country more transparent than any other to the basic archetypes of human conflict and experience. For Israel is merely reproducing to-day a very old drama in modern costume — while, in the scorching light of the Judean hills, eternity looks on through the window of time.

TEL AVIV – CHARTRETTES
August 1948 - *January* 1949

CONTENTS

xi

PART TWO

SUSPENSE (1939-1945)

PART THREE

THE BIRTH-PANGS (1945-1948)

BOOK TWO: CLOSE-UP

BOOK THREE: PERSPECTIVE

BOOK ONE

BACKGROUND

" For I never knew so young a body with so old a head "—The Merchant of Venice.

PART ONE

CONCEPTION AND GESTATION

(1917–1939)

CHAPTER I

ROMANTICS AND ROUTINE

Jewry as a freak of history — Freak character of the
Balfour Declaration — Its motives: the subjective factor in
history — Its meaning: an exercise in applied semantics
— What is a "national home"? — The romantic and the
trivial planes of History: Prophets versus Civil Servants

I

ISRAEL, then, is a freak of history. When writing about the
events, past and present, which led to the resurrection of the
Jewish State, adjectives like "unique" and "unprecedented"
are difficult to avoid. But "unique" is a tiresome adjective,
probably because it refers to an experience which can be fitted
into no general scheme and has no claim to general validity. On
the other hand, freak phenomena are merely the extreme exten-
sions of normality. Thus the peculiarities of the Jewish character,
that apparently unique blend of pride and humbleness, spirit-
uality and cupidity, inferiority complex and over-compensation,
calculated cunning and dripping sentimentality, could probably
be induced by a team of determined psychiatrists in any community kept for no more than a couple of generations under hot-
house conditions approximating those of the Polish ghettoes.

The Jewish neurosis is an extreme response to an extreme
"stimulus of penalizations" to use Professor Toynbee's expression; like symptoms can be found in the Parsees in India, the
Armenians in Turkey and in any orphanage or institution for
problem children.[1] Similarly, the mystical attachment of the
Jews to their ancient country must be regarded as an extreme case
of the homesickness of expatriate communities, mixed with mankind's archaic yearning for a lost paradise, for a mythological
Golden Age, which is at the root of all utopias — from Spartacus'
Sun State to Herzl's Zionism. And finally, anti-semitism is merely
a specific form of xenophobia determined by religious, social and

---

[1] Cf. the oriental proverb about one Greek being worse than ten Jews, and
one Armenian worse than ten Greeks.

3

economic factors. Thus analysed down into its prime factors, the Jewish fate seems no longer unique. It is nevertheless unique in the sense that it displays certain human tendencies in an unprecedented concentration, and carries human destiny to unheard-of extremes. For, after all, there is no other example in history of a community which has been chased round the globe quite as much, which has survived its own death as a nation by two thousand years, and which, in between *autos-da-fé* and gas chambers, kept praying at the proper season for rain to fall in a country on which they have never set eyes, and drinking toasts to " Next year in Jerusalem " during the same astronomical stretch of time, with the same untiring trust in the supernatural.

To put it in a different way : we know that at some point quantity changes into quality, and the " very rare " into the " unique ". According to the teachings of the quantum theory, if a golf ball were suddenly to start off towards the hole without being hit, this would not constitute a miracle but merely what is called a " statistically highly improbable event ". In the same way the rebirth of Israel is not a miracle, but it is, there is no getting around it, a " statistically highly improbable event ".

Now an improbable event is bound to lead to further improbable events, until the area of the disturbance gradually returns to normality. The ball which started rolling towards the hole on its own upsets the routine of the whole tournament. The appearance of the freak-movement of Zionism on the political scene was bound to produce a series of freak-reactions. It culminated in the famous Balfour Declaration, one of the most improbable political documents of all time. In this document one nation solemnly promised to a second nation the country of a third.

No second thoughts can diminish the originality of this procedure. It is true that the Arabs in Palestine lived under Turkish overlordship ; but they had been living there for centuries, and the country was no doubt " theirs " in the generally accepted sense of the word. It is true that the Arabs had vast underpopulated territories at their disposal and the Jews had none ; that the Arabs were a backward, the Jews a forward, people ; and that the latter claimed to have received that country three thousand years earlier from God himself who had only temporarily withdrawn it from them. But arguments of this nature had never before in history induced an act of State of a comparable kind.

The Balfour Declaration was in due time endorsed by the League of Nations, which charged Great Britain to carry out her promise by acting as a Mandatory Power under international supervision. In plain language this meant that the League requisitioned Palestine from its owners to provide the Jews with a permanent abode, and appointed Britain to act as billeting officer.

It is of particular importance to bear in mind the freak-character of this whole series of events, for it is the key to the understanding of all that followed. It was unprecedented that a race should lose its country, and hence its physical nationhood, and yet preserve its identity through two millenniums. It was unprecedented that the " fossilized society " (to borrow another of Professor Toynbee's terms) of Jews, immured in a hostile environment, should reawaken to national consciousness and produce a modern political movement, like green shoots breaking from a petrified forest. It was unprecedented that fifty-two nations should agree to create for a fifty-third a " National Home ". And lastly, the term " National Home " itself was a complete novelty, a term with a curiously sentimental ring, undefined by international law and yet the object of an international treaty of far-reaching importance.

Any departmental head in any foreign ministry in the world could have foretold that to embark on such an entirely unorthodox and romantic experiment meant asking for no end of trouble. And to crown the amateurishness of the whole thing, the Mandate contained two obviously contradictory promises made in one breath: the establishment of a National Home for Jews in an Arab country, but without prejudice to the rights of the Arabs.

2

There exists a voluminous literature discussing from all possible angles the exact meaning of the Balfour Declaration and the motives which prompted the Lloyd George Cabinet of 1917 to issue it. Both questions are of more than technical interest, for they show in rare concentration the importance of what one may call the subjective factor in history — as distinct from the objective, social-economics factors which historic materialism claims to be alone operative.

Regarding the motives which led to the launching of this

extraordinary document, we have the testimony of Mr. Lloyd George himself.[1]

> " In the evidence he gave before us, Mr. Lloyd George, who was Prime Minister at that time, stated that, while the Zionist cause had been widely supported in Britain and America before November 1917, the launching of the Balfour Declaration at that time was ' due to propagandist reasons ' ; and he outlined the serious position in which the Allied and Associated Powers then were. The Rumanians had been crushed. The Russian Army was demoralized. The French Army was unable at the moment to take the offensive on a large scale. The Italians had sustained a great defeat at Caporetto. Millions of tons of British shipping had been sunk by German submarines. No American divisions were yet available in the trenches. In this critical situation it was believed that Jewish sympathy or the reverse would make a substantial difference one way or the other to the Allied cause. In particular Jewish sympathy would confirm the support of the American Jewry, and would make it more difficult for Germany to reduce her military commitments and improve her economic position on the Eastern front."

The Zionist leaders, according to Lloyd George's evidence, promised " to do their best to rally Jewish sentiment and support throughout the world to the Allied cause. They kept their word." [2]

It was an honest deal. On the face of it it looks as if it had been a cynical deal. In fact the opposite is true ; if the deal is to be qualified at all, it was a romantically sentimental, and not a cynical one. The men responsible for it, such as Lloyd George, Lord Balfour, President Wilson, General Smuts, were Bible lovers. They were profoundly attracted by the Old Testamentarian echoes which the Zionist movement carried ; and they had historic imagination. If one reads Lloyd George's evidence carefully, one is led to suspect that he deliberately overstates the opportunistic motivations of the Balfour Declaration — as if trying to cover up the romantic impulses behind it. Never in history has the British Empire committed itself to an action of similar grandeur " for propagandist reasons ". The phrase sounds like an excuse, a rationalization, of an act dangerously outside the

---

[1] Palestine Royal Commission Report, H.M. Stationery Office, London, 1937, p. 17. (The page numbers refer throughout to the 1946 reprint.)
[2] *Ibid.* p. 17.

cautious routine of diplomacy. The whole thing was unorthodox, unpolitic, freakish. For one glorious moment the British War Cabinet assumed the role of messianic providence. Politics was lifted from the trivial to the romantic plane.

3

That moment did not last long. Civil servants, colonial officers, military administrators are not at home on the romantic plane. The Balfour Declaration was a statement of poetic inspiration; translated into administrative prose it sounded bewildering and impracticable. The wording of the document itself already betrayed a considerable uneasiness on the part of its authors. Why the curious expression " National Home ", whose vagueness was bound to lead to endless complications and disputes ? The Royal Commission comments :

> " We have been permitted to examine the records which bear upon the question and it is clear to us that the words ' the establishment in Palestine of a National Home ' were the outcome of a compromise between those Ministers who contemplated the ultimate establishment of a Jewish State and those who did not." [1]

An ambiguous diplomatic phrase based on a compromise of this type is called in French a " nègre blanc ". The concept of a National Home was, from its beginning, a white negro. It was a logical misfit and an administrative absurdity. It could be made to appear white or black according to the political constellation of the moment, for nobody knew what it really meant. To General Smuts, who had been a member of the Imperial War Cabinet at the time when the Declaration was launched, the national home meant " in generations to come a great Jewish state rising there once more ".[2] To Mr. Winston Churchill it meant something quite different :

> " When it is asked, what is meant by the development of a Jewish National Home in Palestine, it may be answered that it is not the imposition of a Jewish nationality upon the inhabitants of Palestine as a whole, but the further development of the existing Jewish Community . . . in order that it may become

---

[1] Royal Commission Report, p. 18.   [2] *Ibid.* p. 18.

a centre in which the Jewish people as a whole may take, on grounds of religion and race, an interest and a pride." [1]

Mr. Ramsay MacDonald's Government in 1930 reiterated Mr. Churchill's interpretation that a National Home *in* Palestine was a different thing from the converting of the whole of Palestine into a National Home, and issued a White Paper which the Jews called a Black Paper, and which practically put an end to all Zionist hopes. The Arabs triumphed. The Jews protested.

Three months later the negro once more changed colour. In February 1931 Mr. Ramsay MacDonald published a letter to Dr. Weizmann which seemed a complete reversal of the policy announced in October 1930.

In May 1939, six months after Munich, Mr. Chamberlain's Government issued another White Paper in which the National Home was interpreted as meaning that the Jews were to remain a permanent minority in Palestine, deprived of the right of immigration and of the right to the free purchase of land. This interpretation was rejected by the Mandatory Commission of the League of Nations and provoked the wrath of the opposition, and particularly of the Labour Party. Mr. Churchill called it a " base betrayal, a petition in moral bankruptcy " ; Mr. Morrison went one better by describing it as "a cynical breach of faith, a breach of British honour ".[2]

Five years later, in 1944, the Labour Party's Annual Conference declared that " there is surely neither hope nor meaning in a ' Jewish national home ' unless we are prepared to let the Jews, if they wish, enter this tiny land in such numbers as to become a majority ". Another year later the Labour Party took power and promptly adopted a policy which, according to its own definition, deprived the National Home of both hope and meaning. According to the school of semantics to which Mr. Bevin belongs, a home was defined as a place which you are not permitted to enter. It is an absurd story which could serve as an illustration of the disastrous effects of that crime unlisted in international law, the abuse of words.

The story could equally well be told from the Arab angle, and would sound equally absurd. To the Arabs it was promised that nothing would be done in Palestine to " prejudice their civil and

---

[1] Royal Commission Report, p. 24.
[2] Debate in the House of Commons, April 26-27, 1939.

religious rights ". It is true that " political rights " were not expressly mentioned in the Mandate, but who could earnestly assume that this omission would imply the Arabs of Palestine being deprived of them ? On at least three occasions in thirty years the Arabs had been promised the setting up of a legislative body, the cessation of Jewish immigration and a check on Jewish economic expansion ; but each time the negro had changed colour again before the promise was implemented. The Jews found it absurd to be forcibly debarred entry into their so-called " Home "; the Arabs found it absurd that they should be granted the right of self-determination only after foreign Jews had become a majority in their country. There can be no doubt that the Jews were harder and more tragically hit by these oscillations of policy than the Arabs. But we are not at present concerned with the humanitarian aspect of the problem. The point under discussion is the clash between the romantic plane of history on which the Balfour Declaration and the renaissance of Israel were originally conceived, and the trivial plane of political routine.

4

The history of Palestine during the thirty years of British Mandate moved along the line of intersection of these two planes. British rulers and Zionist pioneers lived in different worlds, spoke a different language, obeyed a different psychology. The Jews thought in terms of the prophecies of Isaiah ; of Tolstoi, Marx and Herzl ; of the miraculous rebirth of Israel. The British Colonial administrators thought in the terms of the British Colonial Administration. Isaiah, Tolstoi and the Jewish renaissance were cloud-cuckoo-land to them. Most of them had seen service in India, the Sudan or elsewhere in the empire ; they knew how to build roads, keep public security on a reasonable level, and how to cope with native populations. They had, in their earlier career, often come across individual cranks or religious sects who lived in cloud-cuckoo-land, and they knew that the correct attitude was discreetly to ignore them unless they became obnoxious. In Palestine these unhappy administrators were faced with a new and unprecedented situation. Here the romantic crank-idea was embodied in the international constitution of the country. Their task was to help " the establishment of a national home ", whatever that might mean.

The guiding principle of every colonial administration is maintenance of the *status quo*, mitigated by such slow and gentle reforms as are absolutely necessary. In Palestine Civil Servants were called upon to carry out a revolution by transforming a predominantly Arab country into a Jewish one. To conceive such an idea, for propagandistic or other reasons, in a Cabinet meeting in London was one thing. To project it from the romantic onto the trivial plane, to translate it into humdrum administrative routine, was another. It would have necessitated a team of men with Byronic idealism and Lawrentian imagination. But the men who ruled Palestine were colonial servants of the average type. The impossible stipulations of the task before them acted as a permanent irritant.

Without that absurd National Home business Palestine would have been a country easy to rule and pleasant to live in. For the Jews Zionism was a messianic inspiration. For the British Administration it was simply a damned nuisance.

CHAPTER II

THE TRIANGLE: VIEWED FROM THE APEX

Gentlemen in morning-coats arrive — The Jewish Agency :
rise of a shadow government — Attractions and repulsions
in the psychological triangle — The weight of imponderabilia — The Marxist view of Palestine history — The
" diabolic " view — The " psycho-somatic " view.

The facts : policy on two levels — Indecision and unconscious bias — Public security and the lures of appeasement — Summary

I

THE psychological conflict began almost immediately after the
completion of the British conquest of Palestine. The country was
under military rule, exercised by the O.E.T.A. (Occupied Enemy
Territory Administration), headed by Sir Ronald Storrs, later
Governor of Jerusalem, and one of the most subtle and determined
opponents of the Zionist enterprise. While the inexperienced
military administrators were still trying somehow to sort out the
muddle inevitable in a freshly occupied territory, a most curious
and, from a regimental point of view, unprecedented body descended upon them from London. It called itself the Zionist
Commission, and was found, to the general dismay, to be officially
sponsored by His Majesty's Government. Since the creation of
the world, military administrations have hated the interference of
civilian bodies, even if these belonged to their own people and
Government. In this case, however, the civilians in question
were neither members of the Government nor even British ; they
were a body of Jewish gentlemen in top-hats and morning-coats,
with unpronounceable names and peculiar accents. These strange
visitors at once put forward the most extraordinary demands,
such as that they should participate in the military administration ; that they should select, and supplement the pay of, Jewish
candidates for the Police ; that they should be allowed their own
military defence force, and that Hebrew should be recognized as
an official language.

The impact of this meteoric burst from the romantic plane in the British officers' mess may be imagined. It is described with gentle irony in the Royal Commission's Report:

" One unhappy result of this situation was that some of the Civil Servants in Palestine did not, as in the United Kingdom or in India, stand entirely aloof from religious faction or political strife, but found themselves in some cases forced into the position of partisans to represent the Arab cause. There was at the time no one else who could represent their case, while the Zionist Commission was touring the country." [1]

This first contact between the British Administration and the Zionist bodies foreshadowed the whole future development, the chronic clash between the two incompatible planes.

Article 4 of the Mandate had stipulated that

" an appropriate Jewish agency shall be recognized as a public body for the purpose of advising and cooperating with the Administration of Palestine in such economic, social and other matters as may affect the establishment of the Jewish national home and the interests of the Jewish population in Palestine, and, subject always to the control of the Administration, to assist and take part in the development of the country. The Zionist Organization . . . shall be recognized as such agency."

This stipulation was another white negro. The existence of an independent public body with the function to " advise ", " cooperate ", " assist " and " take part " in the business of government was a permanent headache for the rulers of the country; it gradually became an obsession and ended in perse-cution mania. For within a few years the Jewish Agency, by force of circumstances, had developed into a shadow Government, a state within the State. It controlled the Jewish economic sector of the country, it had its own hospitals and social services, it ran its own schools, its own intelligence service with virtually all Jewish Government officials as voluntary informers, and con-trolled its own para-military organization, the famous Haganah, nucleus of the future Army of Israel.

There were two possible ways of looking at this situation. One could regard the Jewish Agency and its institutions as the

[1] *Op. cit.* p. 115. The Royal Commission's Report, most of which was written by Sir Reginald Coupland, is probably the only historical classic in English letters published by H.M. Stationery Office.

embryo of the future Jewish State growing in the Mandatory Administration's womb. Or one could regard it as a cancer growth spreading through the tissues of the legal Government. But pregnancy is an uncomfortable condition. Even the minority among the Government personnel sympathetic to Zionism were bound to regard the existence of this Jewish shadow Government and shadow army as a constant administrative nightmare.

Other psychological factors contributed to the steady worsening of relations between British Administration and Zionist bodies The Jews were justly proud of their pioneer achievements, of the rapid transformation of a derelict country of empty deserts and malaria-infested swamps into an oasis with a quasi-utopian social structure. The collective settlements in the Jezreel valley, in Sharon and Galilee, where people lived in messianic communities, where the use of money was banned and Socialism was practised in its purest form, represented quite unique feats of social planning. But achievement is not necessarily accompanied by modesty, particularly if it is systematically exploited by propaganda, both for political purposes and for collecting funds. All young pioneer countries have a tendency to self-congratulatory boastfulness, a tendency which contrasted most unhappily with the British cant of understatement and mumbling self-restraint. Even though he recognized the Jews' achievements, the average Briton in Palestine could not help loathing what he regarded as Jewish conceit and showing off, while the average Jew could not help regarding his British rulers as cold, hostile prigs, if not worse.

This mutual aversion was paralleled by the traditional and spontaneous attraction which the Arab way of life holds for the Englishman. It is the result of a number of converging psychological factors : the lure of the desert, of a lackadaisical, traditionalist form of life, of nomad romanticism, courtesy and hospitality. To these must be added the Lawrence-cult of a certain type of British Colonial official, and, on a different level, the common addiction of Arab and Englishman to the *status quo*, their common dislike of violent change, of any kind of bustling efficiency. In short, the natural affinity between Arab and Englishman was matched by the spontaneous aversion between Englishman and Palestinian Jew. " Somehow we like the Arabs even though they fight us and we dislike the Jews even if our interests run together ", confessed a sincere and pro-Zionist Englishman.

According to the Royal Commission's Report, in 1936, at a

time when Hebrew had been officially and *de facto* the language of the Jews in Palestine for almost twenty years, out of 270 British officers in the First Division of the Civil Service 20 could speak both Arabic and Hebrew, 106 could speak Arabic, and 6 Hebrew.[1] These figures express more forcibly than any political arguments the lack of interest shown by the British bureaucracy in the Zionist revival. Relations between the Administration and the Jewish bodies were mostly hostile, sometimes cooperative, always cold and distrustful. Social contact was entirely lacking. At the last semi-official British reception which this writer attended in 1945 — a big after-dinner party given by the British Council in Jerusalem — of the hundred-odd guests present, about one-half were Arabs, one-half English and three were Jews.

The social structure of the Arab and Jewish communities increased this trend. The Arabs in Palestine had a feudal class with old and extremely attractive traditions of manners and hospitality. The Jews had no aristocracy and no patrician bourgeoisie, only a homogeneous lower-middle-class of Eastern European small-town origin. They drank no cocktails, they rarely relaxed, and they had no social graces. The results are summed up in a remark by a candid British official: " There are two societies in Jerusalem, not three. One is Anglo-Arab and the other is Jewish. The two just can't mix." [2]

If the average British Civil Servant in Palestine tried at least not to let his sympathies and aversions interfere with the carrying out of his duties, his wife felt under no such obligation of restraint. She loathed the sweating crowds of Tel Aviv and loved strolling through the Arab shuks; she found the Jewish settlements hideous, the deportment of the young Jewesses in bloomers deplorable, the wives of Jewish Agency officials with whom she occasionally had to go to tea vulgar and boring, and Zionism in general a rather unmentionable subject. And as the social climate in all colonial countries is made by women, the distaste of the Palestine version of the mem-sahib for all things Jewish would have had its steady, insidious effect on the men, even if the other factors mentioned had not already impressed upon them a marked, though not always fully conscious, anti-Jewish and pro-Arab bias.

There were of course remarkable exceptions. At least three among the High Commissioners of Palestine, Lord Plumer, Sir

---

[1] Royal Commission Report, p. 120.
[2] R. H. S. Crossman, *Palestine Mission.* London 1947

Arthur Wauchope and Lord Gort, were men in the great tradition of the British Colonial Administration, painstakingly fair. If not always capable of a full understanding of Jewish psychology, they made up for it by truly Christian tolerance and patience. One of the first Chief Secretaries of the Palestine Government, Sir Wyndham Deedes, became after his retirement a fervent supporter of the Zionist cause ; a number of other leading Civil Servants, though often the target of Jewish hostility and suspicion, did what they could in a quiet way to counterbalance the effects of high policy and administrative bias. But by and large, the lower one descended in the hierarchy, the more noticeable was anti-Jewish feeling, which on the lowest level, that of the Palestine Police, reached scandalous proportions. With Black and Tan veterans in leading positions, riddled with former members of Mosley's Blackshirts, the Palestine Police was one of the most disreputable organizations in the British Commonwealth.

In short, and once more making allowance for individual exceptions, by the end of the 'twenties the Jewish National Home had become, to repeat Josiah Wedgwood's sad and paradoxical statement, " the land of anti-semitism *par excellence* ".

2

It is necessary to stress these trivial psychological factors, for in their cumulative effect they were largely responsible for the tragic developments to follow. In fact the fate of Israel, as that of the Jews in general, was determined as much by psychological as by social and economic forces. In the last analysis, of course, both Jewish and Colonial-British mentality may be reducible to historical developments. But short of going back to the Saxon conquest and the destruction of Jerusalem by Titus, and taking only the period since the First World War into account, one may plausibly defend what may be called a " psycho-somatic view of History ". In this view — which dominates the present book — events were only indirectly determined by oil policy, or by the successive threats of Nazism and Stalinism ; and more directly by the subjective factor in history — that margin of chance, psychological imponderabilia, ideological and irrational trends, which orthodox determinists always tend to overlook.

In the Marxist view, Palestine was a simple problem : the Jews were tools of British imperialist expansion at the cost of the oppressed native population. That the Palestine Arabs thrived on this oppression and became the richest Moslem community in the Middle East; that Jewish Palestine was more socialist in its economic structure than Soviet Russia, and that British imperialism would have been as happy to get rid of its " tool " as the " tool " of its wielder, never disturbed the happy gang of believers, — until, in October 1947, Stalin became overnight the patron saint of Zionism, whereupon the ritual of eating words, rending of ideological garments and grovelling in counter-revolutionary dust was duly performed.

·As for the Jews in Palestine, though Socialist in their majority, they could obviously not accept the vulgar-Marxist view of their own function in the world. Instead, they fell prey to what one might call the " diabolic " view of British politics. If on the Palestine postage-stamps the Hebrew lettering appeared in smaller type than the Arabic, they saw in it the sinister influence of the Shell Oil Company. If the wife of the Assistant Deputy Director of the Forest and Fisheries Department snubbed the wife of a Jewish Agency official, she must have acted on instructions from Lady Astor's notorious Cliveden Set. Whenever Arabs rioted, they had been paid to do so by British secret funds. Every tongue-tied, pipe-chewing Englishman was an agent of the Intelligence Service; timid restraint was mistaken for hostility, administrative muddle for diabolic design.

In fact, the main characteristic of British policy in Palestine up to 1939 was the absence of any consistent design. This is true both of high-level policy made in London and of the conduct of affairs on the local level. As regards the former, the contradictory official interpretations put upon the Balfour Declaration, the oscillations and successive brusque reversals of policy, were a clear indication of the embarrassment of Britain's leaders. They had in 1917 somewhat rashly let themselves in for a romantic adventure and did not know how to get out of it. They could not rescind the Balfour Declaration, which had been embodied in the League of Nations Mandate ; but they felt equally unable to implement it. Typical of this indecision is the remark of a top-ranking official in the Palestine Administration who, when the Royal Commission's recommendations for partitioning the country were published in 1937, exclaimed in a bewildered voice : " What a very un-English document ! Who has ever heard of a British policy in Palestine ? "

What both Jews and Arabs believed to be a " diabolic policy "
was in fact the traditional muddling-along policy, guided by some
vague notions of balancing the power of Arabs and Jews, and
maintaining as far as possible the *status quo*   But the whole point
of the Balfour Declaration was to upset the balance by transforming Arab Palestine into a Jewish country.   Hence a conservative
policy aiming at the maintenance of the *status quo* was implicitly
an anti-Zionist policy.   " Implicitly " — because London was prepared to tolerate a reasonable trickle of Jewish immigration, and
merely refused active help for quick and large-scale colonization
through appropriate legislative and administrative measures.   But
what on the London level was indecision and passive unhelpful-
ness was translated on the local administrative level into active
obstruction.

Immigration was gradually strangled by more and more
restrictive regulations.   Although the Mandate stipulated that the
Administration should encourage " close settlement by Jews on
the land, including State lands and waste lands not required for
public purposes ", only about 95 square kilometres of State
Domain land was allotted to the Jews out of a total of 1560 square
kilometres.[1]   The development of Jewish industries was hampered
by the Administration's admittedly " very liberal " policy of
granting import licences for manufactured goods which could be
locally produced.   The financial burden for Jewish education and
health services was left almost exclusively to the Jewish Agency,
although the Government's revenue was derived largely from the
Jewish taxpayer — so that the Jews were obliged to finance
directly their own schools and hospitals, and indirectly those of
the Arabs in addition.   The number of Jews employed in Government services and in the Police was considerably below their
proportional strength.   The gravest omission of the Administration, however, concerned public security.

" To-day it is evident ", the Royal Commissioners reported in
1937, " that the elementary duty of providing public security
has not been discharged.   If there is one grievance which the
Jews have undoubted right to prefer, it is the absence of
security." [2]

A full seven years earlier, in 1930, the Permanent Mandates
Commission of the League of Nations had stated :

[1] Information supplied by the Israeli Ministry of Economics.
[2] Royal Commission Report, p. 148.

C

" The charge against the Palestine Government that it has not fulfilled by actual deeds the obligation to encourage the establishment of a National Home has been notably reinforced by the fact that the Government has shown it is unable to provide the essential condition for the development of the National Home — security for person and property."

In 1920, 1921, 1929 and finally from 1936 to 1939, Palestine was in the throes of what were euphemistically called " disturbances ". The range of this word comprised Arab violence on any scale, from local riots to organized massacre and guerilla warfare. The Administration's task was of course extremely difficult and delicate. It was caught between two antagonistic races, was accused by both of favouring the other side ; and had to muddle through without any clear policy being laid down for it. To provide public security for isolated Jewish settlements surrounded by Arab villages, or in the rabbit-warren of the old cities of Jerusalem and Safed, was technically not an easy matter. Under these circumstances it is understandable that the Police occasionally blundered. But the dismal security record of the Palestine Administration over a quarter of a century was more than a series of blunders. Repeated warnings of the League of Nations Mandatory Commission about the unsatisfactory state of public security were rejected in a high-handed manner, and no serious attempt was made to get at the root of the evil by curbing the power of the acknowledged instigators of these periodic outbreaks, the Grand Mufti and his clan. On this issue the verdict of His Majesty's Royal Commissioners was so damning that in any democratically ruled country it would have led to the immediate resignation of the Government : " If one thing stands out clear from the record of the Mandatory Administration, it is the leniency with which Arab political agitation, even when carried to the point of violence and murder, has been treated. . . ."[1]

While Arab terrorism was treated with tolerance, the Administration played a curious cat-and-mouse game with the Jewish self-defence organization, Haganah, about which more will be said later. Yet even on this dark chapter of Britain's Mandatory record no " diabolic " interpretation should be construed. Except in a few isolated cases, and in the lowest ranks of the Palestine Police, no deliberate *mala fides* was involved. In London there reigned indecision and muddle ; left without clear directives, the local

[1] Royal Commission Report p. 101

administration acted according to its own lights and to its anti-Zionist bias. It could have removed the Mufti from his post, dissolved his " Higher Arab Committee " and replaced it by moderate elements. But such a policy would have meant a considerable upheaval. The Administration preferred to go on trying to come to terms with the extremists, whom they believed, rightly or wrongly, to enjoy the largest local support. The only real stumbling-block in the way of coming to such an understanding was Zionism. If Jewish immigration was throttled and the obligations towards the National Home were gradually whittled down, all would be well. Nothing in the instructions from London indicated that such a course was not contemplated. The result of these considerations was a policy of appeasement of the Arab extremists, carried out in the hope that sooner or later the only obstacle to full collaboration would disappear. This attitude was in turn interpreted by the Arabs in the over-simplified way that the Administration welcomed Arab opposition, including violence, to strengthen its hand against the Zionists.

Had the Administration been less blinded by emotive bias, they might have foreseen this disastrous result of their attitude. They should have known that a chance remark from a British official to an Arab village mukhtar betraying some anti-Jewish sentiment would grow in the oriental mind into a direct encouragement to a pogrom. Repeatedly Arab crowds, swooping down with knives and swords on Jewish quarters, yelled " the Government is with us ", or even carried banners to this effect. Nothing would be more unjust than to take this claim at its face value and to believe that the Government really condoned murder and violence. But the point is that the Arabs did believe that this was the Government's intention; and to have permitted this belief to grow is a valid indictment of the Mandatory Administration. To quote once more the Royal Commission :

". . . the official tendency in Palestine to take up a defeatist, almost an apologetic attitude on this cardinal issue (Zionism) had helped to foster a belief in the Arab mind that the National Home was not an immutable point of policy and that, if Arab resistance to it were sufficiently obstinate and forcible, the Mandatory power might presently be worried or even frightened into giving it up ".[1]

[1] *Ibid.* p. 80.

3

It was necessary to analyse this point in some detail, for it illustrates the importance of the psychological factor in the gradual drift of Palestine from muddle to catastrophe. In summing up the preceding pages, several steps should be clearly distinguished.

Firstly, a decision of great imaginative sweep is taken, and a solemn engagement entered into, on what we call the Romantic plane of history, where time counts in centuries and obstacles become dwarfed from an exalted bird's-eye view.

Secondly, the process thus started is continued on the Trivial plane of humdrum political routine. As far as Cabinet policy is concerned, the transition from one plane to another manifests itself in a sort of hangover after the debauch of imagination, a gradual whittling down of the original conception, in indecision and hesitation. If Lord Balfour's pronouncement sounded like a new promise from Sinai, the subsequent interpretations of it sound rather like the hummings and hawings of the Pharisees.

Thirdly, a further step down from the muddle and indecision of Cabinet-level policy in London to the muddle-cum-emotional bias (partly unconscious, partly grotesque in its human triviality) on the Colonial Administration level. In a climate saturated by emotion and prejudice, psychological imponderabilia assume a fateful importance. Under their cumulative effect, ambiguous directives acquire an unconscious twist, and storm-centres of misunderstanding and distrust are created. These in turn react on the next higher level, and influence Cabinet policy. A vicious circle is started, with fateful and unforeseeable consequences.

CHAPTER III

THE TRIANGLE: THE CONFLICT AT THE BASE

Foundations of Israel — The problem of historic justice —
Various conceptions of it — The variables of time and value
— Only relative criteria applicable.

The sell-out of the effendi class — Legislation protecting the tenant — The myth of the dispossessed Arab —
The mess of pottage — Social structure of Arab society.

Influence of Jewish colonization on Arab development
— Statistics — Summary: the ethical aspects of the conflict — The Arab case — Jewish self-righteousness and
cultural isolationism

I

By the middle 'thirties it was no longer a question whether
Zionism was a good idea or a bad idea, whether it was desirable
or not — the 500,000 Jews in Palestine were no longer a political
theory but a fact. They occupied a compact portion of the land;
and though still outnumbered by the Arabs at the rate of two to
one, they had become, in economic strength and social achievement, the senior partner in that unhappy concern. The foundations of the future State of Israel had been laid. A brief analysis
of these foundations seems all the more indicated as Israel is
practically the only State in existence for which all the data for
such an analysis are on record and readily accessible.

Virtually all sovereign States have come into being through
some form of violent and, at the time, lawless upheaval which after
a while became accepted as a *fait accompli*. Nowhere in history
— whether in the time of the Migrations, the Norman Conquest,
the Dutch War of Independence, or the forcible colonization of
America — do we find an example of a State being peacefully born
by international agreement. In this respect, again, Israel is a freak.
It is a kind of Frankenstein creation, conceived on paper, blue-
printed in the Mandate, hatched out in the diplomatic laboratory.
But, in the last phase of its birth-process, violence was the decisive

factor ; and, as with other nations, its existence is ultimately based on an accomplished fact at the expense of the original native population.

The Balfour Declaration, as we said before, was a promise by one nation to a second of the country of a third. It may be argued as a mitigating factor that when the Arabs, by the force of British arms, were liberated from Turkish rule, the history of the Middle East started as it were from scratch. Palestine in 1917 was an under-populated area of deserts and swamps ; and the leaders of the Arabs were at the time quite willing to have it colonized by Jews, on condition of gaining sovereignty over the remainder of the vast liberated territories from the Indian Ocean to the Turkish border. The Emir Feisal, son of the Caliph, even signed an agreement with the Zionist leader, Dr. Weizmann, pledging cordial cooperation between the future Arab State of Greater Syria and the Jewish National Home. As Greater Syria never came into existence the agreement never became valid, and the fate of Palestine was ultimately decided by force.

The term " historic justice " is vague and undefined. Unlike the criminal code, it has no solid frame of reference ; its axioms and criteria depend entirely on what philosophy one adopts. From a Darwinistic point of view, historic justice is the survival of the fitter race at the expense of the weaker. From the point of view of Jewish religion, Israel is the fulfilment of a promise from Sinai, and hence an act of Divine Justice. For the legalist it is founded on a promise from Downing Street endorsed by the League of Nations, and hence on international law. For the Marxist dialectician it is the replacement of a mediaeval feudal structure by a modern socialist one, and hence in accord with the laws of historic progress. For the philanthropist it is a haven for a persecuted homeless race, and hence to be welcomed. For romantic traditionalists it is the defilement of a primitive and patriarchal pattern of life by the bustle of mechanized civilization. And finally, from the point of view of national sovereignty and self-determination, Israel is a historic injustice.

Each of these views is based on a different system of reference and is surrounded by its own " universe of discourse ". If these universes get mixed up, polemics are bound to end in a hopeless jumble. The discussion about the problem of Palestine for the last two decades has been a classic example of semantic confusion aggravated by emotional bias. The fact is that historic justice cannot be measured by absolute standards, only by relative and comparative scales.

As the process of history is irreversible, all judgment becomes a function of time. Yesterday's act of violence is to-day's *fait accompli* and to-morrow's legal *status quo*. Hence, the definition of historic justice depends on which point in time is regarded as zero hour.

Which, then, is the zero hour for Palestine ? Its forcible conquest by the Hebrew tribes from Canaanites, Jebusites and Philistines ? The expulsion of the Jews from it after Bar-Kochba's revolt in the second century ? Its conquest by Arab nomads in the seventh, or by the Ottoman Turks in the sixteenth ? The entry of Allenby's troops in 1917 with the Balfour Declaration in one pocket and Wilson's fourteen points in the other ? The British White Paper of 1939, or the British recognition of Israel in 1949 ?

Historic justice thus appears as a function of two variables : the point in time chosen, and the criteria of value applied. Judgment will firstly depend on how much of the past is taken into account as evidence : whether its starting-point is the Maccabean conquest, the rule of the Caliphs or the Battle of the Negeb. It will, secondly, depend on the judge's views about the relative value of the reduction of Arab infant mortality by immigrant Jewish doctors, as compared to the Arabs' right to their own way of life without alien interference.

The idea of justice is based on a fixed system of reference ; the presence of the two variables of time and value turns the whole concept of " historic justice " into a subjective and arbitrary one ; in fact reduces it to a contradiction in terms. History cannot be judged by the application of any rigid code of ethics ; it can only be represented in the manner of the Greek tragedy, where the antagonists are both right in their own terms of reference and in their own universe of discourse. In the tragedy of Jews and Arabs in Palestine both were in the right, and the spectator could do no more than extend his sympathies to one party or the other, according to his subjective values and emotional bias.

Accordingly, the analysis of the moral foundations of Israel must be confined to a limited period — *e.g.* from the British conquest of Palestine to the new State's Declaration of Independence — and judgment can only be based on comparison with other examples of the conquest of a native country by European colonists. By these limited and relative standards the injustice done to the Arabs of Palestine still remains an undeniable fact; but it will appear as a relatively mild injustice compared with historical precedents, and the methods of Jewish colonization as relatively fair and humane.

2

The fundamental fact about the Jewish colonization of Palestine is that it was carried out neither by force nor by the threat of force, but, contrary to popular belief, with active Arab connivance. No Arab was ever forced to sell his land — whether it was the estate of a rich effendi, or *masha'a* land, *i.e.* the collective property of a village. Nor is it correct to regard the Arabs as naïve victims of the lure of Jewish gold. Arab political propaganda thundered ceaselessly against the sale of land to Jews. At the same time, the policy of the Mandatory Administration was deliberately aimed at discouraging such sales by administrative and legislative measures of increasing severity.

The first British Transfer of Land Ordinance dates from 1920; it was amended in 1921; became in 1929 the Protection of Cultivators Ordinance, which again was amended in 1932 and in subsequent years; the last Land Transfer law dates from 1940. The one exclusive purpose of this long series of legislative acts was to protect the Arab farmer and tenant against the consequences of land sales to the Jews, either rashly undertaken by the proprietor himself, or by big landowners over the tenant's head. The first of these ordinances prohibited the transfer of land to " others than residents in Palestine "; the second added the proviso that consent to the sale should only be given after the Director of Lands was " satisfied that any tenant in occupation will retain sufficient land in the district or elsewhere for the maintenance of himself and his family ". The subsequent ordinances were designed to cover any possible loopholes, to make the eviction of tenants on land sold by the owner impossible, and to prevent by all legal means the creation of a dispossessed landless Arab proletariat. In the last of these ordinances, dated February 1940, Jews were debarred from acquiring land in 63 per cent of the area of Palestine, and restricted in 32 per cent; in its practical effects the ordinance amounted to the prohibition of the purchase of land by Jews in 95 per cent of their National Home.

The Palestine Mandate had imposed upon the British Administration the dual obligation to facilitate the "close settlement by Jews on the land" and at the same time to safeguard "the rights and position of other sections of the population". The Land Transfer Acts were exclusively concerned with the second of these stipulations to the more and more complete neglect of the first, until, in the end, Palestine became in 1940 the only country in the world, besides National Socialist Germany, in which Jews were denied the right to acquire land. The official justification for this series of laws of increasing rigour was the protection of the Arab tenant-farmer against displacement. In fact, however, the "landless Arab", who so prominently figured in anti-Zionist propaganda, was more a political slogan than a reality. According to the official reports of the Palestine Administration, up to the 1st of January 1936 altogether 664 valid claims for resettlement were received from Arab tenants who had become dispossessed by the land being sold over their heads. In 1936 altogether nine valid claims for Government tenancies were received from landless Arabs, in 1937 six claims, and from then on the Administration was able to report to the Mandatory Commission that no further claims had been put forward.

It should be repeated, then, that the Jews acquired the stretches of land which became the economic and strategic foundation of their State not by force, but by free consent of the owners : Governmental legislation was exclusively designed to safeguard owners' and tenants' interests. The Arabs sold voluntarily, and had the fullest possible protection against acting rashly or being taken advantage of. If despite all warnings and restrictions they persisted in selling, they did it with open eyes.

Was it then a repetition of Esau selling his birthright to Jacob for a mess of pottage ? As far as the feudal landowners are concerned the answer is undoubtedly yes. The structure of Arab society in Palestine never emerged from a state of mediaeval feudalism. At its top stood a small aristocracy of landowners, a typically Levantine élite, grown up in the traditions of the decaying Turkish Empire of whose corrupt effendi class they formed the Palestine branch. Many of them had served as officers in the Turkish Army ; they had been educated in Cairo or Beirut, had acquired the outward polish of European culture, mainly in the form of familiarity with the works of Maupassant and Claude Farrère, and were living, mostly as absentee landowners, on the proceeds of their domains. These few families and their clans

of more distant relatives and retainers played the part of the
political parties and groupings in modern countries. The Husseinis, the Nashashibis, the Khalidis and about half a dozen other
clans held the country under their complete economic and political
sway. They led the opposition against Zionism, and at the same
time sold their land to the Jews, through middlemen, at high
profits. In 1948 it was the same effendi class which called their
followers to a holy war against the Jews, and when the first shots
were fired sneaked away to Beirut, leaving the masses leaderless
and thereby sealing the fate of Arab resistance in the civil war.
The effendis were the political leaders, administrators and vocal
chords of Arab Palestine. If they sold their birthright for a mess
of pottage they could not claim to have acted in ignorance as
Esau did.

As in the neighbouring Arab countries, the Third Estate
carried as yet no political weight. The Arab middle-class of professional men, business men and newspaper editors were a thin
layer sandwiched in between the feudal landlords on the one hand,
with, on the other, the politically illiterate but easily fanaticized
mass of hard-working fellaheen and the leisurely drones of the
shuks.

The second main source of Jewish land acquisition was
masha'a land, representing the communal property of the fellaheen
of an Arab village. It was mostly land which the villagers were
unable to cultivate for lack of irrigation or tractors, or because of
their reluctance to adopt modern methods of cultivation and their
lack of capital for doing so. By selling a portion of their waste
land, the fellaheen were able either to improve the exploitation of
the rest, or to start some kind of a business in town.

The paradox of a considerable portion of the land passing
gradually into Jewish possession while at the same time the
number of " dispossessed " Arabs remained insignificant, has its
simple explanation in the fact that most of the land acquired by
the Jews, both from the great landowners and from the villagers,
had been uncultivated before. Thus the two main continuous
stretches of territory, the coastal plain and the valley of Jezreel,
which became the material foundation of the Jewish State, had
been, before the arrival of the Jews, mostly a wilderness of sand-
dunes, marshes and stony desert, with here and there a malaria-
infested warren of mud huts or a village in ruins, whose population
had died out of disease. The expansion of Jewish colonization

did not cause a shrinkage of Arab-cultivated land, nor a displacement or impoverishment of Arab farmers, but the direct opposite.

A few statistical figures may illustrate the process.[1] The Jewish area of citrus culture — Palestine's main export — expanded from 10,000 dunums in 1922 to 155,500 in 1937. The Arab citrus plantations expanded in the same period almost to the same extent — from 22,000 to 144,000 dunums.

The Arab area of fruit-trees in hill districts which in pre-Zionist days were regarded as uncultivable, increased from 332,000 dunums in 1931 to 832,000 in 1942.

Generally speaking, agricultural production per head of the total non-Jewish population rose (in round figures) from £4 : 10s. in 1922 to £7 in 1938. This in spite of the fact that in 1922 Arab Palestine was almost purely agricultural, while in 1938 a considerable sector of the population had migrated to the towns, so that agricultural production *per capita* should normally have gone down — instead of which it increased by more than 50 per cent. This spectacular increase both of the area of land cultivated by Arabs, and of its yield, was due firstly to the capital flowing into Arab hands from Jewish land purchases;[2] secondly, to the rapid growth of the internal market for agricultural products through Jewish immigration; thirdly, to the fall of agricultural taxes from $12\frac{1}{2}$ per cent of the revenue to $3\frac{1}{2}$ per cent of the revenue, made possible by the prosperous state of the Palestine exchequer thanks to the Jewish taxpayer; and finally, to the modernization of primitive Arab agriculture and the rapid decrease in animal and plant pests under the influence of modern Jewish agricultural methods.

If one revisited Palestine at intervals of five or ten years, as the author had occasion to do between 1926 and 1948, one was struck each time by the apparent jumps both in the progress of reclaiming the waste land which had lain fallow and deserted during the centuries of Turkish misrule, and in the rise of the living standard of the population. This progress was even more conspicuous in the case of the Arabs, who had started from a lower level. The transition from mud huts to stone houses, from

---

[1] See *Memorandum on the Influence of Jewish Colonization on Arab Development in Palestine*, Jerusalem, 1947; *Statistical Handbook of the Middle East*, Jerusalem, 1944; and the Royal Commission's Report.

[2] Before Zionist colonization started the price of land ranged from £P5 to £P15 per dunum; in 1944 it averaged £P80 per dunum.

the rabbit-warren of Old Jaffa to the spacious avenues of the
modern town represented a more striking contrast than the more
homogeneous growth of Tel Aviv or the growth of the Jewish
agricultural settlements, which, impressive though they were,
remained more or less true to the same style and pattern.

Parallel with this growth of Arab prosperity, however, grew
an urban industrial proletariat, a far less welcome sight to the
tourist's eye. Previously, Arab poverty had been hidden inside
the windowless, one-room mud huts (housing parents, children
and donkey) of the villages, which looked picturesque and unreal
from a distance. Now it was displayed in the slums of industrial
towns like Haifa, where a whole suburb of shacks built of rusty
petrol tins dismayed and shocked the visitor. Inevitably in Arab
Palestine, as in other parts of the world, a slow drift had set in
from village to town, from farming to industrial employment, from
the monotony of rural life to the cinema and café. But this was
not a consequence of any forced displacement caused by the Jews,
nor even directly connected with the founding of Jewish industries,
which did not employ Arab labour. It was simply the industrial
age slowly dawning on Palestine, and was only indirectly connected with Zionist colonization which, through influx of capital
and competitive example, inspired the beginnings of Arab in-
dustrialization. The Arab drift from village to town coincided
with the inverse movement of the Jews' return to the land. This
curious cross-current of tendencies in the two races was a historical
chance, and not a result of conscious scheming. Similar chance
constellations were, as will be seen, to play an important part in
the birth of Israel.

To sum up. Had Jewish immigration been confined to the
towns and to industrial occupations, the Jewish State would never
have come into existence. The decisive factor was the conquest
of the land, both in the metaphoric and literal sense. Without
possession of the strategic key positions along the coastal belt and
in the valley of Jezreel, and of the frontier outposts scattered over
Galilee, Judaea and the Negeb, the Jews would have been unable
to defend themselves. Without their achievement of transforming
desert, swamp and dune into the material basis of the National
Home, they would have had no moral claim to its possession.
They had started building their country from scratch, in the
wilderness, which had been unexploited by its native owners and
had been willingly yielded by them against material benefits,

despite every warning and legal and administrative hindrance. The rich sold their land out of cupidity, putting greed above the national interest which they purported to represent. The villagers sold their land because they put their well-understood material interest above political considerations which were alien to them. They were capable of wild outbursts of religious fanaticism when the village priest chose to preach holy murder in his Friday sermon in the mosque ; but as natives of a feudal country which had been somnolescent under Turkish rule since the middle ages, they had never acquired a national consciousness in the political sense. We are always apt to forget that nationalism is a product of a relatively recent, post-feudal European development. Neither clan-allegiance, nor religion, nor hatred of the stranger, is sufficient to give structural coherence and the capacity of coordinated action to a people. The Arabs of Palestine were an amorphous mass — peace-loving, tradition-bound, illiterate, divided by blood feuds and clan rivalry ; time and their feudal rulers deprived them of their chance of becoming a nation.

Into this stagnant country the Jews burst like an explosion. They gained control of the land, not by force or fraud, but because they were the harbingers of the twentieth century in a country which had virtually stood still since the fifteenth. They did not dispossess or victimize or exploit its native owners, but substituted themselves for the former by virtue of a historic fatality. They did not come, as other Europeans had come to dark continents before them, with shotguns, glass beads and fire water ; nor with missionaries either. They meant no harm to the Arabs ; nor were the benefits which the latter reaped intentional on the part of the Jews. They came pressed by persecution and by hunger for a land of their own ; and though the methods of their conquest were ethically less objectionable than any previous conquest in history, this was due more to the force of circumstance than to subjective merit. They were the relatively decent and humane executors of the amoral workings of history. And that is all we have set out to prove, and thought necessary to prove, in view of the distorted partisan accounts, both from the Jewish and anti-Jewish sides, of the beginnings of the State of Israel.

3

To complete the picture, a few more facts should be entered on both sides of the ethical balance-sheet of Jewish pioneering.

On the credit side mention must be made of the influence of Zionist colonization on Arab vital statistics. After centuries of stagnation the Arab population of Palestine doubled between 1922 and 1942 — in round figures, from 600,000 to 1,200,000. This striking development was due partly to the work of Jewish hospitals and doctors, partly to the Government's health services which were mainly financed by Jewish taxes, and partly to the immigration of Arabs from neighbouring countries attracted by Palestine's higher wages and standards of living. The following figures will illustrate this process.[1]

Infant mortality decreased between 1921 and 1939 in Transjordan by 7 per cent, in Egypt by 9 per cent and in Palestine's Moslem population by 27 per cent.

Egypt's population increased in the same period by 25 per cent, Palestine's Moslem population by 75 per cent (Transjordan unknown).

Within Palestine Moslem vital statistics vary in different regions according to the density of the Jewish population in that region, i.e. the establishment of Jewish medical services. The following table shows the interdependence of the Jewish population figures in rural areas and Arab infant mortality in 1937–39. The town names stand for capitals of rural sub-districts.

	Jaffa	Haifa	Ramleh	Safed	Ramallah	Bethlehem
Per cent of Jews in total population	71·9	52·3	22	9·9	0	0
Arab infant mortality per thousand live births	81·4	118·7	114·8	177	171·5	176·4

In terms of expenditure, the Mandatory Administration spent on medical services in 1934–35 £166,000, the Jewish Agency £350,000, while there was no expenditure by Arab organizations. On combating malaria by the draining of marshes, the Jews had spent up to 1935 £403,000, the Palestine Government £86,500, the Arabs nothing. Compared to the neighbouring countries, health expenditure per head in 1936–37 was: Palestine £0·161 (index 100),

[1] For sources cf. footnote 1 on p. 27

Iraq £0·077 (index 47·8), Transjordan £0·051 (index 31·7).[1]

The general Arab standard of living rose as spectacularly as the vital statistic figures. Between 1922 and 1939 the annual consumption of principle commodities per head had risen by 85 per cent, and gross production in agriculture and industry per head by 150 per cent. Wages in 1936 for Arab skilled labour in Palestine ranged from 5s. to 12s. per day, for unskilled labour from 2s. to 3s. 6d. In the same year, wages in Syria ranged from 1s. to 2s. 6d., and in Iraq factory labour was paid round 1s. a day, regardless of qualifications. Finally, Government revenue rose from just over 1 million pounds in 1921 to over 4½ million pounds in 1939–40. The flourishing finances of the Palestine exchequer were due mainly to Jewish immigration, and benefited mainly the Arab sector. Thus Government expenditure on schools rose from round £100,000 in 1931 to over £200,000 in 1939–40, in other words it was doubled within ten years. Of this expenditure 82 per cent went to Arab schools and 18 per cent to Jewish schools, which were mainly financed by Zionist organizations. In the same period of ten years the number of Moslem literates rose from 76,000, or 11 per cent of the Moslem population, to 170,000, or 18 per cent.

This last figure shows that despite all relative progress, the cultural standard of the Arab population was still shockingly low, particularly compared to what one may call the 200 per cent literacy of the Jews — the latter being usually at least bilingual. The same contrast prevailed between Jewish and Arab infant mortality, standard of living, housing conditions. The striking percentual increases in the statistics quoted should not obscure the fact that though considerably better off at the end than at the beginning of the British Mandate, and rich compared to their fellow-Arabs in neighbouring countries, the Moslems of Palestine still lived in appalling material and cultural poverty.

[1] For curiosity's sake we may quote the following statement by the Colonial Secretary of the Chamberlain Cabinet, Mr. Malcolm MacDonald, under whose tenure of office the White Paper of 1939 was issued, and who can hardly be suspected of Zionist sympathies :

"If not a single Jew had come to Palestine after 1918, I believe the Arab population of Palestine to-day would still have been round the 600,000 figure, at which it had been stable under Turkish rule. It is because the Jews who have come to Palestine bring modern health services and other advantages that Arab men and women who would be dead are alive to-day, that Arab children who would never have drawn breath have been born and grow strong."

4

We have discussed at some length the positive aspects of the
Jewish colonizatory enterprise in its repercussions on the Arab
population. The negative aspects are more difficult to substantiate
by statistics or concrete facts. Once again we have to switch from
one historical plane to another, from a system of values expressed
in health statistics and economic standards to a different system
defined by psychological relations and cultural patterns.

We said before that, unlike other colonists, the Jews brought
no glass beads or rum ; but they brought no missionary Bibles
either. This absence of the missionary approach is a characteristic of Zionist colonization. It bestowed considerable benefits
on the Arabs ; but these benefits were not intentional, and thereby
lost much of their moral value and their convincingness as a
political argument. The patronizing tone of Zionist propaganda
produced an effect contrary to its aim and psychologically neutralized any material advantage which the Arabs derived from the
advent of the Jews. The Jews argued and proved that by developing the country's derelict wastes and industrial potential they
were not taking the Arabs' house away but adding a new storey
to it, as it were. The Arabs answered that this may or may not
be so, but that in any case they refused to have an alien nation
living " on top of them ". The Jews argued and proved that by
their building up and moving in the Arabs were much better off
than before. The Arabs answered that this may or may not be
so, but that in any case they hadn't asked the Jews to bestow
benefits on them ; and that all they wanted was to be left alone.
I have tried to sum up elsewhere this very strong and natural
reaction of the average educated Arab to Zionist arguments ; it
boils down to this :

" We don't care whether you pay and we don't care for your
hospitals and schools. You must understand that this is our
country. We want no foreign benefactors. We don't want to
be patronized. We want to live in our own way, and we want
no foreign teachers and no foreign money and no foreign habits
and no smiles of condescension and no pats on the shoulder
and no arrogance and none of your shameless women wriggling
their buttocks in our holy places. We don't want your honey
and we don't want your sting, — get that straight. Neither
your honey nor your sting. . . ."

The novel from which this speech of a member of the Arab intelligentsia is quoted was written in 1945. A short time later, Azzam Pasha, Secretary of the Arab League, put the Arab case in the following words before the Anglo-American Committee of Enquiry :

> " The Zionist, the new Jew, wants to dominate, and he pretends that he has got a particular civilizing mission with which he returns to a backward, degenerate race in order to put the elements of progress into an area which has no progress. Well, that has been the pretension of every power that wanted to colonize and aimed at domination. The excuse has always been that the people are backward and that he has got a human mission to put them forward. . . . The Arabs simply stand and say ' NO '. We are not reactionary and we are not backward. Even if we are ignorant, the difference between ignorance and knowledge is ten years in school. We are a living, vitally strong nation, we are in our renaissance ; we are producing as many children as any nation in the world. We still have our brains. We have a great heritage of civilization and of spiritual life. We are not going to allow ourselves to be controlled either by great nations or small nations or dispersed nations."

On its own level the argument is unanswerable. It is based on the premise that every people has a right to live in its own way, even if it is a primitive, anachronistic way which carries its own doom. To ask whether this premise is " right " or " wrong " is meaningless. History carries a whip in its hand, and in this case the Jews, its traditional victim, were the whip. No effort of humanity and understanding on their part could have possibly hidden this fact from the native Arabs. As it happens, the operation was less painful than in other cases, and in a crudely material sense even beneficial to the victim. But only in this crudely material sense. No effort on the part of the Jews could have induced the Arabs voluntarily to acquiesce in their fate.

But the point is that the Jews hardly made any effort in that direction at all. " The Arabs " represented for them a political headache, not a human and moral problem. They paid lip-service to the necessity of a mutual *rapprochement*, but in practice did little about it. Palestine was their promised land, doubly promised from Mount Sinai and Downing Street, and they came to take possession of it as its masters. The presence of the Arabs was

D

a mere accident like the presence of some forgotten pieces of furniture in a house which has been temporarily let to strangers. They had no intention of removing them unless they got in their way. They meant no harm to the Arabs; all they expected of them was to sit still and watch them taking the country over and running it in their own efficient way to everybody's benefit. Unlike other colonizers, they did not exploit cheap native labour; they simply excluded the Arabs from their own hermetically sealed economy. This was hardly to be avoided, because one of the fundamental aims of Zionism was to reverse the top-heavy social pyramid of the Jews in the Diaspora; the Jews, as a nation, must have their own solid base of farmers and manual workers in all spheres of production. Only the planters of the pre-Zionist Jewish immigration employed Arab labour in their orange groves; but this was regarded as a betrayal of the national ideal, and the old planters, too, were gradually forced to replace Arab by Jewish labour. Theoretically, the Jewish trade unions were open to Jew and Arab alike; practically, little effort was made to attract Arab members. Theoretically, the extreme Zionist left preached a united front of the Arab and Jewish proletariat to liberate the fellaheen from their feudal exploiters. In fact, however, each Jew, Marxist or not, regarded himself as a member of the chosen race, and the Arab as his inferior.

Except for Jewish doctors and health service personnel, who played a considerable part in the improvement of Arab health standards, particularly in the rural areas, the Jews took no active steps to bring modern culture and civilization to the native population and to narrow the gap between the two races. The material benefits which came to the Arabs were an accidental by-product of Jewish economic expansion. The language of the Jewish schools and university, of books and newspapers, was Hebrew — and hence inaccessible to the Arabs. The Jews published no books or periodicals in Arabic. The cultural life of the two communities was confined to watertight compartments, as their respective economies were. The Jews made no effort to bring European culture to the Arab masses, nor to adapt themselves to those aspects of oriental life which would have enriched their own cultural pattern and at the same time made them appear less provocatively alien to the country. They did not learn from the Arabs to build cool and spacious houses which would fit the climate and landscape; they brought with them their architecture of the Polish small town and of German functionalism of the 'twenties. Their dress, food, manners and general way of life were transplanted like a prefabricated pattern from their lands of origin. Some of these were improvements in the country's way of life ; others unfitting and in bad taste. There was no cultural symbiosis between the two races. The Jews came as conquerors. It was a fair and humane conquest, but a conquest nevertheless.

Most of these things were objectively inevitable. The illiterate Arab masses, living under the complete spiritual sway of the village priest, were impervious to the voice of the twentieth century. They had no desire to organize themselves into trade unions, nor to study Marxist pamphlets and fight feudalism. The Jews were a minority, and to assert themselves against a hostile and backward majority they had to show their physical strength or perish. Their Marxist phrases and their talk of mutual understanding were bound to remain lip-service, for had they conceded the subjective justice of the Arab case they would have had to renounce their aim. Short of that, they could in fact do very little to alter the course of events. Nevertheless, had they shown a little more discretion and less self-righteousness, more adaptability and a broader interpretation of their pioneer mission — the effort, even if rejected, even if ultimately hopeless, would have made a great difference, particularly for the later internal development of the State of Israel. For the narrow and self-satisfied cultural isolationism with which Israel became imbued during this period of pre-natal conditioning has left a strong mark on its character and spirit — as will be seen later in more detail.

CHAPTER IV

THE TRIANGLE: THE JEWISH ANGLE

The pre-Zionist community — The old settlers — Their
warning example — Planned socialized character of Zionist
colonization — Rousseau, Marx, Tolstoi and the Bible —
Begging bowls and high finance — Summary: the pre-
natal conditioning of a nation

I

WE have discussed a number of aspects of the Zionist venture
which made it an unprecedented phenomenon in the history of
colonizatory enterprises. The last and probably most important
aspect remains to be mentioned: the planned, collective, national-
ized character of this colonization.

During the last decades of the nineteenth century a steady
trickle of Jewish immigrants had come into the country. They
were the forerunners of modern Zionism, and most of them came
to the Holy Land drawn by a religious, not a national, ideal. Some
settled in the ghetto of Old Jerusalem, subsisted on charity, and
spent their life in prayer. Others became planters; their land
and capital were provided by Jewish philanthropic societies, of
which the most important was the Jewish Colonization Association
(I.C.A.) financed by "the Baron", Edmond de Rothschild. These
old settlers or "I.C.A. colonists" were not Zionists in the political
sense. They were tolerated by the Turks, on friendly terms with
the Arabs, and had become Levantines in their way of living.
They employed Arab hired labour — at first because no Jewish
labour was available, and later because Arab labourers were
cheaper and had no troublesome ideas about trade unions, Zionism
and Socialism. They viewed political Zionism with suspicion and
disfavour, and feared that a large influx of Jewish immigrants with
political pretensions would endanger their good-neighbourly
relations with the Arabs.

When, in 1903, His Majesty's Government offered the Zionist
Organization the territory of Uganda in British East Africa for the
establishment of a Jewish State, a great controversy broke out in

Jewry between the " Ugandists ", who were in favour of accepting the offer, and their opponents, who insisted that the Jewish National Home could only be in Palestine. It is a historical curiosity that at that time the Jews in Palestine itself, with very few exceptions, were fanatical " Ugandists ".

". . . It was a degrading and distressing sight to see all those people who, after all, had been the first to build up the Jewish Palestine of that day, publicly denying and repudiating their own past. . . . The passion for Uganda soon became associated with a deadly hatred for Palestine. . . . In the community centres of the first Jewish colonies young men educated in the *Alliance Israélite* schools denounced Palestine in the French language, with a vain pathos and a false enthusiasm, with a shameless contempt which I cannot describe in words. Their only name for Palestine was 'a land of corpses and graves', a land of malaria and eye-diseases, a land which destroys its inhabitants. Nor was this the expression of a few individuals. Indeed it was only a few individuals here and there in the villages and towns who remained loyal and did not associate themselves with the abusive and decrying masses. We know the names of these individuals. . . . The whole of Palestine was in a state of ferment. . . . All opposition to Uganda came from outside of Palestine. In Zion itself all were against Zion. . . ."

Thus writes Shlomo Zemach in his *Introduction to the History of Labour Settlement in Palestine.*[1] I have mentioned this episode, usually slurred over in Zionist histories, because it shows the enormous difficulties which faced the first Zionist pioneers in Palestine. They came into a semi-savage, disease-ridden land under a corrupt and effete Turkish administration, and had to defend their first collective settlements not only against Bedouin robbers and the deadlier assault of typhus and malaria, but also against the hostility and derision of the existing Jewish community. On the evidence of contemporary records, these levantinized old settlers, who led a parasitic existence on " the Baron's " grants, despised manual labour, quarrelled, bribed and cheated, were a thoroughly unpleasant type. A product of the Eastern European ghettoes, transplanted in space but not transformed in spirit, they were a warning indication of the thwarting influence of ghetto life on social character. Their example showed

[1] Published by the Youth Department of the Zionist Organization, Tel Aviv, 1945.

at the same time that religious fervour has not necessarily a positive influence on social behaviour — for even the worst crooks in the crooked communities of Old Jerusalem or Rishon le Zion were strictly and zealously orthodox.

2

The old settlers nevertheless fulfilled a historical function. Their example, by effect of contrast, drove home to the Zionist settlers how not to build their National Home. It gave birth to " the idea of the spade ", to the revolutionary conviction that Israel could only be reborn as a nation if it acquired a social structure like all other nations, with a solid base of farmers and manual labourers. The promised land could only become theirs in the literal sense if they tilled its soil with their own hands; " If I spend not my strength I shall not gather the crop ", wrote the Hebrew poet Byalik. In order to become " normalized " the Jews had to reverse the social pyramid of the ghetto where for centuries they had been denied access to all productive occupations and condemned to the parasitic existence of money-lenders, traders and middlemen. The successful reversal of the pyramid is illustrated by the fact that in 1943, as against 55 per cent of the population employed in manual labour, only 11 per cent were engaged in commerce, the traditional occupation of the Diaspora.[1]

This new insight shaped the whole character of the Zionist movement. It gave rise to the movement for a " return to the land " — a neo-Rousseauism which, in the special case of the Jews, was not a romantic whim, but anchored in historical necessity. It gave birth to the slogan of *kibbush avodah* — literally translated, "the conquest of labour". In a narrower sense this meant the struggle to force the old settlers to employ Jewish workmen; in its wider sense, the effort to redirect the sons of Polish lawyers and shopkeepers into the manual labour of direct production.

Once this necessity was recognized, it was developed with typical Jewish exuberance into a new cult, the almost mystic worship of manual work, of " labour which ennobles ". This cult in its turn became ideologically fused with Marxist class-conscious-

[1] *Memorandum on Jewish Development under the Mandate*, submitted by the Jewish Agency for Palestine to the Anglo-American Committee of Enquiry, Jerusalem, 1946.

ness on the one hand and with Tolstoian ideas on the other, the whole resting on traditional Jewish messianism with Palestine as its Promised Land. This curious ideological blend, a synthesis of national renaissance and socialist utopia, became incarnated in its purest form in the collective settlements, which give Israel its unique character as a social experiment. In a less radically purist form it became the guiding star of the Palestine Labour Movement and of Zionist colonization in general.

Led by these principles, the Jewish migration became a planned and socialized enterprise. It was centrally financed and directed by an international body, the Zionist Organization. Every two years the democratically elected delegates of the Zionist Congress met in Europe to decide the broad outlines of colonizatory policy, while in Palestine the Zionist Executive and Jewish Agency (the two were practically identical) formed, as already mentioned, a shadow Government under the Mandatory Power.

Within the Jewish Agency, as also in the Zionist Organization at large, the Labour Party and trade unions occupied a dominant position. Thus both Jewish industry and agriculture in Palestine had from the beginning a planned socialist character. More than half of Israel's industrial enterprises are owned and run on a cooperative basis by the trade unions.[1] In agriculture the older citrus plantations are privately owned, but the mixed farming areas are mostly State property. They were acquired by the Jewish National Fund, are the "inalienable property of the nation", and are leased to collective or individual settlers for long periods with option of renewal. Thus land speculation is eliminated in the greater part of the rural areas, and the development both of a landowner class and of rural paupers made impossible. Nor is there a place for usury, the curse of the farmer in oriental countries. The settlers get their land from the National Fund, and their capital investments from the Foundation Fund (Keren Hayesod), from cooperative workers' banks and other public institutions, at a low fixed rate of interest. They market their produce through a nation-wide workers' cooperative and buy their commodities through a similar organization. The workings of this socialized system of economy will be discussed later. The essential point is that from the very beginnings of modern Zionist colonization the experiment was run on planned collective lines.

Of particular interest was the financing of the Jewish National

[1] Cf. Book Three, Chapter I.

Fund (*Keren Kayemet*), the main instrument of land acquisition
in Palestine.   One of the chief arguments of anti-Zionist propaganda was that the Arabs were being edged out of Palestine by the
gold of Jewish High Finance.   In fact, however, though big
donations were frequent, the *Keren Kayemet's* main source of
income was the pennies and cents and francs and zlotys dropped
by Jews all over the world into its blue collecting-boxes — begging
bowls for the purchase of a kingdom.   It looks like an ironic
punishment of the worshippers of the golden calf by their old
desert God that they had to purchase their country acre by acre
on the instalment plan.

As for Jewish high finance and the great banking houses, their
contributions were never on a decisive scale, but rather in the
nature of a few thousand pounds paid as philanthropic conscience
money.   Had Jewish high finance weighed in with large-scale
transactions aimed at influencing political developments, it is
conceivable that they could have achieved sufficient pressure at
least to mitigate the immigration bar of 1939.   But the fact is that
Jewish financiers were reluctant to touch political Zionism, for
fear of endangering their position in their own countries.   This
was the cause of much bitterness on the part of the Zionists.   And
yet the socially positive features of Israel are due to the fact that
it has come into being not through the action of financial pressure
groups, but by the pioneering efforts and financial sacrifices of
the Jewish masses.

3

To sum up.

The existence of the State of Israel is based on the colonizatory
achievements of Jews extending over a period of thirty years from
1918 to 1948.

The mystic attachment of the Jews to Palestine was transformed into a legal claim by the Balfour Declaration and the
League of Nations Mandate.   But unlike Shylock's claim to the
promised pound of flesh, the Zionist case is based, both materially
and morally, on the sacrifices and achievements of the Jewish
pioneers.   Unlike any previous colonizers, the Jews acquired their
land not by force or by threat of force, but for hard cash from
willing sellers.   Most of the land thus acquired was waste land
which the pioneers reclaimed with the work of their hands, paying
heavy toll to tropical disease and hostile raiders.   Unlike any
previous colonizers, they did not exploit cheap native labour. but

took their pride in becoming " hewers of wood and drawers of water ". They brought material prosperity to the native population, but no cultural values — and no possible consolation for the fact that they were gradually taking the country over. The pressure of persecution in Europe, and their superior civilization, made their victory inevitable and in this sense " historically just ", while according to other standards of value the fate of the Arabs remains a pathetic injustice.

In fifty years' time, when Israel's history is counted from the day of its birth on May 15, 1948, few will take an interest in the struggles and shocks to which it was exposed in the pre-natal stage. Yet nations, like individuals, retain characteristic traces of these experiences. Whatever shape the culture of the new State of Israel may take, its pattern and values will reflect the formative influences both of the early pioneer days, which we have discussed in the preceding chapters, and of the tragic suspense and birth labour of the decade starting in 1939, to which we now turn.

PART TWO

SUSPENSE
(1939 – 1945)

CHAPTER V

THE PALESTINE MUNICH

The collapse of a dream and the beginning of a nightmare
—Antecedents of the White Paper — The Mufti's rebellion
and its reward — Decline and fall of the Middle East
experts

The philosophy of appeasement — Implications of a
Round Table Conference — Mitigating circumstances of
British policy — On disbelieving atrocities — Relativity of
ethical judgment

I

1939 was a landmark for the world in general and for Israel in particular.

For humanity at large it was the year in which the Second World War began. For Israel it was the year in which the death sentence of over six million Jews was pronounced, and their escape to Palestine barred by the Chamberlain Government's White Paper.

This crucial document, on which the fate of the National Home hinged, and the whole Palestine controversy was centred for a decade, was issued in May 1939. Its main points were, firstly, that after a last batch of 75,000 Jews, to be admitted to Palestine between 1939 and 1944, further immigration was to be subject to Arab approval — in other words, barred virtually for ever. Secondly, it empowered the High Commissioner to prohibit the sale of land by Arabs to Jews in specified areas — which areas were defined in the Land Transfer Regulations of 1940 so as to cover practically 95 per cent of the country. It finally provided for the establishment within ten years of an independent Arab State in which the Jews were not to exceed one-third of the population — in other words, condemned them to a perpetual minority status.

Thus, at the very moment when the extermination of the European Jews began, the doors of Palestine were slammed in their faces, while those already inside Palestine, who had come on the strength of the British undertaking that they would find there a National Home, found themselves trapped and condemned to live in " one more precarious oriental ghetto ".[1] It was the collapse of a dream and the beginning of a nightmare which was to last to the end of the British Mandate. For the Jews in Palestine the fate of their European kin was not a matter of abstract solidarity ; they had come from Central and Eastern Europe, and every single one of them had left relatives behind — parents, brothers and sisters whom he knew trapped in German-occupied territory and doomed to some atrocious form of death. This nightmare lasted during the whole six years of war, when Palestine was cut off from communication with Europe, and the half-million Palestine Jews lived in uncertainty about the fate of their families, until at last, in 1945, the Red Cross began to publish lists of the survivors in the extermination camps. Such sustained psychological pressure must inevitably find violent outlets ; rage and despair gradually transformed the law-abiding pioneer country into a second Ireland.

Before we turn to the events which the White Paper brought in its wake, a few words must be said about the causes which had led to its inception. As we saw, British Cabinet policy during the twenty years which followed the Balfour Declaration was one of hesitancy and irresolution, while the local administration in Palestine gradually developed a marked anti-semitic bias. In 1937 the Royal Commission, in the most thorough assessment of the Palestine problem so far made, had reached the conclusion that the Mandate was unworkable, and had recommended the partition of the country as the only possible solution which " if it offers neither party all it wants, offers each what it wants most, namely freedom and security . . . and the inestimable boon of peace ".[2]

Partition meant " that the Arabs must acquiesce in the exclusion from their sovereignty of a piece of territory long occupied and once ruled by them ".[3] It meant, on the other hand, that the Jews had to content themselves with a fraction of the National Home which they had been promised — in fact about one-twentieth of the territory originally covered by the Balfour Declaration. It was not an ideal solution, but in view of the incompatibility of the conflicting claims, it was the only possible

[1] Mr. Churchill in the White Paper debate, May 1939.
[2] Royal Commission Report, p. 296.
[3] *Ibid.* p. 296.

solution.[1] It was to be finally endorsed, after ten years of needless torment and bloodshed, by the United Nations, and implemented by a short but decisive test of strength.

Shortly after publication of the Royal Commission's Report, however, fresh Arab riots broke out in Palestine. They were met by the Administration with the same leniency which the Report had castigated in unmistakeable terms,[2] and were allowed to develop into a miniature rebellion which lasted until the beginning of 1939. The Arab guerilla bands operated from the hills, holding their own villagers for ransom, swooping down on isolated Jewish settlements, and systematically assassinating the members of the moderate Nashashibi clan. They were financed by the Grand Mufti (who had meanwhile made his escape to Syria) and his clan, the Husseinis, traditional enemies of the Nashashibis.

According to British estimates, the number of the guerilla fighters never exceeded 1500.[3] They were mostly mercenaries recruited from Syria, and led by a Levantine adventurer named Fawzi Kaukaji. Ten years later, in April 1948, the same Fawzi Kaukaji was to lead the so-called Arab Liberation Army, which was defeated by the still illegal Haganah forces after a fight of three days. He subsequently fled to Syria and returned in June as commander of an invading army operating in Galilee. This time he was defeated in two days, and pursued by the Israeli forces into the Lebanon. The parallel is relevant. In 1938-39 a small band of Arab guerillas was able to hold out for two years against His Majesty's Forces in Palestine. In 1948 an Arab army led by the same commander was driven from the country in a few days by the unseasoned Israeli troops. In 1938 Kaukaji was a rebel without official outside support, while the British troops had the equipment of a regular armed force. In 1948 he had the support of five sovereign Arab States, while the Israeli Army fought alone on five fronts. The conclusion can hardly be avoided that the British effort to end the Arab disturbances of 1936-39 was not a whole-hearted one. Rather it once more

" helped to foster a belief in the Arab mind that the National Home was not an immutable point of policy and that if Arab resistance to it were sufficiently obstinate and forcible, the

---

[1] It may be mentioned in passing that this writer has advocated partition in word and print for the last twenty years.　　　　[2] Cf. p. 17.
[3] Cf. i.a., H. J. Simson, *British Rule and Rebellion*, London, 1937.

Mandatory power might presently be worried or even frightened into giving it up ".[1]

The Royal Commission's observation proved prophetic. The White Paper of May 1939 could only be interpreted as a capitulation of the Mandatory Power before the Grand Mufti's guerillas.

" It seemed that Jewish self-restraint during the trying years of the disturbances had been penalized, and Arab aggression rewarded. The inference that violence was the surest method to achieve political success was inescapable. The sinister lesson sank deep into the consciousness of Arabs and Jews alike." [2]

The " Palestine Munich ", as the White Paper was called by its Labour critics, came nine months after the European Munich. But while the Chamberlain Government, in leaving Czechoslovakia to its fate, had the excuse of retreating before the most efficient war machine that Europe had ever seen, it had no similar excuse in terms of expediency for going back on Britain's pledge to the Jews. The Arabs in 1938 were much weaker than in 1948 — Syria and the Lebanon were still under French, Transjordan under British, Mandate ; and Major Glubb, Commander of the Arab Legion, was not yet detailed to be a crusader in Islam's Holy War. If the combined forces of the Arab States could be beaten by Israel in 1948, nobody can seriously pretend that a fraction of them could have represented a threat to British interests in 1939. And yet, strange as it seems in the light of subsequent events, strategic expediency was the argument, and the only argument, for the " cynical breach of faith", to quote Mr. Churchill, the " base betrayal ", to quote Mr. Morrison, of the Chamberlain Government in May 1939.

The clue to this fantastic miscalculation of the relative strength of Jews and Arabs in 1939 — and again in 1948, when Foreign Office experts confidently predicted the collapse of Israel within a matter of days — is a psychological one. The myth of the irresistible Arab Holy War is a deeply ingrained belief of Christianity. Its unconscious, archetypal roots are probably fed by school-book memories of the Moorish and Turkish conquests, and by romanticized versions of the Revolt in the Desert. " We dearly love the

[1] Royal Commission Report, p. 80.
[2] Political Memorandum submitted to the Anglo-American Committee of Enquiry by the Jewish Agency for Palestine, Jerusalem, 1946.

bogey of a fanatical army of millions of desert Arabs yelling
' Allah ! ' and putting infidels to the sword, and I imagine the
idea must have started about the eleventh century during the First
Crusade." [1]

The working of the archetype on the allegedly sober strategic
mind may be illustrated by a grotesque and fairly unknown
episode from the First World War. Early in 1917 a few thousand
Senussi tribesmen raided the Libyan desert from Tripoli. They
were beaten and dispersed without difficulty by some second-line
British Territorials scraped together from the Canal zone. With
that the incident was over, and no further fighting occurred in
the Libyan desert until the next World War twenty-five years
later ; but the myth of an impending Holy War

" tied up on the Western Frontier for over a year some 30,000
troops badly required elsewhere, and caused us to expend on
desert railways, desert cars, transport, etc., sufficient to add
2d. to the income-tax for the lifetime of the present generation.
It is very difficult to decide now who actually was to blame for
this state of affairs — probably the Intelligence Department in
the first place, as they imbued the soldiers with the idea that if
the Senussi penetrated to the Nile Valley the whole of Egypt
would rise in a holy war against us, which, to say the least, was
a gross and absurd exaggeration. . . . For months our troops
remained facing a perfectly empty desert . . . and they continued to do so until at last the authorities decided very regret-
fully that the Senussi was a myth. . . ." [2]

Two years later, in 1919, the bogy cropped up once more.

" Telegrams were showering in on me to the effect that
hordes of Arabs, estimated at 40,000, were marching on Cairo
and Alexandria from the Libyan Desert . . . but after a two
days' patrol that covered the greater part of the north-west
portion of the Western Desert, I failed utterly to find anything
in the nature of an organization, and wired back to that effect.
I was not believed, for the Powers that Be in Cairo had faithfully
predicted that a rising of Arabs would be the natural sequence
of events ; and as a nation we have definitely a marked Arab
complex." [3]

[1] C. S. Jarvis, *Three Deserts*, London, 1936. Major Jarvis held various
commands in the Libyan desert during the First World War, and was Governor
of the Sinai Peninsula from 1923 to 1936.
[2] Jarvis, *op. cit.*   [3] *Ibid.*

E

Ten years later the Arab complex still continued to play havoc with British strategy, regardless of the change of government.

" The danger of an Arab Holy War is now being used more intensively than ever by officials in the Colonial Service and in the various Middle Eastern Embassies as an argument against the acceptance of the Anglo-American Report. But history does not substantiate this line of argument. . . . Europeans tend to overlook the fact that the difference between the Lebanon and Saudi Arabia is much more pronounced than the difference, say, between France and Bulgaria. . . . The last quarter century abounds in examples of local Arab disturbances. None of them ever produced any unified action in the Arab states. Even Lawrence's desert campaign, stripped of its legendary aspects, was from a military point of view a modest affair. The Druse revolt, the Palestine revolt, or Rashid Ali's revolt in 1941, found no mass-echo in the surrounding countries and retained the character of large-scale but localized riots — a major nuisance to the British commander on the spot but of no strategical significance." [1]

This traditional over-estimation of Arab unity and military weight was reinforced by an emotive tendency to wishful thinking among British oriental experts. Generations of Pashas and Beys from Surrey and Kent had devoted their lives to the Arab cause, and had become emotionally identified with it. The Zionist adventure meant to them a wanton imperilment of their great vision of an Arab renaissance under British patronage, the object of their patient labours and sincere devotion. It was impossible for them to realize that potentially the Arabs were already beaten by the Jewish intruders on the oriental scene. Their ideology was a blend of imperial strategy and Arab romanticism. Untouched by Marxist temptations and ignorant of the elementary facts of sociology, it never occurred to them that their dream of the rebirth of the Arab Caliphate was an anachronism, that a national renaissance was impossible as long as the Arab countries retained their mediaeval, feudal structure of corrupt landowners and poverty-stricken, illiterate masses. Not until ten years later did the dream dissolve under the impact of the Arab League's defeat by the improvised armies of the Jewish State.

It was in fact the Arab experts of the Foreign Office who

[1] *A Palestine Munich*, by R. H. S Crossman, M P., and Michael Foot, M P., London, 1946.

lived in cloud-cuckoo-land, and not the pioneers of streamlined Jewish messianism. Sociologically, the latter were the harbingers of the twentieth century in the Middle East ; under their impact British Orient strategy collapsed like a house of cards.

It could not, of course, be expected that the men on the spot should admit, even to themselves, that what they had been building with such patient effort was a house of cards. They were the men who could quietly say during a discussion : " My dear sir, I have known this country for thirty years . . ." ; who spoke several Arab dialects, who " knew the oriental mind " and had spent more nights in Bedouin tents than the intimidated partner in argument had drunk glasses of whiskey in his life. In fact, they didn't even say all this, they conveyed it by gazing in silent modesty at the glass in their hand. Gradually, in the course of decades, the wishful thinking and emotional bias of the men on the spot, the Abdul Rahman Hendersons and Glubb Pashas and Clayton Effendis, became the axiom and doctrine of British Middle East policy.

Mr. Chamberlain's Government had, for reasons beyond the scope of this book, embraced a general philosophy of appeasement. The experts said that the Arabs represented an impressive power, the Jews a minor nuisance on the oriental scene. This was apparently borne out by the fact that for years now the Arabs in Palestine had been riotously truculent, the Jews timid and law-abiding. The obvious inference was that the Arabs had to be appeased, the Jews left to their fate with a murmured regret. After all, Mr. Chamberlain had said in as many words that a Great Power like Britain could not be expected to risk war for the sake of a small country like Czechoslovakia. How, then, could one expect her to risk a Holy War against forty million Arabs for the sake of half a million Jews ? The warning of the Royal Commission that " to repress a Jewish rebellion against British policy would be as unpleasant a task as the repression of Arab rebellions has been " [1] went unheeded, as did similar warnings by Mr. Churchill and the Labour Party.

2

The motives behind the Chamberlain Government's Palestine policy became evident during the preliminaries to the launching

[1] Royal Commission Report, p. 103.

of the White Paper. In February 1939 the Government called a Round Table Conference of Arabs and Jews to London. The proceedings of this Conference were marked by two significant innovations. Firstly, when the Palestine Arabs refused to sit at one table with the Jews, the British Government endorsed this affront and agreed to conduct separate negotiations with the two parties. Secondly, His Majesty's Government invited not only representatives of the Jewish and Arab populations of Palestine, but also representatives of the Governments of Egypt, Iraq and Saudi Arabia. Never before had a British Government, when negotiating with Egypt, or any other Arab State, invited the neighbouring States to participate in the parley. By taking this diplomatically unprecedented step the British Government intended to demonstrate that Palestine was not merely the concern of its local population, but of the Arab world at large. As a rule, a Colonial Power will do everything to rebuff attempts by outside parties to interfere in its administration ; in this case interference by sovereign Arab States in Palestine affairs was directly invited. The course was set for a policy which the Foreign Office was consistently to pursue in the years to come. The initiative of giving the Arab States a *locus standi* in Palestine was followed by the initiative for the creation of an Arab League which, torn by internal conflict and dynastic rivalries, remained a diplomatic fiction in all respects but one : the fight against Zionism. The presence, on British invitation, of the neighbouring Arab States at the Round Table Conference of 1939 was the prelude to the presence, with active British support, of their invading armies in Palestine in 1948.

3

The Chamberlain Government's policy was, indicted as contrary to international law by the League of Nations Mandates Commission, and in words of rarely heard vehemence from all sides of the House of Commons. The White Paper aroused a storm of protest from the United States, and has done more harm to British prestige than any other single political decision in many years past. It was an inhuman policy from the point of view of morality, and from the point of view of expediency a serious blunder. But the picture would be one-sided were we to ignore the arguments in its favour, which at the time carried considerable weight.

Great Britain was faced with a war for which it was unprepared ; and it was the Government's duty to clear the decks for action with the ruthlessness which the emergency demanded. The Axis Powers had been very active for some years in the Arab countries, where British influence was on the wane. By sacrificing the Jewish National Home the Chamberlain Government hoped to regain some of the lost ground and to neutralize Arab hostility during the coming conflict. That this calculation was erroneous, as Rashid Ali's pro-Axis revolution in Iraq, the attitude of the Egyptian Court and General Staff, of the Syrian and Palestine Arabs later proved, does not alter the fact that, thanks to the advice of its Arab experts, the Government was honestly convinced that it had no alternative but to play the Arab against the Jewish card.

If we switch from the plane of expediency to the plane of humanitarian considerations, the main feature of the White Paper policy was lack of imagination — the inability of the British mind to conceive that Hitler's atrocious threats against the Jews were meant in earnest. The fear of impending massacres was shrugged off as exaggeration and Jewish hysteria. I have written elsewhere about the psychological defence-mechanisms responsible for the phenomenon of this stubborn " disbelief in atrocities " which is particularly pronounced in Anglo-Saxon countries.[1] This phenomenon influenced not only British policy in Palestine, with bitter consequences to the Jews, but was equally characteristic of Britain's general attitude to Nazism, Fascism and, later on, to Soviet totalitarianism ; with equally bitter consequences to Czechs, Poles, Balts and the world at large. Rarely has the cry " Father, forgive them, for they know not what they do " attained a more tragic significance than in the policy of the Anglo-Saxon Powers between the wars. The Jewish refugee tragedy was merely one episode in this general pattern.

For, and this is the third point to be made, Britain's undeniable guilt in barring the Jewish escape road to Palestine can only be seen in its proper perspective by comparing it to the policies and actions of the other big Powers of the day. Germany was trying to impose her New Order with a savagery unseen in Europe since the Dark Ages. Russia had in 1939 concluded her own super-Munich with Hitler, and was deporting Poles and Balts by their

[1] *On Disbelieving Atrocities*, " The Yogi and the Commissar ", London, 1945.

hundreds of thousands to Central Asia and the Arctic labour camps. The United States, mainstay of democracy, were still rubbing their eyes and washing their hands of Europe in lease-lend soap. It was a time, as somebody put it after the conclusion of the Nazi-Communist alliance, when all " isms " had become " wasms ". Europe had become a jungle and the British Government was howling with the wolves. Compared with the gigantic scale of perfidy of Stalin's pact with Hitler, and with the savagery of Hitler's massacre of the Jews, the White Paper appears as a relatively minor sin, and essentially more a sin of omission than a calculated one.

To put the callous policy of the Mandatory Power on a par with the barbarity of Hitlerism, as the Jewish terrorists did in their slogan of the " Nazi-British ", is of course unjust and stupid. It expresses that incapacity to make distinctions of degree which characterizes the mental climate of our age, and is by no means restricted to fanatics. The slogan of the " Nazi-British " is on a par with those of the " Social-Fascists ", " Judeo-Bolsheviks " and the rest. The British White Paper regime in Palestine cannot be measured by absolute ethical standards ; it must be judged against the background of the moral depravity of Europe at the time. And lastly, the scales of justice would be biassed if the Palestine Administration's responsibility for the drowning of the 800 refugees of the *Struma* were not weighed against the thousands of Jewish children and adults who found a haven on the British Isles thanks to the dogged efforts of English Quakers, trade unionists and philanthropic societies.

This warning should be constantly borne in mind during the following sections which deal with the grim facts produced by British policy in Palestine from the outbreak of the war to the termination of the Mandate.

CHAPTER VI

THE LITTLE DEATH SHIPS

The League refuses to endorse the White Paper — Jewish
denial of its legality — The death-blow — Let the children
come unto me — The one spy in a hundred — " Nothing
whatever will be done ".

Assandu, Assimi and *Tiger Hill — Pacific, Patria* and
Milos — Atlantic and *Salvador* — The *Struma* — The
blindness of the heart.

The little death ships and the rise of terrorism

I

THE story of Palestine from May 1939 to the end of the war is
essentially the story of Jews trying to save their skins, and of the
efforts of the Mandatory Power to prevent this through an immigration blockade maintained by force and diplomatic pressure.

In June 1939 the White Paper came up for discussion before
the Permanent Mandates Commission of the League of Nations.
The Commission found unanimously that it was incompatible
with the construction put on the Mandate in the past by the
Mandatory Power itself, while the majority found in addition that
it was incompatible with any possible construction which might
be put on it. Now, according to Article 26 of the Mandate, " the
consent of the Council of the League of Nations is required for
any modification of the terms of this Mandate ". The Council
of the League was to meet in September 1939 ; but meanwhile
the war broke out and it never met. As the Mandatory Commission (and leading politicians of all parties in Britain itself) had
found that the White Paper amounted to a very definite modification of the Mandate, Britain's new policy could only gain legal
validity by the League's consent ; and this consent was never
given. The Jews, therefore, had reasonable grounds for denying
the White Paper's legality. This was the juridical basis of the
Jewish Agency's refusal to consider immigration exceeding the
White Paper quotas as " illegal ", or activities designed to facilitate the rescue of the doomed Jews of Europe as unlawful, even

55

if they contravened administrative ordinances based on the White Paper.

The first of these ordinances was a death-blow to all hope of rescuing the most directly threatened portion of Europe's Jews, those in Germany and Poland. At the outbreak of the war the Government decreed that people from Germany or German-occupied Polish territory were not to be admitted into Palestine (except the small number of those who already held pre-war immigration certificates, and valid immigration visas in addition). Before the outbreak of war, that is before these regulations had come into force, the Jewish Agency had asked for the immediate admission of 20,000 children from Poland and of 10,000 young men from the Balkan countries. The requests were rejected, and the Polish-Jewish children went to Maidanek and Auschwitz instead.

In May 1940, when the new regulations banning the admission of Jews from German-occupied territory were already in force, the Jewish Agency made a new application — supplication would perhaps be the correct term — for the exemption of children and certain adults of known identity from the deadly ban. Fantastic as it sounds, it took the Mandatory Administration nearly two years to make up its mind on this issue. All exceptions in favour of adults were refused. The concession regarding the children came too late.

It is essential, not only in the present context but for the whole development of Anglo-Jewish relations, to bear in mind that the Jews in immediate danger of life were those in German-occupied territory; that precisely these people's escape to Palestine had been declared " illegal " by the Mandatory Administration's wanton decrees; that consequently to help " illegal " immigration had become the supreme ethical commandment for every Jew inside or outside Palestine. For it can hardly be contested that the pretence of administering a National Home for people who are not permitted to enter it, even when in danger of life, was a moral perfidy and legally absurd. One may imagine the effect, under these circumstances, of official Palestine Government announcements like the following, made on November 20, 1940 :

" H.M. Government are not lacking in sympathy for refugees from territories under German control. But they are responsible for the administration of Palestine, and are bound to see to it that the laws of the country are not openly flouted. Moreover, they can only regard a revival of illegal Jewish immigration at the present juncture as likely to affect the local situation most adversely, and to prove a serious menace to British interests in the Middle East. . . ."

The " menace to British interests in the Middle East " was specified on a later occasion (see p. 63) as affecting " security and food supply ". The second argument is too frivolous for serious consideration (Palestine was one of the best-fed countries during the war). As for security, that is, the danger of Jewish refugees acting as Nazi agents — a practically unknown occurrence during the whole war — the obvious answer was to keep refugees whose loyalty was not completely ascertained in safe internment for the duration, instead of condemning, under the pretext that there might be one spy among a hundred refugees, the whole hundred to extermination. This same argument about the possible " one spy in a hundred " has served the Soviet Government as a constant pretext for refusing to admit Spanish militiamen, International Brigaders, persecuted Communists or any other category of refugees into Soviet territory, and for condemning the populations of entire republics (Crimeans, Tchetchens, Volga Germans) to deportation. It is the classic argument of ruthless totalitarianism against the claims of humanity. Yet to the Jewish Agency's supplications to let the condemned men in under any conditions of screening or internment before their fate was consummated — the reply was that internment was " not a desirable solution ".[1]

In fact the whole argument about security was merely an awkward pretext. The Government's real motive was their fear of " upsetting the Arabs " which had grown into an obsession, into a policy of fanatic appeasement as it were, carried to an extreme where it lost all touch with reality. British Middle East strategy had been built on a myth ; British decency and humaneness were sacrificed to a bogy. The Government's attitude was bluntly summarized in a communication from Lord Cranborne to the Jewish Agency in May 1942 which declared : " In pursuance of the existing policy of taking all practicable steps to discourage illegal immigration into Palestine, nothing whatever

[1] D. Trevor, *Under the White Paper*, Jerusalem, 1948, p 29 See footnote on p. 63

will be done to facilitate the arrival of Jewish refugees in Palestine ".[1]

The date of this communication should be noted. At that time the death trains had started rattling through Eastern Europe and the mass extermination had begun. Three months earlier the Jewish Agency had communicated the relevant facts in their possession to the Palestine Government. The Government could not claim ignorance ; only the mitigating circumstance that they had eyes which saw not, and ears which heard not.

2

The practical consequences of this policy were, in the words of an American writer, that in Palestine

" over half a million Jews waited with open arms for their tormented kin . . . while over the Mediterranean and Black Seas unclean and unseaworthy little cargo boats crept from port to port or tossed about on the open waters, waiting in vain for permission to discharge their crowded human cargoes. Hunger, thirst, disease and unspeakable living conditions reigned on those floating coffins. . . . There is a list of mass tragedies already available ; incomplete though it certainly must be, it is sickeningly long." [2]

Out of this list of mass tragedies only a few shall be mentioned here. Even before the promulgation of the White Paper, in March and April 1939, three refugee ships — the *Assandu*, *Assimi* and *Panagia Konstario* — packed with Jews who had escaped from Germany and Rumania, reached Palestine and were refused permission to land. In the House of Commons Mr. Noel-Baker asked the Colonial Secretary, Mr. Malcolm MacDonald, what would happen to these people. Mr. MacDonald said they had been sent back to where they came from.

Mr. Noel-Baker : " Does that mean to concentration camps ? "

Mr. MacDonald : " The responsibility rests with those responsible for organizing illegal immigration." [3]

The theme was set and remained unchanged for a decade , its

---

[1] M Samuel, *Harvest in the Desert*, Philadelphia, 1944.

[2] Statements and Memoranda, presented by the Jewish Agency to the Anglo-American Committee of Enquiry, Jerusalem, 1947, p. 296.

[3] Debate in the House of Commons, April 26-27, 1939.

variations in officialese were repeated over and over again, to the accompaniment of the rumbling of the death trains and the hissing of chlorine let into the gas chambers.

As human imagination is indifferent to the fate of an01.ymous masses and only responds to detail, it may not be out of place to quote here a passage from an open letter by this author, written under the emotive impact of the events described : [1]

> " Try to put yourself in the place of a Jew of your own age on the jetty of Haifa, shouting and waving to a relative — your son for instance — on the deck of one of those ships. He is not permitted to land ; the ship lifts anchor to take its doomed hysterical load back to where it came from. The figure of your boy grows smaller ; a few years later you hear that he has been gassed in Oswiecim. If, instead of Smith, your name were Schmulewitz, it might have happened to you. Something on the same lines happened, among others, to a man whom I met in Palestine two years ago ; he told me that his mother and three brothers had been killed ' by German sadism and the British White Paper '. His name is David Friedman-Yellin, and he is the head of the so-called Stern Gang."

The hunting down of "illegal immigrants" became gradually an obsession with the Palestine authorities. At the time when refugee ships were being turned back to their port of origin, a special Ordinance authorized the Palestine Coast Guards to shoot " at or into " any ship suspected of bringing illegal immigrants and refusing to turn by.[2] The prophecy of Philip Noel-Baker, that under the new policy the only way to stop refugees would be " to tell those kindly British soldiers to shoot them down ",[3] came true ; on September 1, 1939, the first two refugees were killed on board the immigrant ship *Tiger Hill* by fire from a police coastal cutter. From that date to the end of the Mandate such incidents became a regular occurrence.

[1] " Open Letter to a Parent of a British Soldier in Palestine ", *New Statesman and Nation*, August 16, 1947.

[2] Palestine Gazette Extraordinary, April 27, 1939

[3] " If the Secretary of State's policy is now adopted, the illegal immigration of these tortured people from Germany and elsewhere will enormously increase The Jews of Palestine will go by the tens of thousands down to the beach to welcome and to cover and protect their landing. The only way to stop them is to tell those kindly British soldiers to shoot them down. . . . For that, if for no other reason, this policy is bound to fail "—Debate in the House of Commons, April 26-27, 1939.

When the war began it became technically impossible to turn refugee ships back to their country of origin. And yet they kept arriving; no White Papers and Ordinances could abolish the will to survive. In November 1940 two derelict tramp steamers, the *Pacific* and the *Milos*, managed to get as far as Haifa with 1800 survivors on board. The majority among them were Zionists trained in agricultural work who at the eve of the war had been waiting for their turn on the immigration quota; several hundreds among them had relatives in Palestine. As they could not be sent back to Germany, the Government decided to deport them to the tropical island of Mauritius for the duration of the war. In order to kill the last spark of hope in the deportees' minds, the Government took pains to point out that even *after* the war entry into Palestine would be refused them:

> " Their ultimate disposal will be a matter for consideration after the war, but it is not proposed that they shall remain in the colony to which they are sent *or that they should go to Palestine*. Similar action will be taken in the case of any further parties who may succeed in reaching Palestine with a view to illegal entry." [1]

But the deportees never sailed to the Indian Ocean. They were transferred from their two unseaworthy ships to the British steamer *Patria*, and were to sail from Haifa on November 25, 1940. At 9 A.M. on that day the passengers blew up their ship. Over two hundred of them were torn to bits, or drowned a hundred yards from the shore of their promised land. They had reached their journey's end. They were not even threatened with deportation back to Europe; only to a tropical island without hope of return. But these people had become allergic to barbed wire. When a person reaches that stage he is past listening to the reasonable voice of officialdom which explains to him that he should never have escaped, or saved his wife and children, as " a revival of illegal Jewish immigration at the present juncture " was " likely to affect the local situation most adversely ".[2]

The whole Jewish population of Haifa had been watching the preparations for the *Patria*'s departure and saw her blow up. Among them was a boy of fourteen named Eliyahu Ben Hakim, who lived in Panorama Street on Mount Carmel and saw through his

[1] Palestine Government Statement, November 20, 1940. My italics.
[2] *Ibid.*

field-glasses the corpses floating in the water, and women without arms or heads being dragged into boats by fish-hooks. Four years later the boy shot Britain's Resident Minister, Lord Moyne, in a street in Cairo and was duly hanged.

Altogether 260 persons were drowned in this incident. The day before the tragedy another hell ship had arrived : the 800-ton paddle-steamer *Atlantic*, carrying the survivors of the Jewish community of Danzig, together with other refugees from Austria and Czechoslovakia, and their wives and children, 1880 persons in all. Typhus had broken out on the ship, and during the last twelve hours of the journey to Haifa fifteen passengers had died on board. They were still fishing for the corpses of the *Patria* victims in Haifa harbour, but this did not deter the Palestine Government from having the new arrivals deported. They were taken off board to the concentration camp of Athlit, and a fortnight later, on Sunday, December 8, were dragged out by force from their huts in the camp and shipped off — the majority naked, as they offered passive resistance and had to be carried one by one on stretchers amidst scenes of mass hysteria — to the island of Mauritius.

They stayed on that malaria-ridden tropical island for five full years, until August 1945. During the first two and a half years the male deportees were kept in cells in an old French prison, while the women lived in corrugated-iron huts, twenty-four to a hut. They were allowed to see each other three times a week for two hours Fifty children were born on the island. One hundred and twenty-six persons, or round 10 per cent of the deportees, died of tropical diseases.

And still more ships were on their way towards the land which was still called the Jewish National Home. In December 1940 a 75-foot sailing-boat, the *Salvador*, carrying 350 refugees from Bulgaria, reached the Turkish coast. By that time the Palestine Government had communicated to the Turkish authorities their refusal to grant entry permits to Jews from occupied Europe. Accordingly the Turkish authorities refused to admit into their territory refugees not already possessed of a Palestine visa. The *Salvador* was permitted to take food and water, and then turned back to the high seas. She was dismasted in a storm, and 231 of her passengers — men, women and children — were drowned. The survivors were brought back to Istanbul and were still refused Palestine visas. One part of them was forcibly sent back to Bulgaria under German occupation. The remaining 70 embarked on yet another refugee ship, the s.s. *Darien*, and managed to reach Haifa four months later, in March 1941. As the vessel was on the point of sinking, the refugees had to be landed. Thus were 70 out of 350 allowed to survive.

The effect of the Government's declared policy that " nothing whatever will be done to facilitate the arrival of Jewish refugees " is expressed by the following immigration figures :

1938 .	. 13,000		1942 .	. 3,700
1939 .	. 27,500		1943 .	. 8,500
1940 .	. 8,000		1944 .	. 14,500
1941 .	. 6,000			

As the German armies progressed through Europe, one country after another became " enemy occupied territory " from which, according to the Immigration Ordinance of 1939, no Jew was permitted to enter Palestine. As for countries not yet occupied by the enemy, the White Paper had authorized the immigration of the last batch of 75,000 at a rate of 15,000 a year. But as a measure of retaliation against the continued trickle of " illegals ", like the shipwrecked passengers of the *Salvador*, who had dared to survive without official consent, even the immigration quotas for refugees from non-occupied territories were withheld for the decisive half-year periods October 1939 to March 1940, and October 1940 to March 1941. The latter period immediately preceded the German occupation of the Balkans. Except for a few hundred emergency permits, which mostly came too late, no Balkan Jew was given the chance to save his or her skin by the only escape route still open.

The crowning episode in this series of " stupid, callous and inhuman acts " — Lord Davies in the House of Lords on March 11, 1942 — was reached with the sinking of the *Struma*. This 180-ton Danube cattle-boat lurched into the harbour of Istanbul on December 16, 1941, practically a wreck, with 769 passengers crowded in cages on a deck measuring 60 feet by 20 feet. A number of them were on the verge of insanity. The boat stood in the port of Istanbul for more than two months. During this time the Jewish Agency in Jerusalem made frantic efforts to obtain Palestine visas for the passengers ; or at least for a selection among them ; or at least for the children under 16 — so that the Turks might permit them to land. The first request the Government

refused on grounds of security and food supply. The second
alternative the Government refused, because to make a selection
would be too cruel a task. The third alternative, to let at least the
children go, was supported by the fact that some time ago His
Majesty's Government had agreed to permit the entry of a limited
number of children from Rumania and Hungary into Palestine.
To this argument the Government replied that this ruling would
not automatically apply to the children on the *Struma*, and that
a special decision would have to be taken with regard to them.
Meanwhile two months had passed ; on February 24 the Turkish
authorities, at the end of their patience, turned the vessel back
to the Black Sea. Within a mile of the Turkish coast the tragedy
of the *Patria* was repeated ; the ship sank with all its passengers,
including 250 women and 70 children ; there was one survivor.

It should be added that while for all adults on board the
Government's refusal to grant them visas was final, the children
between the ages of 11 and 16 were reprieved — at least in theory.
After two months' delay the Jewish Agency was informed by the
Chief Secretary of the Palestine Government that the children
of the age categories mentioned would be allowed into Palestine.
But the ship put out to sea nine days later with all the children
on board, who were duly drowned with the rest. After the event
the Jewish Agency asked to be informed whether the Palestine
Government had communicated to the Turkish authorities its
decision to grant the children visas. The Palestine Government
gave no answer to this question. The British Government spokesman in the parliamentary debate which followed kept equally
silent on this point. Indirect evidence suggests that the Palestine
Government never informed the Turks of its willingness to take
care of the children, and never asked that they be permitted to
land.[1]

Procrastination of the same kind continued, with the same tragic
results. In the middle of 1943 the British Government finally
agreed to grant visas to all Jewish refugees who managed to escape
to Turkish territory. The Jewish Agency was confidentially
informed of this decision, but it was never made public, presum-

---

[1] The full evidence regarding the *Struma* and the documents relating to it
have been published in Daphne Trevor's *Under the White Paper*, Jerusalem,
1948. Miss Trevor, who is employed in the Press Department of the Israeli
Foreign Ministry, had access to the State archives ; her book contains the most
complete collection of documentary material relating to the period 1939–45.

ably because the Government was apprehensive that if its generosity were to become known, too many Jews would be tempted to escape. For a full nine months the decision was not communicated to the Turkish authorities, despite repeated queries from the latter. When the communication was finally made, in 1944, it was once more too late ; the fate of the Jews from the Balkans had been sealed.

During their two thousand years of exile, never have more Jews been murdered than in the two years from 1942 to 1944 ; never have they been more in need of a national haven. They were denied it by men otherwise kind and well-meaning, who had become victims of a strange obsession, a mirage of the desert. Not only were Jews denied direct access to the Promised Land, but even neutral countries were discouraged from granting them a temporary refuge — for fear that after the war they would again gravitate towards Palestine. In April 1943 the Swedish Government was prepared to admit 20,000 Jewish children from Germany, provided that the British and U.S.A. Governments guaranteed to take charge of them after cessation of the hostilities. This guarantee was delayed until the end of 1943, by which time the relations between Sweden and Germany had so deteriorated that it was again too late. As a reason for the delay the Colonial Secretary stated in the House of Lords that the British Government did not see its way to offering the children " a country of ultimate refuge " ; as for Palestine, it was " not possible for H.M.G. to go beyond the terms of policy approved by Parliament " — meaning the terms of the White Paper.[1]

Similar opportunities arose, and were rejected, in connection with the rescue of Rumanian and Hungarian Jews. In the course of a conversation in 1944, a high official of the Foreign Office, exasperated by Zionist insistence in thinking up scheme after scheme to rescue Jewish families from the crematoria, exclaimed to the future Foreign Secretary of Israel : " Where should we be if the Germans should offer to dump a million Jews on us ? "[2]

There was no evil intent behind these words and acts. The sins committed were mainly sins of omission, prompted by the timeless curse of mankind, blindness of the heart. Their effect was summed up in this laconic sentence of the Jewish Agency's memorandum to the Anglo-American Committee of Enquiry : " There can be little doubt that substantial numbers who are dead

[1] Trevor, *op. cit.* p. 86.   [2] *Ibid.* p. 122.

to-day, certainly tens of thousands, might have been alive if the gates of Palestine had been kept open ".

When victory came at last, European Jewry had been virtually exterminated : six millions were dead, one survived. Yet the survivors were still denied entry into Palestine ; and the policy of forcible deportations — to Cyprus or back to Germany — was resorted to once more. Three years after the end of the war, six months after the end of the British Mandate and the proclamation of the Jewish State, there were still 12,000 survivors of the weary odyssey kept behind barbed wire on the island of Cyprus, *anno Domini* 1948.

3

A few days after the *Struma* went down in the Black Sea, posters of a new kind appeared all over Palestine in Hebrew and English. They showed a photograph of the High Commissioner, and bore the caption :

MURDER

SIR HAROLD MACMICHAEL, known as High
Commissioner of Palestine, wanted for the
murder by drowning of 800 refugees on
board the *Struma*

Jewish terrorism had started in earnest. It had grown out of the terror of the sea, the gaping mouths of the drowning, the deaf-mute gesture of their splashing hands. The drifting corpses gave blood-poisoning to the nation. The measured utterances of officialdom were answered by the rattle of the automatics of fanatic gunmen. Lawlessness had become the supreme law of the Holy Land.

F

CHAPTER VII

THE RISE OF HAGANAH

The *Shomrim* : Hebrew Buffalo Bills — The twilight of
illegality — Haganah during the Arab revolt — New watch-
towers go up — Wingate, Lawrence of the Hebrews.

The negro changes colour — Arms searches and arms
trials — His Majesty's loyal Jewish terrorists — The death
of Raziel — The illegal war effort.

The triangle in the war — Jewish first and second
thoughts — British second and third thoughts — The
Arabs : no more " bonjour ".

Rommel *ante portas* — The second Anglo-Jewish honeymoon — Skull and double-crossbones — The show-trials
— The cancer in the war effort

I

THE official title of Israel's Army is *Z'va Haganah*, Army of
Defence. The title was chosen for reasons of tradition and
considerations of party politics. For Haganah, " Defence ", was
for thirty years the name of the illegal Jewish militia in Palestine ;
it was and remains essentially an organ of the Socialist Labour
Party. Like everything else in Israel, the evolution of this body
from a kind of romantic band of Wild West rangers into the
regular army of the new State was determined by all sorts of
complex ideological trends. It is as much a product of the hard
pressure of necessity as of spiritual factors.

In the 1870s, when the first Jewish agricultural colonies were
founded under Turkish rule, there was no public security in
Palestine ; the law of the country was the law of the desert. The
killing of unbelievers, raids and pillage were hallowed customs
among Bedouins and villagers alike. The Turkish administration
hardly bothered to keep up even the pretence of any lawful order.
If the Jewish colonists were to survive, they could do so only by
proving to their Arab neighbours that they were not " sons of
death " — that is, cowards — but men able and willing to fight.
Physical valour was the only means to gain the Bedouin's esteem
and thus to achieve peaceful relations on a local scale. Moreover,

66

in order to avoid getting involved in interminable blood-feuds with a neighbouring tribe or village, the early settlers preferred cudgel and knife to shotguns.

In his *History of Jewish Self-Defence in Palestine*, Eliahu Golomb (1879–1946), one of the first Jewish " Watchmen " and later Commander of the Haganah, gave a series of sketches of those legendary times.

" In those days there were no buses. Even a mule was an exceptional luxury. The settlement was often completely isolated and special steps had to be taken to ensure the food supply. The settlers had to ford ditches and flooded wadis after the heavy rains, and pass alone through Arab villages bringing food from the nearest town. . . .

" The Arabs of the neighbourhood of a new Jewish village, having sold to the settlers the land on which the village was erected, afterwards tried by constant raids to make life impossible for them ; and by chasing them away, to regain possession of their land — in addition to the houses erected on it. In Petakh Tikwa, there was an additional source of trouble. Two tribes wished to sell part of their land to the Jews, and when the settlers purchased from one tribe only, the other began to attack the settlement. Since they knew that the Jews observed Saturday as the day of rest, they staged all their attacks on the Shabbath. Stamper (one of the early ' Watchmen '), a scrupulously observant Jew, had often to summon the settlers to their posts straight from the Synagogue, to defend the settlement with cudgels and knives."

These " Watchmen ", in Hebrew *Shomrim*, were a kind of Hebrew cowboy or Wild West ranger. Their name was taken from the Bible: "Watchman, what of the night?" They rode on horseback, wore Arab headgear and spoke fluent Arabic. They had familiarized themselves with Bedouin law and Arab custom, and were highly respected among the Arabs. Many of them had become blood-brothers of influential tribal elders, and were called in to arbitrate in disputes or settle blood-feuds. A number of the Israeli leaders are veteran *Shomrim*, among them the Prime Minister, Ben Gurion, once a farm labourer in the lower-Galilean village of Sedjera.[1]

Among Eliahu Golomb's reminiscences are stories like the

[1] Incidentally, the villagers of Sedjera are *Gerim*, that is pure-blooded Russians from the Caucasus who embraced the Jewish faith some generations ago.

following one which, with due allowance for the growth of legend, is characteristic of the atmosphere of those days.

" Judah Rab [one of the old *Shomrim*, and a friend of Golomb's] one day saw a Bedoui on horseback riding past Petakh Tikwa, and, as the watchman on duty, he hailed him and offered him hospitality, according to local custom.   The Bedoui however rode on, taking no notice.   The next morning he turned up again, and this time he rode straight up to Rab and accepted his invitation.   It then transpired that this Bedoui was a Jew from Arabia who had lost his mare and gone in search of her.   His search had taken him as far as Damascus, where he had found the mare.   Having come to Damascus, he thought he might as well visit the Holy Land.   He had by chance ridden into Faja, an Arab village in the neighbourhood, where the villagers told him about the new Jewish settlement.   So he had turned his mare towards Petakh Tikwa, but when he had reached it on the previous night he had been disappointed to see no Jews about, only '*F'ranji* ', Europeans.   He had thought that the Arabs had made a fool of him and had promptly returned to Faja village to take his revenge   At length the villagers had convinced him that there existed Jews of the European kind as well as oriental ones like himself.   So he had come back to see what they were like.

" Judah Rab confirmed to him that the settlers were indeed Jews who had lived in exile in Europe, and had now returned. The Bedoui thereupon said ' I will remain with you for a year '. And so he did.   His name was Joseph ben David, or, in its Arabic version, Yussuf ibn Daoud.   He joined the ' Watchmen ' of Petakh Tikwa and taught the settlers some new tricks.   Like all Bedouin, he had a rifle, but never used it in a fight   ' The rifle,' he would say, ' is a weapon for women.   Anybody can shoot with a rifle.   The sword and the spear are the arms for a man.'

" On one occasion there was a raid by the strong Abu Jarmana tribe which had come to Petakh Tikwa to graze their flocks and to steal corn.   Yussuf ibn Daoud was among those who rode out to ward off the attack.   He speared the sheikh of the tribe and rode into their camp shaking his spear and carrying the corpse of the sheikh across his saddle. . . . This Bedoui Jew, like his Sephardi comrade Ben Maimon, a native of Jaffa, and Stamper and Katz and the rest of the men of Petakh Tikwa, made a great name for the Jews and made the Arabs accept the fact that it would not be possible to drive them off the land. . . ."

These Jewish Buffalo Bills were the forerunners of Haganah. In 1905 a new wave of immigrants came into the country after the pogroms of Kishinev and Cholon. Many of these young men had been members of the Jewish self-defence organizations in the pogrom-threatened small towns of Russia. They brought to the rugged Watchmen of the old settlements their European experience and founded the first country-wide para-military organization, *Hashomer*.[1]

The immigrants of 1905 were not only conscious political Zionists, but having been brought up with the generation of Russian students which led the abortive revolution after the Russo-Japanese War, they were at the same time revolutionary Socialists. With their arrival the Jewish self-defence movement assumed a political character.

2

The next transformation came after the First World War when mass immigration started in earnest. The days of the romantic and somewhat individualistic Watchmen were over. Within the framework of the planned enterprise of colonization self-defence had to be put on a democratic mass scale, and become the para-military equivalent of a popular conscript army. The urgent need for it became evident during the first serious Arab riots of 1920 and 1921, in the course of which scores of Jews were killed and several hundreds wounded

This was at the very beginning of the British Mandate. Obviously the Mandatory Government had two courses open to it : either to put permanent garrisons into every Jewish settlement and outpost, or to legalize some form of Jewish defence organization. The first alternative would have put a heavy burden on the British Forces and the British taxpayer. The second course would probably have led to Arab claims for some form of armed organization of their own. So the Administration, by way of compromise, while refusing to give the Haganah its official sanction, tolerated its existence. This state of affairs continued for thirty years, until the end of the Mandate. The Jewish Defence organization became another white negro, which changed its colour according to the political situation.

Thus, in theory, the Jews were not allowed to possess any arms, except for a few old-fashioned shotguns which were issued

[1] *Ha-shomer* (plural *shomrim*), the watchman

after the 1921 disturbances to isolated settlements. These were to be kept in sealed cases and only opened in a serious emergency —for which they would have been useless anyway. The authorities knew quite well that an isolated settlement of, say, a hundred Jewish men, women and children, surrounded by thousands of Arabs from the neighbouring villages and hills, could not be defended except by automatic weapons. For the Jews to respect the letter of the law would have been straight suicide, as subsequent events abundantly proved. Their only means of achieving security was to smuggle in arms and to hide them in the settlements. The authorities were well aware of this, and not only tolerated this practice, but at times even issued " illegal " arms to Haganah. At other times, when the political constellation changed, they swooped down on the settlements, confiscated the arms and inflicted, as will be seen, quite fantastic sentences on their possessors.

It was an unhealthy state of affairs for both parties concerned. Haganah, forced into illegality, led a kind of semi-underground existence; its thousands of members lived in a conspiratorial twilight. The effects of this habit lingered on even when Haganah became transformed into Israel's regular army. Both leaders and rank and file had been conditioned during the course of a whole generation to bypass the law, and as this was at periods directly encouraged by the British rulers, while at other times it was punished with the utmost severity, respect for the law was gradually destroyed.

The first serious test for Haganah came during the disturbances of 1929. For six days, from August 23 to August 29, Arab mobs all over the country, incited by the Grand Mufti and the village priests under his sway, ran riot against the Jews. The old Jewish communities of Hebron and Safed, which relied on British protection and had no Haganah units of their own, were practically wiped out. The state of public security provided by the Mandatory Government can be gathered from the Royal Commission's Report which mentions that Hebron, a town with a population of several thousands, had one British Police officer. Over 60 Jews, including women and children, were killed there, and more than 50 wounded; and " only the courage of the one British Police officer in the town prevented the outbreak from developing into a general massacre ".[1] On the other hand, the Haganah-protected

[1] Royal Commission Report, p. 50.

rural settlements repulsed all Arab attacks, regardless of how isolated and heavily outnumbered they were — and notwithstanding the fact that a short time before the outbreak the British authorities, acting on one of those sudden and mysterious brainwaves to which the official mind is subject, had withdrawn even the sealed shotgun cases from the settlements, thus leaving them, in theory, completely defenceless. Only three or four settlements (among them Hulda, whose name should be retained), which were insufficiently equipped with illegal arms, suffered heavily in damage and casualties.

The experience of 1929 had taught Haganah, in the words of a Zionist pamphlet, that "where the Jews had illegal arms, they successfully resisted attack. Where they had none, they were slaughtered." [1]

3

Then came the disturbances of 1936–39, culminating in the Arab revolt. By that time Jewish communal settlements were dotted over the whole country : in the Judaean hills and the Jordan Valley, on the borders of the southern desert and up in Galilee — the stronghold of Fawzi's guerilla bands. These isolated outposts, some of them defended by only a score of men, full of tempting women and fat cattle, were the obvious target for the Arab guerillas. Yet not a single Jewish settlement was evacuated or taken. An even more remarkable fact is that at the peak of the Arab revolt new Jewish settlements were founded in the very heart of Arab-controlled territory — in the hills of Zebuloun, right on the Syrian border, and even on the eastern, Syrian shore of the Sea of Galilee. They were a demonstration of the stubborn resolve of the Jews to continue their peaceful conquest of the country, revolt or no revolt. The order of the day was summarized by one of the Zionist leaders :

"Let us retaliate, not by aggression and revenge, but by giving an additional spurt to our constructive work. For every one of our comrades who falls, let us build a new collective settlement. Instead of evacuating the positions we hold, let us conquer another piece of desert, reclaim another swamp, and found new villages in Israel."

The process of founding new "points" — collective settlements — in insecure areas was developed by Haganah into a

[1] M. P. Waters, *Haganah*, London, 1946.

stereotyped routine. At night Haganah detachments occupied the "point" — generally a stony hill in the desert which had seen no plough since Biblical times. At dawn a convoy of lorries would arrive with prefabricated stockades, prefabricated living-huts, plumbing, shower-bath and kitchen equipment ready for assembly ; and, travelling on a caterpillar carrier, the centre of the new settlement : the watch-tower, with its searchlight, whose cyclopic eye was to survey the surrounding terrain and send its twinkling signals to the nearest settlement ten or more miles away.

Haganah as a fighting force has always been guided as much by ideological as by strategical principles. Its second main slogan during the 1936–39 disturbances was " *Havlagah* ", the Hebrew word for " self-restraint ". It was a striking contrast to all traditions of civil warfare, to Arab vendetta ethics, and to the aggressive tooth-for-tooth mentality of the Jewish extremist groups. And in fact it was in protest against the ideology of " self-restraint " that an extremist group split off Haganah in 1938 and founded the *Irgun Z'vai Leumi* (National Military Organization). Under these circumstances and pressures, to maintain the line of *Havlagah* was probably the most remarkable achievement in the history of the future Israeli Army. Instead of the usual trite military do-and-die exhortations, the leaders of Haganah repeated indefatigably the same maxims :

" Your duty is to beat off attacks, but not to let the smell of blood go to your heads. Remember that our meaning is in our name, Defence, and that our only aim is to provide security for creative work. Your organization is subordinate to this ideal ; it is the instrument that enables us to live and work ; it is the servant of our purpose ; it must never become its master."

The effects of the military and ideological discipline of this illegal body of arms smugglers and conspirators were recognized in the Royal Commission's Report :

" It is true . . . that in times of disturbance the Jews, as compared with the Arabs, are the law-abiding section of the population ; and, indeed, throughout the whole series of out-breaks, and under very great provocation, they have shown a notable capacity for discipline and self-restraint." [1]

It was the heyday of Anglo-Jewish cooperation ; never had the negro appeared a snowier white. It is true that Haganah was

[1] Royal Commission Report, p. 87.

still illegal, and was to remain so to the end ; but it was a tongue-in-cheek, almost affectionate kind of illegality. Whenever British Police or troops, visiting a Jewish settlement after a fight, politely enquired how things had gone, they were told that the attack of, say, five hundred Arab raiders had been repulsed with the dozen or so 12-bore rifles in the sealed cases ; and they accepted the apparent miracle without blinking an eye. The real arms and signalling apparatus had of course meanwhile been tucked away. Had the authorities made a search and found the arms, they would have had to confiscate them and arrest the settlers. But they made no searches in those days. During the same period scores of Arabs were hanged or sentenced to many years of prison if found in possession of a rifle. Justice in Palestine had become a function of the political situation ; in fact a mockery. In this case the scales were weighted in favour of the Jews ; after 1939 it was to be the other way round.

4

Towards the end of 1936 the Administration went one step further by appointing a number of Haganah men to act as a Supernumerary Police Force, with the main task of defending Jewish settlements. Some members of Haganah now enjoyed a legal status ; but the organization itself remained theoretically illegal. Another year later cooperation was carried even further by the Military. Most British units had a Jewish " interpreter " attached to them, who was in fact a liaison officer between the British troops and the Haganah in that region. Then, late in 1937, Captain Orde Wingate — later Brigadier Wingate of Burma fame — arrived in Palestine. He came as a young intelligence officer, but already possessed of those unorthodox ideas in strategy which made his Chindit campaign one of the most brilliant adventures of the war. Apart from having his own ideas about strategy, Wingate was a fervent Zionist of a mystical brand. After an arduous campaign against the brass-hats, he obtained permission to recruit members of Haganah for his " Special Night Squads ", and to lead with their help his own guerilla war against the Arab gangs.

The Special Night Squads played an important part in protecting the pipe-line to Haifa and in clearing Fawzi's bands out of Galilee. The experience thus gained by a picked élite of Haganah men proved invaluable ten years later. They had learned to beat the Arabs at their own game of ambushing and hit-and-run raids. In particular, they had learned to take advantage of the Arabs' reluctance to fight, or even move, at night — which was to become the most important single factor in the defeat of the latter in 1948. But, above all, the Jews discovered, much to their own surprise, that they were better fighters than the Arabs — not because the Arabs were less brave, but because modern European Jews had a greater capacity for initiative, improvisation and coordinated action than their primitive adversaries.

The personality of Orde Wingate played an important part in these events. The Jews of Palestine had developed an attitude of hostile suspicion towards the English; but they had the characteristic Jewish capacity to fall into opposite extremes of gratitude and enthusiastic loyalty to the Gentile who proved himself a friend. After a few months young Captain Wingate became the most popular Englishman since Balfour among the Jews in Palestine. The boys in Haganah, whom he submitted to a rigorous and unorthodox training, worshipped him. They loved him for his eccentric habits, his laconicism, his fluent mastery of Hebrew and knowledge of the Bible. Stories about Wingate made the round, and after his death in Burma grew into legends. He had come to be regarded by the Jews as one of their own, a Lawrence of the Hebrews.

The mystic touch in Wingate's relation to Israel became even more evident when, ten years later, in the middle of the Arab-Jewish war, his widow Lorna visited the country and, circling in a tiny aeroplane over a Jewish settlement while it was being attacked by Arab troops, dropped Wingate's favourite Bible to the defenders.[1]

5

Approximately till the end of the 1920s, the Jews in Palestine were dependent on the protection of British arms. During the next decade Jewish defence became gradually self-reliant and was no longer in need of British help. By the end of the Arab revolt, in 1939, Haganah knew that in the absence of British troops they would not only be capable of holding their own against the Arabs, but also of defeating them. The Jews were still a minority of roughly one to two, but they controlled the economic key positions of the country, had large continuous areas as well as a great

[1] Cf. Book Two, Chapter II.

number of isolated outposts in their possession, and had gained
the upper hand in terms of military power. While nine out of ten
people in England, including the people who made British policy,
believed that the British forces in Palestine were protecting the
Jews against the Arabs, they were in fact potentially fulfilling the
opposite function. Potentially — for the Jews had no aggressive
intentions, provided they were permitted to continue immigrating
and colonizing the land.

This was precisely what the White Paper of 1939 no longer
permitted them to do. The revolt of the Arabs was defeated, and
rewarded by the virtual abolition of the National Home. The
Anglo-Jewish honeymoon had come to an end. The men of
Haganah, comrades in arms of yesterday, had reverted overnight
to the status of dangerous criminals.

Before the negro had changed colour, Arabs found in possession
of arms were sent to jail or to the gallows, Jews were winked at.
Within six months from the issue of the White Paper the routine
of the Palestine military courts had changed to the exact opposite.
During the autumn of 1939 and the spring of 1940 British Police
and Army swooped down on Jewish settlements and Haganah
training camps, confiscated their arms and arrested the leaders.
The most notable of these actions was directed against the Judaean
settlement of Ben Shemen, which served as an agricultural board-
ing-school for 450 refugee children from 6 to 17 years of age. It
had repeatedly been attacked by Arab gangs. In January 1940
Police search unearthed 27 rifles, 5 submachine-guns with
ammunition and 23 grenades concealed under a tiled floor. On
April 22 a British military court sentenced eight members of the
staff to prison terms ranging from three to seven years. There
was no suggestion even on the part of the prosecution that the
arms were intended for any purpose other than for defending the
school against recurrent Arab attacks. The prosecution was in
fact careful to point out that no aggressive intentions were imputed
to the staff, but that the letter of the law had to be respected.

A similar fate overtook Wingate's famous Night Squads. One
of these units, whose members had all volunteered for service in
H.M. Forces at the outbreak of the war, was rounded up by the
police during one of its regular training exercises. The sentences
inflicted by the military tribunal were : prison for life for one man,
and ten years of imprisonment for each of the remaining forty-two
men of the unit. Again the prosecution did not deny the loyalty

of the accused's intentions, and the verdict explicitly stated that
" intention [*i.e.* subversive intention] played no part in the
charge ".

More examples of a similar kind could be quoted. But this
is the point where tragedy became transformed into tragi-comedy.
While the military courts imposed these fantastic sentences, confidential negotiations were carried on between the British Army
authorities and the Jewish Agency. Nothing that happened in
public between the Government and Haganah from this date on
can be taken at face value. Both were now playing the classic
oriental game of double-crossing. We have seen how the ambi-
guities of the Mandate had undermined the authority of the law,
subordinated jurisdiction to political considerations, and thereby
in fact reduced the whole administration of justice to a façade
of unctuous pretence. The Twice Promised Land had become
a country rather like the Abyssinia of Evelyn Waugh's *Black
Mischief*.

Thus it became the practice to conclude agreements and
formal " truces " between the Administration, or some branch of
the Administration, on the one hand, and Haganah or Jewish
terrorist groups on the other. Men were put into jail for life or
for ten years, quietly released a year or two later, put into British
uniform to carry out some dangerous mission, and another year
or two later put back into jail again. The forty-three Haganah
members, for instance, whose trial we have just mentioned, first
had their sentences halved by the G.O.C., and, a little over a year
later, appeared in British uniforms on the battlefields of the
Middle East. When, in 1941, British troops invaded Vichy-held
Syria, they needed a vanguard of Commandos familiar with the
lay and language of the land. The obvious solution was to use
volunteers from the Jewish settlements along the Syrian border.
Haganah was approached to provide these, and provided a group
of its shock troops who crossed into Syria, disguised as Arabs,
ahead of the regular forces. Their task was to blow up bridges,
cut communications in the frontier area, and so on. They acquitted themselves well. One of the group was Moshe Dayan,
son of a Jewish Labour leader from the agricultural settlement
Nahalal. Just a year before, he had been sentenced to ten years
by a British military court. In the Syrian campaign he lost an
eye and a finger serving with the British Army. But as the Palestine
censorship, for reasons to be explained later, suppressed all

mention of the fact that Jews had played a part in the Syrian campaign, he remained for public purposes an amnestied criminal. In August 1948 Dayan, still a slim youth under 30, with a black patch over one eye, was appointed military commander of the Israeli Army in Jerusalem. His opposite number was Brigadier Leash, of the Arab Legion, a former British Police officer in Palestine. Most of the Israeli Army leaders have similar careers behind them.

While the military courts continued to dole out decades of prison terms for the possession of illegal arms to members of Haganah, a party, among others, of twenty-three Haganah men left Haifa in a motor-boat in May 1941 with the task of blowing up the oil refineries at Tripoli. They were commanded by a British officer, Major Sir Anthony Palmer, and were equipped, by request of the military authorities, with their own " illegal " arms, as Middle East Command had at that time few arms to spare. Their boat, the *Sea-Lion*, was never heard of again, nor were any of the men.

The underhand dealings between British authorities and Jewish terrorists were of an equally picturesque nature. In 1939 most of the leaders of the Irgun Z'vai Leumi, including the terrorist commander-in-chief David Raziel, were arrested and taken to the detention camp of Latrun. When war was declared on Germany, Irgun offered a " truce " to the authorities, which was accepted. In May 1941, when the Mufti and Rashid Ali proclaimed their Holy War against Britain from Baghdad, a special party of Irgun terrorists was flown by the British Army to Habaniyah, the British-held airfield near Baghdad. The party consisted of David Raziel ; Jacob Viniarsky, *alias* Meridor ; a Sephardi and a Yemenite Jew. Their task was to get into Baghdad disguised as Arabs, to blow up oil installations, and to kidnap His Excellency the Grand Mufti. On May 20, 1941, Raziel was killed during an air bombardment and the action subsequently called off. He was buried in the British military cemetery in Habaniyah ; the inscription over his grave describes him as " Captain David Raziel ", with the shield of David underneath.

It is a little-known fact that the first commander of the " terrorist thugs " of the Irgun died in British service and was buried with military honours. Had this not been the case he would doubtless have shared the fate of Viniarsky-Meridor, who was rearrested by the Palestine Government three years later and deported to

Eritrea.   He was released in 1948, and shortly afterwards re-arrested by the Israeli Government — for being involved in the smuggling of arms in contravention of the U.N.O. Truce regulations.   The Holy Land is not an ideal school for forming law-abiding citizens.

6

For a better understanding of this bewildering oriental fantasia, the policies pursued during the war by the various parties concerned must be shortly summarized.

The Jewish attitude was summed up in 1939 by David Ben Gurion, later Prime Minister of Israel, in the formula : " We shall fight with Great Britain in this war as if there were no White Paper.   And we shall fight the White Paper as if there were no war."

That the Jews had every interest to side with Great Britain against their mortal enemy, Hitlerism, is self-evident.   It is equally evident that they had to continue to fight the immigration bar imposed by their allies and rulers.   And thirdly, they were naturally determined to get the whole political benefit of their war sacrifices.   As soon as war broke out, some 130,000 Palestine Jews of military age of both sexes voluntarily registered for armed service in H.M. Forces.   But they registered not directly with the British authorities,[1] but through the Jewish Agency, which compiled the list of volunteers for a Jewish regiment.   A Jewish regiment had already fought under British command in the First World War.   Now the intention was to create a similar corps — recruited exclusively from Palestinian Jews — which, apart from fighting the enemy, would become an invaluable asset for Zionist propaganda, strengthen the national consciousness, provide the Jews with expert military training, and thereby become a potentially decisive factor in a possible local showdown after the war.

This was precisely what the British were determined to avoid at any price, even at the price of leaving the sources of Jewish manpower and war enthusiasm untapped.   Once Britain had, rightly or wrongly, set her course on the White Paper policy, i e. on a lasting settlement with the Arab world at the expense of Zionism, it was better to have no Jewish Army than to risk

[1] As Palestine was a Mandated Territory its citizens were not subject to conscription.

creating a kind of Trojan horse. Furthermore, Jewish eagerness to get to the head of the queue in the anti-Axis fight was considered likely to push the Arabs even further into the arms of the Axis. The Government's policy was to avoid every irritant to Arab public opinion, such as the very mention of the word Zionism ; the faintest suggestion that the war was being fought for the sake of the Jews ; and any criticism of the pro-Axis activities of the Grand Mufti. Even the fact that the Nazis were persecuting Jews was to be kept as far as possible secret, as likely to awaken Arab sympathies for the former. British Middle East Arab broadcasts featured items such as the allegation that Hitler was employing a Jewish house physician, followed by some mention that the Royal Household drank Arab coffee. The implication was evidently that Hitler was harbouring pro-Jewish sympathies, and hence a bad man, while the King of England took the opposite, correct view of the Jews, and was a good man.

The Arabs, as the third party in the triangle, were in the most advantageous position. They played a simple waiting game to see which party proved the stronger, and to side with it at the proper moment. It was a natural policy for an oriental country designed to achieve the maximum immunity from European interference by following the way of least resistance, and by exploiting the clash of interests between two European camps. In the spring of 1941, when France had fallen, when Britain stood alone and her chances were at the lowest ebb, the Mufti and Hitler's puppet Prince Rashid Ali called for a Holy War on the side of the Axis. The response of the other Arab States, garrisoned by Allied troops and still doubtful about the final outcome, was lukewarm, and confined to telegrams of official sympathy, the usual student demonstrations and platonic assertions of the solidarity of the Arab world. The swift collapse of the Rashid Ali revolt should have shaken British faith in Arab strength and solidarity ; but once more the experts disregarded the warning.

While the Iraqis revolted, the Syrians and Lebanese accepted — because of the obvious weakness of France — the rule of Vichy with a little less hostility than subsequent Allied rule. A confidential British intelligence digest of the period described all the main Syrian political parties as being in Axis pay. (The one notable exception was the Populist Party, which disintegrated after the murder of its leader by Arab extremists.) The Egyptians

suffered the use of their country as a British base with the sullen
hostility which characterized Anglo-Egyptian relations both before
and after the war. The arrest of the Egyptian Chief of Staff at
the moment of his intended departure from Cairo airport with a
brief-case full of British military secrets, and the British ultimatum
to King Farouk, supported by a detachment of tanks milling round
the gardens of the Royal Palace, are episodes too well known to
need detailed description.

In Palestine itself the respective attitudes of Jews and Arabs
were expressed in figures of voluntary recruitment : while despite
all official discouragement more than 30,000 Jews joined the British
forces, the corresponding number of Arab volunteers, out of a
population twice as big, was 9000 — in other words, the ratio of
Jewish to Arab volunteers was as six to one. Despite the White
Paper with its immigration bar and promise of an independent
Arab State in Palestine, despite the extremes to which the policy
of appeasement was carried by the turning away of Jewish refugee
ships, the Arabs remained hostile and unconvinced. Portraits of
the Mufti were distributed openly throughout the country and
displayed in Arab homes ; entire Arab villages refused to comply
with black-out regulations, for Arab whisper propaganda had told
them that Axis bombers would spare them and destroy only Jewish
settlements. In the days of El Alamein mysterious chalked signs
kept appearing on Jewish houses ; they were meant as indications
that this or that Arab citizen had staked his claim to the house in
question, to be redeemed when Rommel's victorious troops had
chased both the British and the Jews into the sea. But as the
parallel trend in the neighbouring countries indicated, anti-British
feeling existed independently of the Zionist issue. It was the
natural expression of the desire for independence, and of the
traditional anti-European attitude of Islam. To assume that once
the stumbling-block of Zionism was removed, Arab xenophobia
would cease, was a miscalculation as naïve as the belief that once
the stumbling-block of the Sudetens was removed the Nazis
would become peaceful citizens of Europe. A century of British
and French experience in Egypt, Syria and other Arab countries
was convincing proof that even if the half a million Jews in
Palestine were made to vanish from the face of the earth, anti-
European agitation would at once find another peg. The following
text of a leaflet which was distributed in Syria during the anti-
French riots of 1945 is typical of hundreds of others :

" If you wish to avoid further calamities, and
If you have a noble Arabic heart in your chest, and fresh
    Arabic blood in your veins, and
If you are anxious to do your duty towards your country —
    then you must do the following :
No more ' bonjour ' or ' bonsoir ' or ' au revoir ' or ' pardon ',
No more French newspapers or French magazines or French
    culture,
No more French goods."

By substituting for " French " the words " English " or
" Jewish ", according to the case, one gets the general atmosphere
of Arab nationalism.

These, then, were the three principal protagonists on the
Palestine stage during the war. The intricate oriental game was
further complicated by splits and conflicts inside each of the three
camps. The British military authorities and various intelligence
branches played a game which frequently clashed with the policy
of the Civilian Administration. The anti-Husseini cliques in the
Arab camp tried to destroy the Mufti's prestige on grounds of his
alliance with Hitler, much to the distaste of the Palestine Administration. Finally, the bitter hatred between Haganah and the
Jewish terrorist groups led to a squalid game of denunciations,
kidnappings and double-crossings which the Administration was
delighted to exploit for its own purposes.

A full chronicle of the part-tragic, part-grotesque and sometimes quite surrealistic events which were produced by this
complex field of forces would be rather like the detailed verbal
description of an oriental carpet. We must confine ourselves to
picking out some of the main threads.

7

As mentioned before, the Jews wanted a Jewish regiment under
British command, and the Mandatory Administration was determined not to have a Jewish regiment at any price. Out of this
conflict of policies the most paradoxical consequences followed.
The 130,000 young Jews and Jewesses who had registered as
volunteers with the Jewish Agency became the target of an official
discouragement campaign. The very mention of the existence
of the Jewish Agency's recruiting office was banned by the censor.
Moreover, any news item associating Jews with the war effort

G

was suppressed. This led to absurdities like the following two censored items.[1] The words suppressed by the censor are in square brackets, and those substituted by the censor in round brackets.

" 30.1.43. Tel Aviv, Saturday.—' The Army still wants recruits ', declared the Deputy District Recruiting officer yesterday afternoon, when he called upon a large audience in the Mograbi Cinema to look upon themselves as recruiting agents.

" The rally and cinema display was featured by films of views from the Russian front, and a picture devoted to Winston Churchill. [Jewish and Scottish] (Two) military bands performed."

Or :

" 18.1.42. Tel Aviv.—Men who have been trained for port work are invited [to apply to the Jewish Agency's recruiting Department] to register in connection with the formation of a [Jewish] port operating company. A re-organized [Jewish] port operating company is to be formed for service with the British military forces, and all persons with port experience and training and those wishing to serve are invited to register immediately [with the Jewish Agency recruiting office in Jerusalem, Tel Aviv and Haifa]."

To avoid any possible misunderstanding, the item refers to a specifically *Jewish* port operating company, which the Army wanted, and whose formation had been approved by the military authorities. The impossible task which the Palestine Government had set itself was to recruit Jews in their National Home on the understanding that they were to forget that they were Jews, that no reference was to be made in Press or public to this inconvenient fact, and that no credit whatsoever for their actions should accrue to the Jewish community. Two more examples of this :

" 1.7.43.—Palestine [Jewry] was represented in the United Nations march past reviewed by the Governor of Bombay on April 27. . . ."

" 17.6.43.—The tenth anniversary of Pales Press Co., Ltd., was celebrated yesterday when the management entertained members of their staff at a reception. . . . The staff presented

[1] The Editor of the *Palestine Post* has collected several hundred similar curiosities ; a selection of them is published in Trevor, *op. cit.*

the management with a cheque of £50 to be used as a donation for the [Jewish] underground press in occupied territories."

As one writer has put it,[1] the war effort of the Jews in Palestine was the best-kept secret of the war in the Middle East. No mention of the Jewish Commando units in the Syrian or Libyan campaigns, of the fifty Haganah volunteers parachuted into enemy territory (half of whom were never heard of again), was permitted for several years to appear in the local Press. As for words like " Zionism " or " National Home ", they fell under the censor's axe even if uttered by Winston Churchill. On July 30, 1941, a parliamentary question by Mr. Lipson, " Whether His Majesty's Government still adhered to the policy of establishing a National Home for Jews in Palestine ", was answered by the Prime Minister, who stated that there had been no change in the policy of His Majesty's Government with regard to Palestine. Question and answer were both stopped by the Palestine censor.

Despite systematic discouragement, insults and sneers, out of the 130,000 whose original registration with the Jewish Agency's recruiting office had been ignored, round 30,000 Palestine Jews served, as already mentioned, in the British forces. They did so, needless to say, not for love of the English, but to fight the Axis and to serve their own well-understood interests. After five years of a grotesque tug-of-war between the Jewish Agency and the British authorities, in the course of which British Cabinet decisions were reversed under pressure of the local Administration, and the question whether Jewish R.A.S.C. drivers in the Libyan desert should be allowed to paint a Shield of David on their trucks was an object of grave deliberations at G.H.Q., the Jews were finally permitted, in the autumn of 1944, to form their own " Jewish Brigade Group ".

Jewish perseverance had scored against the set policy of the Administration a victory which had been more difficult to achieve than draining marshes or defeating Arab raiders. The Palestine Administration had been overruled mainly by Winston Churchill's personal intervention. Yet within the framework of British Middle East policy from 1939 to this day, the Palestine Administration was logically right. The veterans of the Jewish Brigades became, exactly as the Administration had foreseen, the nucleus of the future Israeli Army and the decisive factor of the Arab defeat,

---

[1] Pierre Van Paassen, *The Forgotten Ally*, New York, 1943.

which, as things were, amounted to a defeat of British policy.

If the policy of the Palestine Administration, as expressed in its censorship regulations, was to suppress all reference to the Jewish war effort, any allusion to the Mufti's pro-Axis activities was equally taboo. After the collapse of the Iraqi revolt the Grand Mufti had betaken himself to Berlin, from where he broadcast anti-Allied propaganda in Arabic, organized the levy of an S.S. regiment of Bosnian Moslems, prepared memoranda about the campaign to exterminate the Jews and pursued other activities of a similar nature, which led to his subsequent inclusion in the British List of War Criminals. The following is a sample from the Mufti's Arabic broadcasts from Berlin, recorded by the United States Monitoring Service on March 4, 1944 : "Arabs ! Rise as one and fight for your sacred rights. Kill the Jews wherever you find them. This pleases God, history and religion. This saves your honour. God is with you." [1]

Obviously the only sane propaganda line for the British would have been to mobilize Arab public opinion against the Mufti's party in Palestine. In view of Arab jealousies and dissensions this would have been all the easier to do, as condemnations of the Mufti were readily forthcoming from his rivals among the Arab princes and statesmen, including Emir, later King, Abdullah of Transjordan. Instead of being used as weapons to discredit the Mufti, these statements were, strange as it sounds, barred by the Palestine censorship. The two following items, among many others, may serve as examples (words suppressed by the censor in square brackets, words inserted by the censor in round brackets).

[" 15.3.42. 'DISCREDITED AXIS TOOL.' New York, Sunday (ANA).—Haj Amin, ex-Mufti of Jerusalem, who is now shuttling between Rome and Berlin collaborating with the Axis in anti-democratic propaganda, has lost his prestige in the Arab world, according to the Emir Abdullah of Transjordan.

" The Emir told Cyrus L. Sulzberger, correspondent of the *New York Times*, in an interview, that Haj Amin was now regarded merely as an Axis tool who had sold himself to the Italians."]

The whole item was suppressed by the censor ; the Palestine Arabs were not allowed to know that Abdullah, son of the Caliph Hussein and the most popular Arab prince in the Middle East, condemned the Mufti for siding with the enemy.

[1] Quoted from B. C. Crum, *Behind the Silken Curtain*, New York, 1947.

" 18.3.42.—New York, Tuesday (AN).—Violent attacks on [Haj Amin el-Husseini, the ex-Mufti of Jerusalem, for his association] (those who cooperate) with the Axis are published by the Arab press throughout the United States. ' This is our war . . .' writes *Al-Hoda*. ' Anyone who helps the enemies of America and her allies is our enemy, whether he be [Mufti, Patriarch] (religious hater) or layman.' "

8

Two main threads in the oriental carpet remain to be shortly summarized : the continuation of the double-dealings between Administration and Haganah, and the growth of Jewish terrorism.

In the summer of 1942 Rommel's Afrika Korps had driven the British forces back across the Libyan desert into Egypt. In Russia the German troops were advancing rapidly towards the Caucasus. A giant pincer movement threatened to crack the Middle East like a ripe nut in its claws. It was the last major military crisis of the Allies. Stalingrad, Alamein and the invasion of North Africa were still events in the unknown future. Egypt was threatened by immediate peril and, if Egypt went, Palestine could not be held.

As always at critical moments, when British and Jewish interests were simultaneously threatened, the British Military and the leaders of Haganah got together over the wagging heads of the Palestine Administration. The Afrika Korps in 1942 was a unifying agent, as Kaukaji's bands had been in 1937–38 ; a second Anglo-Jewish honeymoon on the level of military cooperation began. A few weeks after the sinking of the *Struma*, and after Lord Cranborne had communicated to the Jewish Agency that His Majesty's Government's policy was, and would continue to be, " that nothing whatever will be done to facilitate the arrival of Jewish refugees in Palestine ", along another thread of the carpet agreement was reached between Haganah and a special branch of Middle East Headquarters, known as G.S.I.(J.), and commanded by Major-General B. T. Wilson. The agreement provided for the arming and training of Haganah guerilla groups which were to operate as a maquis in the case of Rommel's entry into Palestine. These groups were set the task of cutting German communications in the rear of the withdrawing British forces in southern Palestine ; of establishing a secret radio network throughout the country to keep contact with the Allies during the German occupation; and so on. At the same time, the Jewish Agency's intelligence service in the other Arab countries was to be put at the disposal of the British Army. It was a purely military agreement with no political conditions attached to it; for it was naturally not in the power of a secret branch of the British Army to abrogate the White Paper or change immigration policy.

It need not be emphasized that it required more than ordinary courage for a Jew to volunteer for such a task. A Frenchman parachuted into France or a Greek into Greece could hope to merge with the colourless mass of the politically indifferent crowd. But in a Nazi-occupied Palestine every Jew would be suspect — provided that he lived to be suspected. On the other hand, the chances of a general massacre were such that to take additional risks hardly made much difference. In theory at least, for in practice it is easier for most people to trot meekly to the slaughter-house with the rest of the crowd. These considerations are mentioned because they illustrate the predicament and the state of mind prevailing among Jews in any Nazi-occupied territory. Considerations of this kind decided habitually over-cautious Jewish mothers to embark with their children on the small, unseaworthy death ships, or to take to the forests of the Ukraine and Poland with Jewish guerilla bands; or the meek inhabitants of the Warsaw ghetto to rise and die in hopeless revolt.

A considerable part of the population of Jewish Palestine are refugees, who have only survived and finally reached its forbidden shores by having at one time or another taken the additional risk and played for all or nothing. This is one of the decisive factors in the gradual transformation of the once peaceful and law-abiding pioneer community into a nation with an unusually high proportion of terrorists and bitter Maccabeans.

Fortunately, however, for all concerned, Rommel was beaten back and the Palestine maquis did not come into being. The whole episode ended with a typically Palestinian twist. The British had established a secret training school for the prospective guerillas of Haganah in the hill country south-east of Haifa. After the victory of Alamein, when it became clear to the Haganah volunteers that their services would not be required and that the honeymoon was at an end, they broke one night into the training-school and made off with the arms in it — a considerable haul. Since the aftermath of the Wingate episode before the military courts, Haganah had lost its innocence and was getting wise to the game. Henceforth they were going to play it with all the cynicism of the policy applied to them.

As the tide of the war had turned and Jewish help was no longer needed, the Police and the military courts set to work again to discover secret arms whose existence had been no secret a few months before. Among their more spectacular feats were arms searches in isolated settlements like Hulda [1] and Ramat Hakovesh, carried out in the manner of major military operations (Ramat Hakovesh, a settlement of 140 men, was surrounded by a task force of 800 Indian troops) and with a new provocative brutality. The searches were the Administration's first serious attempt to smash Haganah in good and earnest. They caused immediate mass protests and riots, which showed that a thorough combing-out for illegal arms of the one hundred-odd communal settlements, not to mention the towns and villages, would lead to a full-dress Jewish rising. This the Palestine Government could not afford, either strategically or politically. The attempt to crush Haganah had for the time being to be abandoned.

Instead, the Administration resorted to the eccentric and rather un-British expedient of staging several show-trials, of which the most spectacular was held in August 1943. Two British privates, Stoner and Harris, both of whom had previously committed a variety of crimes, including forgery, theft and desertion, were court-martialled on a charge of being in illegal possession of 300 American rifles and 125,000 rounds of ammunition, with the intent to sell them to the Chairman of the Jewish Agency, David Ben Gurion. The court-martial lasted no less than thirty-four days; American newspaper correspondents in Cairo were specially invited to attend; the whole affair was conducted in a blaze of publicity and in an atmosphere of theatrical unreality reminiscent of Russian show-trials. Ben Gurion was assigned the diabolical role of Trotsky : he had been recognized, from a photograph, as a man seen by one of the accused in a Haifa café, in the company of the chief of a vast arms-trafficking gang. This gang was described by the defending officer as a subsidiary of the Jewish Agency and the "cancer in the Middle East war effort". Counsel for the defence proceeded to explain that it was necessary to broadcast this fact to the Allied nations so that they should be able to revise their policy towards the Jews. He concluded by declaring that the two accused soldiers "should be made world-

[1] Cf p. 71.

famous " because, thanks to them, facts had been unearthed about the attitude of the Jews towards the war effort which might affect the policy of His Majesty's Government.

By that time the atmosphere and language in the military courts and in the officers' messes had by far surpassed what one might call the normal degree of anti-Semitism, and was showing the definite influence of National Socialist ideology. The " vast conspiracy ", the " cancer in the war effort ", the unearthing of a sensational " truth about the Jews " were not improvisations of a misguided and over-zealous defending officer, but the core and purpose of a carefully staged and broadcast show-trial. The trial was to serve the twofold aim of exonerating the Palestine Administration's dark record, from the *Struma* to the cold pogrom against Haganah, while at the same time discrediting Palestine Jewry in the eyes of world public opinion. This tendency culminated in the famous order of the day of the G.O.C. Palestine, Lieut.-General Sir Evelyn Barker, of July 26, 1947, which put all Jewish premises out of bounds for British troops, imposed a ban on fraternization with Jews, and ended with the words :

> " I appreciate that these measures will inflict some hardship on the troops, yet I am certain that if my reasons are fully explained to them they will understand their propriety and will be punishing the Jews in a way the race dislikes as much as any, by striking at their pockets and showing our contempt for them."

The plain facts behind the show-trials are that Haganah did, of course, purchase " illegal " arms wherever they could lay their hands on them, and that Stoner and Harris had very likely negotiated about arms sales with members of Haganah (though the story about the Chairman of the Jewish Agency discussing such matters in a Haifa café is an obvious fabrication designed to provide a missing link in an incomplete chain of evidence, according to the classic practice in show-trials of this sort). That Haganah was buying illegal arms, just as they were bringing in illegal refugees, was a fact known to the Administration for a quarter of a century ; tolerated at periods, penalized at others, but certainly no news. The sensational staging of the trials had nothing to do with the administration of justice or the maintenance of law and order — of which illegal Jewish arms had, as we saw, formed an integral part ; they served purely political purposes and were part of a deliberate smear-campaign waged by the

Palestine Administration against the Jewish National Home.

It may not be without interest to note that, at the precise time when the military court in Jerusalem broadcast its tale of the Jewish cancer in the war effort to all those willing to listen, the first Haganah volunteers for British intelligence work in Nazi-occupied Europe were parachuted into the Balkans in a suitable absence of publicity.

CHAPTER VIII

THE RISE OF TERRORISM

" An eye for an eye " versus " Thou shalt not kill " —
Polish revolutionaries and " coloured Jews " — The eti-
quette of terrorism — Abraham Stern, the gunman poet —
The split between Irgun and Stern — Death of Raziel
and Stern — Arrival of Menachem Beigin — Friedman-
Yellin's escape from Latrun — Haganah's illegal war
against the terrorists — Kidnappings and denunciations —
Ambiguity of the Zionist attitude

I

THE ideological background of Jewish terrorism, as well as the
ethical problem which it posed for the renascent nation, will be
discussed in a later chapter. At present only the main events in
the rise of the terrorist movements will be outlined.

It will be remembered that during the Arab Revolt of 1936–39
Haganah's set policy was expressed by the slogan *Havlagah*,
self-restraint. Rejection of this policy and a belief that not
passive defence but only active retaliation would act as a deterrent
to the Arabs were the main causes which led to the foundation of
Irgun Z'vai Leumi. Haganah adhered to a Socialist philosophy
and obeyed the orders of the Socialist-controlled Jewish Agency.
Irgun owed political allegiance to the Revisionists, the extreme
nationalist wing which in 1935 had split off the official Zionist
Movement and founded its own " New Zionist Organization ".
Haganah had a kind of semi-legal status which varied according
to the political constellation; Irgun was from the beginning
organized on the strictly conspiratorial lines of a terrorist underground movement. Its relations to the New Zionist Organization
were much looser than those between Haganah and Jewish
Agency; Irgun was virtually an independent military organization
which only took orders from its own " High Command ". Its
rank and file was recruited from the Revisionist Youth Organization *Betar*, and from the " coloured Jews " — Yemenites and
Sephardis — for whom its flowery, chauvinistic phraseology had

a particular appeal. These oriental Jews were eventually to constitute about one-half of Irgun's total strength, while the leaders were almost exclusively young intellectuals who had grown up in the Polish revolutionary tradition. This created the peculiar ideological climate of Irgun — a mixture of that quixotic patriotism and romantic chivalry which characterized the Polish student revolutionaries, with the archaic ferocity of the Bible and the Books of the Maccabees. It found its literary expression in the remarkable Bible-and-gun poetry of Abraham Stern, a student of the Hebrew University in Jerusalem, who, together with his fellow-student David Raziel, was the initiator of Irgun.

Up to the inauguration of the White Paper policy, the Irgun concentrated its activities on smuggling illegal immigrants from Central Europe into Palestine. It received active help and arms from the Polish Government, who wished nothing better than to get rid of their Jews and to embarrass the British. Its first large-scale terrorist action took place in February 1939, when, after a series of Arab outrages against Jewish civilians, Irgun members hurled bombs into the crowded Arab markets of all the big towns of Palestine at a prearranged hour, killing scores of Arab men, women and children. Never before had Jews retaliated with indiscriminate murder, and the condemnation of the act by the Jewish Agency and the Zionist bodies abroad was genuine and spontaneous. Haganah issued leaflets against Irgun headed by the Sixth Commandment : " Thou shalt not kill ". Irgun's secret radio-transmitter answered with Exodus xxi, 23-25 : " Life for life, eye for eye, tooth for tooth, hand for hand, burning for burning ". The fight between the two rival resistance groups was on. In this first phase it was merely an ideological battle, fought with Bible quotations in the illegal Press and on the illegal air.

In the summer of 1939 the leaders of Irgun, including Raziel and Stern, were arrested. Several of them were tortured by order of a certain Police Inspector Cairns. Irgun first sent a warning, then passed " sentence of death " on Cairns, which it communicated to the Mandatory Government. Despite elaborate precautions, Cairns and a second inspector were killed by an Irgun bomb in August 1939. It was the first anti-British terror act of the Irgun and it displayed already all the features of rocambolesque etiquette, the strict observance of an elaborate " code of honour ", which was to characterize its actions till the end. This self-imposed code included, *inter alia*, the rules that no British military installations were to be damaged for the duration of the war; that before attacking an administrative building or Police station due warning must be given in writing or by telephone, so as to enable its occupants to evacuate it; that during each " military action" the "soldiers" of Irgun must wear armlets in lieu of uniform; that "executions" must be preceded by a verdict of Irgun's "military court" and communicated in proper form to the accused; that after each action Irgun must take public responsibility for it by means of posters and radio announcements; and, finally, the unconditional refusal to engage in acts of violence and retaliation against members of Haganah or any other Jew. In exchange, Irgun claimed that prisoner-of-war status should be accorded to its men if captured by the British.

Legally, of course, the whole construction was absurd. But until its final dissolution in September 1948, Irgun strictly observed its own code. The discipline among its members was exemplary, and no actions were perpetrated except by order of the leaders.

2

At the outbreak of the war a formal truce was concluded, as mentioned before, between Irgun and the Palestine Government; it lasted until the *Struma* tragedy. The leaders of Irgun were released from detention and employed on special military missions for the British forces, much in the same way as members of the Haganah. Raziel's death in action during the Iraqi revolt in May 1941 has already been related.

This truce led to a split in the Irgun, with fatal consequences for Israel. Abraham Stern, the fanatic gunman-poet, denounced the truce as a capitulation and left the Irgun, taking with him the greater part of its cadres and arms. Thus came into being the " Fighters for the Freedom of Israel ",[1] commonly known as the Stern Gang. The Sternists were believers in unrestricted and indiscriminate terror. They derided Irgun's scrupulous observance of underground etiquette as quixotry and phoney warfare. Irgun concentrated after the truce on the destruction of Police stations and Government offices, trying to avoid casualties as far as possible; the Sternists ambushed British policemen and soldiers, and shot them at sight. Both terrorist groups made a

[1] In Palestine the group is usually referred to by its initials as " L.E.H.Y " (*Lohmey Heruth Israel*).

point of assuming public responsibility for each of their actions, but even without this the public and Police knew at once which group had committed which act, so different were their methods and objectives.

During the decisive years of the war, from 1939 to the end of 1943, terrorism was no more than a sporadic nuisance. All in all, 8 Jewish, 6 Arab and 11 British policemen were killed during this period. Abraham Stern himself was trapped by police in his hiding-place in Tel Aviv and shot in the back " while trying to escape ", according to classic tradition. The gang was temporarily broken up and a number of its leaders arrested with the active cooperation of Haganah. Irgun had not yet recovered from the death of Raziel and the consequences of the split ; thus until the beginning of 1944 both terrorist groups were temporarily out of action.

In 1943 Menachem Beigin, a young Revisionist lawyer from Warsaw, arrived in Palestine with General Anders' Polish Army. An exceptionally gifted organizer and propagandist, he succeeded within a few months in resurrecting the Irgun. At about the same time the Stern Group managed a series of spectacular escapes. Twenty of its leaders broke out in November 1943 from the concentration camp at Latrun, after digging a tunnel 45 yards long through rocky ground. The tunnel had electric ventilation and lighting, and for some time after was shown to trustworthy tourists with a certain pride by the British personnel of the camp. The escape was planned and led by Abraham Stern's successor, science graduate David Friedman-Yellin. Shortly afterwards two more Sternists managed to break out by equally ingenious methods from the Central Prison in Jerusalem.

The leaders of the Jewish Agency have accused the Mandatory Administration, in more or less veiled terms, of having deliberately let the Stern leaders escape in order to exploit the renewal of terrorism against the Jewish community, and to intensify the internal strife among the Jews. This is another pattern of the oriental carpet; it illustrates how far mutual distrust had gone. The British accused the Jewish Agency of being a cancer in the war effort; the Agency had an equally " diabolic " theory of British connivance in the terrorists' escape. For a variety of technical reasons, the theory is highly improbable, and a more natural explanation for the recurrent escapes is to be found in the slackness and muddle of oriental prisons. The story ends with another typically Palestinian twist : five years later, after the murder of Count Bernadotte, members of the Stern Group staged a no less spectacular jail-break, and this time it was the Israeli Government who became the object of diabolic suspicions.

Thus early in 1944 both terrorist groups were ready for action again. Irgun blew up a number of Government offices and Police stations, and captured a sizeable haul of arms ; on May 15, 1944, they even succeeded in temporarily occupying the Government Broadcasting Station in Ramallah. They continued to give warning before each attack so that, as far as can be ascertained from Press reports, the number of British Police killed in all these actions did not exceed two. It is worth mentioning that a letter from Dr. Weizmann expressing " grief as well as horror and indignation " about Jewish terrorism, and published by the London *Times* on February 18, 1944, was banned by the Palestine censor.

The Stern Group meanwhile was pursuing its own line of direct action. In August 1944 an abortive attempt was made on the life of the departing High Commissioner, Sir Harold Mac-Michael, whom the Jews of Palestine held personally responsible for the *Struma* disaster and for the Administration's anti-Jewish policy. In September, four Police stations were attacked and a Police constable murdered. In October Britain's Resident Minister in the Middle East, Lord Moyne, was murdered in Cairo by two members of the Stern Group, both under 20. One of them was Ben Hakim — the boy who had watched the blowing up of the *Patria* in Haifa harbour [1] and, according to a statement of members of his family to this writer, had never recovered mentally from the consequence of the shock. Both young men were hanged.

The Moyne murder shook the Zionist world to the core. The Jewish leaders felt that if terrorism was allowed to continue, not only the British public, but world opinion would turn against them. To avert this danger, the Jewish Agency mobilized Haganah against Irgun and the Stern Group ; while the official Zionist bodies and the Hebrew Press exhorted the public to cooperate with the British Police against the terrorists. But the great majority of the Jews in Palestine turned a deaf ear to these appeals. They disapproved of terrorist methods, but at the same time refused to act as informers against their own people, or to

[1] Cf. p. 60 f.

deny shelter to hunted men. To cooperate with the Police in the
tracking down of political outlaws creates, even under normal
conditions, a dilemma for the normal citizen. In Palestine both
the citizens and the conditions had long passed beyond the stage
of normality. The Police no longer felt compelled to hide its
anti-Jewish feelings ; each week brought new tales of third-
degreeing of Jews, and new public insults.[1] The authority which
the Jews were told to defend was the authority which upheld the
White Paper, the immigration and land transfer laws, the savage
sentences of the military courts. The policy of the Administration,
which for years had turned law and order into a mockery, was
beginning to bear its poisoned fruit.

3

It was a different matter with Haganah. Its members were
subjected to an intensive political as well as military training.
They saw in the terrorist groups not only a danger to Zionism,
but also a political rival and ideologically the arch-enemy. Above
all, they were a disciplined body of men, and if the Jewish Agency
ordered them to collaborate with the Police they had no choice
but to obey the order.

As Haganah was itself an illegal body, without official status
and without legal arms, it was obviously not in a position to arrest
terrorists. All suggestions of the Jewish Agency that some form
of legal status be accorded to specially picked anti-terrorist

---

[1] The following censored report from the *Palestine Post* of 21.9.45 is
characteristic of the atmosphere prevailing at that time (words suppressed by
the censor in square brackets) :

" A serious charge against a British Police Constable, No 1100, has been
lodged with the Attorney-General and the Inspector-General of Police by
Mr. George T. Elia, the Jerusalem lawyer.

" Mr. Elia complained that while walking in the Street of the Prophets,
at 11.30 P.M. on Sunday night, he was jumped upon by a dog. As he tried
to drive the animal off, a British Constable in uniform allegedly asked : ' Who
gave you permission to speak to another dog ? ' [When] Mr. Elia replied
that he was afraid of the animal, [the Constable allegedly said : ' Anyhow,
shut up, you dirty, bloody Jew.' Mr. Elia said that he was not a Jew and
produced his identity card, to which the Constable is reported to have remarked, ' Anyway, you're a dirty native.' The lawyer protested,] and was
taken to the Machne Yehuda Police Station, where the Constable wanted to
arrest him and pushed him into the lock-up. When Mr. Elia wanted to get
in touch with a superior officer, the Constable allegedly hit him in the eye,
rendering him unconscious."

Haganah squads were rejected by the British authorities. This put the leaders of the Agency into the unenviable dilemma, either to sit back, watch the ineffectual attempts of the Police to track down the terrorists, and be accused of passive complicity ; or to turn their own resistance movement, the nucleus of the future Jewish Army, into a body of temporary Police informers. They chose the second course, with consequences which will be discussed later. During the months following the Moyne murder, a list of the names and hiding-places of round four hundred leading members of Irgun and Stern Group was handed over by the Political Department of the Jewish Agency to the British authorities. Haganah furthermore made a practice of warning the Government of terrorist actions in preparation, and, for instance, prevented the Government's Secretariat in the King David Hotel in Jerusalem from being blown up at that time. All this, however, did not suffice to stamp out terrorism ; so the paradox was carried one step further when the illegal Haganah proceeded to enforce law and order by the illegal means of kidnapping and trapping their underground rivals. In December 1944 and January 1945, special Haganah detachments abducted from their homes a number of young men, who were mostly not directly connected with terrorism but members of the Revisionist Party, and suspected of being in the know about terrorist arms caches and hiding-places. The kidnapped men were put into Haganah " prisons " — that is, into a guarded house in one of the politically reliable collective settlements — and were interrogated by Haganah Intelligence men. The third-degree methods employed during these interrogations were in some cases on a par with those sporadically used by the Palestine C.I.D. Political Branch. The seed which the Government had sown kept producing its poisoned flowers. In the general atmosphere of mock-legality and official double-dealing, no group or party could remain immune against the germs of moral corruption.

Though the kidnappings were stopped as they attracted too much public attention, collaboration between Haganah and British Police against the terrorists continued for roughly one year — from the Moyne murder in October 1944 until Mr. Bevin's first fateful statement on Palestine in November 1945. This time, however, there could be no question of a honeymoon, as in the days of the Arab Revolt or of El Alamein ; it was a partnership, enforced by circumstances, which both parties equally detested. No credit was given to the Jewish Agency, either during or at any time after this period, for the loathsome task which it had considered its duty to undertake. Nor did the arms searches, arrests of Haganah members and military. trials cease. While Haganah men hunted down terrorists they continued to be hunted themselves. A highlight in this tragi-comedy was the arrest in January 1945 of a young Haganah member, acting as special bodyguard to Mr. Shertok, and his sentence to six months' imprisonment for being in possession of a revolver and fourteen cartridges. Mr. Shertok was head of the Political Department of the Jewish Agency in whose offices the fight against terrorism was centred.

In spite of all this, the uneasy partnership continued until the end of 1945. It ended after a series of terrorist attacks against Police Headquarters in Jerusalem and Tel Aviv, in which more than ten people were killed. The collapse of their hopes that the end of the war.and the victory of the Labour Party would bring a change in Britain's Palestine policy made the Jewish leaders realize that it was hopeless to fight terrorism as long as the underlying cause was not removed. On December 30, 1945, Messrs. Ben Gurion and Shertok informed the British High Commissioner that any further efforts by the Jewish Agency to assist in preventing such acts " would be futile ".[1]

This implicit admission, three months after VJ-Day, that even the cautious tacticians of the Jewish Agency had reached the end of their tether, inaugurated a new phase in Palestine's history which was to last to the end of the British Mandate. From now on, the uneasy collaboration between Agency and Government was

[1] The full text of the Jewish Agency's announcement to the Palestine Press about its interview with the High Commissioner was as follows :

" It is learned that during the interview Mr. Ben Gurion and Mr. Shertok declared that the Jewish Agency completely dissociated themselves from the murderous attacks on Government and Army establishments perpetrated on Thursday night. They expressed their profound sorrow at the loss of life caused by the attacks. But, they stated, any effort by the Jewish Agency to assist in preventing such acts would be rendered futile by the policy pursued in Palestine by His Majesty's Government, on which the primary responsi-bility rested for the tragic situation created in the country, and which had led in recent weeks to bloodshed and innocent victims among Jews, Britons and others. The Jewish Agency representatives added that it was difficult to appeal to the Yishuv to observe the law at a time when the Mandatory Government itself was consistently violating the fundamental law of the country embodied in the Palestine Mandate " (Trevor, *op. cit.* p. 176).

replaced by an equally ambiguous underhand partnership between Haganah and the terrorists.

None of these dealings have so far been disclosed and explained by official British or Jewish spokesmen. This reluctance of the Jewish leaders to assume public responsibility for their decisions during a critical period of Palestine history was to create a chain of misunderstandings and an atmosphere of mistrust, both inside the new State and in the outside world. It was the main cause of that ambiguous twilight in which the birth of the new State was shrouded, from the murder of Lord Moyne to that of Count Bernadotte.

PART THREE

THE BIRTH-PANGS
(1945–1948)

CHAPTER IX

THE DISPLACED NATION

The victory of the Labour Party — Great expectations —
And shattered illusions — Anatomy of the D.P. — A Labour
M.P. in the Jewish Hades — " This nation must emigrate "

I

On May 8, 1945, Germany capitulated. In July the General
Election brought the Labour Party into power, supported, for
the first time in its history, by an absolute majority in the House
of Commons. Not only was Fascism defeated, but Socialism had
triumphed in the still most powerful country of Western Europe.
The common people on the Continent, emerging from the nightmare of six years of war, looked to Socialist Britain for hope and
guidance. They felt that a new era must open in Europe, and they
turned their expectant gaze towards red Downing Street from
where the new revelation must come.

In the series of bitter disappointments which befell, one by
one, - Greek Liberals and Spanish Republicans, German anti-
Fascists and Polish war veterans, and the progressive forces of
Europe in general — in this funeral procession of shattered
illusions the Jews, to paraphrase a famous statement by Mr. Bevin,
took once more the head of the queue.

Of Europe's estimated pre-war Jewish population of seven
millions, only one survived.[1] Out of the surviving million, 300,000
were in Western Europe, with a fair chance of rebuilding a normal
life. The remaining 700,000 were driftwood, human debris floating on the surface of the receding flood. One hundred thousand
of them lived in so-called Displaced Persons Camps.

A Displaced Person, commonly referred to as a D.P., is an
abstraction. To study this abstraction, and to " examine the
position of the Jews in those countries in Europe where they have
been the victims of Nazi and Fascist persecution, and the practical
measures taken or contemplated to be taken in those countries to

[1] Excluding the U.S.S.R.

enable them to live free from discrimination and oppression ",
was one of the tasks set to the Anglo-American Committee of
Enquiry appointed by the Governments of the United States and
the United Kingdom in December 1945.

The reality behind the abstraction, which the Committee
discovered in the course of its descent to the Hades of Central
and Eastern Europe, may best be conveyed by the following
extracts from the report of one of its members.[1]

" During ten days, each of my colleagues [on the afore-
mentioned Committee] had smelled the unique and unforget-
table smell of huddled, homeless humanity.   The abstract
arguments about Zionism and the Jewish State seemed curiously
remote after this experience of human degradation.   A door had
slammed behind us ; now a nightmare, dimly apprehended in
reports and interviews and newspapers, had become our
everyday life, and everything else was a dream.   Policies which
seemed sane enough in the White House or in Downing Street
struck these wretched people as sadistic brutality.

" What had we actually discovered ?   First, that there were
about 98,000 men, women and children in the Assembly Centres
in Germany and Austria.   Some of these centres were camps,
but many of them were blocks of houses or even good hotels
commandeered by the military authorities for the purpose.
Where they were surrounded by barbed wire, it was at the
wish of the inhabitants, who felt safer when they were divided
from the Germans by a fence.   The living conditions of these
people and their food were far better than those of the Germans
or the Austrians.   There was nothing to complain of here, and
for the most part they made no complaint on this score.   When
they talked, as they did, of inhuman treatment, they meant
simply the inhumanity of keeping them where they were, in
the country of the people who had murdered 6,000,000 of their
kinsmen.   When they refused to work, or left their quarters in
a filthy state, or even smashed the whole camp to pieces, it was
always for the same reason.   They were afraid — neurotically
afraid — of being kept where they were.   To tidy the room,
to put curtains in the windows, or to work, would be an act of
submission to the intolerable present by men whose only life
was a dream of the future.   This they refused to do.   A pathetic
but obstinate determination to survive made them assert that
each day in Germany must be lived as though it were the last
day, when food is eaten hurriedly, when bags are packed ready

[1] R. H. S. Crossman, *Palestine Mission*, London, 1947.

for the journey out of the Land of Egypt and into the Promised Land.

"These 98,000 people, most of them Polish Jews, had been deported to a foreign country whose language most of them could not speak. They had been rescued by our armies from the gas chambers. If the war had gone on a few weeks or even a few days longer, none of them would have been alive. Nearly all of them were the isolated survivors of families which had been wiped out. A large number, when the war ended, had walked hundreds of miles back to their home towns to find themselves the sole survivors of the Jewish community; living ghosts returned from the grave to reclaim property which had long since been shared out. So they had trudged back to the camps.

"Even if there had not been a single foreign Zionist or a trace of Zionist propaganda in the camps, these people would have opted for Palestine. Nine months had passed since VE day, and their British and American liberators had made no move to accept them in their own countries. For nine months, huddled together, these Jews had had nothing to do but to discuss the future. They knew that they were not wanted by the western democracies, and they had heard Mr Attlee's plan that they should help to rebuild their countries.[1] This sounded to them pure hypocrisy. They were not Poles any more; but, as Hitler had taught them, members of the Jewish nation, despised and rejected by 'civilized Europe'. They knew that far away in Palestine there was a national home willing and eager to receive them and to give them a chance of rebuilding their lives, not as aliens in a foreign state but as Hebrews in their own country.

"Before I reached Vienna I had often asked myself whether these people would still want to go to Palestine if America opened its doors. I soon learned that this question was academic. They knew and I knew that America was not prepared to open its doors. Their one hope of escape from hell was Palestine. If they were told that they might have to fight the Arabs in Palestine, they replied — not unreasonably — that they were willing to take the risk. Better to die fighting as members of a Hebrew nation than to rot away month after month in Assembly Centres in Germany, run by British and Americans who talked of humanity but shut their doors to human suffering.

[1] In the House of Commons, as remote from the Jewish Hades as the moon, the British Prime Minister had suggested that the D P.s, instead of going to Palestine, should collaborate in the rebuilding of Europe.

" Talking to the camp leader [of a D.P. camp near Villach on the Austro-Italian frontier], I learnt their history. These were Jews who had returned to Poland from the gas chambers of Auschwitz. Thence they walked in twos and threes southward into Czechoslovakia and southwards again into Austria. The grapevine — those mysterious rumours by which Displaced Persons get their news — had told them that the way over the Italian passes was still open and that from Italy they could get a boat to Palestine. But by the time they got to Villach in their twos and threes, the British Army had closed the frontier and forbidden anyone to approach within five miles. They had been shepherded by British soldiers into the disused prisoner of war camp at the end of the town, and for seven months they had lain in the camp looking at the frontier.

" They disliked our coming, and who would blame them ? They regarded the British officials as prison warders. They knew of Mr. Bevin's remark and they could not appreciate the humour of being accused of ' pushing to the head of the queue ' by a statesman who forbade them to go to Palestine and offered them no other homeland. The camp policeman, elected by the inmates, was a Polish boy of sixteen who had spent six years of his life in concentration camps. His had been the survival of the fittest, of the personality able to cajole, outwit, or bribe. I asked him if he had relatives in America and he replied that his mother was there. I asked him whether he wrote to her, and his handsome face contorted with passion. ' I have cut her off, root and branch. She has betrayed the destiny of my nation.' I asked him what he meant and he replied : ' She has sold out to the Goy. She has run away to America. It is the destiny of my nation to be the lords of Palestine.' I asked him how he knew this was the Jewish destiny and he replied : ' It is written in the Balfour Declaration.'

" It was useless to argue with that boy. He was the product of his environment, of six years under the S.S. in concentration camps and nine months under the British at Villach. For all I know he is still there, lying in his bunk, gazing out at the exquisite snow-mountains and the frontier just five miles away. and still brooding on the fact that if he tries to cross it he will be shot by a British soldier.

" Our discussions in Vienna drove us to one conclusion. There was no possibility of sending these 98,000 people back to their own countries, because they had no countries of their own. Their roots had been torn up by the Nazis, and they could not be replanted in their native soil. Nor was it possible to resettle them in Germany or anywhere else in Europe.

" We had observed that morale was always highest in the centres where a *Kibbutz* (a group community training itself for the new life in Palestine) had been organized. The Kibbutzim were a moving spectacle. In an environment of utter hopelessness, the Zionist faith expressed itself in self-organization and self-discipline. Their own civilization and communal life as Jews had been destroyed. Their homes, their synagogues, their libraries, everything had perished. But here in the camps a new community was growing up in anticipation of the new life in Palestine. To destroy the *Kibbutz* would be to break the only values which prevented these people from degenerating, as many in the concentration camps had degenerated, into subhuman beastliness. But what country other than Palestine would permit group movement and group settlement ? We knew of none. And we were driven to the conclusion that if these 98,000 human beings were to be saved, they must be allowed to go where they wanted to go and where their needs and neuroses would be understood.

" But speed, we all agreed, was essential. In the nine months since VE day an appalling demoralization had set in which could not be halted by good food or accommodation or educational facilities. Every month which passed, accelerated this process of moral decay and of corrosive bitterness against Britain and America. I remember calculating with an ingenuous optimism that if our report were finished by the end of April, the movement should have been completed by August at latest. . . ."

The month of April to which the author refers is April 1946. During the twenty-five months which passed between that date and the termination of the British Mandate, the British Government rejected all proposals for the transfer of the 98,000 to Palestine.

After Austria, the Committee visited Poland, and heard witnesses from Hungary and Rumania. As to the first country mentioned —

". . . on a rough calculation, about 300,000 Polish Jews out of 3,250,000 had survived the massacre. Just nine out of ten had been killed. The vast majority of Polish Jews were determined to emigrate. Poland had become a Jewish graveyard, and anti-semitism was still strong despite the efforts of the Government to combat it. Restitution of property, essential if the Jews were to rebuild their lives, had not been put into practice and would undoubtedly create a new wave of anti-Semitism if it were."

The plight of the Jews of Rumania was described by one witness to the Committee in these words :

> " ' I would like to say a few words about the frame of mind of the people who return from deportation. They return home and they do not find the rest of the members of their family. It is a very rare case if more than one member from each family returns. They find their homes destroyed, their places of work destroyed. Their first task is to search and investigate into what happened to other members of their family. They under-take long journeys when they hear that, in some far corner of the country, someone may have some information about a member of the family. Then, when after long investigations they find that it is hopeless to investigate any further, a crisis enters their lives. There are two courses they can take at this period. One is that a great number of them commit suicide. I have no official figures, but in my own home town there were fifteen such people who committed suicide after liberation, as they had no further purpose for living. The second course is to flee. They do not want to remain in the place of the catastrophe. A Jew can no longer remain in the city where he used to be happy with the other members of his family, and where he can now see, in the face of every man he looks upon, a possible murderer of his family. In my opinion this is the deeper reason for the great mass movement which we are experiencing all over Europe to-day.'
>
> " ' All that is left,' he went on, ' is the diseased rump of Eastern European Jewry. If this diseased rump is permitted to fester and rot in Poland, Hungary and Rumania, it will infect those countries with virulent anti-Semitism. Our civilization and culture have been destroyed. The limbs of Jewry have been torn off and its eyes pulled out. The only hope is to remove the wretched survivors before they do any harm to themselves and to their Gentile neighbours. It is of course possible for the armies and the Governments to close the frontiers of eastern Europe. But if that is to be the policy, we should be under no illusion that it condemns three-quarters of a million survivors of the Nazi persecution to immediate hopelessness and to a lingering death. . . .'
>
> " As a European I found it hard to accept the inevitable conclusion. Could it really be true that, apart from the western democracies where the Jewish communities had always been insignificant, no single European country could be expected to revive its Jewish community ? Could Hitler really have accomplished his aim ? "

A few months later, when the Committee's enquiry was completed, the author had found the answer to his question : " I realize now that in this sense Hitler has won. He has created in central and eastern Europe a Jewish nation without a home. This nation must emigrate."

CHAPTER X

THE ROAD TO DISASTER

New factors on the post-war scene — Labour's Palestine
pledges — The struggle for the rescue of the 100,000 —
The impact of American opinion — Haganah's conversion
to terrorism — Bevin's first statement on Palestine —
Appointment of the Anglo-American Committee.
   The Committee's report — The arguments for its
rejection — The end of Balfour's vision

I

THUS, the first new factor which emerged at the end of the war
was the existence of a " displaced nation " — a negative nation,
as it were, moulded not by organic growth but by outside pressure.
It was no longer a question of individuals wishing to emigrate for
individual reasons ; it was a modern repetition of the exodus
from Egypt.

The second new factor was that the Jews of Palestine emerged
from the war with a new national consciousness, a unity of purpose
overriding party conflicts and internal feuds — in other words,
with all the positive characteristics of a nation reborn.

These two halves of a race in fermentation strove towards each
other with the irresistible impulse of a chemical reaction, of an
electric current between opposite poles. No obstacles could
prevent its flow. When one channel was blocked, it found ten
others in its blind, groping, irresistible progress.

The third new factor affecting the Palestine problem was the
polarization of the globe into an Eastern and a Western half, with
Palestine, as usual, as one of the nodal points of the new field of
forces. Until the end of the war, British policy in the Middle
East was determined by considerations of preventing the Axis
from getting a hold over the Arabs. From the end of the war
onwards it was determined by similar considerations of preventing Soviet Russia from getting a hold over them. The
guiding rule remained appeasement of the Arabs at any price ;
the only difference was that the Russian threat had been substi-

tuted for the Nazi threat as a justification for continuing the White Paper policy. It will be seen that Mr. Bevin's apparent realism in handling the Palestine problem was in fact as irrational as Mr. Chamberlain's attitude to Hitler or the Mufti. The main difference was one of accent : while Mr. Chamberlain's unconscious prejudices were of a somewhat pale and watery nature, those of Mr. Bevin expressed themselves in a more dynamic and virile manner.

The fourth new factor was the Labour victory itself — that is, the victory of a party more strongly and explicitly committed to a pro-Zionist policy than any other. Support for the national home had been incorporated into Labour's war aims as early as 1917, and reasserted during the following two decades, at successive Party Conferences, on no less than eleven occasions. When the Chamberlain Government issued the White Paper this was not only condemned in the most violent terms by the Party, but it was also made clear by the future Lord President that this policy would not be binding upon any future Labour Government :

". . . it ought to be known by the House that this breach of faith which we regret, this breach of British honour, with its policy with which we have no sympathy, is such that the least that can be said is that the Government must not expect that this is going to be automatically binding upon their successor . . ."[1]

During the same debate Mr. Philip Noel-Baker, the future Minister of State, uttered his prophetic warning :

" The Jews of Palestine will go by the tens of thousands down to the beach to welcome and to cover and protect their landing. The only way to stop them is to tell those kindly British soldiers to shoot them down . . . for that, if for no other reason, this policy is bound to fail. . . ."

One year later the Labour Party entered the Coalition Government. It now had its full share of responsibility in the conduct of the war, but its policy towards Palestine remained unchanged, except in so far as the European massacre made the Party take an even more radical line in favour of Zionism. In 1944 the annual Labour Party Conference resolved :

[1] Mr. Herbert Morrison, in the House of Commons Debate on the White Paper, May 1939.

"There is surely neither hope nor meaning in a 'Jewish National Home' unless we are prepared to let the Jews, if they wish, enter this tiny land in such numbers as to become a majority. There was a strong case for this before the war. There is an irresistible case now, after the unspeakable atrocities of the cold and calculated German Nazi plan to kill all Jews in Europe."

Again a year later, in 1945, a few weeks before the Labour Party came into power, the later Chancellor of the Exchequer, Dr. Hugh Dalton, stated :

"It is morally wrong and politically indefensible to impose obstacles to the entry into Palestine now of any Jews who desire to go there. We consider Jewish immigration into Palestine should be permitted without the present limitations which obstruct it. . . ."

Breaches of electoral promises are no novelty in politics. But these were not electoral promises in the usual sense ; they were expressions of a policy which the Party had consistently advocated for a quarter-century. The Jewish electorate is from the Labour point of view insignificant, and considerations which make the Zionist issue an important one in American presidential elections do not arise in England. Nor does the classic argument that it is easy to take an idealistic line for a Party as long as it is in opposition, but difficult to implement it when in power, apply in this case. The Party did not step into power straight from the Opposition, but had been sharing the power and responsibility of the Coalition Government for five years. During these five years, while it reasserted its maximalist support for the Zionist case, its leaders in the Cabinet had access to all reports, official and secret, concerning Palestine, and both the opportunity and the duty to familiarize themselves with all aspects of the problem. When their position changed from shared to exclusive responsibility, they could not claim ignorance as an excuse for their sudden and complete reversal of policy.

2

Germany had capitulated on May 8, 1945. On June 18 the Jewish Agency applied to the Palestine Government for the allocation of 100,000 immigration permits "in order to meet the most

urgent claims and in view of the untenable position of the surviving Jews of Europe ". Thus started the long and bitter
struggle for the " Rescue of the 100,000 " on which gradually
the whole Palestine question came to focus

The Agency's application remained without effect. In July the
new Government came into office. The King's speech at the
opening of the new Parliament kept silence about Palestine. So
did, for almost six months, the Government, whose members had,
immediately before the elections, so urgently pressed for the
abolition of all immigration restrictions.

In September the President of the United States received a
report from Mr. Earl Harrison about the plight of the Jewish
D.P.s, and wrote a letter to the British Prime Minister, urging on
him the immediate admission of the 100,000 into Palestine. The
President's letter, according to a later State Department communiqué, remained unanswered.

At about the same time a campaign started in the British Press
which centred round two main points : firstly, that the admission
of Jewish D.P.s into Palestine would " set the Middle East aflame ";
and, secondly, that if the Americans made proposals for a British
policy in Palestine, they should be prepared " to take their share
of responsibility in carrying them out ".

Both arguments were officially inspired, and were to be repeated
for years to come by the Government's spokesmen. They sounded
plausible enough to the British taxpayer, who did not remember
that the bogey of " setting the Middle East aflame " had already
been used by Mr. Chamberlain in 1939, and did not know that to
prevent immigration into Palestine would be a policy much more
costly in terms of manpower, casualties and loss of British prestige
than to permit it. The Government, on the other hand, knew these
facts from its military advisers on the spot ; the reasons which
prompted it to adopt a policy which members of the Cabinet
had described only a few weeks before as " morally wrong and
politically indefensible " will be discussed later.

The first consequence of the Government's repudiation of its
pledge to allow Displaced Jews into Palestine was to incense
American public opinion and to endanger the granting of the
urgently needed American loan. At a mass rally, before an
audience of 45,000, New York's Mayor La Guardia advised the
British Ambassador, Lord Halifax, that " if Britain wants credit,
the best way to get it is the indication that the borrower knows

how to keep his word ". The fate of the 100,000 began to act on world opinion like a pebble thrown into a pond. Its ripples soon grew into waves which threatened to drown Britain's prestige and economic future. The British Press asserted that the whole storm was artificially stirred up by Zionist propaganda. This certainly played an important part, but it was merely that of the lock-gate which opens the sluice. And behind the dam were Dachau and Belsen, of which the first authentic pictures and reports were flooding into the world's conscience.

On September 24 Dr. Weizmann disclosed that instead of 100,000, the Colonial Office had offered him 1500 immigration certificates, with the comment that " they were the last available under the White Paper ". Indignation and tension rose both in Palestine and on the political front in the U.S.A., whose five and a half million Jews now constituted the bulk of what survived of the Jewish race outside Russia. In Palestine a procession of 60,000 people was headed by survivors from Belsen and Buchenwald in striped convict pyjamas. In America reactionary isolationists and Communist sympathisers gloated in unison over " Albion's latest perfidy ".[1]

At the same time Haganah and the Jewish Agency underwent a gradual and reluctant conversion to terrorism. During the first days of October it became known that the Government intended to deport some forty oriental Jews to their countries of origin, Iraq and Syria. As anti-Semitism was rapidly growing in the Arab countries, the fate which awaited these people was prison or worse. They were detained, together with another 170 illegal immigrants from different countries, in the Athlit detention camp. On October 10 armed Haganah men descended on the camp, overpowered the garrison, and freed the inmates ; in the course of the action one British constable was killed. It was the first time an Englishman had fallen victim to Haganah since the beginning of the Mandate, and the first act of armed revolt on Haganah's part.

Hitherto the Jewish Agency had restricted the activities of its militia to the defence of settlements, the smuggling in of immigrants, and the fight against the terrorist groups. Now a decisive

[1] It is of some historic interest to note that during this critical period of Anglo-American relations, when the Palestine issue assumed suddenly a mass-psychological weight capable of tilting the scales one way or the other, the American Zionists at the last minute decided, in the interest of Western solidarity, to vote for the loan.

change of political strategy took place. The Agency leaders and the Hebrew Press began to refer to Haganah as the "Jewish Resistance Movement". Though everybody concerned knew that this was merely a new name for Haganah, the leaders stuck to the tenuous fiction that the Jewish Agency and the Jewish Resistance Movement were two independent bodies.

Ten days after the Athlit coup Haganah staged its first country-wide sabotage action. On the night of October 31, 1945, the railway system all over Palestine was paralysed by the simultaneous blowing up of bridges and junctions in over a hundred places. At the same hour police patrol ships exploded in the ports of Jaffa and Haifa, and bombs went off in the Haifa oil refineries. The number of victims — six killed — was relatively small; but none of the casuistry used in the official statements of the Jewish leaders could alter the fact that Haganah had embarked on an underground warfare whose methods were hardly distinguishable from those of Irgun.

A fortnight later, on November 13, came Mr. Bevin's first official statement on Palestine, followed on the same day by a Press conference. The essential point of the statement was the appointment of an Anglo-American Committee to make recommendations for the future of Palestine. This was exactly the eighteenth fact-finding committee appointed by His Majesty's Government; and as the Labour Party was committed to abolishing the immigration bar, the embittered Jews of Palestine suspected that the only purpose in appointing the Committee was delay and prevarication; — a suspicion which subsequent events proved correct. The tone and manner of the statement appeared to the Jews insulting; they particularly resented Mr. Bevin's fatal crack that they should not "push to the head of the queue". But worst of all was the refusal to admit the 100,000 D.P.s, and their implicit condemnation to remain indefinitely in the camps. Even the continuation of the dismal trickle of 1500 immigrants a month was made dependent by the Foreign Secretary on the "generosity of our Arab friends" — as if to drive home to all concerned that the Jews were in Palestine not by right, but on sufferance. The statement was a catastrophe for the Jews; under its shattering effect it remained almost unnoticed that the continuation of the monthly quota of 1500, however conditional, meant nevertheless a symbolic breach of the White Paper. This was, however, hardly more than an alibi for the Government against the accusation

I

that it was continuing Mr. Chamberlain's policy.

On the day following Mr. Bevin's statement, the Jewish National Council called a protest strike, and the Chief Rabbinate a Day of Prayer and Fasting, marked by the blowing of the ram's horn in the synagogues. There were violent outbreaks all over Palestine, with 9 Jews killed, 37 British soldiers hurt, and a number of Government offices demolished. The Government retaliated by deploying some 15,000 troops of the 6th Airborne Division, the Brigade of Guards and other units, to carry out arms searches in three settlements in the plain of Sharon and in Samaria, in the course of which 8 settlers were killed. The Jews in their turn hit back by blowing up Police headquarters and electric power stations all over the country.

The year which had brought peace to the world ended with the first encounters in the sub-war between the British Foreign Office and the future State of Israel.

3

" The Anglo-American Committee of Enquiry regarding the Problems of European Jewry and Palestine " was, as already mentioned, the eighteenth committee to study Palestine, but the first in which the problem of European Jewry was linked to that of Palestine. Such was the feeling of urgency in American public opinion about the fate of the D.P.s, that the Committee was requested to complete and furnish its report within 120 days from the inception of its enquiry. It actually did so in less. At an official luncheon in London, given in honour of the Committee, Mr. Bevin pledged his word that if its report were unanimous he would do everything in his power to implement it. The report was unanimous, and was never implemented.

The Commission's Report was published on April 20, 1947. It was divided into short-term and long-term recommendations. The main points of the former were the recommendation that 100,000 immigration permits be immediately granted to displaced Jews and that the land sale regulations of 1940 be rescinded. These two recommendations for immediate action meant in fact the abrogation of the White Paper of 1939. The long-term recommendations were : extension of the British Mandate under United Nations Trusteeship with the gradual development of self-governing institutions, and the temporary continuation of

Jewish immigration according to Article 6 of the Mandate, pending the new trusteeship agreement under U.N.O. In fact the long-term recommendations of the Committee left the door open to any kind of ultimate solution ; it explicitly rejected the conversion of Palestine into a Jewish State, and did not even mention partition.

The first official reaction came from President Truman who, immediately after the publication of the Report, made an enthusiastic but, in view of British susceptibilities, rather tactless statement. It endorsed the Committee's short-term recommendations, and rubbed salt into Foreign Office chilblains by gleefully pointing out that the Committee had " recommended in fact the abrogation of the White Paper of 1939 ". About the long-term recommendations the President was rather vague ; about American cooperation in implementing the Committee's report he was silent.

This gave the British Government an excellent pretext for torpedoing the whole Report. On May 2 and on June 12 the Prime Minister and the Foreign Secretary, the former in the House of Commons, the latter at the Party Conference in Bournemouth, gave a number of reasons for the Government's refusal to implement the recommendations of the Committee which it had appointed. Mr. Attlee declared that it " would not be possible for the Government of Palestine to admit so large a body of immigrants " without American help, and, furthermore, made the admission of the D.P.s dependent on the condition that the " illegal armies in Palestine " (meaning the Haganah) be " disbanded and their arms surrendered ".

This, again, sounded reasonable and fair to the uninformed public. The fact is, as the Government's critics pointed out in the debate, that to disarm Haganah without simultaneously disbanding the armies of the Arab League would have been neither fair nor reasonable. To accept a one-sidéd disarmament while the League was openly threatening the Jews with extermination would clearly have been suicide for the latter — and this the British Government knew as well as the Jews did. But the fact that Haganah was an " illegal " army, while the armies of Egypt, Syria, Iraq and Transjordan, who two years later were to invade Palestine, enjoyed international respectability of a sort, enabled the British Prime Minister, on this as on later occasions, to make an absurdity sound plausible. As members of the Anglo-American Committee subsequently disclosed, the proposal to make the disarmament of Haganah a condition for the admittance of the 100,000 had been discussed and rejected by it as a logical and moral impossibility. In other words, the Prime Minister made acceptance of the Committee's report dependent on a condition which the Committee itself had rejected.

The Prime Minister's arguments for refusing to admit the 100,000 were complemented and rounded off by the Foreign Secretary's statement at the Party Conference one month later. It was the first Conference since the Party's ascent to power. At the previous Conference the delegates had cheered the resolve that " immigration into Palestine should be permitted without the present limitations which obstruct it ". Now they cheered with equal gusto when Mr. Bevin told them that the D.P.s' transfer and resettlement would cost the British taxpayer two hundred million pounds ; that in order to get them into Palestine he would need " to put in another division of troops there, which he was not prepared to do " ; and that the reason why the Americans were so keen on dumping Jews into Palestine was that they did not want " to have too many of them in New York ".

The Foreign Secretary's first argument, about the two hundred million pounds, was flatly untrue. From the beginning to the end of the British Mandate the transport and resettlement of immigrants was exclusively paid for out of Zionist funds and never cost the British taxpayer a penny. Later on Mr. Bevin was forced to admit his error which, whatever its causes, had the effect of giving the British public the impression that it had to pay fantastic sums to get Jews into Palestine — who, once there, immediately started shooting at their benefactors.

As for the additional division to protect the immigrants, the Jews in Palestine, far from needing British protection, were in a position to take the country over whenever the British withdrew. This was not only proved by events two years later, but (as will be seen in the next chapter), was already known to the British Government at the time when the Foreign Secretary made his statement. The fact is that no division, company or platoon was needed to let the D.P.s in ; but no less than five divisions, in addition to units of the Royal Navy and Air Force, were subsequently needed to enforce a policy of keeping them out. After Mr. Bevin's Bournemouth speech it became clear, not only that it was the latter policy which the Government had decided to carry out, but also that it had decided to go " all out " against Haganah and the Jewish Agency, and to liquidate the Zionist adventure once and for all. The proof came a fortnight later, when, on June 29, 1946, the Government arrested 3000 Jews in key-positions and embarked on wholesale military operations against Jewish settlements

From here onward the road led straight to disaster — to the undoing of half a century of patient British achievements in the Middle East and the drowning of Balfour's great vision in the blood and squalor of a second Ireland in the Levant. Before we turn to the depressing story of the last two years of the British Mandate we must try to analyse the reasons which prompted the Labour Government to adopt a policy which stood in glaring contradiction to the Party's principles and pledges, and led to a series of political defeats, all of which had been predicted as inevitable consequences of such a policy, by members of the Government itself.

CHAPTER XI

THE PSEUDO-MACHIAVELLIANS

The Sphinx without a secret — The vicious circle of
bureaucracy — A Foreign Office plan for the Middle East
— The re-education of British public opinion — The
machiavellian fallacy.

    The shift in the Palestine balance of power — Zionist
Bolsheviks and Jewish Fascists — The oil controversy —
The intrusion of the archetype

I

UNLIKE in detective stories and in the diabolic interpretation of
history, the safest guess for the solution of a political puzzle is
always the most trivial one. Most of the episodes in English
history which puzzled the world from Queen Elizabeth's day to
British policy between the two World Wars can be reduced to a
homely mixture of inertia, departmental muddle and bureaucratic
routine. His Majesty's Governments and Ambassadors have at
all times played the part of Wilde's Sphinx without a Secret.

Thus the first answer, though not a complete one, to the
question why the Labour Party's Palestine policy changed into its
exact opposite in the short period between the General Election
in July and Mr. Bevin's statement in November, is that the
Government had changed, but the Foreign Office and the Arab
experts had not.

The layman's idea of the purpose of a Committee of Enquiry
is that it should enquire into the suitability or otherwise of the
policy pursued by those responsible for administering the territory
in question. But the layman's idea does not necessarily coincide
with departmental routine. The Anglo-American Committee's
report was not judged by the members of the Cabinet on its
merits, but in the light of the comments of the Civil Servants and
departmental heads to whom it was previously submitted. These
comments, according to the testimony of a British member of the
Committee, amounted to " a concise summary of the case against
the report ".[1] It could not be otherwise, since these were the men

[1] Crossman, *op. cit.*

responsible " for administering the territory in question ", and it
was only logical that they should do all in their power to demolish
a report whose conclusions amounted to a demolition of their
policy.   Thus the Anglo-American Committee's report in 1946
shared the fate of the Royal Commission's Report in 1937.   " We
had sat in judgment weighing all the conflicting views, including
that of the British officials.   Now, at the moment of decision, the
officials gave judgment on our judgment." [1]

This vicious circle, bewildering as it appears to the common
sense of the average citizen, was by no means an exceptional
consequence of the Palestine tangle.   The appointment of a
Commission of Enquiry into some disturbing problem always
sounds reassuring to the democratic citizen, and in as many cases
as not this reassuring effect is all that it produces, — particularly
if the object of the enquiry is colonial or prison administration.
If its conclusions whitewash the Government, or do not go beyond
the proposal of some mild palliatives, all the better, and they may
even have a chance of being implemented.   If the conclusions are
disturbing, the report can be shelved " for further consideration ".
The channels through which it passes are often identical with
those whose workings it criticizes or tends to reform.   In short,
such committees are frequently what harsh critics of the regime
call " democratic eyewash ".   To become efficient instruments of
democracy, it would be necessary that an undertaking by the
Government which appoints them should be included in their
terms of reference ; or otherwise that final judgment should rest
with a body separate from the executive power.

It is not pure chance that Palestine has been the object of
enquiries and recommendations by more commissions and committees than any other British imperial headache, and that their
recommendations never resulted in a constructive policy.   For
Palestine was, as we emphasized in the first chapter, an unorthodox
affair, a freak phenomenon, and, for this reason if for no other,
the pet aversion of permanent officials and heads of department.
It was at the same time a test for the ratio of imagination to routine
in every Government which had been called to cope with it.   It
was finally a test for the capacity of a Government to adapt itself
to a rapidly changing situation — for in no other country had the
balance of power been so startlingly reversed in so short a time
as through the transformation of Haganah from the meek home

[1] *Ibid.*

guard of a precarious minority to the weightiest military factor in the Middle East. It is on this last test that the Labour Government fell down most heavily. A powerful minority in the Cabinet had formed, with the help of the permanent officials and of their personal bias, a definite opinion as to what should be done in Palestine in the interest of all concerned ; and no Anglo-American or United Nations Committee, neither independent advice nor the plain language of facts, could deter them from their fixed course.

The Anglo-American Committee was a truly independent body of men, half American, half British, of various professions and parties. The majority of its British members was definitely not in sympathy with the political aspirations of Zionism. Yet their conclusions, based on a thorough and independent survey of facts, stood at right angles to the course of British policy — like those of their predecessor, the Royal Commission, and their successor, the U.N.O. Fact-Finding Commission. In consequence, all of them had to be ignored.

" This [the Anglo-American Committee's] assessment of the situation was in flat contradiction to that of the permanent officials. . . . That, I am sure, is why Mr. Bevin, despite urgent requests, could find no time to see Sir Frederick Leggett [H.M.G.'s representative at the International Labour Office and a close collaborator of Mr. Bevin] and myself at any time during the whole summer. To see us would be waste of time, unless the Foreign Secretary were prepared to take seriously our assessment of the situation. That meant reviewing afresh his whole Middle Eastern policy." [1]

And this Mr. Bevin was not prepared to do at any price, and whatever arguments spoke for it. The very fact that the Foreign Secretary refused even to talk to members of a committee appointed by his own Government, and whose recommendations he had pledged himself to implement, is proof of the unalterable course he had set himself.

What was that course ? The same which the permanent officials and Arab experts had urged upon all Governments for the last twenty years, the same which had decided Mr. Chamberlain to issue the White Paper and the Palestine Administration to close the gates of Palestine to Jews in the hour of their need : to remove the stumbling-block of Anglo-Arab understanding, the nigger in the Levantine woodpile, from the political scene — not

[1] Crossman, *op. cit.*

by doing the Palestine Jews any harm, but merely by curbing their political aspirations towards autonomous statehood. For this purpose their numerical increase by immigration and their strategical expansion by the acquisition of more land had to be prevented. Instead, they were to have a guaranteed minority status in an independent Palestine Arab State linked to Great Britain by a pact of friendship and mutual assistance, in exchange for British military equipment and perhaps a financial subsidy — as in the case of Transjordan and Iraq. Thus peace would come to the Middle East and the Arab States could be turned into a reliable bulwark against German or Soviet expansion, as the case may be, with British airfields dotted over the map, and Arab oil peacefully flowing across the deserts. The Jews themselves would be much better off under this arrangement, for once the Arabs ceased to fear their domination and were generally appeased, they would no longer be hostile to the Jews, with their " guaranteed minority status ".[1]

To put this programme into effect, two obstacles had to be overcome. Firstly, the Jews in Palestine, thanks to British leniency, had grown too strong and presumptuous. To clear the way for an all-round settlement on the proposed lines they had to be taken down a peg. The necessary measures for doing this were contained in a plan which had been submitted to the National Coalition Government by Sir Harold MacMichael, High Commissioner of the *Struma* period, and since elaborated in detail by the various service departments concerned. It comprised the forcible disarmament of Haganah, the breaking of the various monopolies and economic key positions of the Jewish trade unions, the smashing up of the Jewish State within the State, the dissolution of the Jewish Agency and, if necessary, the arrest of the Jewish leaders. This plan was tentatively put into operation on June 29, 1946 ; its consequences will be seen in the next chapter.

The second difficulty was the existence of certain idealistic pledges passed at Party Conferences, and the equally unrealistic statements in the past of the Party's leading members who were now in the Government. This could only be overcome by patient

---

[1] This pet formula of officialese never lost its pleasing sound, despite the experiences of the Armenian, Greek, Syriac, Kurdish, Maronite, Hindu, Moslem, Sikh and other national or religious minorities in the East — not to mention those of Europe. Translated from the language of officialdom into that of historic fact, a " guaranteed minority status " is equivalent to that of a " licensed persecutee ".

prevarication, by the appointment of Committees of Enquiry, the Consultation of Experts, and other approved means of playing for time, until public opinion and the attitude of the Party came gradually round to a more realistic attitude, re-educated by reasoned speeches from the Government, the eloquence of the Press, and the benevolent despotism of the Party Whip.

All this sounds extremely machiavellian. The only snag in the whole conception was that it was utterly divorced from reality. It was in fact a pseudo-machiavellian cloud-cuckoo policy. But the puritan British mind always feels sinfully flattered when, instead of inconsistency and muddle, cynical ruthlessness and machiavellian cunning are imputed to it. It is precisely this lack of ruthlessness and imagination which makes the British politician behave in such a way that, if he cannot be taken for a philanthropist he should at least be taken for a sinister Grey Eminence. The secret of the sphinx, made impenetrable by conscious cant and unconscious mannerisms, is its mediocrity. Mr. Chamberlain was not a machiavellian but a business man from Birmingham. Mr. Bevin is not a machiavellian but a trade union boss who regards the world as a slightly enlarged Transport House. They are not Renaissance princes, but somewhat flat-footed pseudo-machiavellian burghers.

2

There are circumstances in history when the leaders of a nation or political movement feel compelled to sacrifice morality to expediency. What possible reasons of expediency may have compelled the Labour Cabinet to adopt a policy which was bound to expose them to the same charge of a " cynical breach of pledges " which they themselves had brought against the Chamberlain Government a few years before ?

One of the fundamental rules of expediency is to " back the winning horse ", or to " play the strongest card ", among those available, against the main enemy. This principle induced the Chamberlain Government, in its struggle against the main enemy, Germany, to appease the Arabs and sacrifice the Jews. The same principle has been invoked to justify the Labour Government's siding with the Arabs against the Jews in its efforts to stem Russian expansion. But if in 1939 Mr. Chamberlain may have had some excuse for falling victim to the myth of Arab might and power created by the Middle East experts, Mr. Bevin in 1945 had no excuse for believing the Arabs to be the stronger party, or a bulwark of any strategic value against the Russians. The most authoritative view on this subject was probably that of the British G.O.C. Palestine. In March 1946 this post was held by General J. C. D'Arcy. He stated his views on the relative strength of Jews and Arabs to members of the Anglo-American Committee of Enquiry as follows :

" 1. Speaking purely from the military point of view, he could enforce a pro-Jewish solution without much difficulty.

" 2. In enforcing such a solution, the Haganah could be most helpful.

" 3. In the event of a pro-Arab solution, he would have to contend with a " highly efficient " military organization (the Haganah). He would require three army divisions and from four to six months to break the back of the opposition. Even then, some measure of underground resistance would persist.

" 4. In enforcing a pro-Arab solution, Arab support, he was afraid, would be of no value.

" We discussed with him what would happen if British troops were withdrawn from Palestine.

" ' If you were to withdrew British troops, the Haganah would take over all Palestine to-morrow,' General D'Arcy replied flatly.

" ' But could the Haganah hold Palestine in such circumstances ? ' I asked.

" ' Certainly,' he said. ' They could hold it against the entire Arab world.' " [1]

The last High Commissioner of Palestine, General Sir Alan Cunningham, expressed a similar opinion. Speaking of Haganah, he said to members of the Committee : " My own feeling in the matter is, that it really cannot be destroyed — even if the Government should wish to do so." [2] The cumulative effect of the public and secret information gathered by the Committee in the course of their investigations is summed up by Crossman as follows :

" An Arab expert in Cairo told me that the Haganah was the most powerful military force in the Middle East, apart from the British Army, and has completely transformed the balance of power. He added that if we withdrew from Palestine the Haganah would overrun the country and hold it for some years

[1] Bartley C. Crum, *Behind the Silken Curtain*, London, 1947. Mr Crum was an American member of the Committee. [2] *Ibid.*

at least. No one here in Jerusalem challenges that view. Even those who dislike the Jews most pay tribute to their military efficiency." [1]

The fact that without British intervention on either side the Jews were in a position to impose their own solution must therefore have been known to the British Cabinet. In terms of pure expediency, the Jews being militarily the stronger party, there was no apparent logical justification for Labour's refusal to implement their pledge to them.

It may be argued against this that the Jews, though physically stronger, were less reliable as an ally against Russian expansion than the Arabs. Strange as it seems to-day, similar arguments had already been used in Mr. Chamberlain's days to prove that the Jews of Palestine, many of whom were of German origin and imbued with German culture, would be less reliable in the fight against Nazism than the Grand Mufti and the Arab effendis. It is a characteristic of the conscious or unconscious anti-Semite that he always assumes the Jew to be on the side of his enemies. For Hitler all Jews were agents of Bolshevism and of the pluto-democracies. For the French and English anti-Semite, all German war refugees were Nazi agents. The Palestine Government's policy was, as we have seen, supported by the same argument. With the advent of Mr. Bevin at the Foreign Office, the D.P.s automatically transformed themselves from Nazi agents into Bolshevik agents.[2] The fact that the Nazis killed Jews did not affect the war-time distrust of Jewish refugees. The fact that for thirty years, from 1917 to 1947, the Soviets persecuted Zionism as a Fascist Movement and imperialist tool — with arctic deportation camps as an equivalent for the gas chambers — was equally unable to dispel the suspicion that they were a Russian fifth column in the Middle East.[3]

---

[1] Crossman, *op. cit.*

[2] It should be noted that Soviet and Comintern policy remained violently hostile to Zionism until two years after the period under review. It changed abruptly in October 1947, for reasons to be referred to later

[3] Cf. Crossman, *op. cit.* : " I dined with a group of middle-grade British officials and their wives. Two of them spent the evening trying to convince me that the Jewish Labour movement here is Bolshevik and can't be trusted. Actually, the Labour movement here, from what I've seen of it, is fanatically anti-Bolshevik, and as good a potential ally of the British Labour movement as were the Vienna Socialists. But nothing I said did any good at the dinner. These people ' knew '."

The same half-conscious bias worked in the opposite directior when it came to the assessment of Arab reliability against Germany or Russia. Since the First World War, when Turkish rule wa: replaced by Anglo-French domination in the Levant States, Arab policy, however confused, has remained self-consistent on one basic issue : the natural tendency to play one European power against the other. During each of the Syrian rebellions against the French, British arms from Palestine found their way as mysteriously into the rebels' hands as French arms did during the anti-British revolts in Palestine. Italian and German arms and funds were accepted with equal readiness when Anglo-French domination seemed to be on the decline :

" Whatever the Arab politicians might say to the British diplomatists, there was no reason to believe that the Arab attitude would be any more favourable in a third world war than in the second. Every Arab State, since British power has sharply declined, would be bound in the event of war to avoid siding actively with us. . . . I asked Jemal [Jemal Effendi el Husseini, one of the Palestine Arab leaders] a series of questions on his attitude to the Mufti and the Arab attitude to the war. He answered with calculated candour, explaining why an Arab patriot could not help being indifferent and expressing his conviction that the Mufti had always acted in the interests of his people, and that when he was in Germany that is just what he was doing. After today's evidence, anybody who thinks that the Arab leaders are not prepared to accept any sort of help in order to get rid of the British is just refusing to face facts." [1]

If British estimates of the respective value of Arabs and Jews as a potential ally against Russia were to be taken at face value and not as what they are, rationalizations of an emotional prejudice, then the controversy about Zionism would have become as " polarized " between pro- and anti-Russians as, say, the controversy about Poland, or about Mihailovitch and Tito. In other words, the fellow-travellers would all have been pro-Zionist — as they actually did become overnight in November 1947, when Russia changed her line about Palestine. The fact is that the alignment in the Arab-Jewish issue was determined primarily by irrational motives, and cut across the two camps. If a person is emotionally for the Arab and against the Jew, he will rationalize his attitude with equal ease whether he is pro-Soviet or anti-Soviet.

[1] Crossman, *op. cit.*

If he is anti-Soviet, he will explain that the Jews cannot be trusted because they are Bolsheviks. If he is pro-Soviet, he will explain that the Zionists cannot be trusted because they are Jewish Fascists. In both cases the rationalization of the bias will be entirely sincere.

The last rationalization of the pseudo-machiavellian is usually a somewhat shamefaced reference to the fact that while there may be some philanthropic arguments in favour of the Jews, the over-riding argument in favour of the Arabs are the oilfields in the Iraq and Saudi Arabia. In fact, this argument cuts both ways, just like the previous one. King Ibn Saud's budget is almost entirely derived from British subsidies and American oil royalties. The Iraqi Government is in a similar position. Soviet roubles cannot compete in attraction with dollars and pounds ; and both countries being under the direct menace of the proximity of the Soviet frontiers, know only too well that to do business with, and receive subsidies from, the Western democracies is one thing, to come under Communist rule another. The Arab oil countries are as dependent on Western financial support as the Western Powers are on the Middle Eastern oil ; loss of the oil royalties would mean immediate bankruptcy for both Iraq and Saudi Arabia, and no Arab Government is willing to commit suicide for the sake of a cause which does not affect its interests except in a remote and sentimental manner. No patriotic sentiments were able to prevent the Arab ruling class in Palestine itself from continuing to sell its land piecemeal to the Jews ; it was fantastic to believe that Ibn Saud or the Iraqi Government would face bankruptcy and revolt in their own countries to prevent a compromise solution in Palestine — provided they knew that the Western Powers were determined to carry it through.

Against the belief of the " diabolicians ", Britain did not sacrifice the Jews to her oil interests. The opposite is true : oil interests served as a pretext for her sincere wish to liquidate her Zionist commitments. It was the British Government which went out of its way to bring the oil-possessing Arab States into the Palestine dispute by inviting them to the Round-Table Conference in 1939, and by uniting them a few years later in the Arab League, a cardboard monster which turned out to be as anti-British as it was anti-Zionist. The aim of this policy, grown out of the roots of the Arab myth, of the wish-dreams of the Cairo officials, was, as far as it can be summed up in concise terms, not that Arabs should fight or massacre Jews, but rather that the Arabs should be put into a position from which they could blackmail Britain into an anti-Zionist policy. The Foreign Office experts wanted to see the Arabs strong so as to be able to justify, before their own conscience and in the eyes of the world, the abandonment of the Zionist experiment as a hopeless and doomed cause. They believed in Arab strength, and tried to bolster it up to justify their belief. They wanted to be bullied and blackmailed out of their commitments to the Jews, and they created the instrument for Arab bullying and blackmail. It was not a diabolic but a pseudo-machiavellian policy, concocted from emotional prejudice and stale Foreign Office recipes.

To sum up : the abrupt change of Labour policy towards Palestine after the war was not a case of sacrificing principle to circumstance or morality to expediency. All arguments of expediency were refuted by subsequent events which were the outcome of a situation of which the Government had full knowledge. Expediency was not a prime mover of this policy but its excuse and rationalization *post factum*. Its prime mover was, apart from the factors already discussed, an irrational bias of archetypal power which found its most remarkable expression in the person of the Foreign Secretary.

CHAPTER XII

JOHN BULL'S OTHER IRELAND

Mr. Bevin's 18th Brumaire — The Master Plan leaks out — Arrest of the Jewish Agency leaders — Operations against the settlements — Passive resistance — The anti-climax.

Anxious improvisations — Morrison Plan and Bevin Plan — Palestine referred to U N O.

The lowest common denominator — Terror and hypocrisy — The deportation orders — The blowing-up of the King David Hotel — Haganah and Irgun

I

MENTION has been made in the previous chapter of the British plan, first proposed by Sir Harold MacMichael, to break up once and for all the Jewish State within the State by disarming Haganah, dissolving the Jewish Agency, mass arrests and similar draconic measures.

As things go in Palestine, a sufficient number of documents were intercepted by Haganah Intelligence to keep the Jewish leadership posted in some detail on the decisive blow planned against them; a collection of photostatic copies still lies in the State Archives of Israel awaiting publication. It is significant, however, that a number of prominent Service chiefs, among them the last two High Commissioners, Lord Gort and Sir Alan Cunningham, were opposed to the whole scheme, as they realized that it could not be successfully completed without aerial bombardments of Jewish towns and settlements to break the people's resistance. Two remarks made by Sir Alan and General D'Arcy to the Anglo-American Committee are significant in this context. At an official reception in Jerusalem one of the British members of the Committee asked the G.O.C., Palestine:

" ' Are you implying, Sir, that it is impossible for His Majesty's Government to disarm the Haganah ? ' General D'Arcy replied : ' You cannot disarm a whole people. I rather think the world will not stand for another mass murder of Jews.' " [1]

Sir Alan Cunningham was even more explicit :

" No, I shouldn't want to see the Agency disbanded. I am not one of those who underestimate it. The Palestine Government may not like it, but it cannot ignore it : it is a force to be reckoned with, and my own feeling in the matter is that it really cannot be destroyed — even if the Government should wish to do so." [2]

A number of similar statements could be quoted to demonstrate the division of opinions which prevailed in the top-level strata during the decisive months before the 29th of June 1946. It was not so much a disagreement on the policy to be pursued as a widespread reluctance to face the consequences of its implementation. This led to a typical British paradox. The Foreign Secretary and his extremist advisers in Cairo and London had their way in formulating policy ; but found themselves unable to carry it out in practice. Half-way through the planned operation, which began with the arrest of the leaders of the Jewish Agency on June 29 and was meant to end with the breaking up of Haganah and all Jewish political institutions, they had to call a halt. And by stopping half-way they sealed their ultimate defeat.

A fortnight before it actually started, Haganah's illegal radio transmitter, the Voice of Israel, revealed its knowledge of the impending action. The military operations were to be aimed at forty-nine Jewish towns and settlements, and foresaw, in addition to the use of motorized infantry and armoured cars, the intervention of artillery and units of the Royal Air Force to put down resistance in Jewish settlements in case of necessity. A black-list of several thousand leading personalities earmarked for arrest was included in the operational plan.[3] The broadcast ended with a

---

[1] Crum, *op. cit.*   [2] *Ibid*

[3] A reference to this plan, corroborating the disclosures of the Haganah broadcast, was made in Mr. Crossman's speech in the House of Commons on July 1, 1946, two days after the operation had started with the arrest of some 3000 leading Palestinian Jews :

". . . The course which the Government are now pursuing can only lead to war. It will not stop the violence. It will precipitate violence. . . . Why am I so certain ? Because of all the military experts in the Middle East not one pretended that if this plan, which after all has been on the cards for some time, were carried out, it would stop at the arrest of 2000 leaders. No, this is the plan for the liquidation of the Haganah, and that means the liquida-

K

characteristic flourish : " The document is now public property. Let the Yishuv,[1] the Diaspora and the whole world know what Bevin, Attlee and their henchmen are preparing for us, and let the world know that we shall fight."

To show that they meant business, the day after the announcement Haganah disrupted road and railway communications all over the country, cutting Palestine off from the neighbouring states. One day later the Stern Group attacked the Government's railway repair shops in Haifa, leaving 11 out of the 30 attackers (including several girls) dead on the field. Another day later Irgun kidnapped five British officers as hostages for two of their own men under sentence of death. The Government countered by the usual method of surrounding Jewish settlements with troops and the mass arrest of settlers, causing the usual number of dead and wounded ; but the initiative had been wrested from them by the resistance movement. When, a fortnight after it had been made public by Haganah, the master plan to liquidate Jewish opposition was put into operation on June 29, it had lost its element of surprise and went off at half-cock, as it were. The headquarters of the Jewish Agency was occupied, its leaders arrested, together with some 3000 officials of the Hebrew Labour Party, the Trade Unions, Cooperatives, Communal Settlements and so on ; but all the important commanders of Haganah had by that time gone underground, and most of the arms stores had been removed to new hiding-places.

The main reason, however, for the miscarriage of Mr. Bevin's 18th Brumaire in Palestine was Haganah's strategy of combining active with passive resistance. Active sabotage was the task of its mobile striking force, *Palmakh* — a commando formation which had gradually grown out of Wingate's Night Squads. But the real strength of Haganah rested with its mass membership of some 40,000 settlers in over a hundred collective settlements dotted all over the country.

Twenty-seven of the settlements were surrounded and searched

tion of a large number of men, women and children in Palestine. . . . I ask the Cabinet to refer to the secret minutes of our report, which are available in the Foreign Office. Unless I am completely wrong, any large-scale arrest of this sort was a preliminary to a large-scale campaign, and no expert I met in Palestine advised that the campaign could be avoided. . ."

At this point the speaker was pulled up on a point of order for the impropriety of quoting from secret documents.

[1] Yishuv : the Jewish community of Palestine.

during the first three days of the operation by a task force estimated at three divisions. The task which they were supposed to
carry out was to confiscate arms, to arrest the " ringleaders ", to
break down resistance. But when the spearhead of tanks or
armoured cars broke down the gates of a settlement, and the
troops advanced in formation with fixed bayonets — " looking
either thunderously grim or patently scared " [1] — they found no
resistance, only the startling sight of, as one official communiqué
put it, " men and women lying on the ground with legs and arms
interlocked, and refusing to move ".

Instead of the expected battle, the soldiers were confronted
with the grotesque task of dragging the passive resistants, in some
cases several hundred of them, one by one, into barbed-wire cages
for interrogation. When at last they got them there, with a fair
number of men and women bruised and wounded in the process,
the second anticlimax came : the settlers, to the last man and
woman, refused to be interrogated, refused to give their names
and answered all questions relating to their identity with the
monotonous statement : " I am one of the Jews of Palestine ".
All that the bewildered commander could do was to pick out at
random a certain proportion of the settlers and carry them off
" for further investigation " — which proved as fruitless as the
first. Sometimes tear gas and oil jets had to be used to overcome
this passive resistance ; but apart from some rough-housing,
pilfering and the standing joke of scrawling swastikas on the
walls, the troops found no occasion for any martial activity, and
were on the whole kept under restraint by their officers. Some
arms were unearthed in the settlements ; but Haganah being a
kind of conscript militia, with arms dispersed in small quantities
at the most unlikely hiding-places, the programme of " disarming
the Jews " as conceived by orthodox military minds, would in fact
have meant digging up the whole country from Dan to Beersheba.

Thus the first phase of the operation, which was intended to
be the decisive one, had only confirmed the old experience that
a resistance movement based on the passive support of an entire
nation cannot be defeated by any traditional military operation
short of a total extermination policy. And as neither the British
Government nor British public opinion was prepared to accept
the latter alternative, the great operation was bound to peter out
in inconclusive skirmishes. Moreover, once it had become clear

[1] Trevor, *op. cit.* p. 129.

that Jewish resistance could not be broken except by a wholesale massacre, it could be predicted that the Government was, in the long run, doomed to defeat.   Like all resistance movements, the Palestine underground had the decisive advantages of anonymity, invisibility and ubiquitousness — which sooner or later must lead to a process of attrition and demoralization of the regular occupying force.

2

The aftermath of the " 18th Brumaire " was a series of anticlimaxes.   The action produced the usual Storms of Protest and Cries of Indignation.   These, in a typically Palestinian manner, became focussed on the person of 69-year-old Rabbi Fishman, Acting Head of the Jewish Agency Executive, who, when arrested on June 29, which was a Sabbath, was refused the privilege of walking to jail, and forced to break the Law of Moses by riding there in a car.   The alleged statement of a soldier : " I walloped him ", referring to the venerable rabbi, made particularly juicy headlines.

The other after-effects of the misfired operation were in the same strain.   Among the approximately three thousand people arrested there was not a single prominent terrorist or Haganah leader — or if there were any, they could not be identified.   They were released in batches, including the members of the Agency Executive, who were freed on November 5.   His Majesty's Stationery Office published the text of some intercepted code telegrams which were meant to prove what needed no proof, namely, that there was collusion between Jewish Agency and Haganah.   The telegrams, full of curious cover-names, sounded phoney — and though in fact they were authentic, completely missed their effect.   It became increasingly obvious that neither the Police nor the military were able to track down the terrorists or Haganah leaders, and that the situation was from week to week getting more out of hand.

From the abortive attempt to crush Jewish resistance to the end of the Mandate, the British Government no longer acted on any consistent plan ; its policy was a series of *ad hoc* measures and improvisations.   The first of these was the so-called Morrison Plan, a scheme of Cantonization prepared by the Colonial Office before the Labour Government had come to power ; it had been rejected by the Anglo-American Committee after years of slumber in a Colonial Office file, and was suddenly produced now by the Cabinet as a new solution, like a rabbit out of a hat. Its basic feature was to bar entry by Jews into 83 per cent of Palestine, and to make immigration, even in the remaining 17 per cent, dependent on the British High Commissioner's ruling. The admission of the 100,000 was made dependent on acceptance of this plan. The scheme was outlined by Mr. Herbert Morrison in the House of Commons on July 30, and promptly rejected by Jews, Arabs and the White House.

The next rabbit was a new Palestine Round Table Conference in October. The invitations to it were rejected both by the Jews, whose leaders were still detained in Palestine, and by the Palestine Arabs ; the only people to attend were delegates of other Arab States. The Conference having proved futile, it was adjourned till better days. In the meantime, the Middle East experts of the Foreign Office had a new machiavellian brain-wave and tried to set up a puppet Jewish Agency as a kind of satellite Government. A number of Jewish public figures with anti-Zionist leanings were approached for this purpose, but to no avail.

The next idea of the Foreign Office, in September 1946, was to ask those members of the Jewish Agency who had not been arrested for " informal talks " to London, where they were offered a bargain : if they gave up promoting illegal immigration their arrested colleagues would be released. A more maladroit proposal could hardly have been made ; and once more the rabbit vanished back into the hat.

The last of these anxious improvisations which had to serve in lieu of a policy was the so-called Bevin Plan, submitted to the truncated Palestine Conference on February 7, 1947. It envisaged the admission of 4000 immigrants per month for two years, after which period further immigration would be made dependent on an arbitration tribunal to be appointed by the United Nations — that is to say, on a cumbersome procedure and on all sorts of international hazards. After a further three years the Jewish minority would come under the domination of the Arab majority in a unified and independent Arab State. In short, the Bevin Plan of 1947 was another re-hash of the White Paper of 1939, and was met by the same unconditional refusal on the part of the Jews.

Ten days later, on February 18, 1947, the Foreign Secretary stated in the House of Commons that the Government had decided, in view of the Mandate having proved unworkable, to submit the problem to the judgment of the United Nations.

3

There is a kind of symbiosis or mimicry at work, not only between married couples, but also between chronic antagonists. The negative relationship, like the positive, leads to a mutual adaptation to and imitation of the opponent's methods and idiosyncrasies. In the war against totalitarian Germany the Allies were gradually forced to adopt the methods of total war, from the broadcast lie to saturation bombing and Hiroshima. It is impossible to fight ruthlessness with considerateness, guile with sincerity. Opponents in battle, like partners in understanding, must meet on a common plane — which is inevitably that of their lowest common denominator.

During the last two years of the Mandate the relations between English and Jews were confined to the lowest common denominator of both. The Mandatory Administration and the Jewish Agency vied with each other in ruthless action covered by a film of oily hypocrisy. In the poisoned atmosphere of the Holy Land, through a process of mutual contamination, each brought out the evil latent in the other. During a mass screening of the total population of Tel Aviv, which lasted four days, the British troops divided the " sheep " from the " goats " by marking them like cattle with different coloured dye on their foreheads ; they heiled Hitler in Jewish settlements and desecrated synagogue walls with swastikas. The Jews in their turn called Britons Nazis in pamphlets and posters, and in a Press interview a Jewish writer declared that every Englishman killed meant a holiday in his heart. A British court sentenced a Jewish schoolboy to flogging for carrying illegal leaflets ; Jewish terrorists kidnapped and flogged British soldiers who had fought in the European war. British officials hanged four Jewish maquisards, denying them the last farewell to their families and the spiritual comfort of a rabbi's presence ; Jewish terrorists hanged two British sergeants in an orange grove, booby-trapping their dead bodies. Fanatic Jewish gunmen killed British soldiers in their sleep ; drunken British soldiers shot passing Jewish civilians in the back. The British Administration passed emergency laws which turned the country into a Police State, abolished Habeas Corpus, legalized detention without trial, the deportation of Palestine citizens to British colonies in Africa,[1] the hanging of people for membership of an illegal group without any specific crime being proved, or even charged, against them. The Jewish underground countered the reign of legalized terror by individual terror which made every Briton's life unsafe in Palestine.

On the top level both parties deplored acts of violence, declined responsibility for them, and vied with each other in issuing statements of sickening hypocrisy. Two examples, (a) and (b), will illustrate the degree of insincerity which both sides had reached.

(a)

On August 13, 1946, His Majesty's Government announced that the practice of interning illegal immigrants (who managed to reach the country despite the naval blockade) in Palestine detention camps would be discontinued, and that such entrants would be deported in future to " Cyprus or elsewhere ". This decree came one year after the end of the war, four months after the Anglo-American Committee's recommendation for immediate admission of the 100,000, and a few weeks after the pogrom of Kielce, which had only too clearly demonstrated the truth of the Committee's finding that for the Jews of Europe there was no return. It should also be remembered that the Committee's report had stressed that for the overwhelming majority of European Jews Palestine was the only country to which they could and wished to go, thereby refuting the hoary allegation that illegal immigration was the artificial product of a Zionist racket.

The immediate consequences of the deportation order were as follows.

On August 11 two ships had arrived in Haifa within two hours of each other. Both were sailing-boats ; one with an auxiliary motor, the other without. The first, which carried only canvas, was called the *Yagur* ; her 758 passengers included 350 women, 50 of whom were pregnant ; she had been at sea for twenty-nine days. The second, called the *Henrietta Szold*, with 450 passengers, had been at sea for fifteen days. All the passengers came from concentration and D.P. camps with the only expectation of

---

[1] Since October 1944 the Palestine Administration had adopted the legally unique practice of deporting without trial politically suspect Palestine citizens to the Sudan and Eritrea.

changing residence from a D.P. camp in Germany to an internment camp in Palestine. The new decree destroyed this sanguin-
ary hope; on August 13 an official communiqué announced that
"transfer of illegal immigrants from the *Henrietta Szold* and
Yagur to two transports has been successfully completed, and the
latter sailed from Haifa for Cyprus this morning".

The communiqué was silent about the circumstances of the
successful completion of transhipment, which were as follows.
On the eve of the operation a whole infantry division, reinforced
by Sherman tanks, had moved into the port, to cut it off from the
city. Two cruisers of the Royal Navy,[1] escorted by several
destroyers and a screen of Police launches, surrounded the immigrant boats. One foreign correspondent cabled to his paper:
"It was considered unnecessary to have anti-aircraft guns". The
deportees, weakened by the journey, offered only passive resistance
when they were led into the wire cages of the British transports,
ironically belonging to the category known as Liberty Ships.

While their transhipment was being carried out, thousands
of Jews in Haifa streamed towards the port. The situation of the
troops became critical, and they opened fire. Three people were
killed: a boy of 15, a girl of 19 and a man.

The next refugee ship to arrive was the 300-ton caique
Palmakh with 600 passengers. The Royal Navy captured the
ship at the fourth boarding attempt. The immigrants on board
entrenched themselves behind barricades. The boarding party
finally gained control of the vessel by using tear-smoke grenades
and oil sprays against them. During the operation one refugee
was killed and several wounded. About thirty young men and
women jumped overboard and swam towards the shore. They
were pursued by Police launches. The swimmers' arms were
branded with German concentration camp numbers. They
refused life-belts and resisted being pulled into the Police boats.
Four young men, who had swum over a mile, yelled that they
preferred drowning to deportation. They could only be saved
after soldiers had jumped into the water, knocked them out and
fastened ropes around them.

These were the first consequences of the deportation order in
terms of human suffering. It is against this background that the
official statement[2] by which the Government justified the deporta-

---

[1] H.M S. *Mauritius* and H.M.S. *Ajax*.
[2] Statement issued by H M.G. on 13.8.1946.

tion order should be appreciated. It opened with the affirmation that " no country in the world has been a better or more consistent friend of the Jewish people than Britain " and informed the world at large that " in Britain there are no pogroms ". After describing in moving terms the Government's "patience, forbearance and humanity ", it called the mass exodus of Jews fleeing from the Polish pogroms and the German D.P. camps a sinister traffic organized by " unscrupulous persons " — agents whose sole aims were " to exploit the sufferings of these unfortunate people ", and to annoy the Palestine authorities. As neither security reasons nor the shortage of food could any longer be invoked as arguments, as in the case of the refugee ships during the war, the continuation of the same policy was now justified on the grounds that admission of refugees placed " a severe strain on the administration ", threatened civil war and a break-down of government, and was " likely to have an adverse effect on the hope of a general settlement ". The fact is that civil war broke out, and government broke down, precisely because they refused admission to the refugees.

(b)

The hypocrisy of the Government which fought refugees with tear gas while posing as the best friend of the Jews found an equal in the hypocrisy of its opponents. The Jewish Agency had travelled a long way from the days when Haganah's first commandment was law-abiding self-restraint. The Arab revolt had been rewarded by the White Paper; Haganah's loyalty with a pat on the shoulder and a kick in the pants. The lesson had sunk in deeply with both the leadership and the rank and file. Step by step Haganah had changed its methods from helping immigration and accumulating arms for defence, to the sabotaging of railroads, the blowing up of Police launches and attacks on R.A.F. stations used for patrolling the seas. All this, Haganah claimed, was not terrorism but part of their activities to aid immigration ; it could hardly be expected, however, that the authorities should recognize such subtle distinctions.

Moreover, since the end of 1945, when the Agency leaders had declared all attempts on their part to fight terrorism under the prevailing political conditions to be futile, the relations between Haganah, Irgun and Stern Group had become extremely ambiguous. While the Agency leaders and other official Jewish

bodies issued one public statement after another condemning
terrorism in sonorous language, Haganah at times quarrelled, at
others collaborated with the other terrorist groups. While collaboration thus alternated with mutual denunciation between the
rival underground groups, the Zionist leadership adopted the
classic attitude of the right hand not knowing what the left hand
is doing. By this double-faced policy the leaders of the Zionist
movement, as so often happened in its history, spoiled and discredited their otherwise perfectly good case. The ambiguity of
their statements was not lost on the members of the Anglo-
American Committee.

" To-day ", writes Crossman, " Ben Gurion gave evidence,
and made a bad impression on the Committee. . . . He seems
to want to have it both ways, to remain within the letter of the
law as Chairman of the Agency, and to tolerate terror as a
method to bring pressure on the Administration . . . to claim
constitutional rights for the Jewish Agency as a loyal collaborator with the Mandatory, and simultaneously to organize
sabotage and resistance." [1]

On July 22, one month after the arrest of the leaders of the
Jewish Agency, the King David Hotel in Jerusalem, seat of the
offices of the Government's secretariat, was blown up by members
of the Irgun. According to the Irgun practice, a warning of the
impending explosion was given by telephone twenty-five minutes
before it took place. The warning was disregarded, and the fact
that it had been given only admitted by the Government two
months later, in the indirect form that no such warning had been
received by anyone at the Secretariat " in an official position with
any power to take action ". The fact that the warning was given
cannot erase the moral responsibility for the act ; but to omit
mention of it would be to distort the evidence in the opposite
direction. In the explosion 91 persons — Britons, Jews and
Arabs — were killed, and 41 injured. The Hebrew Press the
next day was unanimous in condemning the outrage ; *Davar*, the
Labour daily, mouthpiece of the Jewish Agency, wrote :

" The entire Yishuv has been shocked to the core by
the criminal and abhorrent distortion given yesterday to the
struggle of the Jewish people by a gang of dissidents. This

[1] Crossman, *op. cit.*

criminal massacre has no reason and no atonement. . . . It is a crime committed not only against the many dead and wounded, but against the Jewish community and its future."

Yet in this case the gang of dissidents had acted on orders from Haganah. And Haganah was under the direct orders of the Jewish Agency. It is true that four members of the Agency Executive were at the time in detention, and its Chairman, Ben Gurion, absent in Paris; the resulting disorganization and confusion must be counted as a mitigating factor in judging the official Jewish attitude. But the King David episode is merely an extreme example of the general policy of the official Zionist bodies. They preached resistance but denied indignantly acting against the law; they alternately tolerated, fought against or engaged in terrorism, according to the opportunity of the moment, but all the time carefully maintained the fiction of being guardians of civic virtue. Unlike the Irish rebels, the French resistance or the Jewish terrorists, they never had the courage to go underground and to harmonize their words with their acts. They had learned their lesson in hypocrisy from the Mandatory Administration; and the habits once acquired were partly carried over into the newborn State.

But here, too, psychology has to be taken into account as a mitigating factor. What to the outside world appeared as calculated hypocrisy, was often merely the outward projection of an inner conflict in the minds of the leaders of the Jewish Agency. True to their social-democratic tradition, they were, like the Austrian and German Social Democrats, profoundly reluctant to risk all they had built up in years of patient labour by embarking on open revolt. More precisely, like their brother-Socialist parties they regarded open fight as a last resource, and kept on trying, hoping against hope, to achieve their aims by negotiation and compromise, supported by half-hearted threats and token acts of violence. The German Socialists never fought; the Austrians fought when it was too late. The Jewish Agency would probably have shared the same fate if the terrorists and the extremist element within Haganah had not forced the pace, and had not the British withdrawal confronted them with the choice to fight or perish. Even a short time before the final decision, informal negotiations took place between members of the Jewish Agency and of the British Government, in which the former indicated their willingness to accept the modest compromise of an increase of the monthly immigration quota from 1500 to 4000, under a continued British Mandate, and to postpone the final solution *sine die*.

It was more than anything the intransigent attitude of the Labour Cabinet, its insistence on a kind of " unconditional surrender " of the Jewish Agency, which prevented a compromise and brought the crisis to a head.

Without Mr. Bevin there would probably be no State of Israel to-day.

CHAPTER XIII

THE MIRACLE OF LAKE SUCCESS

Britain rejects the U.N. recommendations — The miracle of
Russo-American agreement — Palestine becomes a test
case for U.N.O. — The Marx Brothers at Lake Success.
    Evacuation of British civilians — Reactions of Arabs
and Jews — More bombs, hangings and prison breaks —
The Farran case — *Exodus* in reverse

As we approach the date of the termination of the British Mandate
and the proclamation of the Jewish State, the events which
constitute the " Background " of this chronicle move nearer to
the focus of the present, and overlap to an increasing degree with
the " Close-up " reports in the second part of this book. We shall
therefore accelerate the pace, and record only the main outlines
of the events which took place during this period of transition.

I

On February 18, 1947, the Foreign Secretary had referred the
Palestine problem to the United Nations. The United Nations
Assembly met on April 28, and on May 15 appointed a new
commission — the nineteenth — to find a solution for it.
The " United Nations Special Commission on Palestine " —
U.N.S.C.O.P. — headed by Judge E. Sandstroem (Sweden) and
composed of members of eleven nations, sojourned in Palestine
from the middle of June to the end of July. On September 26
U.N.S.C.O.P. submitted its majority report to the General
Assembly, which adopted it on November 29, 1947.

The conclusions of the report were essentially the same as
those reached by the Royal Commission ten years earlier : the
Mandate was unworkable and Partition the only possible solution.
And, as in the case of the Royal Commission's and the Anglo-
American Committee's reports, the British Government, having
asked for independent advice and received it, rejected it out
of hand. On December 11, Mr. Creech Jones made public
Britain's refusal to implement U.N.S.C.O.P.'s majority report,

without offering any alternative policy; and at the same time announced that His Majesty's Government had decided to bring the Mandate to an end, and to withdraw from Palestine.

The United Nations' general debate opened in its Palestine Committee on October 4. It was to be full of surprises and almost surrealistic turns, true to the traditions of the Holy Land. During the first days the great enigma was, what attitude the Soviet Union and its satellite countries would take. The first clue was given on the fourth day of the debate, when first the Polish, then the Czech delegate, Jan Masaryk, supported Partition on the basis of the U.N.S.C.O.P. Report. Then came the modern Palestine miracle, which made even those who took no interest in the problem hold their breath. Within two days of each other, on the 12th and 14th October respectively, the United States' and the Soviet Union's delegates both came out in favour of Partition, and for the first time in U.N.O. history found themselves together on the same side of the fence.

It looked as if for once the United Nations were in a position to solve an international problem in a harmonious, business-like manner; and once they started on this road, who knows how far they might travel ? So Palestine again became a test case; that seemed to be its perpetual fate. That U.N.O. did not pass the test was in this one exceptional case not Russia's, but Britain's, fault.

On October 17 the British delegate, Mr. Creech Jones, made his long-awaited statement, the gist of which was that

"His Majesty's Government would not accept responsibility for the enforcement, either alone *or in cooperation with other nations*, of any settlement antagonistic to either the Jews or the Arabs or both, which was likely to necessitate the use of force."

The crucial passage is the one in italics. To make its meaning quite clear, it has to be taken in conjunction with repeated official British statements to the same effect, and in particular with the Foreign Secretary's reply to a question on this matter in the House of Commons on January 2, 1948 :

Mr. Warbey (Socialist, Luton): "Do I understand from what the Foreign Secretary has just said that if the Security Council were to decide that collective enforcement action was necessary in respect of Palestine, this country would not take its share as one of the members of the United Nations ? "

Mr. Bevin : " That is what the Hon. Member must understand. . . ."

From here onward British policy can no longer be qualified
as muddled, short-sighted or pseudo-machiavellian; it became
plainly surrealistic. Six months earlier Mr. Bevin had asserted
that he had no right to impose immigration on Palestine " by
force " ; but he had taken for granted the right to exclude immigration by force. Britain had rejected the Anglo-American and
the United Nations Committees' recommendations on the grounds
that she could not carry them out alone; now that international
assistance was offered, she refused even to take her share along
with others. Six months earlier the Foreign Secretary had re-
nounced Britain's Mandate on the grounds that the claims of Jews
and Arabs were irreconcilable and agreement between them
impossible ; from now onward British spokesmen kept repeating
that Britain would only support a solution which conciliated
Jewish and Arab claims, and was based on agreement between
the two. To appeal for the judgment of an international body
in order to stop two parties from quarrelling, and then to reject
the judgment because it meant enforcing peace between them,
was no longer diplomacy but sheer Harpo Marx logics.

The remaining six weeks of the U.N.O. debate took place in
the same Marx Brothers atmosphere. The vote was to take place
on October 21 ; but Mr. Creech Jones' statement, like a poisoned
arrow, threw the State Department into fits; the miracle of
Russia's consent changed into the nightmare of having to side
with her against England. The White House took a somewhat
detached view of this, the State Department did not ; the shooting
war in Palestine became transformed into a tug-of-war in Washing-
ton. The heaves and tugs exerted from there in opposite directions found their visible expression in the somewhat jerky
behaviour displayed by the Central American banana republics
and by such parties to the Palestine dispute as Siam and Liberia.
On the day before the first vote was to take place, the anti-
Partitionist convictions expressed by the delegate from Cuba
were taken as an indication that the United States delegation were
lobbying for votes against their own resolution. Two days later
events took a new turn : instead of taking the decisive vote, the
Palestine Committee appointed three Sub-Committees : one to
elaborate the Partition plan, a second to deal with Arab proposals,

a third with the poetic task of " conciliating Arabs and Jews ".
—" Because of the convolutions of the lengthy debate ", the
Palestine Post commented, " by the time it came to voting, most
delegations were not sure what they were voting for ".

The Sub-Committees settled down to work ; the Arab Sub-
Committee was composed of delegates of eight Moslem States
and of Colombia. " The only reason Snr. Gonzales agreed to
serve with the Arabs, was to appease the leader of his Government's opposition, who is a wealthy Arab immigrant to Colombia",
the *Palestine Post* informed its readers.

In the Partition Sub-Committee the miracle of Russo-American
agreement was repeated. By November 11 the Sub-Committee
had agreed in detail on the boundaries of the proposed Arab and
Jewish States, and on the modalities of the transfer of power. On
November 14 the British delegate, Sir Alexander Cadogan, rejected this Soviet-American plan, declaring that British troops
would not be available for the enforcement of the proposed
settlement. A week later the Sub-Committee had a new plan
ready, in which the modalities of the transfer of power were altered
to suit the British delegate's previous objections. Sir Alexander
Cadogan rejected it, declaring that the transition regime under
U.N.O. tutelage now envisaged in the proposal " would create a
division of authority between Britain and the United Nations,
which in turn would create confusion and disorder and have
disastrous consequences. . . ."

Furthermore — and this declaration contained the clue to all
that happened afterwards — the British delegate announced that

> " So long as my Government will continue to hold the Mandate
> for Palestine, they must insist upon their undivided control of
> that country. . . . The transfer of authority by the Palestine
> Government to the councils of government or their representa-
> tives would in practice amount to the implementation of this
> scheme by His Majesty's Government which, failing an Arab-
> Jewish agreement, they are not prepared to undertake."

The meaning of this announcement was not fully appreciated
at the time, but became disastrously evident in Palestine during the
months to follow. It meant, in practice, that until the day when
Britain gave up the Mandate, she would continue in " undivided
control " of Palestine, refuse the gradual transfer of authority
either to U.N.O., or to the Jews and Arabs, and thus create a legal,

administrative and security vacuum — a procedure unprecedented in history. Its motto was that of the French monarch seeing his world crumble : " *Après moi le déluge* ". Thus began the last melancholy chapter of British rule in the Holy Land, a manœuvre directly responsible for the war which followed — and which may be conveniently referred to as Operation Deluge.

To meet Britain's new objections, the recommendations of the Sub-Committee were redrafted for the third time, and on November 24 the United States delegate came out with a massive speech in favour of it. It was accompanied by an equally massive criticism of " British policy, which has not been entirely helpful, and which has made the work of our Committee difficult ". Two days later U.N.O.'s Palestine Committee approved the Partition plan by 25 votes to 13, and rejected the Arab plan by 29 votes to 12. The British delegate consistently abstained from voting, the U.S.A. and U.S.S.R. consistently voted together.

The final decision now rested with the General Assembly, where a two-thirds majority was required to pass the resolution. The result of the ballot in the Committee had shown that the pro-Partitionists were just one vote short. On the 27th it became known that the Siamese delegate, who had voted against the resolution, had been dismissed by his Government for unknown reasons. But on the same day the Philippino delegate, who in the Committee had abstained, made an enigmatic speech which was neither here nor there. Once more the rebirth of the Jewish State after two thousand years hinged on one vote — that of the gentleman from the Philippine Islands.

On the 27th the Chief Rabbi of Jerusalem urged the Jewish Community to pray at the Wailing Wall. That seemed to work, for the delegate from Haiti, who the previous day had declared that he would vote against, received last-minute instructions to reverse his attitude. It also became known that the Chinese delegate had been instructed to abstain, the Greek delegate, who had previously abstained, to vote against. Other delegates cabled and telephoned for instructions to their respective Governments, from Costa Rica to Afghanistan, from Iceland to Peru. During the three days between the vote in the Committee and the final vote in the Assembly, not less than twelve delegates changed their minds about the rights and wrongs of the issue. It looked as if the Marx Brothers were playing General Post in the lobbies of Lake Success, for the stake of the future of Israel.

L

The result of the historic vote on November 29 was : 33 for the Partition resolution (including the U.S.S.R., U.S.A. and France) ; 13 against it (the eleven Moslem countries, Cuba and Greece) ; and 10 abstentions (including Britain, alone among the Great Powers, and alone among the countries of the British Commonwealth, all the rest of which voted for).

On that evening and during the night Jews danced and sang in the streets of New York and Tel Aviv, of Belgrade and Vienna, in the D.P. camps in Germany and in the fortress-settlements of Galilee. In the synagogues prayers of thanks were offered for the resurrection of Israel. It was Jewry's V-day — the first since the time of the Maccabeans.

On the morrow of the decision the Palestine Arab Higher Committee decided on a three days' strike ; synagogues and Jewish houses were burnt down in Aleppo, and seven Jews were murdered in a convoy ambush near Tel Aviv. The civil war had begun ; and the focus of events shifted back from Lake Success to Palestine.

2

During the months preceding the United Nations' decision the Anglo-Jewish sub-war had reached its climax. Hangings, kidnappings, murder and deportations had become daily occurrences.

On January 31, 1947, the Government had decided to evacuate from Palestine all British women, children and male civilians in non-essential jobs. British journalists, business men and clergy, if they wished to stay behind, would do so at their own risk. It was the first plain indication, a fortnight before Mr. Bevin referred the problem to U.N.O., that Britain was unable to cope with the terrorists, and was preparing to pull out of Palestine.

The reaction of the various parties concerned to this momentous event was psychologically significant. The British business men sent a cable of protest to the Cabinet declaring that the evacuation " constituted a surrender to the terrorist elements " — which in fact it did. The Arab Press could not believe that British might and power had been defeated by Jewish resistance, and suspected some particularly diabolic scheme behind the evacuation order :

" Can you conceive ", wrote *Falastin*, " of such a state of affairs in a country ruled by Britain and where she has mustered 100,000 soldiers, that is one fully equipped soldier to every five

Jews ! By Allah, if we were asked what was the greatest lie ever told, we would say that it is the reason given for the evacuation. . . . No, the . . . Government is taking advantage of terrorism for its own imperialistic aims in Palestine. It is turning the country into a military camp and thereby threatening the peace of the world."

Most revealing of all was the reaction of the official Jewish circles and newspapers. They were furious that the end of British rule, for which they had clamoured, had been brought within sight not by prayers in the synagogues and Agency protests, but by the action of the rival " dissidents ". Thus the *Palestine Post*, mouth-piece of the Jewish Agency, wrote : [1]

" If . . . the consequences implied in the evacuation order take their repressive and demoralizing shape, the effect upon the psychology of this country's citizens, as well as upon their social and economic life, may well be disastrous. . . . It beggars thought that any government should desire so to flatter a group of dissidents or so to drive a hard-working and peace-loving people to unwilling association with methods it hates and condemns."

The immediate antecedents of the evacuation order were in the best Palestinian cloak-and-dagger style. On January 24 the G.O.C., General Barker, had confirmed sentence of death on a member of Irgun, Dov Gruener. On the 26th the condemned man refused to appeal for the King's clemency ; on the same day Irgun kidnapped two Englishmen, a judge and a former army officer, as hostages for Gruener One day later, on the 27th, the G.O.C. granted a stay of execution for Gruener so that his case might be taken to the Privy Council. One day later, on the 28th, the two Englishmen were released. The judge declared that he had been treated with courtesy, given a bed, good food, cigarettes, and a book to read (which happened to be a novel by this author). He professed that he felt no resentment against his captors, who had kept his wig as a souvenir.

The subsequent events were in a less decorous style. Dov Gruener was hanged three months later under particularly revolt-ing circumstances, to which reference has been made earlier.[2] After the evacuation of the civilians the country was gradually transformed into an armoured camp. Jews were evicted from the

---

[1] On February 2, 1947.   [2] Cf. p. 134.

residential quarters in Haifa, Jerusalem and Tel Aviv without being offered alternative accommodation. The blocks thus freed were transformed into British Security Zones — small fortified enclaves surrounded by fantastic tangles of barbed wire and sandbagged barricades, locally known as " Bevingrads " or " British ghettoes ". Yet none of these precautions could stem the tide of terrorism.

On February 10 three members of Irgun were sentenced to be hanged — on the sole charge of having been found in possession of arms on December 29, 1946, the night when British Army personnel had been flogged by terrorists in retaliation for the caning of a young Irgun boy. On March 1 twelve British soldiers and Police were killed when the British Officers' Club in one of the " Security Zones " of Jerusalem was blown up under cover of machine-gun fire. The next day statutory Martial Law was put into force in Tel Aviv and parts of Jerusalem. For over two weeks 240,000 Jews — about 40 per cent of the total Jewish population — were denied postal, telephone, telegraph and motor transport services, and completely cut off from the outside world. No goods or persons were allowed to leave the Martial Law area ; all public services were closed, and life was paralysed. It was a measure of collective punishment, whose only effect was to increase the number of recruits and sympathizers for the terrorist groups. The attackers of the Officers' Club were never caught, and during the whole Martial Law period terrorist action continued. On March 16 the Press Offices of the Jewish Agency were blown up by a time-bomb ; it was believed that this and a series of similar bombings were the work of a counter-terror squad within the British Police Force, composed of former members of Mosley's Blackshirts.

In April four terrorists were hanged, among them Dov Gruener. Two others succeeded in blowing themselves to bits in their prison cell, before they could be hanged, by means of smuggled hand-grenades which they pressed under their armpits. All of them had refused to take part in their trials, and had sat through the proceedings reading the Bible or reciting the Psalms of David. The executions were followed by a new wave of assassination, bomb-throwing and mine-laying, which caused fourteen deaths within the next few days ; on the scene of each attack the terrorists left a hangman's noose as their signature.

On May 6 a Jewish boy of 16, suspected of being a member of

the Stern Group, was abducted from a street in Jerusalem by a group of plain-clothes policemen, working under the orders of Major R. A. Farran, D.S.O. He shouted for help ; passers-by tried to rescue him, but desisted when the men produced their Police cards.

" The boy appears to have been taken to an isolated spot outside the city and tortured to death. No trace has been found of the body. The incident created a deep stir. Several weeks later it became known that Major Farran had escaped to Syria, and that a request for his extradition had been made. He was actually handed over, but escaped from military detention at the Allenby Barracks in Jerusalem, apparently with the assistance of members of the special anti-terrorist squad to which he belonged. He subsequently surrendered to the police." [1]

Farran was tried by a military court-martial on October 1, 1947, having previously been released from his Police duties so that he could revert to Army status. At the court-martial counsel for the defence objected to having the defendant's diary produced as evidence on the grounds that the diary was part of his defence ; the objection was granted. Farran's superior officer, Colonel B. Ferguson, refused to testify about certain statements which Farran had made to him, on the grounds that his testimony would be self-incriminatory. (Colonel Ferguson resigned from service a short time later.) On October 2 Farran was acquitted. On his arrival in Liverpool harbour he was cheered by a crowd of several thousands. His memoirs were serialized by a popular English Sunday paper. His brother was killed by a letter-bomb sent by the Stern Group.

The last episode to be recorded in this weary tale is Irgun's attack on the penitentiary in Acco, which led to the escape of over a hundred political prisoners (and some Arab criminals who took advantage of the occasion) through a hole blown in the massive walls of the Napoleonic fortress. Several of the attackers were wounded, and subsequently captured and hanged. Their death was avenged by Irgun with a barbarity surpassing everything the country had previously seen : two British soldiers, Sergeants Martin and Plaice, were found hanged in an orange grove, with booby-traps attached to their dead bodies.

During all this time more refugees kept arriving at the shores

[1] Memorandum presented by the Jewish Agency to the United Nations Special Committee on Palestine, Jerusalem, 1947, p 42.

of Palestine — and leaving it again in the cages of British deportation ships. The circumstances of these unique naval engagements
were always more or less the same. The little hell-ships were
spotted at sea by R.A.F. patrols, escorted to Haifa by units of
the Royal Navy, and the passengers forcibly transferred to the
deportation ships by marines and airborne troops. As a rule,
their resistance was overcome by tear gas, oil jets and baton
charges. As a rule, there were one or two dead and a score or so
wounded and trampled down, with women screaming and babies
suffering the shock which made them later on into interesting cases
of refugee-neurosis. The legal aspect of the deportations was not
without a touch of grim humour : when writs of Habeas Corpus
were filed before Palestine courts on behalf of the refugees, the
courts upheld the deportations after members of the administration had stated in evidence that the granting of permission to land
would be " prejudicial to public security ". The bearing on public
security of the battles for their transhipment, of the riots,
bombings and assassinations, which were their direct consequence,
seems in each case to have escaped the court's attention.

The war was over, the floods had receded, the Government had
changed ; yet this human wreckage was still being aimlessly tossed
about as " illegal immigrants ". After about twenty boat-loads
of them had been carried off in the manner described to yet
another concentration camp — their fifth or sixth or tenth — the
Government decided that it had been carrying leniency too far.
Cyprus was too near to Palestine, and the D.P.s interned there
might think that they had, after all, made some headway towards
their ultimate destination ; which in turn might encourage others
to follow their example. The obvious solution was to deport the
D.P.s, not to Cyprus, but back to Germany. In July the 4300
passengers on board the refugee ship with the symbolic name
Exodus 1947, after three of their number had been killed in
boarding operations off the coast of the National Home, were
shipped back as prisoners aboard three British transport ships
across the Mediterranean, round the coast of Spain, through the
English Channel and across the North Sea to Hamburg, port of
the country which had become their national cemetery. The
journey in the blistering heat lasted forty-six days of which
twenty-five days were spent off Marseilles, the French Government having offered asylum to the deportees, which the latter,
with a few exceptions, refused. Each stage of the journey was

spot-lighted by the world Press ; for weeks on end Britain was the target of more humiliating comment by her friends and foes alike than at any other time in recent history.

It was indeed an exploit as pointless as it was symbolic. His Majesty's Government seemed to have taken it upon themselves, by reversing the *Exodus,* to turn back the tide of history.

CHAPTER XIV

THE CIVIL WAR

The showdown begins — The battle of the convoys —
Infiltration from the neighbouring countries — Ambiguous
status of the Arab Legion — British arms deliveries to
Transjordan and Iraq.

Haganah goes into action — From convoy defence to
punitive raids — The storming of Castel — The victory of
Mishmar Ha'emek — The blood-bath of Deir Yassin — Its
extraordinary repercussions — The Arab exodus — The
surrender of Tiberias — The battle for Haifa — The surrender of Jaffa — The Jews take Safed, Beisan and modern
Jerusalem — They lose the Old City and five settlements

I

MEANWHILE the United Nations Commission had arrived in
Palestine, and with the beginning of the Palestine debate in
October 1947 a temporary lull descended on the country. The
interlude in Lake Success constituted the dividing line between
the Anglo-Jewish struggle which had preceded it and the Arab-
Jewish struggle which followed the passing of the Partition
resolution in the Assembly.

The final showdown began on the day after the historic vote;
it passed through a series of continuous gradations from raids and
riots to full-scale civil war, and from there to the war of intervention of the six Arab States against Israel. This last phase began
on the day of the termination of the Mandate, May 15, 1948;
until that date the civil war was fought in a country still, on
Britain's insistence, under " undivided British control ",[1] and in
which the British Government of Palestine remained "responsible
for law and order ".[2]

The initial phase was characterized mainly by Arab attacks on
Jewish motor-vehicle convoys on the main arterial roads; by
street fighting on the Jaffa–Tel Aviv border and in the Old City

---

[1] Cf. i.a., statement by Sir Alexander Cadogan on November 21, 1947.
[2] Cf. i.a., statement by the Colonial Secretary on December 11, 1947.

of Jerusalem ; and by bomb outrages in crowded places. The strategically most important aspect during this phase were the attacks on the convoys which aimed at paralysing Jewish road traffic, cutting off Jerusalem's life-line to Tel Aviv and starving out the isolated Jewish settlements in the Negeb and in Galilee. The battles of the convoys fought in this period at the gorge of Bab el Wad, where the Jerusalem road emerges into the plain, and along the roads to Galilee and the Negeb, were probably the most cruel and savage encounters of the whole struggle. To this day the roadsides of Palestine are littered with the carcasses of burnt-out motor-buses, their wheels pointing to the sky like the legs of dead horses. At least once a week a Jewish convoy with food supplies for Jerusalem or the settlements would run into an Arab road-block or mine and find itself surrounded by a mob of several hundred Arabs who riddled the passengers with machine-gun bullets and set the buses on fire. There were, as a rule, few survivors, as those who sought protection in the buses were burnt alive, the others mowed down.

The British authorities refused to provide escorts for Jewish convoys because, as a senior Government official informed the Jewish Agency on December 3, "that might be interpreted as British implementation of partition ".[1] At the same time, they refused to authorize the Jews to provide their own protection for the convoys by using the armoured cars of the Settlement Police ; they even refused to allow the passengers, or at least the drivers, to carry arms.

On January 22, to quote one example among many, seven Jewish Settlement Policemen, travelling in an open tender because of the ban on armoured cars, were killed in an Arab ambush and their dead bodies mutilated. Seven days later, on January 29, a Colonel Nelson at British H.Q. informed representatives of Jewish settlements in the same vicinity that they could not use armoured cars " since it arouses the Arabs ".[2] On December 21 the Under-Secretary of State for the Colonies had informed the House of Commons that the Government did not consider the arming of Jewish bus drivers advisable, " since the carrying of firearms by vehicle drivers does not constitute effective protection ". So the convoys often had to proceed without any protection whatsoever. When the Executive of the Jewish National Council, whose

[1] Memorandum presented by the Jewish Agency to the United Nations Palestine Commission, Jerusalem, 1947, p. 6. [2] *Ibid.* p. 8.

members were obliged constantly to travel between Jerusalem and
Tel Aviv, improvised armoured plating on their car, the car was
confiscated by British Police on completion of its first journey.
The logical result of all this was that on an average fifty Jews were
killed per week, mostly by travelling in unprotected convoys, and
that in some cases over fifty were killed on a single convoy. The
conditions which prevailed during this period are further illustrated by incidents like the Government's solemn assurance, on
Thursday, December 25, that their security forces were taking
care of the Tel Aviv–Jerusalem road which would now be kept
open and safe, and the ambushing and assassination on this
same road of seven Jewish travellers the next day. It should be
noted that this vital road is all in all 40 miles long, and can be
easily patrolled by a relatively small number of modern police
cars.

The probably most tragic incident occurred, symbolically, on
the slopes of Mount Scopus. The Hebrew University and the
great Hadassah Hospital both stand on this hill, separated from
the Jewish quarters of Jerusalem by Arab suburbs. In December
Arab snipers had continually attacked Jewish road traffic to the
Hospital and University, and killed one nurse, wounding several
others. Yet at a Press conference on January 21 the Government
spokesman placidly explained that "armoured escorts are not granted
to ambulances because ordinary considerations of humanity should
render them immune to attacks ". Again the inevitable happened :
on April 13 a convoy carrying hospital and university personnel
was ambushed on its way to Mount Scopus. In the attack 77
Jews were killed, among them the Director of the Hospital, and
20 wounded.

The Arab intention behind these attacks was obvious : the
Jews were to be forced off the highways of Palestine. Once this
aim was achieved, the Jewish enclaves of Jerusalem, in the Negeb
and in Galilee, as well as the isolated settlements dotted all over
the country, would be cut off, made defenceless, and would have
to be evacuated. The impossibility of Partition would thus be
proved, and the whole plan would collapse. The British attitude
was equally evident : to protect Jewish road traffic, or to legalize
Jewish self-protection on the roads, would amount to " enforcing
implementation of the partition plan " and was therefore not
feasible. It is true that the Government was responsible for order
and public security, but as long as the Jews stayed at home and

did not travel on the roads the security of most of them was assured As for those enclaves which depended on supplies by road transport, the Government's advice was that the Jews should evacuate them. Among the positions which the Government officially advised the Jews to evacuate for reasons of security were the Old City and the old Commercial Centre of Jerusalem, and the entire Negeb.

On February 15 the United Nations Palestine Commission submitted a Special Report to the Security Council, which pointed out that " powerful Arab interests, both inside and outside Palestine, are defying the resolution of the General Assembly, and are engaged in a deliberate effort to alter by force the settlement envisaged therein ". The first attempt towards this end had been the battle of the convoys. It was soon followed by the next stage : the infiltration of Arab guerillas, openly recruited by the Egyptian and Syrian Governments, across the frontiers of Palestine and by sea. Ragged strangers kept appearing in increasing numbers in Arab villages and towns — a reminder of the invasion by German tourists of Spain before the Civil War. They were referred to by the neighbouring Arab Governments as Volunteers, and were in fact, apart from a small number of professional officers, the riff-raff of the bazaars in Cairo, Damascus and Baghdad, hired for the Holy War for a shilling or two per day.[1] As the Palestine Arabs showed little willingness to fight, most of the sniping, ambushing and guerilla warfare was done by the foreign volunteers. It was typical of this state of affairs that after the first serious clashes had occurred between Arabs and Jews in Tiberias (on the 11th and 14th March) the heads of the two communities arranged a truce, the Arab delegates stating that the attackers of the Jewish quarter were " strangers who had forced their way into the town ".

Infiltration of irregulars from Syria had already played a decisive part during the Arab revolt of 1936–39. At that time the British authorities had kept their number down by fortifying the Syrian border (by the so-called Teggart Line) ; now their attitude was one of strict neutrality, of " non-intervention against foreign intervention ", true to the pattern of the Spanish war. Thus on January 16 Associated Press reported from Damascus that Syrian irregulars were sifting by the hundred across un-

---

[1] The Iraqi and Syrian irregulars captured later on by the Israeli Army stated that their pay had been between £3 and £5 a month.

guarded sections of Palestine's northern frontier.   On January 19
the Jewish Agency warned British G.H.Q. that 800 armed Syrians
were concentrated at Irbid in Transjordan, and were preparing
to cross into Palestine at Sheikh Hussein or over the Allenby
Bridge — which they actually did two days later.   They moved
into prepared camps at Tubas in the Samarian hills.   Yet in his
statement in the Commons a week later (February 4) the Colonial
Secretary gave the impression that the invaders had taken the
Government by surprise.   On January 30 another 800 armed
Arabs crossed into Palestine from Transjordan, escorted by Arab
Legionaries.[1]   On February 5 Associated Press reported from
Damascus that " 600 trained Syrians had crossed the Jordan on
Tuesday (3.2.48) night, and moved into prepared positions 60 km.
inside Palestine ".   On the 9th *Davar* reported that another 1000
Arabs, armed with light artillery and automatics, had crossed into
Palestine unhindered between February 5 and 7.   On February 11
the British delegate to the United Nations Palestine Commission
admitted that bands of Arab invaders were " increasingly exercising considerable administrative control over the whole area "
of Samaria.   Apparently these men, who were beyond doubt
Illegal Immigrants, were more favoured by the Administration
than the D.P.s — who were still being deported to Cyprus, on
the grounds that their admission would " be prejudicial to public
security ".

On February 14 Haganah blew up five bridges in Galilee to
check infiltration ; on March 3 the Colonial Secretary told the
House that 5000 Arabs had invaded Palestine since November 29,
and on the 16th he added that Fawzi el Kaukaji, leader of the Arab
revolt of 1936–39, had " slipped through the border guards " and
arrived in Palestine.   By that time a whole army of irregulars, in
its great majority Syrian and Lebanese, variously referred to as
the Yarmuk Army or the Arab Army of Liberation, was fighting
a pitched three-day battle against Haganah in the Valley of
Esdraelon, while the spokesmen of the Government still repeated, poker-faced, that Britain insisted on being alone responsible
for the maintenance of law and order.

Besides these tourist armies there was encamped on Palestine
soil the regular army of a neighbouring Arab State under British
operational command.   The Arab Legion, this strange military
hermaphrodite, owed allegiance to King Abdullah of Transjordan,

[1] *Palestine Post,* February 1, 1948.

was officered, financed and equipped by Great Britain, and, to make things more complicated, though it wore an alien king's cloth, acted as part of the British security forces in Palestine.

Clashes between Jews and members of the Legion were frequent and inevitable. Thus, on December 15, troops of the Arab Legion attacked a Jewish supply convoy on its way from Tel Aviv to the Children's Village at Ben Shemen and killed fourteen Jews. In Haifa, passengers of Jewish buses were sniped at while passing the Arab Legion camp, sometimes with fatal results. When the Mandate ended, on May 15, the Arab Legion's status as a British security force changed overnight into that of a regular army of invasion — still owing allegiance to King Abdullah, and still under British command.

While tolerating the infiltration and assembly of irregular armies, and maintaining a regular Arab army on Palestine territory, the British Government continued to supply the Arab countries with war material. On December 12-17 the Prime Ministers of the seven Arab States — Syria, Lebanon, Iraq, Transjordan, Egypt, Saudi Arabia and the Yemen — met in Cairo and issued an official statement to the effect that they would support the Palestine Arabs with arms, money and troops, and that their armies would march against the Jews as soon as the British Mandate ended. Yet a short time after, on February 6, 1948, the British Minister of Defence justified British arms deliveries to the Arab countries by explaining that his Government " had no reason to suppose " that arms assigned to Arab States under treaties would "find their way to Palestine ". The statement referred to the new Anglo-Iraqi treaty, signed on January 15, in which Britain undertook to supply "provisions for the forces of His Majesty the King of Iraq, of arms, ammunition, ships and airplanes of modern pattern, such as are in current use by the forces of His Britannic Majesty ".

On March 15 Great Britain signed a new twenty years' treaty of mutual defence and friendship with Transjordan, according to which the latter was to continue to get arms, ammunition, military equipment and other war materials from Britain; should either party become engaged in war the other undertook to come to its aid. It was simultaneously reported that Britain would continue to pay King Abdullah his annual two million pounds grant for the maintenance of the Arab Legion, and that Brigadier Glubb Pasha and his staff would remain in command of the Legion.

2

" In this situation ", the Jewish Agency stated on February 21 in its memorandum to the United Nations Palestine Commission, " the Jewish people in Palestine have come to recognize that only their own forces stand between them and annihilation. Faced with the Government's neutrality in the issue of their survival or extermination . . . the Jews of Palestine have assumed a responsibility which formally rests on the Mandatory Power."

At last the Jewish Agency had awakened to a full awareness of the situation and began to show that determined self-reliance which nationhood implies. This was no longer the mealy-mouthed protest of a committee of lawyers and synagogue elders, but the matter-of-fact voice of a nation at war.

Haganah's operations in these crucial six months developed gradually, as the Arab plan of attack took shape, from local defensive action in the battles of the convoys to retaliation and counter-attack ; and culminated in an offensive which resulted in the conquest of the entire territory of the Jewish State. These operations were partly carried out in areas still under nominal British control, and partly in the vacuum created by the piecemeal withdrawal of the British forces from Palestine.

The first time Haganah forces came out in more or less open action was in the inconclusive skirmishes against Arab snipers on the Jaffa–Tel Aviv border at the beginning of December. For the next few weeks its mobile forces were employed to go to the rescue of convoys which had run into an ambush, and of isolated settlements attacked by Arab bands. It was a harassing job against heavy odds, and the toll in casualties was severe. Thus, for instance, on January 17 a unit of 35 Haganah men rushing to the relief of Kfar Eftzion in the Hebron area was surrounded by Arab irregulars and killed to the last man.

Gradually Haganah went over from passive defence to punitive raids on Arab villages known to harbour irregulars. After a convoy attack originating from the Arab village of Silwan near Jerusalem, in which 7 Jews were killed, Haganah, on December 17, stormed the village and dynamited a number of houses. These actions were based on the example of the punitive methods used by the British Army during the Arab revolt of 1936–39. On January 24 Haganah went into action near Mount Castel on the Jerusalem–Tel Aviv road ; 40 Arabs and 10 Jews were killed, 4

of the latter by British troops.   On February 15 Haganah raided
Beisan, strategic key town at the junction of the Jordan and
Jezreel valleys.

In March events began to move faster as the evacuation of
British troops got under way.[1] The first prolonged battle, a
ten-day attack on the Jewish village of Magdiel by Iraqi troops
entrenched in the neighbouring A. D village of Bir Adas, ended
with the withdrawal of the invaders and peace overtures from the
villagers. In a punitive action on the 13th of the same month,
Haganah destroyed the Arab village of Kafr Husseinia in Galilee,
killing 30 villagers. A few days later its forces began a concentrated drive deep into Arab territory in the Beisan-Jenin area,
striking at villages which were used as bases for attacks on Jewish
settlements in the Jordan Valley. This phase of fluid guerilla
fighting ended on April 2, when Haganah not only raided, but
occupied and held the strategic village of Castel, which dominates
the Tel Aviv–Jerusalem road on the western approaches of the
ancient capital. For ten days Syrian and Iraqi troops, who were
now doing practically all the fighting on the Arab side, counter-
attacked and were repulsed. They finally broke the fight off, after
their commander, Abdul Kader Husseini, cousin of the Mufti,
had been killed in the action.

During the same days the second decisive battle of the civil
war was being fought at Mishmar Ha'emek,[2] a Jewish settlement
in the area where the Jewish Valley of Jezreel borders on the Arab
hills of Samaria. The attackers were the Arab Liberation Army,
personally commanded by Fawzi el Kaukaji, and equipped with
modern British arms, from medium tanks to automatics, which
had found their normal way to the battlefield via the Iraqi and
Transjordan Governments. After holding its ground for several
days, Haganah on April 9 went over to the offensive, took seven
Arab villages, and decisively routed Fawzi's army. The proudest
trophy of the victors was Fawzi Bey's personal staff car, an American luxury make decorated with crescent moons.

During this whole period the two terrorist groups had been
fighting their private war against both Britons and Arabs by
hurling bombs into Arab market-places, blowing up British troop
trains, and participating in the defence of the Old City Ghetto of
Jerusalem. A week after Haganah had taken Castel, a combined

[1] The first 1800 troops left Haifa for Liverpool on March 5, and another
draft of 2000 on the 7th.   [2] " The Watchpost of the Valley."

force of Irgun and Stern Group stormed the Arab village of Deir Yassin in the same area. Two hundred and fifty Arabs were killed in the action, among them a large number of women and children. Later in the same day, groups of Arab men and women captured in the village, including the Mukhtar and his family, were paraded through Jerusalem in open trucks and then turned over to the British Army.

The near-simultaneous Arab defeats in the decisive battle of Mishmar Ha'emek, in Castel and Deir Yassin, and the departure of British troops, started a sudden panicky flight of the Arab population all over the mixed territories of Palestine. It had the character of a landslide. The psychologically decisive factor in this spectacular Arab exodus was the last of the three episodes mentioned. The blood-bath of Deir Yassin was the worst atrocity committed by the terrorists in their whole career, and an isolated episode in the war between Arabs and Jews. It had extraordinary repercussions. The Jewish Agency issued a statement expressing " its horror and disgust at the barbarous manner in which this action was carried out ", and took the unusual step of cabling the statement to King Abdullah of Transjordan, the leading prince in the enemy coalition. The Chief of the Transjordan Royal Cabinet cabled back, not without logic, that as the Jewish Agency spoke in the name of all the Jews of Palestine, it would have to take the responsibility for their acts.

The Jewish Agency's cable was naturally played up by Arab propaganda as an admission by the Jews of their own barbarity, and as a confirmation of all the atrocity tales previously put out. For the next forty-eight hours all Arab radio stations were engaged in non-stop broadcast descriptions of the bayoneting of pregnant women and the impaling of infants, adorned with the lurid detail of oriental imagination. The effect of this propaganda was the exact opposite of its aim : the Arab population was seized with panic, and fled from villages and towns with the pitiful cry : " Deir Yassin ".

On April 17 the first large town with a mixed population, Tiberias on the Sea of Galilee,[1] was deserted by its Arab inhabitants. Three days later British troops evacuated Haifa and withdrew to small fortified enclaves in the port area and on Mount Carmel. As they withdrew, the battle for Haifa, key port of the Levant, with a population of 60,000 Jews and 70,000 Arabs,

[1] The Sea of Galilee is now usually referred to as Lake Tiberias.

began. It was over after one night ; the Syrian mercenaries were routed and the entire Arab population of Haifa, with the exception of some 2000, started their weary trek towards the Lebanon or into the hills of Samaria.[1]

On April 25, after five months of skirmishing on the Tel Aviv borderline, Irgun launched its offensive against Jaffa — second important harbour in Palestine and its biggest purely Arab town, with a population bordering on 100,000. Two days later, when Irgun forces had penetrated to the immediate vicinity of the town centre, Haganah joined in the attack. On the same day the Palestine Government warned the Jews that the British Army would prevent the capture of Jaffa by force. On April 28 British artillery started shelling Jewish positions in Jaffa, and British troops moved into positions between the Jewish and Arab lines. A deadlock followed, which lasted for a fortnight, until the final evacuation of Jaffa by the British. Two days before the evacuation was due to take place, the Palestine Government offered to nego-tiate a truce in Jaffa, but Haganah refused British mediation and insisted on direct negotiations with the Arabs. On May 12 the British left Jaffa. On May 13 the Arab Emergency Committee in the town signed the surrender terms presented by the Tel Aviv area Haganah commander. The Arab population left, as in the case of Haifa and Tiberias ; only some 4000 stayed behind.

It was the same story in the other mixed or purely Arab towns and villages over the whole area allocated to the Jews by the United Nations decision. Safed, key town of Northern Galilee, fell on May 10 — its 12,000 Arabs fled before its 1500 Jews in the wake of the withdrawing British troops. Beisan, last of the Arab towns in Jewish territory, surrendered on May 12, three days before the termination of the Mandate. By the same day the entire 15-mile stretch of mountain highway between Bab el Wad and Jerusalem was in Jewish hands. The British Security Zones of Jerusalem, which comprised the strategically decisive buildings of the modern centre, were occupied by the Jews the day after the British troops left, on May 14. The conquest of the new city was

---

[1] The cable in which the High Commissioner, Sir Alan Cunningham, reported the battle of Haifa, began as follows :

" The Jewish attack on Haifa was a direct consequence of continuous attacks by Arabs on Jews in Haifa over the previous four days. The attack was carried out by the Haganah, and there was no massacre.

" Arabs in Haifa were thus themselves responsible for the outbreak in spite of our repeated warnings."

completed with the capture of the Allenby Barracks, and that of the Arab Sheikh Jarrah quarter two days later. Only the Old City within the walls remained in Arab hands; and within the Old City the ancient Jewish Ghetto formed an isolated enclave.

The only losses suffered by the Jews were five settlements in the area allocated by the Partition Plan to the Arabs. Beit Ha'aravah, an isolated experimental settlement on the Dead Sea, was evacuated without fight.[1] The other four settlements, known as the Kfar Eftzion group, were situated in the purely Arab area between Bethlehem and Hebron. They had been cut off, and constantly attacked for three months by irregulars reinforced by troops of the Arab Legion; supply convoys trying to fight their way through to them had suffered the heaviest casualties in the whole battle of the convoys. On May 13 Kfar Eftzion fell to the Arab Legion; the next day the remaining three settlements surrendered. The surviving settlers were sent by the Arab Legion as " prisoners of war " to Amman; — this was probably the only action of the Government which might be interpreted as an implementation of the United Nations' Partition resolution.[2]

On May 14, when Israel proclaimed its independence, there were only a few thousand scattered Arabs left in the territory of the new State; round 300,000 Arab refugees, deserted by their leaders, lacking both the will and the organization to fight, had sought refuge in the Arab part of Palestine or in the neighbouring states.

[1] This settlement had embarked on the strange experiment of de-salinating the soil of the barren area where Sodom and Gomorrah once stood.

[2] The paradoxical nature of the whole situation is illustrated by the fact that these people had been defending their settlements against attack by Arab bands who had no legal status, and by soldiers of the Arab Legion under British command — at a time when the Legion was still part of the British security forces and responsible for maintaining law and order

CHAPTER XV

OPERATION DELUGE

Security chaos and administrative vacuum — Palestine expelled from the Sterling Block — The vanishing of the Government's assets — The closing down of the oil refineries — Railways, shipping, air transport and postal services cease to function—Operation Deluge completed.

The Jews build their skeleton Government — The flood and the Ark — Formation of the Provisional State Council — The Proclamation of Independence.

Götterdämmerung in Palestine — " Here goes thirty years, gentlemen " — Increasing demoralization and corruption — Aspirins and tanks for sale — Mosleyites at work — The flood of evil

I

THE British Government's refusal to hand over the administration to any local bodies, and to legalize some form of militia which could exercise authority, was designed to create both a state of chaos in matters of physical security and an administrative vacuum in the country.

As regards physical security, the successive evacuation by British troops of towns and rural areas of mixed population without passing on to anybody legal or factual control was inevitably followed by civil war in the town or area in question — be it Haifa, Safed or the plain south-west of Afula. The withdrawal of each British garrison created a local vacuum into which both parties rushed their improvised para-military troops to grab possession of it. The whole plan and manner of execution of this unprecedented abandonment of a country, after a long period of international trusteeship, with no authorized security forces in any area,[1] could produce no other foreseeable result than to set that country, and *ipso facto* the whole Middle East, " aflame ".

---

[1] The only exceptions made were the authorization at the beginning of December of Arab and Jewish police in the Jaffa and Tel Aviv areas respectively, and the handing over of control over the Old City of Jerusalem to the Arabs.

The piecemeal withdrawal of the British troops from successive areas in Palestine began in January and was virtually terminated by May 15, the date when the Mandate was relinquished and the Administration closed down. From May 15 onwards only an insignificant number of troops remained in small enclaves in and around Haifa, waiting for transport, and observing an attitude of scrupulous non-interference in the war raging around them.

Parallel with the withdrawal of the troops proceeded the winding up of the civilian Administration. The melancholy process of closing down one public service after another, and of progressively cutting off the country from all traffic with the outside world, struck its citizens like a methodic preparation for Doomsday or the arrival of the Comet. To make its intentions unmistakeably clear, the British Government repeatedly refused the United Nations Palestine Commission's request to be allowed to proceed to Palestine and prepare for assuring the continuity of the Administration on May 15. It was precisely this continuity which the British Government was determined to avoid, as the following statements will illustrate.

On November 21 Sir Alexander Cadogan had rejected the Partition Sub-Committee's proposal for a United Nations' transition regime because

> " it would create a division of authority between Britain and the U.N., which in turn would create confusion and disorder [sic] and have disastrous consequences. So long as my Government will continue to hold the Mandate for Palestine, they must insist upon their undivided control of that country."

On December 12 the Colonial Secretary, Mr. Creech Jones, stated in the Commons :

> " Britain has made it clear that as she could not take part in implementing the U.N. plan, it would be undesirable for the Commission to arrive in Palestine until a short period before the termination of the Mandate. For reasons of administrative efficiency and security [sic] the overlapping period should be comparatively brief."

On January 30 the British delegate at the United States Partition Commission categorically rejected the Commission's request for the creation of Arab and Jewish militias to ensure security at the termination of the Mandate, and at the same time stated that the British Government could not authorize the arrival of the United Nations Commission in Palestine at a date earlier than May 1 — that is, just a fortnight before the termination of the Mandate.

On February 3 the United Nations Commission once more approached the British Government with a request to be permitted to proceed earlier to Palestine ; the request was once again rejected.

On February 11 the British delegate at U.N.O. stated that Arab infiltrators from neighbouring countries were exercising "considerable administrative control" in Samaria, while Mr. Bevin stated in the Commons that his policy had not yet been proved unsuccessful in Palestine. "It is not yet over," he declared, somewhat ominously.

On February 18 Mr. Creech Jones declared in the Commons that Britain was unable to concur with the United Nations' suggestion to open a port in Palestine for Jewish immigrants : "Thanks to British influence, the Arabs had shown considerable restraint [1] [sic], but if a port were opened this restraint would disappear". He reiterated that Britain could not allow the United Nations Commission to enter Palestine before May 1, "as this was certain to bring about Arab demonstrations". He also added, yet once again, that Britain was determined to maintain "full and undivided authority for security in Palestine up to May 15".

One of the members of the United Nations Commission summed up the situation in the laconic remark : "They have created a vacuum and refuse to hand it over."

And yet only two months earlier, on December 11, 1947, the British Secretary of State for the Colonies, Mr. Creech Jones, had solemnly stated : "The decision of the Assembly is regarded by His Majesty's Government as a court of international opinion. This is not a grudging acceptance . . . we wish our authority transferred to our successors in an orderly manner."

---

[1] The total number of casualties (British, Arabs and Jews) had already amounted three weeks earlier to 869 killed and round 2000 wounded. These figures, published by the British delegation at Lake Success on February 1, covered only the two months' period since December 1, 1947.

By April 3, 1948, the total number of casualties listed by the United Nations Commission had risen to 6187 killed and wounded, Arab and Jewish casualties being roughly equal. The number of British casualties at the same date was 430.

2

On February 22, 1948, Palestine was at short notice expulsed from the Sterling Block. Palestine Jews who had followed the patriotic slogan " Save for Victory " woke up one morning to find that their savings invested in Bearer Bonds and Postal Savings Certificates were frozen in far-off England, and would be inaccessible probably for years to come. The Palestine Government's assets, which, thanks to the country's previous prosperity, had amounted at the end of the fiscal year 1946–47 to over eleven million pounds, shrank rapidly ; for the first time the Government's budget showed a deficit, amounting to five million pounds, in the quarter October–December 1947. Last-minute grants to Moslem " religious funds " administered by the Mufti's Higher Arab Committee, and the debiting of the budget by such items as £2,000,000 for the " maintenance of the Cyprus camps for Jewish deportees ", helped to squander away the assets accumulated mainly through the contributions of Jewish taxpayers ; what remained of them on Doomsday was again frozen in England.

The oil refineries, run by the British-owned Consolidated Refineries Ltd., closed down in mid-April. Palestine was entirely dependent on them for her petrol supply, which amounted to 12 per cent of the output of these refineries. They received about half of their crude oil through the pipeline from Kirkuk, the other half by tankers from abroad. From now on the Company's tankers were employed in the opposite traffic : the existing stocks of crude oil were removed to Tripoli, the refined petrol to Beirut ; the flow from the pipeline was simultaneously diverted to Amman. True to her interpretation of neutrality in the conflict, Great Britain not only continued to deliver arms to Iraq and Transjordan, but also made sure that their armies should be well supplied with fuel ; while the Jews saw an arms embargo enforced upon them and their motor transport left high and dry. The Jewish Government's request that the refineries should be reopened after the truce came into force was rejected under the pretext that there was " not enough Arab skilled labour available in Israel ".[1]

In March all British shipping lines were ordered not to touch

---

[1] The refineries were reopened by decree of the Israeli Government a few weeks later, and seemed to get along all right with only Jewish skilled labour.

in future any Palestine port. At about the same time the Palestine Government refused to grant or to renew licences for the import of goods into Palestine — including agricultural machinery, building materials, books and newspapers. Gradually, step by step, Palestine was isolated from the outside world. Its food supplies depended to a large extent on allocations from the Combined Food Board and the International Emergency Food Council, and formed part of Great Britain's bulk allocations. The Government made no provisions to assure the continuity of these allocations, or to enable the Jews to lay in stocks, which were the more needed as supplies from the neighbouring Arab countries had naturally stopped. The result of this was an inflationary deluge as part of the general picture.

Next came the throttling of air traffic, the paralysing of the railways, the cutting of postal and telegraph communications. Lydda airport, the only one which had facilities for the landing of the four-engined overseas passenger craft used by the big airlines, such as B.O.A.C. and T.W.A., was closed down on April 25. The first notice of warning that no through tickets to neighbouring countries would be issued by the Palestine Railways from the end of that month appeared on February 26; from then onward travel to the neighbouring countries, and later on internal travel, were gradually discontinued as the railway administration wound up. On April 14 the Press published a report of the United Nations Palestine Commission at Lake Success, according to which preparatory steps to continue essential services had been taken by that Commission. On the same day the Palestine Government announced its schedule for the suspension of postal services, " in the absence of any communication from the U.N. Palestine Commission providing for acceptance of responsibility for the continuation of the services ". Surface mail to and from Palestine was accordingly discontinued in April, air mail in the first days of May. At the same date Palestine was excluded from the International Postal Federation.

When Sir Alan Cunningham, the last British High Commissioner, sailed from Haifa on May 14, he left behind him a country without legal government, administration, police or public services, cut off from the outside world and ravaged by war. Operation Deluge was completed.

3

We have reported before how the power vacuum created by the withdrawal of the British security forces was filled in by the successful operations of Haganah, which resulted in the entire territory of the future State being safely under its control by May 15. Parallel to these military operations, the Jewish Agency proceeded to neutralize the administrative vacuum by building up the skeleton of a government and civilian administration.

This task was, on the one hand, made easier by the administrative experience gained under the British Mandate when the Jewish Agency had already functioned as a State within the State, running its own schools, hospitals, and a number of other public services. But this advantage was counterbalanced by the prevailing conditions of civil war. Jerusalem, headquarters of the Jewish Agency, and of the main Jewish institutions and archives, was cut off most of the time from Tel Aviv. Convoys were rare, and travel on them entailed risk of life. The only other means of communication between the ancient and the future capital was a set of short-wave transmitters — and a tiny two-seater training plane, property of the Jewish Agency, which performed perilous hops from an improvised dirt-track runway in Jerusalem to Tel Aviv and back, with one shaky passenger on board. When Israel's first Government was constituted in Tel Aviv on May 14, the Minister of the Interior, Mr. Yitzchak Greenbaum, was stuck in Jerusalem and could not join the Cabinet for several weeks because each time he wanted to board the tiny plane in Jerusalem some Haganah officer on essential duty was given priority over him.

It is against this background that the building up of the new State has to be pictured. The floods were closing in from all sides ; if the Jews of Palestine were to survive as a nation they had to improvise a new Ark and ride against the tides. On January 12 a spokesman of the Jewish Agency told the Press that " the entire plan for the structure of the Jewish State, from the preparation of ministries down to the number of Hebrew and Arabic typewriters necessary, will be ready by the end of this month. The work has been under way since November 29."

The main steps towards the establishment of the new State may be summarized as follows :

On January 19 the chairman of the Jewish National Service

Census Board reported that 72 per cent of the young men in the age-groups from 17 to 25 had registered for " national service "; of the remaining 28 per cent the majority was already otherwise engaged — that is, had gone underground.

On February 17, in the first notice of this kind to appear in the Press, the Jewish Agency advertised for " Candidates required to undergo a course of training as officers in the Police Force of the Jewish State. Command of either Hebrew or Arabic is essential."

On February 27 the Jewish Agency imposed a ban on foreign travel for all Jews between 16 and 40, " who are liable for national service ". At the end of February the Hebrew trade unions published a comprehensive scheme for social security legislation in the future State. On March 1 the *Vaad Leumi* [1] met in Tel Aviv and decided on the broad outline of the composition of the Jewish Provisional Government Council, which was to be " responsible for the forging of the instruments of the local and central Governments. Representatives of Arab communities adhering to the U.N. decision would also be co-opted to the Council." On March 9 the composition of this Council took definite shape ; it was to be composed of 12 members of the Jewish Agency Executive, 14 members of the Vaad Leumi Executive, and 6 of parties not represented on either Executive. In addition, it was stated that " negotiations had started for the setting up of a smaller executive body to act more or less on the lines of a Cabinet ". The offer to Arabs to participate in the Provisional Council was repeated, and the spokesman of the Jewish Agency emphasized that " this was not a platonic offer ".

On March 21 the Jewish Agency Executive decided that the Provisional Jewish Government would begin to function on May 16. On March 31 the Press reported that " hundreds of Jewish men and women were being trained to take over the postal services after the termination of the Mandate ". On April 2 the Jewish National Census Board announced a call-up of all Palestinian Jews abroad. On April 11 the Jewish Agency and Vaad Leumi announced the creation of a Jewish State Fund — which was to start immediately collecting income-tax from the future citizens of the future State. On the next day the Zionist General Council, which was in session in Tel Aviv, resolved " that upon the termination of the Mandatory regime there shall be an end of foreign rule in Palestine, and that the Governing Body of

[1] Jewish National Council.

the Jewish State shall come into being " ; it endorsed the proposed agreement between Haganah and Irgun, and decided to launch a Jewish National Loan. On April 19 the Jewish Agency and Vaad Leumi issued an order to all Jewish Government employees to remain at their posts after the termination of the Mandate.

On May 14 the Provisional Council, which had changed its name into " Provisional State Council ", met in solemn session in Tel Aviv, elected a Provisional Government of thirteen members, and proclaimed the independence of the new State, " whose name shall be Israel ".

4

The Götterdämmerung of British rule in the Holy Land was not in the Wagnerian, but rather in the Dostoievskian style.

In a statement to the foreign Press on October 8, 1947, Britain's last High Commissioner, in answer to a question, had said that it would be " physically possible for Britain to go, leaving nothing to replace her in Palestine ". But it would be, he warned, at the expense of " misery, distress and chaos ". Sir Alan Cunningham could not foresee at the time that it would become his tragic duty to carry out the policy against which he had warned, and to create the conditions which he had predicted — " misery, distress and chaos ".

Equally tragic was the situation of a number of men in the higher and medium ranks of the Administration, who, whatever their bias, had honestly laboured for many years to build up a structure which they were now called upon to destroy. A few of them had been caught by the imaginative appeal of the Jewish pioneering effort ; the majority was emotionally anti-Jewish and pro-Arab — but all of them had come one way or another to identify themselves with the country for whose best they had worked according to their lights ; and none of them had foreseen or desired this dismal and humiliating end. They had to leave without farewell, boycotted by their friends in both camps, hated by both. They could not even, in sincerity, reproach them with ingratitude. The 300,000 Arab refugees in the olive groves, the Jews assailed by armies commanded or equipped by Britain, were the undivided responsibility of the Government whose orders the men in the Administration obeyed.

Characteristic of the general atmosphere of doom was an

incident which occurred during an inter-departmental meeting of high-ranking British Civil Servants. The agenda of the meeting, as of all similar conferences at the time, was " the winding up of the Administration ". In the middle of the conference one of the leading officials, who had seen nearly a quarter-century of service in the country, was seized by a crying fit. He kept repeating the mumbled words : " Here goes thirty years, gentlemen, thirty years. . . ."

In the less reputable layers of the Administration, and particularly in the Police, no such heart-searchings prevailed. To carry out an elaborate task of destruction has inevitably a destructive effect on morale ; and to be garrisoned in a country where one is despised by the population aggravates this effect. The abandoned camps and billets of British troops all over Palestine looked like a panorama of the Sack of Rome, where smashed furniture and broken glass mingled with electric wires and gutted pipes. Thousands of lorries, jeeps and motor-cars, which the authorities could not evacuate or sell to the Arabs, and which they refused to sell to the Jews, lay as gigantic heaps of twisted metal and burnt rubber in deserted car parks all over the country ; the total area of these motor cemeteries must have covered scores of acres. Such senseless destruction goes against human instinct ; hence it is only natural that soldiers, N.C.O.s and officers of the departing army vied in appropriating condemned equipment and selling it to the highest bidder, whether Arab or Jew. Thus Operation Deluge produced, among other phenomena, a black market in British arms and equipment the like of which has rarely been seen in history, and where the purchasing agents of both parties could buy anything from a kilo of aspirin to a 4-ton lorry loaded with kit-bags, as well as radio equipment, jeeps, light field-artillery pieces and even Churchill tanks. It was only human that these properties of the Crown, condemned to be smashed, burnt or dumped into the sea, should be put to some better use — by being converted into a gift for somebody at home, or into a suburban plot for a retired soldier. But it was not an edifying spectacle, and it led to a general demoralization and corruption rare among British troops ; having lost the sympathy of the population, they now lost its respect. It was a melancholy exit, and an undeserved punishment which, as is the rule, smote not the head but the arm which protects it.

Even more distressing was the gradual demoralization in the

Police. The symbiosis of evil in the poisoned atmosphere brought certain disreputable elements in its ranks — former Mosleyites and Black and Tan veterans — increasingly to the fore towards the end. The lurid circumstances of the Farran case have already been recorded; they revealed the existence of a Fascist counter-terror caucus within the Police for which the fight against the Jewish resistance movement became a pretext for committing outrages on a par with those of Irgun and the Stern Group. On February 1 the building of the *Palestine Post* in Jerusalem was destroyed by an explosion; on the 22nd of the same month an explosion in Ben Yehuda Street, the main shopping centre of Jewish Jerusalem, wrecked several buildings, killed fifty-two people and injured over a hundred. In both cases the enquiries instigated by the Government produced no result; the parallel Enquiry Reports of a committee set up by the Jewish Agency named British Police personnel as the perpetrators, and in both cases Arab spokesmen denied having anything to do with the bombings. Responsibility for the second outrage (and by inference for the first) was claimed by the " British League — Palestine Branch ", an offspring of Mosley's " British League of Ex-Servicemen ", in a circular letter sent to a number of British residents in Jerusalem, the text of which, together with a comment broadcast over Haganah's illegal radio station on March 3, appears in the footnote.[1]

Similar influences seemed to be at work within limited groups of the Army. On February 12, for instance, four Haganah men were arrested by an Army patrol, turned loose in the Arab quarter of the Old City near St. Stephen's Gate, and found there three hours later murdered and mutilated. On February 29 British

---

[1]   " THE BRITISH LEAGUE (PALESTINE BRANCH)

" ' Our aim must be to subjugate the World and become its sole Masters by demoralising all hostile Gentiles ' (from *Protocols of the Elders of Zion*, page 63). Thus the vile Jew, backed by International Free Masonry, supported by international Communism and with the help of international Finance, strode into the 20th century. Under the cloak of Zionist ideals, but in reality for the purpose of creating a centre for international intrigue, he claimed the establishment of a Jewish National Home in Palestine. Now Jewish guile was discarded ; no sooner did he feel safely entrenched in Palestine, than his aggressive impulses and ambitions were revealed. With systematic perseverance he acquired the power and the means to dominate the rightful owners of Palestine. But the noble Arab arose at last to fight the unscrupulous enemy. In this hour of their trial, the Arabs will not be alone. We, the British League of Servicemen and Ex-Servicemen, pledge our full support to the chivalrous sons of Araby, who

troops disarmed the personnel of a small Jewish factory on the Jaffa–Tel Aviv border and turned them over to an Arab mob, who killed nine Jews on the spot. A subsequent Government enquiry into the first case stated that

> " although the Company Sergeant Major (in charge of the four murdered Jews) was guilty of an error of judgment in not handing his prisoners over to the Police, — for which suitable action has been taken by the military authorities — it has been clearly established that he released them with their arms at a point where, being on the edge of a Jewish area, he assumed that the four were in no danger ".

The error of judgment of a Company Sergeant-Major who arrests people behind the Jewish lines, puts them on a truck and, instead of handing them over to his superiors, releases them " with their arms " in Arab territory " on the edge " of a Jewish area may have been due to an unusual chain of coincidences, but this did not sound plausible in the middle of a civil war ; the vileness of the incident shook Jewish trust in the fairness — politics apart — of the British Army more than other events on a much larger scale.

have come to liberate their country from the yoke of the Wandering Jew. All of us will join this fight : from the highest to the lowest of Britain's Imperial representatives.

> " Not words alone will help to win
> This noble fight against the Jew ;
> 'Tis deeds which count and gelignite,
> And brave determined guns !

" In the Church of the Holy Sepulchre, on the site where our Lord Christ was crucified by the impenitent ancestors of those very Jews who now aspire to mastery of this country, members of the British League took a sacred vow, dedicating themselves to a Crusade against the Jews. Accordingly, on 22nd February 1948, we attacked the central Jewish quarter of Jerusalem with high explosives, inflicting heavy casualties on the guttersnipes ; over 100 killed and 200 injured — all Jews ! We take pride in announcing that no distinction was made by us between the cowardly, treacherous Hagana gangsters and the murderous Sternists. Jewish women and children, old and young, they will all be annihilated. We will finish Hitler's job !

" Nations of the World, arise and smite the Jews ! Arabs, unite and liberate your country ! Britons, awake and drive out the Jewish-dominated Labour Government! British soldiers and policemen, join the British League! Rule Britannia!

" THE BRITISH LEAGUE (PALESTINE BRANCH)
February 1948."

Haganah Comment· The following statement was made by the Haganah commentator after the reading of the above circular : " We do not believe that all Britons uphold the ' lofty ' ideas of the League. We know that the Fascists are a minority of the British people, and also of the Britons here in Palestine. But we cannot ignore the presence of such a minority in our midst."

For the first time the Jewish Agency in an official statement permitted itself " to place it on record that in this instance it makes a definite charge of murder ", while the Haganah Commander in Jerusalem ordered, after referring to the incident, " all members of the Haganah in Jerusalem from now on to resist with arms any attempt by British forces to search for weapons or to make arrests ".

Again it must be said that after the King David outrage, with its ninety-one victims, after the blowing up of troop trains and the assassination of British soldiers and policemen from ambush — and sometimes in their sleep — by members of the Stern Group, it was only human that groups of men in the Police and Army conspired to retaliate against the Jews, an eye for an eye and a tooth for a tooth. But this had no longer anything to do with the maintenance of law and order ; it was a surrender to the flood of moral evil which Operation Deluge had brought over the Holy Land.

CHAPTER XVI

FROM BALFOUR TO BEVIN

India compared to Palestine — " It's either them or us "
— The five choices before the Labour Government —
Palestine the Seventh Dominion — The missed opportun-
ity of 1945 — The capitulation of common sense.

   Samson among the Philistines — The climate of public
opinion — Its rejection of totalitarian measures — The
buffers of democracy and the boons of the lesser evil

I

WHEN the British withdrew from India after handing over power
to the Moslem and Hindu Governments, they knew that whatever
the rights and wrongs of the past they left that country under the
relatively most favourable conditions which careful constructive
planning could devise, and that if the future was nevertheless to
bring more bloodshed, it was not of their design and making. In
Palestine the exact opposite was the case. Thirty years of labour
were deliberately and wantonly undone within a few months. It
was the capitulation of British common sense before emotional
conviction and traditional prejudice, resulting in a policy which
Mr. Ernest Bevin, supported by a coterie of permanent officials,
had succeeded in imposing on the Cabinet.

   Irrational emotive behaviour always leans towards extremes
(though sometimes it may take the form of extreme hesitancy).
If asked to account for his conduct, the subject will rationalize
his motives by explaining that he had no other choice, all middle
roads having been blocked by circumstances. He lives in a
schematized world, and his schematized reasoning makes him
constantly go off at a tangent. When asked by a friend about the
reasons for his stubborn and uncompromising refusal to let the
refugees from the D.P. camps enter Palestine, Mr. Ernest Bevin
is reported to have answered with profound conviction : " My
dear boy, it's either them or us ". " Them " referred to the Jews
in Palestine ; " us " referred to the British Commonwealth of
Nations.

The real choice before the Labour Government was of course neither between " them and us ", nor between an extreme pro-Arab or pro-Jewish policy, but between a series of possible compromise solutions. A full implementation of Labour's avowed programme — the transformation of the whole of Palestine into a Jewish State — could, in the light of later events, have been carried out without much difficulty by simply standing by while Haganah took over. But to let the Jews take over while they were in a minority would have been a flagrant breach of all democratic principles ; and to wait until the Jews became a majority through immigration would have meant continuation of a mandate which had already become practically unworkable.

The third possibility was Partition, proposed by the Royal Commission as long as ten years ago, adopted by the United Nations Assembly, and in fact the only workable solution — which, moreover, was in accord with the classic traditions of British compromise. It was rejected by Mr. Bevin and enforced by the logic of history, — at the price of entirely unnecessary bloodshed, destruction, and loss of British prestige. The Jewish State, for which Britain had laid the foundations in 1917, was ultimately inaugurated against Britain's will.

It would have been both logical and easy for Britain to act as godfather to the new State. Despite all bitterness, the memories of Balfour were never quite erased. To the very last moment the majority of the Jews hoped that the Labour Government would come back to its senses and that Israel would be allowed to become England's natural ally in the Middle East, united to her by ties of tradition and mutual interest. As early as 1925 Lord Wedgwood had launched the idea of Israel as the Seventh Dominion in the British Commonwealth of Nations. All arguments of humanity and expediency spoke in favour of it. This commonwealth of immigrants would have become a beachhead of European tradition and democracy in the Levant ; a highly industrialized, compact outpost against totalitarian expansion, German or Russian. The airfields and strategic bases which the Western Powers needed at this Clapham Junction of the Orient could be had from the Jews for the asking — it was in the Jews' own interest to have them there. England and France had been gradually edged out of Egypt, Syria and the Lebanon by the hostile pressure of Arab xenophobia ; here it would have been possible to establish a solid base in the proximity of the Suez Canal, controlling the approaches to the Levant, with a European population as a friendly hinterland.

This would not have been an imperialist policy — there was no question of exploiting the Jewish natives, or of using them as a springboard for expansionist conquests. Nor did it mean " playing the Jewish card against the Arabs ". Neither Egypt nor Syria and the Lebanon, Palestine's neighbours to the south and north, had any claim or standing in its problems. To the east, Transjordan's Emir, later King, Abdullah, had always been on particularly friendly terms with the Jews, and had never hidden his eagerness to unite the Arab part of Palestine with his kingdom, while leaving the Jewish part to the Jews. It was not merely the question of a political deal, but a genuine desire on the part of Transjordan's ruler, and the handful of educated men around him, to profit from the presence of the Jews to modernize his country. On his initiative, Palestine Jews built the electric power station and grid in his capital, Amman. Negotiations for other Jewish concessions and pioneering enterprises in the vast deserts of Transjordan (whose total, and mainly nomadic, population numbers only 300,000) had been going on all the time — until the White Paper of 1939 made it clear to the Arabs that Britain disapproved of the presence of Jews in Palestine. Even so, contacts between King Abdullah and the Jewish Agency were continued right until the outbreak of hostilities — paradoxically enough against the wishes, and behind the backs, of the British diplomatic representatives in Transjordan. And finally, Abdullah's Government was the first to enter into peace negotiations with Israel — against the protests of his unwelcome allies in the Arab League. Had British diplomacy not created this phantom body, and dragged Egypt, Syria and the rest into the Palestine issue, Jews and Arabs on both sides of the Jordan would have partitioned the country peacefully between themselves some ten years ago. They would, moreover, in all likelihood have worked out some form of economic federation, connected to the framework of the Commonwealth by elastic but solid ties.[1]

[1] Without going into the details of Arab politics, it should be noted that Transjordan was and is as interested in a solution on these lines as the Jews, in view of the age-old rivalry between the Hashimite and Saudite dynasties, the religious antagonism between its Sunnite tribes and the Wahhabis of the peninsula ; and that the hostility between Egypt and Transjordan is not less marked. Only to the distant European does the Arab world appear homogeneous ; in fact, Saudi Arabia and the Lebanon are countries as different in cultural, social and economic structure as, say, Bulgaria and France.

N

The fellaheen in Palestine would have accepted this solution, as they had accepted the transition from Turkish to British rule, with feelings ranging from indifference to relief. The amorphous character of the Arab masses in Palestine, and their lack of national consciousness, has been described in an earlier chapter ; it was confirmed by their complete apathy and unwillingness to fight. Although superior in numbers and, thanks to the neighbouring Arab countries, in an incomparably more favourable position for obtaining arms than the Jews, they simply emigrated *en masse* and left the fighting to be done by mercenaries and foreign armies. If Partition based on an agreement between Abdullah and the Jews had been imposed, the greater part of the Arabs within the boundaries of the Jewish State would probably have preferred to remain there ; the rest could have been transferred in an orderly manner to the Arab kingdom of Palestine, instead of losing their goods and chattels in panicky flight.

The only forces opposed to this solution were the Mufti and the effendis of the Husseini party, with the village priests who owed allegiance to them. Their solution, stated almost in so many words in the Mufti's testimony to the Royal Commission, was to drown the Jews in the sea ; their policy was alliance with the Axis ; their social programme mediaeval feudalism. They had preached death to Zionism and sold their land to the Jews ; they had preached the Holy War, and when the showdown came were the first to sneak away to Beirut and Cairo, leaving the helpless masses in the lurch. For thirty years Britain had appeased the Mufti, claiming that there was no other way ; a week after the Jericho Conference had proclaimed Abdullah ruler of Arab Palestine,[1] he dismissed the Mufti and appointed a new one in his stead.

When the Labour Government took power in July 1945 the situation was particularly propitious for carrying out Partition in a bloodless operation. The Husseini clan had backed the wrong horse and felt its position tottering. The Mufti was wanted as a war criminal. The Labour victory meant that a Party had taken power which was committed "to put an end to the rule of the corrupt effendi class ", to abolish the White Paper, and to promote unfettered Jewish immigration "in such numbers that they should become a majority ". In these circumstances, had the Labour Party changed its policy from one hundred per cent

[1] In December 1948.

Zionist support to the compromise of Partition, the moderate Arab leaders would have regarded this as a gift from heaven ; and after some oratory about " fighting to the last drop of blood ", and arranging for the reasonable amount of rioting which is *de rigueur*, would have accepted the solution imposed " by brute force " with quiet realism, — convinced that they had successfully diddled a British Government which had promised the whole of Palestine to the Jews. Never in the history of Palestine, since the beginning of the Mandate, was a more favourable opportunity offered to a British Government for a peaceful solution than at the time when Labour came to power after the victorious termination of the war.

2

Partition, then, was the third alternative choice before the Cabinet — the first, as will be remembered, was the full implementation of Labour's Palestine programme ; the second, continuation of the Mandate on the pre-White Paper basis.

The fourth solution was neither full support for Zionism nor Partition, but merely the admission of the 100,000 Jewish D.P.s recommended by President Truman, the Anglo-American Committee and the elementary demands of humanity. This fourth alternative, already three steps down, as it were, from the official Labour platform, was equally rejected.

The fifth alternative presented itself when Great Britain, after having appointed a Royal Commission and rejected its recommendations, having appointed an Anglo-American Committee and rejected its recommendations, finally took the matter before the United Nations. U.N.O. appointed yet another Commission, whose recommendations were endorsed by the General Assembly ; and once again Britain declined to carry them out, or even to collaborate in their implementation.

The irrationality of this obstinate refusal to accept any compromise solution was matched by the absurdity of mobilizing British warships, airborne divisions and diplomatic machinery to prevent a few thousand wretched D.P.s from getting into Palestine. This policy was doggedly maintained to the very last day of the Mandate, when neither security reasons nor the shortage of food, nor even the danger of " the Middle East going up in flames ", could any longer be invoked for its justification — the Middle East being already as much aflame as it ever can be when six Arab countries breathe fire, brimstone and Holy War.

That this policy could not be explained in terms of logical reasoning and expediency became gradually apparent in a series of symptomatic incidents which revealed the irrational emotions at work. Such symptoms were, firstly, certain passages in Mr. Bevin's speeches which were either simply untrue, like the story about the two hundred million pounds; [1] or grossly insulting, like the jibe about America being so keen on dumping Jews in Palestine because she wanted to avoid having them in New York; [2] or revealingly emotional, like the " staking of his political future on Palestine ".[3] The unconscious source of these outbursts was the conviction that " it's either them or us ". The derogatory tendency towards the Jews was underlined by insinuations about the motives of America's interest in them, and stood in conspicuous contrast to the eulogies of " the generosity of our Arab friends " [4] and to reminders that " the Arabs should not be taken for nobody or nothing ".

Other revealing incidents which could not be explained by any rational motives were the deportation of the refugees on the *Exodus 1947*, not to Cyprus, but to Germany, the very scene of the nightmare which they were trying to escape ; and the continued detention of some 12,000 Jewish D.P.s in Cyprus half a year after Britain had relinquished her Mandate over Palestine, and with it her right to decide who should or should not be allowed to enter that country. While the Mandate was still in force the legal grounds for detaining these people had been that they were illegal immigrants intercepted on their way to Palestine ; from June 11 to July 9 the justification for their detention was that their arrival would upset the truce ; when the United Nations Mediator ruled that there was no objection to their being allowed to proceed to Palestine, the British authorities in Cyprus passed a special law designed to make their continued detention possible with an appearance of legality. It should be remembered that the only legal offence of which these people had been guilty was that, after the destruction of their relatives, friends and possessions, they had committed the imprudence of embarking for a country which they regarded as theirs ; and which has since become it.

It is futile to search for rational causes when faced with acts

---

[1] Statement at the Party Conference at Bournemouth, June 12, 1946.
[2] *Ibid*
[3] Statement at Press Conference, November 13, 1945.   [4] *Ibid.*

of an irrationally vindictive character. How indeed could the continued detention of these human wrecks under abstruse legal pretexts be logically connected with oil policy, the Soviet menace, strategy, morality, expediency or what have you ? It is a puzzle with a simple psychological solution. In his first statement on Palestine Mr. Bevin had warned the Jews not to try to get to the head of the queue ; in his last act of immigration policy he made sure that they should remain at the tail of the queue. The sub-conscious layers of the mind have their own logic and wry humour.

3

Like Samson, bringing down the temple over his head to destroy the assembled Philistines, so Mr. Bevin, in his determination to destroy Zionism, made Britain's Arab policy collapse into ruins. Some of the circumstances which enabled the Foreign Secretary and a small group of men sharing the same convictions to impose their will on Government, Party and country have already been discussed in previous chapters ; a few relevant facts have to be added to complete the picture.

The External Affairs Committee of the Labour Party had given its enthusiastic approval to the Anglo-American Committee's report, and had urged its immediate adoption. And yet a few weeks later the Bournemouth Party Conference, in June 1946, had again ended in a spectacular triumph for the man whom the rank and file acclaimed as " Our Ernie ". Once more the popular, matey trade-union boss proved to carry incomparably more weight than any of the Party's " intellectuals ". However strongly some of his colleagues in the Cabinet ridiculed and resented his Palestine obsession — and some of them made no secret of this in private conversation — they knew that if they forced a showdown they would inevitably be the losers. There was occasionally a muttered threat of resignation, but there the matter ended. Ernest Bevin's ascent to the position of a benevolent despot in the Party repeated a pattern only too well known in the history of the Socialist Movement.

However, the weight of his personality and the support he commanded would probably not have sufficed to reverse the Party's attitude and programme had not the Jews been rapidly losing sympathy with British public opinion as a consequence of the terrorists' outrages. This trend was exploited and accelerated

by the Press (with a very few notable exceptions) in a campaign
partly Government-inspired, and partly carried by ever-latent
anti-Semitic currents. The problems involved in the Palestine
issue were too complex to be judged on their merit by the house-
wife-in-the-street ; the unctuous self-righteousness of Zionist
propaganda left her cold ; but Mr. Bevin's homely jokes about
the Jews found an archetypal echo in the masses. How rapidly
this proverbially tolerant people had become transformed into
the most anti-Semitic nation of the West became evident when a
crowd of thousands thronged to the Liverpool docks to welcome
an ex-officer of the Palestine Police, freshly acquitted of the charge
of beating to death a Jewish boy of 16.

So we have come back to our starting-point, the importance
of subconscious psychological processes, of the subjective factor
in history. British policy in Palestine is not a tale of diabolic
scheming ; it is a case-history for the psychologist.

It is of course possible that our " psycho-somatic " view of
history is mistaken, and that the whole chain of events, from the
Struma to the 15th of May, was the result of a conscious, calculated, machiavellian policy, dictated by reasons unknown to this
writer or to any other student of the problem. In this case the
diabolic conception of the nature of British policy — as described
by Soviet propagandists and by some sections of the American
Press — would be the correct one. This writer believes the
analysis of events presented here to be nearer the truth — though
of course this conviction, too, may be emotionally biassed. For it is
based on the axiomatic belief that there are more fools than knaves
on this earth, whether in Whitechapel or Whitehall.

4

Two Englishmen have done more than any other to bring
about the rebirth of Israel : Lord Balfour and Ernest Bevin. The
first gave the Jews their legal charter ; the second, by refusing
any compromise, forced them to fight it out and thus pass the
test of nationhood.

There is a thread running through this history which one takes
so much for granted that its importance is seldom recognized.
Neither Balfour nor Bevin could fully realize their respective aims.
The cumbersome machinery of democracy with its parliamentary
valves and administrative brakes, prevented, for good or evil, the

total execution of the idea. Only despots, ancient and modern, are able to say : " there shall be a Jewish State ", or " there shall be none " ; " there shall be a Crimean Republic ", or " it shall be erased " ; " this nation shall be exalted, that other cremated ". The elastic buffers of tradition and routine which absorbed the impulse of Balfour's vision neutralized the effects of Bevin's obsession.

When, after June 29, 1946, it became evident that Jewish resistance could not be broken short of totalitarian measures, the Government stopped short of them — and thereby lost the game. At any time between that day and the termination of the Mandate, Tel Aviv could have been bombed into submission, the settlements wiped out, and the three-quarters of a million Palestine Jews rendered as helpless as, say, the population of Lithuania under Russian rule. During the civil war period, when Haganah came out into the open, British non-intervention indirectly favoured the Arabs ; but the direct intervention of a single mechanized division would have decided the issue against the Jews. When the invasion from the neighbouring countries started, the Government favoured the invaders by the continued delivery of arms, by the diversion of oil supplies, by using the Arab Legion to make war on the Jews, while Britain herself remained officially neutral. It was a revolting hypocrisy, but the very necessity of being hypocritical about it, of using indirect, back-door means, is proof that Parliament and public opinion would not have stood for more direct measures. Even at that stage the intervention of a few British divisions or R.A.F. bomber squadrons would have put an end to all Israel's hopes.

Mr. Bevin and his consorts did everything in their power to prevent the Jewish State coming into being ; but the point is that their powers were limited by democratic control and the climate of opinion. This climate was hostile to the Jews but would never allow this hostility to be translated into action on the German or Russian pattern. It is not difficult to imagine what the fate of the Jews would have been if, through a different turn of history, an international body in 1917 had given Germany or Russia the Mandate over Palestine.

Two lessons can be drawn from these considerations. The first is that the cumbersome controls, safety valves, brakes and buffers of a democratic regime make it unfit to carry through to the end any calculatedly ruthless machiavellian policy. Machiavellianism was the natural doctrine of Renaissance princes ; and the equivalent in our time of the Renaissance prince is the totalitarian despot. A trade-union boss may at times imagine that he is Lorenzo the Magnificent ; but Transport House is not the Palazzo Vecchio, and Westminster not the Kremlin ; so he is bound to remain a pseudo-machiavellian.

The second lesson applies to those who hold that there is nothing to choose between Western imperialism and Eastern totalitarianism ; for whom British policy in Palestine or Greece is on a par with German policy in Poland or Russian policy from the Baltic to Rumania. Such false equations are mostly drawn by people who have no experience of either the one or the other, and are consequently unable to appreciate the difference in degree between the fate of ten thousand Jews illegally detained in Cyprus, and that of the as many, or twice as many, millions of living dead in the Arctic labour camps. It is a difference which may sound somewhat abstract to radical idealists living in safety, but not to the people directly concerned. To live under a regime whose inherent structure imposes a limit on its possibilities of doing evil, or under a regime which has no such limits, is a difference which comprises the essence of human progress. Whatever the creeds and ideals in whose name men started revolutions and fought their battles, the real progress achieved was at best always a transition from a greater to a lesser evil.

The Democracies in their present form may be cold comfort, but they are comfort nevertheless. They are the unheated shelters where men, shivering, can still huddle together in the totalitarian blizzard.

BOOK TWO

CLOSE-UP

During the siege of Jerusalem, two old Jews were overheard talking.

" We can only be saved," said one, " either by a miracle or by a natural event."

" And what natural event ? " asked the other.

" The coming of Messiah, of course."

During the first fortnight of the life of the newborn State, it looked as if it would share the fate of the infants under Herod whose tender bodies were put to the sword. May 15, the date of the official termination of the British Mandate, was the appointed D-Day (D for Deluge), on which the armies of five sovereign Arab Nations invaded Palestine from the north, east and south. The days of the new State seemed to be numbered, and speedy capitulation the Jews' only chance to avoid wholesale massacre.

Contrary to all expectations, the men of Haganah held their ground. Between May 15 and our arrival in Haifa on June 4 the main military events had been, first, the unopposed advance of an Egyptian column through the desert to the southern boundaries of the Jewish coastal belt in the area round Gaza, by-passing the Jewish settlements in the Negeb. A second Egyptian column, also advancing through purely Arab territories, had reached the southern outskirts of Jerusalem. In the north the Jews had taken Acco and advanced along the coast to the Lebanese frontier post at Ras en Nakura. Syrian and Lebanese attacks on Jewish settlements in Galilee and the Jordan Valley had been repulsed. There were inconclusive skirmishes with Iraqi troops along the border of the Jewish coastal belt and the hill country of Samaria. The only serious fighting was in the Old City of Jerusalem and on the crucial Jerusalem–Tel Aviv road.

Eleven minutes after the Provisional State Council had proclaimed Israel's independence in Tel Aviv, President Truman had announced the United States' de facto recognition of the new State. Forty-eight hours later the Soviet Union recognized Israel de jure. Guatemala, Uruguay, Poland, Czechoslovakia and other small nations followed suit during the next few days.

On May 17, the U.S.A. delegation at the Security Council proposed that the Council should declare the situation in Palestine a " threat to peace ", according to Article 39 of the Charter, and issue an order to end hostilities within thirty-six hours under threat of sanctions. On May 19, Great Britain at the Security Council opposed the proposal of the United States, which was rejected in the Council on May 22 ; instead of issuing an " order " under threat of sanctions, the Security Council merely " called on " both sides to cease hostilities within thirty-six hours. At the expiry of this time-

limit the Jews accepted the Security Council's call for a cease-fire, the Arabs rejected it. Again the United States and the Soviet Union proposed the application of sanctions against the Arabs, and again the British attitude prevailed ; the Arabs were granted another time-limit of forty-eight hours. When these expired, on May 26, the Jews again accepted, and the Arabs again rejected the cease-fire call. For the third time the U.S.A. and U.S.S.R called for sanctions, and for the third time Sir Alexander Cadogan carried the day. The Security Council refused to call the Palestine war a threat to peace, refused to invoke sanctions, and accepted the British proposal, which preconized a four weeks' truce, to be arranged and supervised by the United Nations' Mediator, Count Bernadotte. It also imposed an arms embargo against both attackers and attacked, against the regular Arab armies which had regular stocks of war material, and the improvised army of Israel which had none.

The time gained through Great Britain's delaying tactics in the Security Council was used by Brigadier Glubb's Arab Legion to shell the isolated Jewish ghetto in the Old City of Jerusalem to bits, to dynamite its last stronghold, the ancient Hurva Synagogue, and to occupy the ruins. This action, as we have seen, was not Great Britain's responsibility, as on the night of May 14-15 the Arab Legion had ceased to be a British security force and become the regular army of Transjordan's independent sovereign. Its com-mander, as was later announced in the House of Commons, had, presumably in the same night, given up his British citizenship and become a Transjordan subject. The British officers, N.C.O.s and technical staff of the Legion were no longer seconded to their duties by the War Office but had transformed themselves into individual volunteers.

Besides the Old City of Jerusalem, the Arab Legion had occupied the strategic monastery and police station at Latrun, which dominated the Jerusalem–Tel Aviv road, and thus isolated the 100,000 Jews in the modern city of Jerusalem from the rest of Israel. On May 30 the Jews suffered a major defeat when they threw untrained troops, mainly boys freshly arrived from the D.P. camps, into an ill-prepared attack on Latrun. They were beaten back without difficulty by the artillery and machine-guns of the Arab Legion, leaving over two hundred dead on the field.

On May 31, Count Bernadotte arrived in Tel Aviv and began his arduous negotiations to secure a truce.

We landed in Haifa four days later. The Old City of Jerusalem had fallen, and the situation at Latrun was still critical. Apart from these two set-backs, the Israeli Army was in control of the whole territory allotted by the United Nations to the Jews ; it had, in addition, conquered the biggest Arab town, Jaffa, and the whole coastal plain, allotted under the Partition plan to the Arabs, from Haifa to the Lebanese border.

I

POMPEI REVERSED

Haifa, Friday, June 4, 1948

After a bumpy flight from Cyprus, which made M. feel sick and the two returning Irgun terrorists on board look humble, a pencilled yellow streak appears, interposed between water and skyline : the coast of Israel. It swiftly expands, and unfolds into the golden dunes of Acco Bay, the pine slopes of Carmel, the suburbs of Haifa spawning over them like a skin-disease ; the oil refineries and behind them two giant petrol tanks like monstrous amphorae of cement.

The great tanks are dry because the flow of Mesopotamian oil has been diverted to Beirut and Amman. The golden dunes are mined. Among the pines of Carmel Arab and Jewish snipers play hide and seek. The weathered wall of Acco's Crusader fortress had a hole blown in it through which the friends of our terrorists made their escape.

But none of this is written over the smiling face of the bay. The whole sunny landscape, this levantine twin-sister of the Gulf of Naples, strikes at once the dominant chord of all journeys into war : it is so completely peaceful.

This intense and perverse peace, superimposed on scenes of flesh-tearing and eardrum-splitting violence, is an archetype of war-experience. Grass never smells sweeter than in a dug-out during a bombardment when one's face is buried in the earth. What soldier has not seen that caterpillar crawling along a crack in the bark of the tree behind which he took cover, and pursuing its climb undisturbed by the spattering of his tommy-gun? This intersecting of the tragic and the trivial planes of existence has always obsessed me — in the Spanish Civil War, during the collapse of France, in the London blitz.

The Dakota, with its load of terrorists, newspaper men and war-volunteers, is preparing to land. This is the moment we have all quietly dreaded since Le Bourget : the Arabs are supposed to be blockading Israel by sea and by air; a landing 'plane is to attacking aircraft what a pigeon is to a hawk, and the

Jewish state has so far no air protection. But there are no Syrian or Egyptian planes in sight. With the relieving bump on the runway the worst is over ; now one can settle down quietly to the routine of another war : to another blackout, more wailing sirens, girls in sweaty uniforms and operations according to plan.

The reflections of the sun on the ripples of the sea, the straight thin shadows of the palm-trees on the sand, register the silent comment of mineral and plant on that novelty in evolution, the human brain.

The airport. As we squeeze one by one through the small port-door of the Dakota and stumble down the wobbly step-ladder, there is a great clicking of Leicas and purring of movie-cameras. The State of Israel is exactly eighteen days old, so all events here are Historic Events and all persons arriving from abroad are Very Important Persons. Elated, we troop to the Customs.

Unlike railways stations, which tell you at once what sort of a town it is in which you have arrived, airport buildings have the same dull, neutral architecture and atmosphere all over the world. Waterloo is London and St. Lazare is Paris, but Croydon and Le Bourget belong to the same aerial no-man's-land. From this rule, Haifa airport is an exception. It is the newborn state's first and as yet only link with the world outside. The signposts with the Hebrew words for CUSTOMS, PASSPORTS, POLICE, LADIES and GENTS are freshly painted and still wet. The newly appointed Immigration Officer has as yet no uniform. Nor has the Customs Inspector ; nor the Police ; nor the Army. All servants of the State, civil and military, wear the same dress : khaki shirt and khaki shorts. This uniformity without uniforms strikes at once a note of drab efficiency. An army without colour and fancy dress deprives killing of its glamour : the soldiers of Israel hold no magic for the female. Nowhere in Haifa did we see young officers dining out with attractive women ; one can't even tell an officer from a private. From the first moment one gathers that this is a colourless, business-like war, in keeping with the drab functionalism of Israel's architecture.

The newbaked officials at the airport are all affable, rattled and inefficient. Here is bureaucracy in a larval state of innocence, before it has had time to spin itself a cocoon of red tape. Soon they will learn to scan with expressionless faces the little booklet

with the names blacklisted by the secret police, refuse explanations with icy politeness, dig for hidden shekels among the
voyagers' dirty shirts, every one a little Elohim. But as yet all is
in a state of virginal muddle, as on the first day of creation, before
the heavens and the earth were divided, when Immigration
Officers, floating on little clouds through chaos, treated the
passengers to cigarettes and brandy. The one who handles our
passports visibly tries to take himself seriously, but without much
success. I imagine that every morning before breakfast he repeats
to himself a Coué formula :

" You are now a Government official in an official Government,
which every day and in every way is becoming sovereigner and
sovereigner."

He looks at our visas ; he feasts his eyes on them ; they are
another symbol of Israel having attained the dignity of statehood.
M.'s and mine are among the ten first visas issued by the Provisional Government's Representation in Paris ; they are written
in Hebrew and French, stamped in with red ink, occupy a whole
page in our passports and have the serial numbers five and seven.
We showed them the same evening to a group of wounded
Haganah men in the military hospital in Haifa. They looked at
them like children at a new toy. We found later the same en-
raptured expression on the faces of people looking at the first
Israeli pound-notes, at aeroplanes with the star of David painted
on their wings, at the new flag, at the first foreign Ambassador
presenting his credentials to the Government. They can't get
over their amazement that these are real aeroplanes, real flags,
real ambassadors.

There is a story about an American Zionist who used to tell
other American Jews about the wonderful achievements of the
pioneers in Palestine — how they drained marshes and made the
desert flourish — without ever having been to Palestine himself.
After thirty years as an ardent propagandist, he was ·at last
persuaded to make a trip to the country. When he saw the first
Hebrew village he looked bewildered, and for a few minutes kept
silent. Then he meekly asked his companions :

" Do you mean to tell me that what I have said in those
speeches is really true ? "

Israel's citizens are rubbing their eyes. It does not often
happen that a dream comes true.

Saturday, June 5, Haifa

Before going on to Tel Aviv we decided to spend a couple of days in Haifa, to see some old friends. So from the airport we drove up in a taxi to the " Sanatorium " on Mount Carmel. In peace-time this was a kind of nursing-home for the imaginary ailments of the rich of Tel Aviv, run with great efficiency by old Dr. Bodenheimer of Berlin, who combined an excellent kosher kitchen with a teutonic furore for cleanliness. It inspired visions of the manageress chasing across the dining-room with a table-napkin after a lone streptococcus floating through the air. The rooms have large balconies with a lovely view over the Bay, and the air is fragrant with the scent of the famous pines of Carmel. On very hot and very damp days, of which Carmel has many, it is rather like entering a bathroom where somebody has just finished having a hot bath with pine-extract — Bathsheba maybe, with Urias holding the towel. But we are at the beginning of June and, as we left the mists of North Wales only a few days ago, the blaze of sunshine is delightful.

After Dr. Bodenheimer had put on his hat to say grace, and the waiters had warned us not to smoke because of the Shabbath, we settled down to our first meal in Israel. Half of the Sanatorium is now converted into a convalescent home for wounded soldiers; the other half of the guests are rich couples from Tel Aviv who are staying here under one pretext or another — in fact because they are frightened of the air raids. People of this unpleasant category exist in every country; why then does their Jewish variety strike us as particularly obnoxious? And why does the Yiddish lilt of the quarrelling voices in the kitchen get more on M.'s nerves than the screaming of Italian women squabbling in the market, or the jabbering of any foreign tourist guide? Probably for the same reason for which newspapers give more prominence to black-market cases if the offender's name happens to be Abramowitz or Cohen instead of Smith. The figure of the Jew squirming in front of the serene, wigged Magistrate evokes a deep archetypal reson-ance in the reader, the sources of which are as obscure to him as the cause of his excitement about the monster of Loch Ness, the radio-signals from Mars, or the beggar who left a million in his will. They all are modern variants of ancient symbols of legend and myth. Mr. Abramowitz is not an individual who has com-mitted an individual offence; he is folklore crystallized as a

o

news-item. If his image in the reader's eye could be X-rayed, it would reveal a modern likeness superimposed on a faded portrait of Shylock ; and underneath that would appear some even more shadowy mythological contours.

And that, of course, is the case, and perhaps the only case, for the Jewish state. The particular social structure and mental pattern which centuries of segregation impressed upon the Jews in the Diaspora, that eery odour of otherliness, of vagrancy and jugglery which surrounds Mr. Abramowitz who comes from nowhere and belongs nowhere, makes him into something super- and subhuman at the same time, a man without a shadow, a product of crystallized folklore. Each time you burn him alive, stick a knife into his stomach or pump gas into his lungs, he pops up again like a jack-in-the-box, with a more horribly ingratiating smile, and offers you a second-hand suit or a share of real estate. This monotonous game has now been going on for some twenty centuries and there is no sign that it will stop in the twenty-first. But now at long last the Jew will be able to say : You don't want me ? All right then, I'll go. . . . The knowledge alone of being able to say that will have a slow but steady healing influence on that oldest social syndrome, the Jewish neurosis.

After dinner, on the starlit terrace of the Sanatorium, we talked to some of the wounded Haganah soldiers. One of them is the cowman of the collective village of Shaar Hagolan in the Jordan valley, south of Lake Tiberias. On the first night of the war, May 15th, they were expecting an attack from Syria, across the Jordan ; so he, with some fifteen others, was lying on a hill in wait for the Syrian tanks. The Arabs had cut off the spring which supplies the water to Shaar Hagolan, and the imported Dutch cows, the pride and main source of income of the commune, were dying of thirst. There was some desultory artillery fire from the other side of the Jordan, and each time the guns were silent, they could hear the cows mooing their complaint in a chorus. " Whenever I heard them," said the cowman wonderingly, " I was unable to make up my mind which was the real reality so to speak : the war and the tanks or the wailing of the thirsty cows in the night."

The cows, the caterpillar crawling on the tree, the smell of the pines in the darkness. And on the other plane, the other reality. Both exist, but they are mutually exclusive ; and in the rare moments when the two patterns of experience clash, perception is deepened and awareness reaches an otherwise unattainable intensity.

Lunch with Abram Weinshall. He says the Jews have already some three thousand killed. The danger of a prolonged war is not defeat, but the gradual bleeding away of the country's youth. Three thousand killed in a total population of about 750,000 after one month of war corresponds proportionately to two hundred thousand Englishmen killed, or six hundred thousand Americans.

But this figure is misleading The majority of the losses occurred before the official war started on May 15th. Since the beginning of the " real " war, the casualty figures have actually gone down.

Abram's son Saul, who had been studying law in London, has been called up by the Israeli Army and arrived back yesterday.[1] His daughter Judy is in the States; her fiancé, a volunteer from Switzerland, was killed in the early days of the war. A couple of years ago, when she was eighteen, she used to write me fervently patriotic letters which, had they been intercepted by the British censorship, would have promptly got her into jail. Abram himself was arrested in 1947, on the sole grounds of having been a member of the Revisionist Party some ten years ago. He spent forty days in the concentration camp of Latrun.

The British evacuation is almost complete. The civilian administration ceased to function on May 15th, the day the Mandate ended. The last troops, some three or four thousand men, are concentrated in little barbed-wire enclaves in and around Haifa.

From the business centre of Haifa, which is downtown adjoining the harbour area, several roads with hairpin-bends lead up to the Jewish residential quarters spread over the slopes of Carmel. In the course of the twenty minutes' drive from downtown to the Sanatorium, one has to traverse three of these British Security Zones. They consist of one or two requisitioned houses in a strategically dominant position, surrounded by a jungle of barbed-wire tangles, and are called " Bevingrads ". In fact they are wire cages, small concentration camps, in which the rear-

[1] While correcting the proofs of this book, I learnt that Saul Weinshall was killed in action, in the spring of 1949, at the age of 22.

guards of Great Britain's Middle East forces live in melancholy self-confinement. The road traverses these enclaves for stretches of a hundred yards or so, and at each point of entry and exit, where the road intersects the barbed wire, there are British check-posts, with arms at the ready. They look at the driver's papers and wave him into Bevingrad, and a hundred yards further there is another sentry who looks at his papers and waves him out ; and each time there is a machine-gun pointed at the car. No words are spoken while the papers are checked, and no smiles exchanged. The Jews try to look impassive, but scorn is written on their faces and their silence has for the sentry a contemptuous ring. The sentry looks equally impassive, his boots are well polished and his movements smart, but he knows that he is the rearguard of an Empire in retreat.

Sunday, June 6th, Tel Aviv

Palestine, a British statesman once said, has the size of a county and the problems of a continent. Within less than forty-eight hours of our arrival, we have tasted samples of a lot of problems. They make a mixed dish, which burns the palate like hot curry.

We asked one of the wounded soldiers in the Sanatorium what he thought of the political prospects after the war. He is a *kibbutznik*,[1] a member of *Hashomer Hazair*,[2] a gentle, dreamy boy. He said : " First we had to get the British out. Now we have to beat the Arabs. And after that, we will have to finish our own fascists, the people of Irgun." " Do you really believe the Irgun are fascists ? " I asked him. " Of course they are." " How do you define a fascist ? " " Oh," he said wearily, " you only have to look at them. They are the type."

The prospect of a civil war did not frighten him in the least. Being a good marxist, civil wars appeared to him as a matter of course in history, and appeals for tolerance as so much sentimental poppycock — just as sincere nationalists a century and a half ago took wars of conquest for granted.

This morning we set out for Tel Aviv in a taxi, and as we watched the traffic on the coastal road, I thought again I was back in the Spanish war ten years ago. The road was teeming with

---

[1] *Kibbutz* : collective settlement ; *Kibbutznik* : a member of it
[2] " The Young Watchman ", left-wing political Party.

trucks and requisitioned passenger buses packed with singing soldiers — in the open trucks they all stand upright holding on to each other, in the buses they sit on each other's knees with elbows sticking out of the windows and their fists banging the rhythm of the song against the tin-plating. All vehicles are camouflaged against air attack by the simple expedient of smearing them with a thick coating of mud; they have the same dirty khaki colour as the soldiers' shorts and shirts. Again that impression of drab efficiency; the Jews have always lacked a sense of colour. The colour in Palestine was provided by the Arabs; but the Arabs have gone. The shuks in Haifa are deserted, the bazaars looted, the houses closed. The camels and the donkeys, the nargilehs and the shoeblack urchins, that heavy cloud of the odour of oriental spices which enveloped the shuks, all gone. The mud huts of the slum villages along the coastal road are dynamited, their population gone. It is another exodus, but the same desolation.

Truck after truck with singing, yelling soldiers. Some trucks are covered with a kind of home-made armour-plating, some other makeshift contraptions are trying to look like tanks. Most of the soldiers have no rifles or kitbags. It is just like the road from Valencia to Madrid in 1936. Everything bears the sign of amateurishness, muddle and enthusiastic improvisation.

The soldiers are all young, sunburnt and visibly feeling on top of the world. So were the Spanish militianos, the Serb guerillas, the soldiers of the French Revolution. Only improvised revolutionary armies know this emotional exuberance. They fight like devils, and when they panic they run like monkeys. They are not blasé like soldiers of a regular army where grousing is a sign of self-respect and a token of reliability. And if there can be such a thing as a just war, then this war of Israel is a just war.

But the snag with all wars is that the phenomena which they produce are only very indirectly connected with the idea or cause in whose name they are waged. Those who are in it do not think in terms of democracy, national self-determination, the Succession to the Spanish throne or the abolition of slavery. They sing, yell, dream of their favourite dish, masturbate and count their lice. They are tough and sentimental, gay and melancholy, selfish and unselfish, according to the same cheap, ready - made pattern. They don't hate the enemy, but they love to wreck the furniture of requisitioned billets and to leave the maximum of dirt behind, as children love to smear filth over the wallpaper in unconscious protest against parental don'ts. All armies breed epidemics of infantilism. It is not the killing aspect of war, but this inevitable degradation, the enforced lowering of the mental age, which makes all soldiery, regardless of the cause for which it fights, into such an un-adult, depressing phenomenon. And the sickly heroics of the home-front are even worse. The old fusspot busybodying as an air-raid warden, the lying poster with 'it all depends on you ", the shortening of our lines and the lengthening of the enemy's communications, Churchill's cigar and Hitler's lock, totem-mask and tabu-sign, the age of the Boy Scout, the triumph of imbecility.

The abrupt changes of landscape on this coastal road, from desert-dunes to orange groves and back to desert again, have always fascinated me. In 1926, when for the first time I travelled from Haifa to Tel Aviv, there was no road, and most of the country was a wilderness. At that time the train took some five hours to cover a distance of seventy miles, and if one travelled by car, one had to make a long inland detour across the hills of Samaria. I was spared this dilemma by being penniless and walked down the coast on foot. I walked at a leisurely rate, avoided the more ill-reputed Arab villages, slept and was fed in Jewish settlements free of charge. If the settlement was a collective one, I even drew the daily ration of cigarettes. Free board and a bed are still being provided by all collective farms to visitors ; but to-day people travel by cars or buses, whereas twenty years ago there were few roads, fewer cars, no hotels or roadhouses outside the towns, tramping was a national sport and the whole country a large family.

Such tramping experiences of one's youth leave one with a partly nostalgic, partly proprietary feeling towards the landscape or country where they took place. In 1926 there were only about a dozen Jewish settlements in the coastal plain between Haifa and Tel Aviv and most of the plain was sand-dunes, desert and marshes. Now there is a continuous chain of them, the highroad runs along a green carpet of artificially irrigated, reclaimed land, with only an occasional patch of sand as an abrupt reminder of the past. And each time we ran across such patches of desert I got that silly proprietary feeling one has when showing one's native town to a tourist. Citizens of young pioneer countries who have seen their rapid transformation with their own eyes, are particularly prone to it. Even the New York highbrow, when showing visitors round, cannot entirely avoid giving the impression

that he has built the Empire State Building with his own hands.
No wonder then that the Israeli citizen, whose individual share in
what has been achieved here is so much greater, and to whom
constructive achievement is historically such a novelty, is still
intoxicated with pride in every acre of reclaimed desert, in every
cow which feeds on it, in every tomato which grows there. To
his forebears in the ghetto a cow was a wild animal, and a tomato
a commodity arriving by some miracle in the grocer's shop. Held
together by a petrified faith, Jews have lived for centuries on
familiar terms with the supernatural, and completely estranged
from nature. Hence their naïve delight in jewish cows and jewish
grass, jewish tomatoes and jewish eggs. They marvel at the chick
which, hardly born, knows already how to peck ; it is a *wunder-
kind* like those other infant prodigies who at seven know chapters
of the holy scriptures by heart. The green pastures of Israel have
sprung from a twofold desert : the waterless land and the arid
past of the nation.

To the outsider, this naïvely self-congratulatory enthusiasm
is at first very moving, then equally tiresome. A friend of mine,
an American newspaper man, who was being taken round by a
Government official, on being told for the twentieth time ·that
Tel Aviv was built on sand, sighed in mock-despair : " I wish
they'd never done it." The official's face closed with a snap ; my
friend was branded an antisemite for life. Extreme touchiness
and lack of a sense of humour are outstanding features of the
pioneer mentality.

We pass the Tulkarem–Natanya crossroads. This is the wasp-
waist of Israel ; the coastal plain here narrows down to less than
ten miles between the sea and the Arab frontier. The front at
present runs some three miles east of the crossroads.

A few villages along the road are still populated by Arabs. Some
of them are even working in the fields ; and a little withered Arab
woman is selling oranges to Jewish soldiers out of a basket on her
back. War is Hecuba to her and she is Hecuba to war. But not
for long. A few weeks later some Arab lads will start sniping
from these villages at Jewish trucks on the road ; the Jewish army
will herd the villagers together, dynamite their houses, and put
the young men into concentration camps ; while the old ones
will tie a mattress and a brass coffee-pot on the donkey, the old
woman will walk ahead leading the donkey by the rein and the
old man will ride on it, wrapped in his kefiye, and sunk in solemn

meditation about the lost opportunity of raping his youngest grandchild. Like all wars, this too is a pageant of half-truths in shining armour. The victor is never entirely in the right, and there are no innocent victims.

Monday, June 7, Tel Aviv

Since we have arrived in the Capital I am even more puzzled by this feeling of unreality. We have had our first air-raids, watched people digging shelters, and read the communiques. But to read in biblical Hebrew that our troops have improved their positions round Mount Canaan and that all is quiet by the Sea of Galilee, is a strange experience. It is almost impossible to believe that Israel is a real state, its army a real army, and this war a real war. It is certainly the most improbable war that modern history has seen. The small voice of the leaders of this Lilliput state is drowned by a world-wide echo ; the puny facts created here throw an enormous shadow ; the clichés of front-reportage are overloaded with historical associations. On one side, the Holy Jehad and the Arabian Nights ; on the other the Bible and the Maccabeans. Each hill or wadi where the Sten guns bark has either seen the sun stand still in Joshua's day or a miracle performed by Christ ; reality is swallowed by the archetype.

But there is another reason for the elusive, dreamlike character of the whole thing. As in all dreams, the symbols presented to the mind have several levels of meaning. What we experience here is a kind of Pompei in reverse. In Pompei, schoolboys playing with marbles were suddenly caught by the lava and petrified into monuments. They were transferred from the trivial to the tragic plane in one abrupt jump. All catastrophes have a similar effect. They demonstrate in a drastic form the otherwise invisible transformation of trivial occurrences into historic facts. For the present is mainly on the trivial, history always on the tragic plane.

The Pompei effect is a sudden telescoping of this otherwise gradual transformation. Man - made catastrophes — wars and revolutions — work the same way. Danton's lifted arm freezes in mid-air into the gesture of a bronze monument. Napoleon's liver and Cleopatra's nose belong at the same time to the trivial and historic planes. In both the creative and the destructive kind of cataclysm the actors are mostly unconscious of the parts they play. They do not know where exactly the two planes meet, how their private idiosyncrasies grow into legends, at what point a subjective gesture becomes a datum of history. People who consciously try to precipitate the effect, to project themselves from the trivial to the historic plane, are usually megalomaniacs or utopian cranks. But in this country everybody is conscious of living through a Pompei in reverse. They feel that they are moving through a lava-stream of history in which all that happens now will be preserved for eternity. Even the schoolboys playing with marbles feel a host of Maccabean spectres looking over their shoulders.

The fascinating and endearing episodes in this mass-production of historic facts are not the Proclamations, speeches and self-conscious gestures of the leaders, but the little hitches which occur in between, the holes in the cloth of history which are patched up by hasty improvisation. There is, for instance, the story of Israel's National Flag. It was told to us, the day we arrived, by an old friend, the painter Karl Rubin (who has since been appointed Israeli Minister in Rumania). It seems that one day a week or so ago, an official advertisement appeared in the Hebrew papers in which artists were invited to submit suggestions for the National Flag of Israel; the time-limit given to competitors for sending in their entries was 48 hours! Rubin got furious, ran to the address indicated in the advertisement, found that nobody there knew anything about The Flag, ran to a second and third address, and finally discovered that somebody had appointed a committee of three little bearded men who were to decide about the future Flag of Israel. The three little men were representing the Left, Right and Centre parties respectively, according to the " party key system " which is a sacred tradition in this country, and which prescribes that in each public body and institution all political parties have to be represented in proportion to their relative strength. He also discovered that none of the members of the committee had had any previous dealings with either art or heraldry in his life. It hadn't even occurred to them that aesthetic considerations had anything to do with their task. A Flag, they explained to Rubin, was a political problem; the task of the member for the Left was to watch that there shouldn't be too many religious symbols on the Flag; the task of the member for the Right, to prevent it from having too much red in it; while the member for the Centre was to balance their conflicting views by taking various bits from the various sketches of the competitors and concocting a sort of coalition flag

— as one formulates a resolution from several draft proposals. So Rubin gave up arguing with them and went to the Government, who were all busy with the War on their hands, and finally succeeded in obtaining an extension of the deadline for the competition, and a half-promise that an artist would be coopted to the committee. But as artists, like all other citizens in Israel, belong to one or the other political party, the coopted member would upset the party key — and there the matter rests for the moment.[1]

The second story is in a similar vein. At one of its first meetings, the Israeli State Council, which functions as a kind of provisional Parliament, elected as its president the veteran Zionist leader, Professor Weizmann. As Israel has as yet no constitution, they could not make him President of the Republic, but it was clear that this was in fact what the election implied. Then came the hitch, the hole in the cloth of History. Firstly, the new President had to be elected in his absence (he only arrived in Israel some four months after its proclamation of independence). However, this somewhat unusual situation was passed over in silence in view of the President's precarious health and equally precarious relations with the Prime Minister, Ben Gurion. Secondly, there was the question of the President's nationality. While the British Mandate lasted, only two years of residence in Palestine were needed to acquire Palestine citizenship; and to become a Palestine citizen was regarded as the patriotic duty of every Jewish immigrant. Though Dr. Weizmann's duties as leader of the world Zionist organization kept him mostly abroad, he could of course have acquired Palestine nationality without any difficulties being raised by the Mandatory authorities. But the fact is that he had never done this, preferring to keep his British passport. So, when the question of his election came up, one of the two Revisionist members in the State Council who represent the Opposition, asked the impertinently pertinent question " whether a foreigner, and an Englishman at that, could become President of Israel ". The Minister of Justice, Dr. Rosenblueth, muttered in embarrassment that he would consider the point; but the matter was conveniently forgotten and the election carried by acclamation.

[1] As I was told later, the reason for the hurry about the flag was that Israel had acquired a few cargo ships — which had got into difficulties with port authorities abroad for having no flag to show.

Last morning, our first in Tel Aviv, we were woken up at 8 A.M. by the crack of a bomb from an Egyptian plane. It fell a couple of hundred yards from our hotel on the sea front — a small 25-pounder anti-personnel bomb — and caused no damage beyond shattering a few shop-windows around. With our memories of the V1s and V2s over London, we took a somewhat snobbish attitude about the Lilliput bombs in this Lilliput war. Yet a week ago forty-one people were killed in a bus queue during an air-raid — rather more than the average number of victims caused by the round hundred times heavier bombs which fell on London.

II

DAVID AND GOLIATH

I

EXACTLY a week after our arrival, on June 11, the first truce came into effect. Four weeks later, on July 9, hostilities were resumed. After ten days, on July 18, the second truce began. It was interrupted, though not officially and only in fact, by the two Israeli campaigns in the Negeb in October and December, and other sporadic outbreaks on other fronts ; these were each time settled by local " cease-fires " and " stop-fires ", which represented, so to speak, square brackets within the round brackets interspersed in the course of the war.

This war between truces, on the instalment plan, was another unique aspect of this unique campaign. It reminded one of those old Wild West serials in which films used to end with the heroine suspended by her flowing hair from a rope-bridge over an abyss, and the caption : " Another exciting instalment will be shown in this theatre next week ". Or, to alter the metaphor, it was David fighting Goliath over six rounds, with the U.N. umpire's gong signalling the end of each round just when things were beginning to warm up. All this may sound frivolous ; but the fact is that this Holy War of Islam, which had for so many years haunted their imagination, was a bitter disappointment to believers in the Arab myth.

It was, because of its many historic echoes, a war more than others obscured by bombastic half-truths. Propaganda, rhetorics and distortion surrounded the scanty facts in a series of concentric layers, and to get at the core of truth was like peeling an onion, sometimes with watering eyes. The outer and most transparent layer of untruth was the series of Arab victories reported during the initial period not only in the British Press, but by most European newspapers, who were uncritically echoing the Arabian Night tales put out by Radio Cairo and Radio Baghdad — effectively helped by the inexperience of the Israeli Press and Public Relations Office. Then, as it became gradually known that the Israeli forces were holding their ground and even going over to the

attack, truth was romanticized in the opposite direction : 750,000
Jews were by a sheer miracle defeating forty million Arabs with the
British Empire thrown in.

This version would have been much nearer the truth if the
Arab countries had been comparable to modern European nations
whose entire manpower and productive capacity are mobilized in
a war. But such comparisons are misleading. The social back-
wardness of the Arab countries makes any coordinated national
effort impossible for them ; their fighting forces are not modern
conscript armies but more like mediaeval mercenary troops —
illiterate, badly trained, of low morale, and quite incapable of
fighting a modern war. With all the bragging and blustering of
the Arab Governments and their inimitable radio announcers, the
total number of troops mustered by the six countries which
launched the Holy War against the Jews was, at a rough estimate,
between 30,000 and 40,000 men; among these, 4000 members of
the Arab Legion, 3000 Lebanese, 3000 to 4000 Syrians, 5000 to
6000 Iraqis, 2000 to 3000 Saudi Arabians, 12,000 Egyptians and
3000 Irregulars under Fawzi Kaukaji. Their overall strength was
thus roughly equivalent to that of the armed forces of Israel,
which had proceeded from May 15 onwards with a total mobiliza-
tion of its manpower on modern lines.

Nevertheless, the odds were heavily against Israel. The forty
million Arabs were after all a reality, if only as a manpower
reservoir hardly tapped but practically inexhaustible. For the
750,000 Jews, on the other hand, casualties were irreplaceable.
Secondly, the maintenance of a disproportionately large army put
a terrific economic strain on the small Jewish community, which
increased as the interminable truce dragged on. Thirdly, and
this was their most serious handicap, if the Arab regular armies
had little modern equipment in tanks, artillery and aircraft at the
beginning of the war, the Jews had none at all. And in the
subsequent race to smuggle in equipment despite the arms
embargo, the Arabs had the advantage of their immense frontiers
and coast-lines defying control by U.N. observers, whereas the
Jews had only an easily supervised coast-line of a hundred miles
and three or four closely watched airports. Finally, the tiny
area of Israel — less than 100 miles long, from 15 to 25 miles
wide — gave them no opportunity for defence in depth and no
chance to retreat. They had to fight with their backs to the wall ;
and that is what won them the fight.

2

It took us over a fortnight to assemble the necessary permits, safe conducts, transport and escort for a tour round the frontiers of Galilee.

Our escort was a young man of German-Jewish origin called Shlomo (Hebrew for Solomon). His surname we never found out, nor that of any of the officers and local commanders with whom we talked and travelled along the fronts. It was all part of the atmosphere of dark secrecy in which Haganah shrouded itself. These men had so long lived underground that the habit of conspiracy had become second nature to them, and now they could not get out of it. The unique practice of keeping even the names of the General Staff and Army Commanders secret had already produced a swarm of pernicious rumours in the foreign Press to the effect that the Jewish Army was run by Soviet generals on active service. At the first Press conference we attended in Tel Aviv the public information officer introduced a young man as the General Officer Commanding Operations without mentioning his name. An American journalist had a crack at him with " How do you spell your name, sir ? " but was told that for " security reasons " the G.O.C.'s identity could not be disclosed. Actually, his name was Yigal Sukenik ; he was the son of a well-known archaeologist at the Hebrew University.

Some weeks later anonymity was dropped ; but at that time not only names but also the addresses of Army headquarters in Tel Aviv and everywhere else were kept secret, which was a source of endless muddle and confusion. As we proceeded on our journey to Galilee, our escort Shlomo would get out in various towns and villages, hail a soldier, go into a conspiratorial huddle with him about the probable whereabouts of headquarters — where he was to get his security briefing and some more permits, if not an additional field security escort. After driving about for a while in quest of H.Q., when Shlomo felt that the trail was getting hot, he would leave the car and continue his search on foot, so as not to betray its location. We were drifting along on our journey in a kind of elusive and fluid universe in which there were no fixed points of support, such as headquarters and responsible commanders, only places " somewhere in Israel " and some Uris and Moshes and Reubens — Big Reubens, Small Reubens, Reubens from Khanita and Reubens No. 3.

We had to go through Haifa again, and there we pieced together the improbable story of the conquest by the Jews of this key harbour and prize city of the Middle East after only a few hours' street fighting, and at the price of eighteen Jewish and less than a hundred Arab casualties. More than to anything else it was due to psychological causes. The 70,000 Arabs of Haifa abandoned the town after no more than a token fight because they had been completely demoralized by the desertion of their leaders and the psychological warfare waged on them by Haganah. One after another the local Arab notables had slipped out by night to Beirut or Cyprus, on motor yachts laden with their families and furniture. Through a system of tapping telephone wires Haganah learned of each of these desertions and was able to announce them immediately in Arabic broadcasts from their illegal radio station.[1]

A few days before the decisive battle, the Arab chief commander, Amin Bey Izzed Din, vanished in a motor-boat towards Beirut under the pretext of fetching reinforcements. By that time Haganah was using not only its radio station, but also loudspeaker vans which blared their sinister news from the vicinity of the Arab shuks. They warned the Arab population to keep clear of the billets of the foreign mercenaries who had infiltrated into the town, warned them to send their women and children away before new contingents of savage Iraqis arrived, promised them safe conducts and escorts to Arab territory, and hinted at terrible consequences if their warnings were disregarded. In the industrial town of Haifa Jews and Arabs had always got on particularly well together, so that after their leaders had deserted them the Arabs were rather more inclined to listen to their Jewish neighbours than to flowery exhortations from abroad.

Thus Haifa yielded to Haganah's first vigorous attack with very little resistance. After the Arabs had left, Haganah discovered several armouries containing machine-guns and huge stocks of ammunition which had never been put to use. In fact, Haifa fell like Jericho had once fallen, with Haganah's loudspeaker vans replacing the trumpets which had made the walls crumble.

It was more or less the same story in the other mixed towns during the civil war period. Everywhere Arab morale collapsed under the simultaneous impact of the desertion of the effendis,

---

[1] Haifa, as will be remembered, fell in April 1948, when Palestine was still under British Mandate.

of panicky rumours and of Jewish improvisation and propaganda. But, above all, the Palestine Arabs lost the civil war without a serious fight for the simple reason that they had nothing to fight for. They had accepted the presence of the Jews a long time ago, and on a local level got on quite well with them — as long and as far as no outside interests interfered. They were an easy-going, peace - loving and individualistic people, with narrow interests and no national consciousness. They cultivated their little gardens, cafés and bazaar-shops, and had no ambitions to fight. They had kept away both from the First and Second World Wars which did not affect their interests; this time, too, they would have been quite willing to let the Jews and the neighbouring Arab princes fight it out between themselves — and perhaps to come in at the end for a little looting and quiet killing, as is the custom in these latitudes. All this was reflected in the probably most typical and instructive episode of the civil war, the battle for Safed.

It is referred to in Israel as the Miracle of Safed — which is in keeping with the traditions of this hallowed centre of mediaeval Jewish mysticism, where the Kabbala originated and in whose surroundings some Jewish families of scholars and mystics have survived in uninterrupted succession since the ancient Jewish State. Besides being a spiritual centre of Judaic tradition, Safed is also the strategic key town of Northern Galilee, and one of the most beautiful places in Palestine — perched on a hill nearly 3000 feet high and commanding a lovely view over the Galilean mountains. We drove up to Safed late in the evening from the Hula region on the Syrian frontier; and as the car climbed up the serpentine road to Mount Canaan, we had alternating views of the Sea of Galilee in the east and the Mediterranean in the west. To the east it was already night, and an enormous orange moon was rising over the lake; while in the west lay a different world of coloured twilight, with the sun just setting in the Mediterranean. Arrived in Safed, we put up in the Central Hotel, from where a whole school was just moving out — evacuee children returning to their Galilean settlement which had been made safe for them again by the latest Israeli advance. The proprietor of the hotel is old Chaim Maiberg, who comes from the stock of the first immigrants of the 1880s. He produced a bottle of the famous Safed arak, which contains no aniseed and does not get cloudy with water.

Although Safed, because of its height, is supposed to be one of the coolest places in Israel, it was so hot that I slept on the balcony. The next morning we set out in search of the local Haganah commander, whose identity and location were of course top secret. When at last we found him in his headquarters in the old city, he turned out to be the son of old Maiberg, whom we had just left breakfasting with his papa at the hotel. Like most commanders of the Israeli Army he was a *sabra* [1] and incredibly young, about 25. Equally typical was the contrast between the bearded, patriarchal, ultra-Jewish father with his little black skull-cap and the blond, good-looking young man with his neutral, " de-salinated " features and the slightly anglicized manners — which he had acquired, together with thirty thousand others of his generation, as a volunteer in the British Army. Young Commander Maiberg explained to us the inside workings of the Miracle of Safed.

The total population of the town at the outset of the battle consisted of 12,000 Arabs and 1500 Jews. The strategic position of the Jews within the town was such that, in the estimate of the commander of the British garrison, they could hold out for not more than two hours after the garrison had been evacuated.

The lay-out of the town is as follows. Safed is built round the slopes of a hill which dominates the main high roads of central Galilee and which, two thousand years ago, was one of the main strongholds of Flavius Josephus' revolt against the Romans. The top of this hill is a fairly even plateau, about 150 yards long and 30-50 yards wide, overgrown with shrubs. This small plateau dominates the whole town and its approaches. A mediaeval fortress once stood here, built on the ruins of some Judean fortress which was probably built on the ruins of some Canaanite fortress. It is called the Matzuba. When the British left Safed the Matzuba was occupied by the Arabs.

Along the gentle slopes down from the Matzuba are spread out the Jewish and Arab quarters. The Jewish quarter occupied about one-third of the conic mantle of the hill, the Arab quarter about two-thirds.

The hill round which Safed is built is surrounded by other hills, all but one of which were in Arab hands. The one exception was Mount Canaan which, apart from its historic echoes, had little

---

[1] *Sabra*: current nickname for Palestine-born Jews, derived from the prickly fruit of the cactus plant.

value for the Jews. On the hill opposite Mount Canaan, and directly to the north of Safed, stands the formidable Teggart Fortress. It is one of a series of steel-and-concrete fortresses built in strategic positions all over the country by General Teggart during the Arab Revolt. The one in Safed is the second biggest in Palestine; it could only be reduced by heavy artillery or aerial block-busters — and the heaviest weapons the Jews in Safed had were three two-inch mortars, whose effect on the fortress would have been about that of pea-shooters.

The British garrison began to prepare for the evacuation of Safed at the beginning of April. Its commander, Colonel X of the 1st Battalion Irish Guards, seems to have been under orders to hand over to the Arabs, on evacuating the town, the Teggart Fortress and the Safed Police Station — which two buildings between them would allow the Arabs to keep every single Jewish house under direct fire. Whatever the political leanings of the officers of the British garrison, it must be assumed that they spent a few sleepless nights visualizing what would happen after they had withdrawn according to plan, since they must have known that the orders for their withdrawal were such as to deprive the Jewish minority of any chance of defending themselves. Colonel X first tried, about a fortnight before the British evacuation of Safed was due, to persuade Haganah to withdraw its men from the town; if this were done the Arabs would guarantee the bodily safety of the 1500 unarmed Jews. It must be assumed that the Colonel either naïvely believed in the chivalry of the Iraqi mercenaries and of Kaukaji's bands who were already in control of the Arab quarter of Safed, or that he thought that even a slender chance of avoiding a massacre, by persuading the Jews to lay down their arms, was better than the certainty of a massacre if they did not.

Haganah refused to withdraw. According to our Haganah informants — among them young Maiberg and a chubby South African war veteran called Harry — the Colonel and his liaison officer, Captain Y, tried almost to the last moment to persuade the Jews to give up both Safed and the only Jewish settlement in the region, a small commune a few miles away called Ein Zeitim, the Olive Spring. Ein Zeitim was cut off from Safed, which in turn was cut off from the rest of Jewish Palestine. Young Maiberg interpreted these efforts as a proof of the machiavellian design of the British to demoralize Haganah by a " war of nerves ". During the last few days a number of rather hectic telephone conversations took place between the British officers and Maiberg or Harry. According to young Maiberg (who, previous to serving in the British Army, had picked up a Scottish accent in a missionary school) these talks were on the following lines:

Captain Y to young M.: "You should really evacuate Ein Zeitim. Every soldier knows that in a tight spot one has to shorten one's lines."

Young M.: "If you were a Jew and had spent years in concentration camps and been beaten up a wee bit, and then were smuggled into Palestine and settled down at last on a farm of your own, you wouldn't leave either, whatever happened."

Captain Y: "Then Haganah must give them an order to leave."

Young M.: "That wouldn't do a wee bit of good. They wouldn't obey any order to leave their settlement."

The Captain gave up; obviously Jewish strategy was different from all other strategy. But, when all is said, the whole Jewish community of Palestine was strategically in such an impossible situation that the only reasonable decision would have been to shorten their lines and clear out of the country. It so happened that their only line of retreat was the sea; and at the other end of the sea they had no bases either. The Arabs of Palestine could run away to Syria, Transjordan, Egypt; they had thousands of miles behind them. The Jews had no other choice but to stay where they were or perish. This was the overall consideration determining the strategy of the Jewish war.

Anyway, on one of the following days Captain Y took a stroll to Ein Zeitim, and when he came back he remarked to young M., in the words of the latter: "Now that I have seen the place and the people, I quite agree that it would be a waste of time to try and persuade them to leave." He seemed to be rather shaken, said young M.

Soon afterwards the Colonel rang up Harry late one night and, in Harry's version of the dialogue, said to him:

"I am really rather worried about what's going to happen when we go."

Harry (in his cosy, slow South African voice): "Whatever happens, you can rest assured that we shall never forget the meanness and trickery of the British."

The Colonel (almost in tears): "You must appreciate our difficulties. All our forces are being withdrawn from Palestine, and we feel that we can no longer control the situation."

Harry : " That's all right, we know that already."

The Colonel : " But, my dear fellow, I'm very worried, very worried indeed."

Harry : " Don't you worry, Colonel. We trust God and ourselves."

(Comment by Harry : " You know I just said that, but really I'm not religious at all.")

In the end neither Haganah nor the Jewish community leaders were officially notified of the date when the British garrison would go and leave the town without any authority in control. On April 16, one month before the termination of the British Mandate, and of the Mandatory's international responsibility for the maintenance of law and order, at twelve noon Haganah scouts reported to young M. an unusual event : the local commander of the Arab irregulars, Adib Shukatli, and the Arab Chief of Police Sidi Qadura, escorted by twenty armed irregulars, had been seen walking into the Police Station, where they were received by the British officer in command.

Approximately at the same hour a Haganah detachment on Mount Canaan was surrounded by British infantry and armoured cars ; and while they were thus cut off from the Teggart Fortress, the fortress itself was handed over by the British commander to Arab troops. As it transpired later, these troops were not even Palestinians, but Iraqis.

This happened round midday. By 3 P.M. the last British vehicle and soldier had left Safed. Even before they left, about 2 P.M., the Arabs started shooting with machine-guns and mortars at Jewish houses from the Police Station. A few hours later, under covering fire from the Teggart Fortress, they occupied the Matzuba, the plateau dominating the town. The battle of Safed was on.

It was a ding-dong battle which lasted for three weeks. Neither Arabs nor Jews like hand-to-hand fighting. They prefer sniping from windows and throwing tins filled with dynamite. The Arabs were in possession of the three strategic positions which dominate the town : the Teggart Fortress, the Matzuba and the Police Station. They outnumbered the Jews by eight to one. With a minimum of planned coordination they could have stormed the Jewish quarter under covering fire from these three positions. They lacked both this minimum of coordination and the guts to make a direct attack.

The Jewish defence was concentrated round three strong points : old Maiberg's Central Hotel, a building called the Commercial Centre and the Technical School. The latter was destroyed by mortar-fire ; the other two, relatively solid three-storey houses, held out to the end and saved the Jewish quarter.

The fight was full of picturesque episodes. Old Maiberg defended his hotel — kosher kitchen, reasonable prices — with the courage of the lion and the cunning of the serpent, as the Bible has it. The flat roof of the hotel is only about 200 feet below the level of the top of the Matzuba. While the British were still in Safed, old Maiberg had been building, at night, brick-and-mortar pill-boxes on his roof. During the day the British Chief of Police kept discovering the pill-boxes and ordering them to be demolished. Old Maiberg took his pill-boxes down in the afternoon and put them up again at night. At the same time he was engaged in fantastic architectural undertakings. He made a hole in the partition wall to his neighbour's garden, erected a brick structure, rather recalling some public urinals in Paris, round the porch of his next-but-one neighbour, built a tiny bridge connecting the porches of two houses further on, and by similar makeshift devices succeeded in constructing from the Central Hotel to the heart of the Jewish quarter a line of supply protected at every point from the machine-guns of the Police Station. Simul-taneously young Jewish boys built a concrete ditch across the slope half-way up between the Central Hotel and the Matzuba. Officially it was a canal serving some irrigation purpose. In fact it was neither a trench, for it lay parallel to the firing lines of the Police Station, nor a tank trap, for no tank could come down that way from the plateau. It was a trap, for barrels filled with dynamite, which old Maiberg was convinced the Arabs would roll down from the Matzuba at his hotel. He knew Arab tactics and he was not mistaken. The ditch and the sheltered passage saved the Central Hotel.

As for the second Jewish stronghold, the Commercial Centre, its fate was touch and go when the Arabs built a tunnel from a house in their own quarter a hundred yards away, with the intention of coming up under the Commercial Centre and dyna-miting it. The Jews were unaware of these activities, even when the tunnel had progressed to within a few yards of their walls.

Then something happened which scientists would call a statistically improbable event, and the old mystic scholars of Safed call a miracle. A 25-pound shell from a Jewish mortar fell exactly over the extreme point of the tunnel and made the earth cave in. We looked around there and found that on an area of roughly a thousand square yards no other shell had fallen. The event is the more improbable as the shell was a freak shell, the Jews having no interest in shooting at the area immediately adjoining their own stronghold. The most curious fact about the whole thing is that when the Arab tunnel caved in the Jews still noticed nothing, while the Arabs, convinced that the Jews had discovered the tunnel, gave the plan up.

After three weeks of this cloak-and-dynamite warfare, the Jews decided that the time was ripe to strike. They struck on the night of May 8; and on the morning of the 9th Safed was theirs. They struck simultaneously at three points : the Matzuba plateau, the Police Station and a minor Arab stronghold, the Shalba building. The Matzuba they stormed round midnight, having climbed the shrubby slopes under cover of darkness — one of the most obliging aspects of Arab tactics is that they rarely send out observation patrols, and that everybody goes to sleep at night. Having reached a promontory of the plateau unobserved, they opened concentrated fire on the Arab trenches ; the latter were manned by sleeping Iraqi soldiers, who ran away with gluey eyes. They left behind three dead ; the Jews lost one man and had ten slightly wounded. It was not an exaggerated price to pay for the key town of Galilee.

The Police Station was taken by Haganah at about the same time, by the classic method of dynamiting a hole in its wall and smoking out the garrison. We have seen these identically shaped holes in the police stations of Safed, Samakh and Acco. It is an almost monotonously repetitive story, and after a while, looking at these holes, one thinks the whole thing is childishly easy. But never have Arab soldiers, even in the most isolated and strategically impossible Jewish strongholds in Palestine, made a hole in the wall and crept into it with two hand-grenades in their belts and knives in their mouths.

The third Arab stronghold, the Shalba building, was taken by the same method. The Jews gained possession of these three strongholds on the morning of May 9, and by May 10 not a single Arab was left in Safed. They fled as they had fled from

Haifa, Jaffa and other places, leaving their houses, goods and chattels behind, and the last cup of coffee half drunk in the tiny china cup.

But the Teggart Fortress was still in Arab hands, and that was a building into whose walls no holes could be blown. It had become curiously silent from the day after the Matzuba had been taken and the civilian population had run away. The Jews thought this silence was a trick to lure them into a rash attack on the fortress. Two days later some young boys came over from Ein Zeitim. They had heard that Safed had fallen, and came to celebrate. In their innocence they believed that the heroic soldiers of Haganah had taken not only the town but the Fortress too. So they walked up to the heavy concrete gates, and on finding them open strolled into the Fortress yelling " Is anybody there ? " There was nobody. The Iraqi garrison had left discreetly the night before without firing a shot. There is one version according to which the Jews of Safed had spread the rumour that Haganah had succeeded in producing atom bombs — not very big ones, just a kind of pocket atom bomb which did not kill 200,000 people as in Hiroshima, but only 20,000 at best. Young Maiberg denied this story indignantly, obviously thinking that it was beneath the dignity of Haganah warriors to employ such cheap tricks. But in view of the psychological warfare methods employed by Haganah in Haifa, Jaffa and other places, the story seems not unlikely. The more so as all Arab prisoners of war seemed convinced that the Jews had a secret weapon called the " adum ", which makes fire spout out of the earth and houses cave in without visible cause.

This, then, is the story of the fall of the holy town of Safed, fortress in the last war of the Jews in A.D. 70, and a proof, two thousand years later, that " rivers may yet flow uphill ".

Two scenes stand out in my memory of our last hours in Safed, like themes from Moussorgsky's " Pictures in an Exhibition ". One is the bleak interior of a disused garage where two incredibly old Arabs, a man and a woman, sat propped up against the back wall like the limp dolls of a puppet theatre after the show is over. The curtain had fallen and they had been forgotten there, left behind by their families as useless ballast, for Allah to take care of them. Whether they had been sitting there for hours, or days, or weeks nobody knew, and they probably knew less than the others. Their world had caved in, for reasons beyond their comprehension, and they simply remained sitting where somebody had dumped them, without speaking, moving or thinking, in a dim, merciful haze. They might have been mummies thrown out of their tombs by an earthquake; the clay jug of water and the morsels of bread beside them on the concrete floor of the garage might have been left there as their ritual fare for the next world.

The second scene is the interior of the old Synagogue of the Ari where three bearded old Jews were sitting, each in the centre of a hermetically closed world of his own, studying the secrets of the Kabbala. One, very short-sighted, bent so closely over an immense folio of Hebrew script that his tangled beard swept slowly across the yellow page and his avidly moving lips seemed literally to lap up and gulp down the inked words off the parchment. A second was loudly chanting a different text from a different folio to himself, while his body performed a series of jerky bows from the hips each time the sacred words Adonai or Elohim came up. The third was wandering up and down between the empty pews and past the altar, holding his text in front of him; now and then he stopped at a striking or puzzling passage and then his murmur would become a triumphant shout, accompanied by a wild waving of his arms, as the right interpretation of the obscure words occurred to him. Each of the three sages was absorbed in his own holy madness; and as untouched by the unholy madness of the war as the two old Arabs waiting in their garage-crypt for Allah's call.

3

So much, then, for the civil war, which lasted until the real war started with the invasion of the regular Arab armies.

In Galilee the invading armies were those of Syria and the Lebanon, with some scattered Iraqi troops thrown in. The shape of Jewish-held territory may be approximately compared to that of a closed fist with only the index and the little finger stretched out. The closed fist corresponds to the compact Jewish area of the Jezreel Valley between Haifa Bay in the west and the stretch of the Jordan from Beisan to Lake Tiberias in the east. The little finger is the coastal belt from Haifa Bay to the Lebanese frontier which the Jews conquered during the first days of the war. The index finger corresponds to the strip of territory stretching out northward from Lake Tiberias to the sources of the Jordan near Dan,[1] including Safed and a whole cluster of old and new Jewish settlements. It was this valuable strip or finger which the invaders aimed at cutting off from the body of Israel.

In the hill country between the two fingers the situation remained fluid ; no serious fighting occurred here until, between the first and the second truce, Haganah took the offensive, occupied Nazareth and cleared the whole area up to the frontier. The Arab troops in this region were Fawzi Bey's ill-organized bands, reinforced by some Nazi ex-prisoners of war, by Croat Ustachis, British deserters and other mercenary riff-raff collected in Beirut. Apart from ambushing Jewish convoys and looting Arab villages, they never undertook any serious action. The clearing up of this Arab pocket between the two fingers by Haganah was more in the nature of a mopping-up operation than of a military campaign.

Nor did the Lebanese undertake any offensive action along the coast towards Haifa. Both the Lebanese and the Syrian armies' efforts were entirely concentrated against the other " finger " — from Lake Tiberias to the upper reaches of the Jordan. Had they succeeded in cutting through this strip, and linking up with the forces in the pocket in and north of Nazareth, Jewish Galilee would have gone ; and with it the main pride and achievement of Zionist pioneering.

The main attempts to cut through the finger from the east were made by the Syrians at Dagania, south of Lake Tiberias, and at Mishmar Hayarden, south of Lake Hula ; while the Lebanese attacked from the west, a little further up, at Ramat Naphtali. In each case the attack was directed against one of the Jewish frontier settlements mentioned, and was repulsed by the local Haganah corps of the settlers, with little outside help. In those early days of the war, having just emerged from underground illegality, Haganah was not an organized army in the usual sense. It had no regiments, brigades or companies ; its only mobile units, the few thousand men of Palmach, were mainly engaged on the central front round Latrun. Haganah's strength

---

[1] The same place represented the northernmost tip of the ancient Jewish State. There is a story that when, during the Peace Conference after the First World War, Lloyd George and Clémenceau came to the question of the frontiers of Palestine, there was no map handy, so Lloyd George, remembering the biblical phrase, suggested that the frontiers should stretch " from Dan to Beersheba " — and so they did.

and resilience rested entirely on the fact that it was a kind of country-wide home guard with a trained nucleus of men in every village, residential quarter and communal settlement. In particular, the communal settlements, dotted in strategic positions along the frontiers and all over the country, served with their stockades and watch-towers and their local Haganah organization as natural centres of resistance both against the attack of irregulars from inside the country and against invasion from abroad.

Measured by European standards, the Arab Holy War was an operetta war. But there was also an epic quality of courage and self-sacrifice in the defence of the communal settlements with their grotesquely inadequate arms against the invading armies. It may be illustrated by a few typical episodes from the battle for Galilee. I quote from my diary.

Sunday, June 20, Dagania

This is my third visit to Dagania since 1927. This oldest of all collective settlements looks lovelier than ever under its fireworks of scarlet acacias in full flower. To M.'s bitter disappointment old Wabash is no longer alive. While I get to work to piece together the story of the battle with the Syrian tanks, she goes off for a swim in the Jordan — which flows past at a stone's throw from the northern fence, fringed on both banks by silent willows and eucalyptus trees, in a green tunnel of leaves. A hundred yards up the road to the east stands a burnt-out Syrian armoured car, watching her.

The low, whitewashed houses between the red and green acacia trees are spattered with shell-holes; but not a single one is completely destroyed. An amazing number of freak shells seem to have bounced off trees and in and out of dining-room windows and doors. Each of them means a cherished near-escape story to some member of the commune. They were bombarded by artillery and from the air for several days, but nobody was killed. Most of the stuff that fell was 50-pounders, with a few 100-pounders thrown in.

The show began with the evacuation by the British troops of the town of Samakh, a mile or so to the east of Dagania, on the southernmost tip of Lake Tiberias. Samakh, which strategically controls the cluster of Jewish settlements south of the lake, is an Arab town within Israel's U.N.O. boundaries. As in Safed, the

Police Station, key building of the town, was handed over by the departing British to the Arabs. The next day, a commando unit of eleven Haganah men dynamited one of the classic holes in its walls, and smoked the Arab garrison out. As usual, this initial Jewish success was the signal for the exodus of the whole Arab population of the town.

A few days later the Syrian invasion began. Samakh was its first obvious target. After three days of intense shelling by Syrian artillery the Jews had to evacuate it. They also had to give up two communal settlements to the south of Samakh, Massada and Sha'ar Hagolan. The defence of the western shore of Lake Tiberias and of the gates of Galilee now hinged on the twin settlements of Dagania Aleph and Dagania Beit.[1]

After several days of artillery fire and air raids, on May 20th, the Syrian motorized spearhead attacked Dagania. The battle lasted from 4 A.M. to 1 P.M. The Syrians attacked with eight medium Renault tanks, deployed across the fields facing the eastern fence of Dagania Aleph and Beit, and supported by some ten armoured cars. The settlers of Dagania had a few rifles with armour-piercing bullets, some bottles with home-made molotov-cocktails, and a number of sten-guns. These sten-guns, the national weapon of the Israeli Army, were manufactured in secret Haganah factories while Palestine was still under British Mandate. They are useful weapons in street fighting and at short range, but of little use at distances over a hundred yards. Apart from the light arms mentioned, the men and women of Dagania had nothing to fight with — except their determination not to leave at any price. They had dug zig-zag trenches, secured with bags of cement and camouflaged with leaves, behind the outer fence of the settlement, and a second and third network of trenches further back among the acacias and palm trees.

The Syrians advanced in a hesitating, undecided sort of way. They sent out several waves of infantry which, as soon as they came within range of automatic fire, turned tail and swarmed back instead of digging in. A couple of armoured cars supported their flank along the road which skirts the lake; one of them was put on fire by armour-piercing bullets, and was left there burning; the other turned back.

Not till about noon did the eight tanks arrive at the outer fence of the settlement. The first one, on the flank nearest the

[1] Aleph = A, Beit = B.

lake, was incapacitated by a molotov-bottle which hit its caterpillar chain. The third broke through the fence, reached the slit
trench, there seemed to hesitate, then slowly veered south as if to
progress parallel to the trench. At that moment it was hit by
two molotov-bottles, thrown simultaneously from distances of
twenty and ten yards respectively. One was thrown by Shalom
Hochbaum of Katowice, Poland, who arrived two years ago in
Dagania after spending altogether five years in thirteen different
concentration and D.P. camps, including Belsen. The second was
thrown by Yehuda Sprung of Cracow, thirty-eight, wife and two
children, twelve years in Dagania, before that a student of law at
Cracow University. He is a thin, timid little man who looks like
a tailor; Hochbaum a burly youngster who resembles Yehudi
Menuhin. Neither of them had seen a tank before in his life.
M. photographed them both on the turret of " their " tank,
which still stands in the same position as at the moment when
it was hit by the beer-bottles with the inflammable liquid, and
one of its crew of two started to climb out, and was finished
off by a sten-gun. The charred fragments of the other are still
inside.

As soon as tank number three started burning, while number
one milled round itself with its chain gone, the other six tanks,
obviously by wireless order, veered round and trundled back
towards Samakh. Two more of them were put out of action
while turning. The attack was over, and they were never seen
again. A few days later the Jews recaptured the ruins of Samakh
and the two abandoned settlements, Sha'ar Hagolan and Massada.
As far as this front is concerned, the war was over.

It sounds simple enough. But a tank at twenty yards distance,
irresistibly advancing with roaring engines and fire spitting from
its turret, is a very frightening sight even for seasoned troops ;
not to mention men like Hochbaum and Sprung who had never
had any similar experience before. Obviously the loss of four
of his tanks out of eight made the Syrian commander decide that
Dagania was an impregnable fortress, probably defended by
" adums ", and made him renounce any further attempt. The
knocking out of those four tanks out of eight at close quarters, with
primitive home-made explosives and without any battle experience, was precisely the kind of test which decides whether a
nation shall live or die. For this kind of thing did not happen in
Dagania alone — it happened independently and almost simul-

taneously in thirty or forty other settlements, all left to their own devices to stem as best they could the planned deluge. It happened in Ramat Naphtali and Mishmar Hayarden, the vulnerable joints of the finger pointing to the north; in Ein Geb east of Lake Tiberias and in Mishmar Ha'emek on the edge of the Arab triangle; in Hulda and Kiryat Anavim at the approaches to Jerusalem; in Negba and Nirim and the other isolated outposts in the Negeb desert.

The following night we visited Ein Geb, which is an example of a different kind. It stands in a little enclave of Israeli territory on the eastern, Syrian shore of the lake. Strategically its position is no doubt the most impossible among all the isolated settlements. The small collective village of 300 souls is perched on the lake and surrounded in a semicircle by hills which are all in Arab hands. From these hills Syrian artillery bombards them at its ease — as if people in the dress-circle of a theatre threw peanuts on the heads of those sitting beneath them in the stalls. The only protection of the settlers of Ein Geb was to go underground, in the literal sense of the word; and this they did. Working at night only, by the light of pocket-torches or of the moon, they built themselves a complete underground village twelve feet down under the earth, with dormitories, a communal dining-hall, kitchen, infirmary and operating theatre; the whole with a solid ceiling of over three feet of earth and cement.

The only life-line of Ein Geb is across the lake; and because of the Syrian artillery on the hill-balconies, the settlers must fetch their supplies from Tiberias at night with their only remaining motor launch — the other was sunk by a Syrian shell. We boarded the little boat after dark at the famous Lido of Tiberias, and had the treat of an hour's moonlight journey across the Sea of Galilee, with *kibbutzniks* from Ein Geb sprawling all over the deck and singing Hebrew songs. The Syrian guns on the dark hills were silent in temporary observance of the truce; we manœuvred into the tiny harbour, and were led at once into the underground village, blazing with electric light, and unbearably hot in spite of the electric ventilators, which milled in the thick, heavy air like a whisk in steaming porridge. We got out into the only slightly fresher air above ground, and were shown around the defences by whispering guides, bending double whenever we had to cross an open stretch for, truce or no truce, Arab snipers can rarely resist taking a pot-shot at a nice sharp silhouette in the moonlight.

The battle of Ein Geb was on similar lines to the attack on Dagania. During three days, even before the official Holy War had begun, on May 10, 11 and 12, infantry and some light tanks and armoured cars milled round the perimeter of the settlement ; and, after suffering some casualties, withdrew for good. The highlight of the battle was a running fight in the hills between two Syrian units, each of which took the other for Jews. The Jewish casualties were throughout amazingly small : two killed in Dagania, five wounded in Ein Geb. This is part of the general pattern of the War of the Settlements, and a tribute to the efficiency of these small, hard groups of men and women, each endowed, apart from the indispensable amount of courage, with intelligence and initiative for self-protection.

The Haganah commander of Ein Geb seems to have been made in the same workshop and after the same pattern as most of the others we have met : he is a *sabra*, with a pleasant open face and good physique, rather taciturn and suspicious at first, but disarmingly naïve and nice once he loosens up ; his English is good with a specific Israeli-*sabra* accent ; he wears no badges or any insignia of rank, and has no surname, only a first name, which I have forgotten.

Since the beginning of the bombardment Ein Geb lives only at night. The bananas are watered at night, the fishing boats leave after sunset and return before daybreak, the cows are milked at night. They are given no greens, to diminish the volume of their milk and thus shorten milking time. As they can't market their produce, the settlers have never been so well fed as they are now.

The children have been evacuated, but all the women stayed and took the same part in the defence as the men ; there is something of a legend about the " Amazons of Ein Geb ". Outside the settlements, however, girls are now generally withdrawn from the front lines because, as one Haganah officer put it, " When they know that there are girls about, the Arabs suddenly begin to fight like lions ". Many Arab prisoners are found to carry photographs of Jewish girls on them, pilfered in some abandoned house, or taken from the wallet of a dead Haganah man.

We all slept on the lawn in an open square at the centre of the settlement, caressed by the full moon and by wafts of the sweetish smell from the corpses in the fields outside the fence. They have not been burnt yet because of the petrol shortage.

Sha'ar Hagolan

This is one of the few communal settlements which had to be temporarily abandoned to the Arabs; and an example of what might have happened to the rest of Jewish Palestine.

The whole settlement gives the impression of a funeral watch. The houses are burnt out. The cement walls which withstood the flames were smashed in with hammers and crowbars. The water-tower has been dynamited; it lies flat on its side like a dead white elephant. One of the settlers, Roth, had assembled a little museum of neolithic finds; he is digging now, heart-broken, for fragments of his potteries and flints among the charred rubble.

Sha'ar Hagolan had three main sources of income : vineyards, banana plantations, and carp-breeding in artificial ponds. Now the carp are dead, floating with their bellies up, for no fresh water has been let into the pond — the first thing the Arabs did was to blow up the pumping station on the Yarkon river. The banana plantations look like wilted steppe grass; they need watering every ten days, and haven't been watered for over two months. The carp have died of suffocation, the bananas from thirst; the cattle have been slaughtered; the tractors dumped into the ponds. The settlement was founded eleven years ago; now they have to start again from scratch.

This pointless destruction has a particularly depressing effect in this hard and scant country. I have seen the desperate struggle of these pioneer settlements with the arid soil, and known the discussions, the privations, the self-sacrifice that went into buying a bull, or a diesel engine to get electric light. The debris of a water-pump in the desert can be a more heart-breaking sight than a corpse.

Sha'ar Hagolan had been evacuated before the Syrians arrived, so they lost only the product of ten years' labour, and no lives. Other settlements were less lucky; their patrols when captured or ambushed met with an appalling end. Which brings me to that most loathsome chapter in all wars, atrocities and atrocity propaganda. The Jews have Deir Yassin on their hands.[1] They gave the village one hour to evacuate the women and children,

[1] Cf. p. 160.

and when the Arabs refused, the women and children perished
with the men in dynamited houses or by machine-gun fire in the
street fighting. But Deir Yassin owes its notoriety to the fact that
it was an exception ; and at least the Jews committed no individual
acts of sadism. Nor did the Arab Legion, whose British officers
had taught them fair treatment of prisoners of war. But elsewhere
the corpses of Jews who had fallen into Arab hands were often
found castrated and with their eyes gouged out. Israeli com-
muniqués and propaganda were silent about this, for good
reason : atrocity propaganda is only effective when it relates to
events at a safe distance ; otherwise it may spread panic, as Deir
Yassin proves. But before leaving Tel Aviv I had got hold of a
collection of photographs which I had passed on to Alexis Ladas
of the United Nations Commission. They showed grinning men
in Arab uniform posing for the photographer with their bayonets
plunged into stacked heaps of naked mutilated corpses, and the
like. Ladas said that legally they were not evidence ; photographs
of this kind never are. But it is difficult to imagine a troupe of
actors making themselves up to look convincingly like Arabs,
getting hold of a pile of corpses and mutilating them to pose for
the photographer. I mention this subject with reluctance ; to
pass over it in silence would mean minimizing the bravery of
Jews going out on lonely patrols or convoy escorts. For this
sort of thing did not start with the war ; from the days of the
first Jewish settlements, when a Jew was found murdered on the
road he had nearly always been mutilated. Yet I have never heard
the matter publicly discussed among Jews in Palestine.

The fact is that one should not romanticize the gentle savage.
The disarming kindness and hospitality of primitive peoples, and
their more or less idyllic way of life, have led to a general, nostalgic
attitude towards them — which passes in silence over the infantile
sadism which is almost invariably found, not only among primi-
tives in the narrower, anthropological sense, but also among rural
populations in the Balkans or round the Mediterranean.

We needed some fresh air in more than one respect. Sha'ar
Hagolan and the surroundings of Lake Tiberias are still under
sea level ; it is here that the deepest depression on the earth's
surface begins, to reach its lowest point at the Dead Sea, 75 miles
further down the Jordan. I could never decide which is the worst
of the things the settlers here are up against : the heat, the Arabs,

.he mean soil or the mosquitoes and sandflies. No ideal, however stable and profound, can make a European become physically acclimatized to these conditions. Adaptation comes only the natural way, with the second and third generations. And these are physically and mentally quite different types from their forebears in Bialystok or Vienna. Israel to-day is a race in transition.

We got the fresh air as we climbed up, past Lake Hula and the sources of the Jordan, into the foothills of snow-capped Hermon. Hermon is the Fujiyama of Galilee; its white cap pops up unexpectedly in the distance after every turn of the road; its peak unfortunately is across the frontier, in Syria. But Metulla, the Jewish frontier village at the tip of Israel's pointing finger, is not a bad place either. The untidy individualism of this straggling, fifty-year-old village is the exact opposite of the spartan drabness of the collective settlements. The people here are a Hebrew variety of the international species of frontier smugglers. They are mostly sturdy, patriarchal, bearded mountain Jews. One of these, Brenner, is a famous local character, who organized the defence of Metulla when Syria was under the Vichy French, and the British proposed to evacuate the village. He runs, among his other unspecified activities, a kind of café-restaurant, but as privileged visitors we were asked into his private plush parlour, and thus stepped from the Syrian frontier straight into Nalevki, Poland in the early eighteen-fifties. After a lunch of fried eggs and goat's cheese, our party advanced across the frontier into Syria, which begins fifty yards behind Brenner's house, and looked for miles very empty. Perhaps we could have walked straight to Damascus. Most frontiers in dead sectors look the same in a war because there are no customs men about to demonstrate national sovereignty; and the snipers in the inconspicuous farm-houses on both sides of no-man's-land are usually having a siesta.

Ramat Naphtali

This is the uppermost vulnerable joint of the finger; a small communal settlement built around a fortress-like old Arab house on top of a hill, which commands the western approaches to the Jordan Valley.

Apart from intermittent heavy shelling, which lasted for weeks, and forced the 52 settlers of Ramat Naphtali to live all together in the Arab house, the Syrians and Lebanese made two

Q

main attacks, the first supported by six tanks. Besides the inevitable sten-guns, the settlers had only two Hotchkiss machine-guns, one of which was out of order when the tanks came. These Hotchkisses, complete with ammunition, had been captured during a Haganah raid into Vichy Syria. But the cartridge-belts had come from Vichy factories where the French workers were sabotaging production, and every other cartridge was a dud.

At the time the tanks arrived the 52 men and women of Ramat Naphtali had already 15 wounded and 4 dead. That left them with 33 able-bodied defenders in the half-crumbled Arab house which had suffered several direct hits. They saw the tanks slowly creeping up in the distance, in single file on the narrow mountain road from Manara; and then something very Palestinian happened. They heard the hum of a plane — one of the tiny two-seater training planes, a dozen of which constituted at that time the Israeli air force, affectionately known as "primuses" after a popular type of petrol-cookers which are noisy, smelly and frequently explode. The primus circled low over the house, and the settlers could see that it carried a woman passenger. It was, as they later learnt, Lorna Wingate, widow of the "Lawrence of the Hebrews". She waved and then dropped a small parcel. It was a Bible in Hebrew which Wingate had carried on him through the Burma campaign where he had met his death.

The tank battle developed much on the same pattern as in Dagania. Before they could deploy from the narrow dirt-track which is the sole approach to the settlement, the first tank was immobilized by armour-piercing bullets. The others promptly began to back, some by driving in reverse gear, some by turning round. Presently the first tank awoke from its torpor and took its place in the rear of the retreating column. They were never seen again.

After the attack had been repulsed, the settlers sent out a night patrol to reconnoitre. One man was wounded and fell into Arab hands. His body was found the next morning by another patrol, with the eyes gouged out and their orbits filled with his testicles. When he was carried inside the house his wife could not be prevented from looking at the corpse; she committed suicide the same night.

During the next lull, the settlers of Ramat Naphtali were evacuated and Haganah took over the defence of what remained of their stronghold. On June 10, the day before the first truce, the Arabs made their last determined attempt to storm the place. They succeeded in taking an advance position in which twelve Jews were caught and killed. After that the Jews counter-attacked and drove them off. We were led to a pathetically ugly little communal grave with the names of the twelve dead men scribbled over a wooden star of David. It was stuck on a pole into the loose rubble over the grave; and through the loose rubble oozed the sickly-sweet smell which we are beginning to know too well. There are also a number of Arab corpses still about in the fields, unburnt and unburied in the heavy heat.

4

A fortnight before, we had met one of the evacuated settlers of Ramat Naphtali convalescing in the Sanatorium on Mount Carmel. He had told us long stories about the fighting, and particularly about the Arab way of launching an attack, which at the time had sounded like malicious exaggerations, but which now, after this tour of the Galilean battlefield, dovetailed with what we had seen and heard like two pieces in a jigsaw puzzle.

Chain smoking on the Sanatorium terrace, his sensitive, un-soldierly face lit up from time to time by the flame of a match, he had told us how, during the first attacks, they had all been nervous, and had opened fire at 500 yards. Then they had found to their amazement that whenever one of the attackers in the line was hit he threw his arms into the air in a theatrical fashion and yelled "Allah", whereupon the line on his right and left came to a standstill, and, shouting to each other, started running back. Now and then one of their clumsy armoured cars advanced, put itself between the stockade and a wounded man, pulled the latter inside and drove back. This was repeated several times; a hesitant advance, one or two "Allahs", reflux, armoured car acting as an ambulance. The Arabs never tried to dig in at the place to which they had advanced. The defenders, becoming gradually accustomed to these strange methods, let the Arabs come up to within less than 200 yards, and took a heavy toll of them. After a few hours the Lebanese became fed up with the whole thing and vanished from sight.

All this recalled like an echo a number of episodes from the Lawrence-Feisal campaign. As far as I can remember, the number of the Arab casualties suffered in any of those skirmishes against Turkish posts on the Hedjaz railway, which in their ensemble constitute the Revolt in the Desert, never exceeded five. Lawrence had to be careful to avoid casualties, because the sight of a single man wounded or dead would demoralize a whole unit, who would simply shoulder their rifles and ride home on their camels. The Lebanese have little in common with the Bedouin of the Peninsula, except that, like all Arabs, they like their battles noisy but bloodless. On the whole, it is a very sensible attitude. If wars must be, they should at least be bloodless. In this respect the comic opera is certainly preferable to the Greek tragedy.

Of all the Arab armies which invaded Palestine only one was a serious fighting force in the modern sense : the Transjordan Legion. The explanation why this was so is simple : the Legion was trained and led by British officers, equipped with modern British arms, operated by a British staff. It was a small but extremely efficient army — Britain's shining toy in the orient. Had the Lebanese and Syrians been as thoroughly trained, and led by British commanders, there is little doubt that, despite Wingate's bible and the self-sacrifice of the Jewish settlers, Galilee would have been overrun. It was not merely out of resentment or querulousness that Israel raised such a fuss about Glubb Pasha and his Anglo-Hashimite Legion. Had it been withdrawn from the battlefield the war in Palestine would have been over in a week.

5

Even so, the periods of actual fighting between the Security Council's truce gongs were short. The first round lasted less than four weeks : from invasion day on May 15 to the beginning of the first truce on June 11. The second round lasted ten days : from the end of the first truce on July 9 to the beginning of the second truce on July 18. After that there were only some minor, and two major, flare-ups : the campaigns in the Negeb in October and December.

The main events of the first round have already been described : the advance of the Israeli Army along the coast to the Lebanese frontier ; the defeat of the Syro-Lebanese attempts to invade Galilee ; the loss of the Old City of Jerusalem to the Arab Legion ; the stalemate on the central front at Latrun ; the successful defence of the Negeb settlements which the Egyptian columns had bypassed ; and the halting of these columns on the southern outskirts of Jerusalem and on the boundaries of the Jewish coastal belt.

During this first and decisive round, Haganah, which had been transformed overnight from an underground resistance movement into a would-be army and was simultaneously assailed on five fronts, had to rely mainly on psychological bluff and improvisation. The secrecy in which everything concerning the newborn army was shrouded, and which so much exasperated U.N. observers and foreign correspondents, including ourselves, was only partly due to the hangover of conspiratorial habits. The main reason for banning all visits to the so-called fronts was the necessity to hide the Jewish army's weakness, and the fact that in a number of sectors no front line existed at all beyond some scattered observer posts. The real front, it should be emphasized again, was the ensemble of the communal settlements. The rest of the fighting, except in the sector facing Glubb's Legion at Latrun, was improvised guerilla warfare and ingenious bluff.

As a last example, take the story of Sarafand. This huge army camp, with billets for a garrison of 30,000, less than ten miles from Tel Aviv, was to be turned over on evacuation to the Jews by agreement between the British Commander and the Jewish Agency, against a consideration of £600,000. This agreement was overruled by a decision from London. The handing over to the Jews was to take place on May 18; on May 15 the British evacuated the camp, which was immediately occupied by troops of the Arab Legion. The camp was protected all round by extensive minefields; a Haganah communiqué on May 20 alleged that before leaving the British had pointed out to Glubb's forces the only safe passage leading into the camp. However that may be, on invasion day the Arab Legion was in possession of the most important army camp in the immediate vicinity of Tel Aviv. They were ousted from it three days later by a typical romantic stunt of Haganah. A number of their picked men climbed on the night of May 18 into the tall eucalyptus trees surrounding the camp, fixed ropes on high branches, and by means of these swung themselves, Tarzan-like, into the camp. The Legionaries, seized by wild panic, took to their heels. The camp was taken at the price of one Haganah casualty.

Haifa fell to a new version of the trumpets of Jericho; Safed to the spectre of the "adum"; a lone settlement in the Negeb was saved by putting up signs with DANGER—MINES, which persuaded the Egyptians, after one look, quietly to bypass it; Dagania held its ground with molotov-cocktails; Ramat Naphtali with a stuttering Hotchkiss; the defenders of the new city of Jerusalem had four 2-inch mortars which they carted round on trucks from one sector to another. Israel's air force consisted at that time of a dozen " primuses "; its navy of two tiny corvettes and a Police launch; its makeshift armoured cars looked like cardboard stage-props; the only mass-weapon of its infantry were sten-guns — apart from which it started the war with exactly 7000 modern rifles. From whatever angle one looks at it, the all too obvious comparison cannot be avoided : it was David's guile which brought Goliath down.

During the four weeks of truce between the first and second rounds the situation had radically changed. The reasons which made the truce into a farce have been pointed out before; and Israel had no scruples about getting round the arms embargo, which, if taken at the letter, would have reduced her to complete helplessness. Her purchasing agents bought and smuggled arms from wherever they could in Europe and America. The bulk of them came, with Russian blessing, by a regular air-lift from Czechoslovakia; the political implications of this development will be discussed later. The fact is that when the second round started on July 9 the Jews were still inferior in arms to their adversaries; but the margin had been narrowed down considerably and was compensated by their superior initiative and organizing power. In the ten days of renewed fighting they scored decisive successes on the central front by taking Lydda, with Palestine's only large airport, the key town of Ramleh, and a dozen or so strategically important villages, including Ras el Ain, with the pumping station for Jerusalem's water supply. The central plain east of Tel Aviv was cleared, the Arab Legion pushed back into the Samarian hills, its hold on Latrun made extremely precarious; most important of all, a new highway from Tel Aviv to Jerusalem had been opened. Simultaneously in the north Nazareth was taken, almost without resistance; the mopping up of the remaining Arab forces in the pocket between the two fingers in Galilee was completed during the next truce, in inconspicuous brackets so to speak. Israel's new air force retaliated against Arab air raids on Tel Aviv by bombing Damascus, Cairo, Amman and the Egyptian base at El Arish. It was a clear all-round victory to the new State.

During these crucial days the Arab Legion was conspicuously restrained in its actions. The area round Lydda and Ramleh was yielded with little fight; it became increasingly evident that Abdullah, having achieved his limited objectives with the occupation of the Arab parts of Palestine, was no longer interested in the war. The total strength of the Legion amounted to only about 14,000; it had already suffered considerable losses; if after the impending break-up of the Arab League Abdullah was to establish his hegemony in the Levant and annex Arab Palestine in the teeth of the furious opposition of his neighbours, the Legion must be preserved intact and suffer no further losses.

When the second truce started, the Arab League no longer existed except on paper. Not only Transjordan, but also Syria, the Lebanon and Iraq had in fact pulled out of the war, in spite of all declamations to the contrary — which became the more flamboyant the less they were backed up by acts. During the two short and spectacular Israeli campaigns in the south, which flung the Egyptians out of Palestine territory except for a few isolated pockets, the other Arab States watched with folded hands and hardly disguised glee the rout of their Egyptian ally.

6

In altogether thirty-seven days of officially legalized warfare the Jews fought for their independence and won it. For the first time since Bar Kochba's revolt against the Romans they were not passive victims, but active promoters of history.

There are few legends which appeal more profoundly to human imagination than the story of David's accepting the challenge of Goliath and triumphing over him. Yet from the close view of the eye-witnesses it must have been a rather grotesque scene when the nimble little Semitic tribesman pirouetted round the half-idiotic giant, victim of his pituitary glands, and, amid the jeers and cheers of the bystanders, knocked the poor brute out with a jagged stone from his sling. Historic justice, we said earlier, is a function of Time and the scale of Values applied; historic grandeur is an equally relative concept, dependent on distance and the angle of perspective. It is accordingly pointless to ask whether this was a grandiose or a puerile war, a drama or a comedy. It was, like all historic events, both; and which side of the picture is put more into relief depends entirely on the observer's system of reference.

To the distant reader of the tabloid Press at his breakfast table it looked as if history had at last met Metro-Goldwyn-Mayer's most ambitious dream by matching the Sons of the Desert in a Holy War against the resurrected Maccabeans.   As a close shot, to keep to the cameraman's language, it turned out to be a phoney war of small and hopelessly inefficient bands of Levantine mercenaries skirmishing against improvised Jewish home-guard units, with a great amount of bragging and bombast on both sides.   But finally, when one got even closer, and the scene dissolved into a slow-motion view of a microscopic landscape, there remained a few hundred people like Yehuda Sprung, settler in Dagania, wife and two children, who, when for the first time in his life he saw a real tank in action, did not run away but threw a bottle at it from ten yards; and thus, in a half-dazed state, crossed the equinoxial line which divides the trivial from the historic plane.   The Punch and Judy scene between the shepherd and the giant; the defence of Ramat Naphtali; and the forlorn wanderings of Stendhal's young Fabrice across the vast, absurd muddle which he later learnt was the Battle of Waterloo, are all located on this invisible dividing line.   The contrast between the tiny scale of the events described here, and their global resonance, underlines the general ambiguity of all historic episodes in their transition from the trivial familiarity of the Present to the heroic perspective of the Past.

III

THE SIEGE OF JERUSALEM

WHEN the British evacuated Jerusalem on May 14 it had already been cut off from the rest of Jewish Palestine for several weeks. It remained a besieged city until June 9, when the Israeli Army succeeded in completing a new stretch of highway, bypassing the Arab positions at Latrun — the famous " Burma Road "

The Old City of Jerusalem, surrounded by a massive wall built in the sixteenth century by Suleiman the Magnificent on antique foundations, occupies a relatively small area in the north-eastern corner of the town. It has a Moslem quarter, a Christian quarter, a Jewish quarter and an Armenian quarter. The Jewish quarter, more a ghetto than a residential district, was from the beginning of the civil war virtually cut off from the modern town. The modern town has a population of roughly 100,000 Jews and 70,000 Arabs. By and large the Arabs are concentrated in the older quarters to the north-west, adjacent to the Old City, while the modern Jewish residential quarters have spread out mainly to the south.

Immediately after the British evacuation, on May 14 and 15, Haganah occupied all the strategic centres in the modern town, including the Arab quarters Musrara and Sheikh Jarrah. Only the Old City, excluding its Jewish ghetto, remained in Arab hands.

During those two decisive days, when the Arabs fled in panic as they had done in Haifa, Jaffa and Safed, Haganah could probably have broken into the Old City and completed the conquest of the capital. This would have meant employing the same methods which they had used in the Arab quarters of the other towns : the ruthless dynamiting of block after block in the rabbit-warren of bazaars and blind alleys, until the panic had reached sufficient dimensions to end all resistance. But that warren contains the Holy Sepulchre, the street named Via Dolorosa, and a number of other monuments of doubtful historic authenticity and aesthetic merit, but of great symbolic value to the Christian world. Curiously enough, had Israel decided to take that course, the Moslem sanctuaries would hardly have been in danger, as both the Dome of the Rock and the El Aqsa Mosque form a separate enclave walled off against the Old City proper. It was more than anything else the reluctance to damage the Christian Holy Places, and to bear the onus of having done this, which restrained the Jews from attempting to storm the Old City, and made them forsake their chance of gaining complete control of the capital.

Three days later that chance no longer existed. On May 18 an armoured column of the Arab Legion reached Jerusalem from the north. It was commanded by Brigadier Leash, a former British Police officer in Palestine. During the next ten days the Christian commanders of the Legion did unto the Jews precisely what the Jews had refrained from doing unto them : they bombarded the Jewish quarter in the Old City to smithereens and dynamited its Holy of Holies, the Hurva Synagogue.

On May 28 the surviving defenders of the ghetto surrendered to the Legion — which had by now established its batteries of 100-pounders in the midst of the hallowed sanctuaries of the Christian world, and had begun to bombard at its ease the Jewish quarters in modern Jerusalem. The bombardment continued during the whole siege of the city. The Vatican, which had so emphatically insisted on the internationalization of the Holy Places, raised no objection to their use as an artillery base. The other Churches were equally silent.

A little less than a week after the British evacuation, and just after Glubb's panzers had begun the shelling of the Jewish quarter, a high official of the Israeli Foreign Office, stuck in beleaguered Jerusalem, jotted down his impressions for the benefit of his colleagues in distant Tel Aviv. He was good enough to allow me to publish this document, though without mentioning his name.[1]

REPORT FROM JERUSALEM

Not for publication

19th May, 1948

" Six days ago the British were still a factor in Jerusalem. Fox-Strangways was still on the phone, soldiers were guarding

[1] The Consular Truce Commission referred to in these notes was one of the diplomatic improvisations of Lake Success. As this Commission never produced any results whatsoever, mention of it has so far been charitably omitted from this chronicle.

the security zones. On May 14th all the British pulled out, and since then they have been dead. They no longer exist even as a concept, and it requires an effort of the imagination to convince oneself that there was ever such a thing as a Mandatory Government. It was impossible to foresee that such a complete change could come about overnight.

" Two hours after the British left, we drove from the Jewish Agency to the French Consulate through King George Avenue, Wauchope Street and Julian's Way. Heavy firing had already started, and bullets were flying across King George Avenue. But this made less of an impression than the utter emptiness of the whole area. Haganah men had taken the place of the Warwickshires at the entrance to Zone B, but apart from them there was not a living soul in sight the whole way. The entrance to the zone in Julian's Way was completely deserted, and a glance down to Mamillah Road and the foot of Princess Mary Avenue revealed nothing. The King David compound looked like a desert. All the barbed wire was still in place, but nothing looks as dead as barbed wire that no longer serves any purpose. We were in a no-man's-land. The British had gone, and there was nothing except the Red Cross sign on the Y.M.C.A. peri-meter to show that anyone was taking their place.

" The atmosphere at the French Consulate was nervous and tense. The Truce Commission was in session. The presence of a Belgian, a Frenchman, an American, a Norwegian and a Spaniard symbolized the United Nations. Every few minutes the telephone rang — to pass some piece of news, to tell the Belgian consul about the fate of his wounded driver, to bring messages from the Arabs, to announce that the Polish consul had disappeared. But it was not only this that made the quiet conduct of negotiations impossible. Bullets were whizzing past or hitting the building all the time. Suddenly a Red Cross man came in panting with the latest news from Kfar Etzion. Repeated efforts were made to arrange a cease-fire for the Arab representatives, who claimed they were unable to reach the Consulate because of the heavy fighting. Meanwhile an aged manservant went round offering arak. The Belgian consul kept twittering, the Frenchman jumping up and down nervily. The American looked solemn, representing the majesty of his government rather than the United Nations, while the Spaniard maintained a posture of prayer and contemplation. When accusations of bad faith started flying like bullets, while it was clear that nothing effective was being done, there was nothing for it but to go. It was like a nightmare, and the drive back was not much better.

" The French Consulate, in an exposed position overlooking Jaffa Gate and Mount Zion, is not the best possible venue for truce negotiations. There are something like fifty people permanently on the premises, including the consul's six children, whose presence in this danger zone adds to their father's nervousness. The Consulate is without electricity, without water or wine, without bread, and now also without a telephone. As its radio installation is out of order as well, it is almost completely cut off from the outside world. The only carrier of food and news is a Jewish member of the consular staff who sallies forth at times like the dove from Noah's ark. The consul, incidentally, has reverted to a practice of Turkish times by starting his own postal service. Quai d'Orsay revenue stamps have been overprinted ' Postes françaises. 20 millièmes ', and there is a special Jerusalem postmark.

" The work of the Truce Commission has been made difficult by a number of circumstances. The Arabs have been reluctant to meet them, and have found all sorts of excuses for putting them off. There is considerable rivalry and ill-feeling between the Commission and the Red Cross, which has proposals and ambitions of its own. On the Commission itself there is something of a split between the American and the other two members. At least as long as the British were here, the American was much closer to their point of view than his two colleagues. To add to the Commission's difficulties, communications between them and Lake Success are rather precarious, depending as they do on the vagaries of the American consul's radio teletype. In consequence partly of these difficulties, but mostly of the difficulties inherent in the situation itself, the Truce Commission has so far achieved nothing. It is true, however, at least of the French and Belgian members, and certainly of the Spanish and Norwegian members of the U.N. staff, that they would be happy to achieve something if they only knew how.

" Morale among the Jews of Jerusalem has not been good. They have been in heaven one day, and down in the dumps the next. This perpetual see-saw is a constant strain on their nerves. The lack of electricity in the city makes it practically impossible to listen to the wireless, and very difficult to print newspapers. The consequent dearth of reliable information breeds rumour — and rumour, as Virgil said, is the swiftest of all evils. It does not matter whether a rumour is good or bad ; there are always plenty of mouths to repeat it, and plenty of ears to listen. The fear of the unknown is also a powerful factor in depressing morale. Only a small number of Jerusalemites knows the effect of artillery shelling, or what a tank is and can do. The Arab Legion has become such a legend, partly owing to our own propaganda against it, that its very name installs fear even among people who ought to know better. But above all it is the consciousness of being cut off from the rest of Jewish Palestine that has a wearing effect on people's nerves. If only they could listen-in to Tel Aviv Radio, or if a few Jewish planes appeared overhead, they would not feel so lonely. As things are, even the leaders of the community do not do enough to set a good example.

" The Jewish civilian authorities have, on the whole, solved distribution problems fairly well. Fair rations are issued to all through the shops, while water is brought to the people's houses. There is a good deal of queue-ing, which in the hot weather and under fire makes the housewife's lot a hard one, and doubt-less some of it could be avoided with better organization. People grumble — but this is inevitable under the circum-stances, and anyway their inalienable right. But they are appreciative of the fact that basic needs are still met : there is no real shortage of bread, and of water I have already written. In fact, if it were not for the shelling and the lack of news and one or two other things, people would probably be fairly happy. When it comes to a really stiff test, they are likely to show more guts than most observers would give them credit for.

" The shelling of Jerusalem, which has gone on pretty constantly for several days, seems to have no purpose except to wear down the nerves of the civilian population. It does not draw off soldiers from street fighting or guard duties, and its damage to buildings is relatively slight. People are getting used to being shelled, but they undoubtedly suffer through loss of their night's sleep, which is bad for the temper and reduces efficiency.

" Communications between Jerusalem and the outside world are bad. There are a few Jewish radio transmitters working, but all efforts have so far failed to provide a transmitter for press purposes. Newspaper correspondents have to rely either on the irregular and unpredictable aeroplane service, or on the radio facilities provided by the American and British consulates. As a result, the Jerusalem story has not been adequately told in the world's press for the past week. Correspondents, moreover, find it difficult to move about ; a group of British correspondents have shut themselves up in St. George's Close, where they obtain no first-hand news of any kind. The suspension of communications of a more personal kind has also been badly felt. It is now nearly three weeks since postal services broke down, and the new Jewish post office has not yet succeeded in forwarding letters in bulk to addresses outside Jerusalem. Most families have not heard from their relatives in other parts of Palestine for a long time; this in a time of general strain, and particularly of worry about sons and daughters who are away fighting, has been a real trial for thousands. Never was the importance of orderly communications more clearly shown than in the phase through which Jerusalem is at present passing.

" The consular corps has been having a trying time. Consuls are no longer accredited to anybody, their exequaturs are not valid; they are living in a vacuum, obsessed with the same worries about food and water and personal safety that afflict the general population. In their plight the telephone is their only weapon and comfort, and they keep ringing each other up to learn the latest news. The Polish consul recently spent four hours in a ditch under Arab fire, until the Haganah came to rescue him. The British consul, soon to be British Political Representative, is the latest addition to their ranks. He has installed himself in a building at the Damascus Gate, effectively inaccessible from the Jewish quarters. His staff are largely recruited from among members of the former Palestine Government, and something of that Government's tone has been noticeable in their communications to the Jewish Agency. . . ."

For three weeks after this report was written the hundred thousand Jews of Jerusalem remained cut off from the world, and under constant shell-fire from the Old City; the average number of casualties in the civilian population was twenty a day. My first opportunity to get into Jerusalem came by a lucky chance just before we set out for Galilee. I quote from my diary.

Monday, June 14

This morning I went shopping, and on the way back to the hotel ran into Alexis of the U.N. Commission, who was just going to inspect the famous new road to Jerusalem. I got into his car with the blue-and-white U.N.O. pennant, which from a distance looks like the Zionist flag.

This new life-line to Jerusalem is the biggest sensation of the war. It is called the Burma Road of Israel, was built in secret, and opened three days ago for military traffic. Haganah have been working on it for about three weeks. It starts at Hulda, which is inside Israel's boundaries and solidly held by the Israeli Army, and joins the old road at Bab el Wad from where onward to Jerusalem it runs through Jewish-controlled territory. The

" Burma Road " is thus a connecting link between the two separate chunks of Jewish Palestine. It was built across Arab territory, and in some stretches at a distance of less than two miles from Arab positions. All work was done at night, in darkness and silence, literally under the nose of the Arab army. Two nights before the truce came into effect the first convoy with supplies reached besieged Jerusalem.

We drove through Rishon le Zion, Ness Ziona and Rehovot — dreary, dusty villages founded in pre-zionist days, which look as if some Jewish suburb in Poland had been flown over on a magic carpet and dumped into the Judaean plain.

At Rehovot we took a secondary road to Hulda, headquarters of the 7th Israeli Brigade, and starting point of the new road. Hulda is one of the collective settlements which suffered most from Arab raids during the 1936–39 riots, and from British raids during the period of the arms search actions.[1] It has been heavily bombarded by the Egyptians; the Children's House was destroyed by a direct hit a few hours after the children had been evacuated; the pride of the settlement, its imported pedigree cattle, were nearly all killed. There are some Communes in Palestine which seem to have been visited by all the afflictions of Job; usually these produce the most lively characters and the friendliest atmosphere. We had lunch in the communal dining hall, now transformed into an officers' mess, with the Brigadier, Rabinowitch, who was Shertok's military adviser at Lake Success, and Major Peter Wolf from London, who formerly served with the British forces in Palestine. When he was demobilized he said to his commanding officer : " Now my second war starts." " Whom are you going to fight now ? " asked the Colonel. " You," said Wolf, " with the Jewish army."

After a very frugal lunch we left our posh U.N.O. car behind and crowded into a jeep to negotiate the new road, with Peter Wolf in charge and an army driver at the wheel. This driver turned out to be a Hungarian, by name of Berger, who had once been goal-keeper of the champion football team " Hungaria ". Before the war he was a driver with a bus company which ran a passenger service across the Negeb desert, while on Shabbath he kept goal for the Maccabi in Tel Aviv. As we drove in a cloud of dust along the rough track of the Burma Road he described to me in Hungarian how it had been built :

[1] Cf. pp. 71, 87.

" We couldn't use any light except electric pocket-torches, and couldn't use drills or bulldozers, otherwise the Arabs over there would have found out what was going on." (" Over there " was a ridge less than two miles away overlooking the valley through which we were driving.) " The boys had to tear the rock apart with their finger-nails. The only tools they were allowed to use were small chisels and wooden mallets to split cracks into the rock. Then there was the question of the dust, which shows in moonlight like a white cloud in the desert. We were very short of oil, but we had to pour gallons of it over the road to make the dust settle. One day an Arab patrol turned up in the wadi which was on the projected track of the new road. The boys went out in three jeeps to chase them away. Only one jeep came back. But no more Arabs were seen in the wadi."

The road became worse; in fact it could hardly be called a road at all. We bumped up and down slopes and wadis, the jeep swaying like a camel and sometimes leaning over at forty-five degrees. Then we came to the critical patch, about which we had been warned beforehand, a very steep incline of sand and loose rocks about a hundred yards long. It was only negotiable downhill in the direction of Jerusalem; on the return journey trucks, cars and even jeeps had to be pulled up the slope on ropes by a giant caterpillar bulldozer. As we went down the slope we were very nearly overturned, and Alexis performed an acrobatic jump out of the jeep and down the slope into a shrub of camel-thistles. This we found the more damaging to the prestige of U.N.O. as the rest of us, ensconced in the back of the jeep, were unable to extricate ourselves. In the opposite direction an enormous bus was being hoisted up the slope by the bulldozer. It was a fantastic sight. The front wheels of the bus were in the air, and the bulldozer looked like a giant terrier shaking and dragging along a giant rat by its teeth.

On the other side of this wadi the road improved. About two miles away we could see the monastery and police station of Latrun; the Arabs holding it were no doubt watching us through glasses and grinding their teeth. They couldn't shoot at us because of the truce; and if hostilities are resumed, Arab artillery may theoretically dominate the road, but to hit a moving target at night will still remain difficult for them.

We rejoined the old Tel Aviv–Jerusalem road at Bab el Wad. As only fifteen miles of excellent road lay between us and Jerusalem, we decided to let permits look after themselves and to drive on into the city. The number of civilians who had, by one means or another, got into Jerusalem since the beginning of the war could be counted on one's fingers.

In less than twenty minutes we passed the last check-post before the city, and after an absence of four years I saw my beloved Jerusalem again. We drove in through Jaffa Road, past the familiar landmarks : the ruins of the modern blocks in Ben Yehuda Street which British Mosleyites blew up in 1947 ; the wing chipped off the King David Hotel which the Jews blew up in 1946 ; and so on. That is the kind of landmark which gives the atmosphere of modern Jerusalem ; the Old City in its immortal glory and beauty we were not allowed to see. Incidentally this is the first time since the destruction of the Temple that Jews have been prevented from worshipping at the giant stones of the Wailing Wall, last relic of Israel's ancient statehood.

Through devious routes, bye-passing road blocks and miles of barbed wire which have turned Jerusalem into a new version of the labyrinth of Minos, we reached the Y.M.C.A. building, now the seat of the extra-territorial Red Cross mission. There we left Alexis to see his U.N.O. colleagues, and drove on to the house of Gershon Agronsky, editor of the *Palestine Post*. His wife Ethel gave us tea, one cup *per capita* — the Arabs have cut Jerusalem's water supply, and the ration per head per day is two gallons for all purposes — washing, cooking, drinking, laundry, and everything else. Normally at this time of year the Jewish Jerusalemite takes half a dozen showers a day and drinks at least a gallon of tea and lemonade.

We apologized for not having brought any supplies, as our visit was improvised, and asked what we should bring next time. Ethel said a lemon and a carrot ; Gershon said cigarettes. They were hungry for food, hungrier for cigarettes, and hungriest for news. As so often under abnormal conditions of life, psychological needs seem to reverse the hierarchy of physiological needs.

Jerusalem has had for weeks no mail and no newspapers from outside. When there is enough fuel to run the printing press, Agronsky turns out a single sheet edition of the *Palestine Post* based on monitored radio news and short-wave messages from Tel Aviv. But there is always room for the famous " Column One — by David Courtney ", *alias* Roy Elston. Elston turned up while we were having tea ; he is Reuter's former Jerusalem

R

correspondent, who gave up his job and was ostracized by the English colony for throwing in his lot with the Jews and attacking British policy in his brilliant leaders in the *Post*. Their pathos and invective is in the direct line of the great tradition of English pamphleteers, from Swift through Lamb to the early Michael Foot; coming from an English gentile they had a considerable effect in keeping up Jewish morale during the critical days. Meeting Elston again after three years, it struck me that he looks the typical Englishman turned native — he is sunburnt, happy, and beginning to develop a distinctly semitic look. While we were talking, Alexis came in slightly shaken: on his way from the Y.M.C.A. to the French Consulate he had been shot at and narrowly missed by an Arab sniper from the Old City. If this isn't a breach of the truce, I don't know what is; but we had to promise that the story would be off the record. Half of what goes on concerning this country is off the record anyway: the British arms deliveries to the Arabs and the desperate efforts of British diplomacy to keep them from collapsing and the war going; the Czech and French arms deliveries to the Jews; the tug of war between the White House and the State Department which causes a continuous series of earthquakes and eruptions in American policy; the fatuous pretence of the United Nations who know that the truce is broken every day in every way by all parties directly and indirectly concerned. The Holy Land is becoming a kind of ethical atom-pile whose poisoned radiations are spreading in all directions over the world.

Almost every single house in the Jewish residential quarters of the new city bears some mark of the Legion's shellfire. The Agronskys have worked out that, measured by the scale of the population of London, Jerusalem has had 2000 killed and 10,000 injured per week since the siege began. When the fighting started Haganah had only four two-inch mortars, and they used the old trick of carting them about all over the city to give the impression that they had more. One Haganah officer said with a melancholy grin: " King Abdullah once boasted that for every shell the Jews fired, the Arabs fired ten. I wish that were true ! "

On the way back we gave a lift to a Palmach girl who turned out to be the daughter of my old friend Ludwig Blum, the Jerusalem landscape painter. What a small country; I seem to know every other face in the streets. Blum is all right except for a hole in the ceiling of his studio made by a grenade which destroyed ten of his pictures. But as it never rains in Jerusalem before the end of October, the hole doesn't bother him.

On second thoughts, what I have said about knowing every other person in the street used to be true, but no longer is. Now that young soldiers dominate the life of the town the whole character of the population seems to have changed. Particularly striking is the high number of dark-skinned young men of oriental type — Sephardis and Yemenites — who, before the war, lived mostly in the poorer quarters. Many of them belong to the formerly terrorist groups, Irgun and Stern, whose cadres are now being gradually integrated into Haganah. But the trouble is that Irgun and the Stern Group have so far only accepted subordination to Government and Army in the territory of Israel proper — in other words inside the boundaries drawn up by U.N.O. — and Jerusalem, which in theory is going to be internationalized, is outside those boundaries. Hence the Irgun and Stern Group claim autonomy for their units here, which leads to permanent friction between them and Haganah. On the surface this may seem merely an internal squabble, but the matter is more serious : for the two extremist groups will never agree to renounce Jerusalem, and in this respect the majority of the population is on their side. The Government will either have to withdraw its original assent to the internationalization of the capital and claim at least the new town for Israel,[1] or the old prophecy will come true and, having forsaken Jerusalem, her right hand will forget its cunning.

There is little doubt that they will choose the first course and in one form or another annex modern Jerusalem ; and then international quarrelling, haggling and mediation will start all over again. No other town has caused such continuous waves of killing, rape and unholy misery over the centuries as this Holy City.

For those, however, who are inside it,' matters appear much simpler ; constantly exposed to its radiations, they live in holy blindness. There is an old Jewish legend : when, after their long siege, the Legions of Titus put fire to the Temple, the Priests threw the keys of Jerusalem high into the air and cried to God : " Stretch out Thy hand, for Thou art now the guardian of these keys ". And in the midst of the flames a hand was seen reaching down from the sky ; its fingers closed over the keys and

[1] This the Israeli Government did a few weeks later.

took them. On May 20, 1948, when the Arab Legion began its attack on the Jews in the Old City, among the many rumours of war there was one passed on among the old men, from bearded mouth to side-locked ear : the ancient keys of the City gates had been found by the Commander of Haganah, in the courtyard of the Hurva Synagogue. Thus the Lord, having sulked with the Jews since A.D. 71, had at last given Jerusalem back to them.

The young in Israel, whether marxist, democrat or chauvinist, are spiritually nourished from the same source of faith. Faith of this type can not only move mountains but at times become a stronger political factor than oilfields; and speak in a stronger voice than materialist dialectics.

IV

THE END OF TERRORISM AND THE
CONSOLIDATION OF STATE AUTHORITY

DURING the last years of the British Mandate and the first months in the life of Israel, the rivalry between the two main resistance movements, Haganah and Irgun, seemed not only to endanger the consolidation of authority in the young State, but also to threaten eventual civil war.

This tension reached its climax in the tragedy of the *Altalena* during the last week of June 1948. The episode is recorded here in some detail because it is the closing chapter in the history of Irgun, and in fact of the whole Jewish terrorist movement. It was the most painful and violent shock to the sensitive structure of the new State, and the crucial test of its political maturity. Whatever the rights or wrongs of the case, the test ended in the voluntary self-liquidation of the terrorist dissidents and the decisive consolidation of the Government's authority.

The *Altalena*, a cargo boat of 5500 tons, carrying 900 Jewish war volunteers and a considerable quantity of arms, had been purchased and equipped by the Irgun Z'vai Leumi. " Altalena " was the pseudonym under which Vladimir Jabotinsky [1] wrote his literary works; the ship's name was a homage to his memory. She sailed from Port de Bouc near Marseilles on June 11, the day the first truce came into effect.

While she slowly made her way across the Mediterranean, dodging detection by day and travelling at night, representatives of Irgun and of the Israeli Government pursued arduous negotiations about the disposal of the arms. The Government insisted that all arms should be surrendered to them against financial compensation. The representatives of Irgun insisted that 20 per cent of the arms should go to Jerusalem, and that of the remaining 80 per cent half should be earmarked for the Irgun battalions in the Israeli Army.

It should be explained that shortly before the proclamation

---

[1] See Book Three, Chapter I : *Jabotinsky and the Revisionist Movement.*

of the State, Haganah and Irgun had entered into an agreement which stipulated the dissolution of Irgun as a military organization and the gradual incorporation, within a limited period of time, of Irgun's seven battalions (about 5000 men) under their own officers, into Haganah, the official Army of Israel. At the time of the *Altalena* episode half of these battalions had already been incorporated into Haganah ; but, rightly or wrongly, Irgun complained that their units were being discriminated against in the distribution of arms and equipment. Hence their insistence that 40 per cent of the *Altalena* arms go to these units.

In itself this demand sounds not unreasonable in view of the fact that the arms had been purchased and transported through the efforts of Irgun alone. But from the Government's point of view it implied a challenge to the exclusive authority of State and Army. The very term " dissidents " had originated through Irgun's refusal to accept the authority of the Jewish Agency ; now that the latter had become the legal Government it was intolerable that a group within the State should act as an independent agent for importing arms and make conditions as to their disposal.

Thus the core of the conflict was a matter of prestige between two formerly rival underground movements, an extremist minority and a moderate majority, the latter of which had now attained the dignity of official Government and Army. Formally, Irgun accepted this state of affairs by agreeing to its own dissolution as a military force. But past grievances kept rankling both among the leaders and in the rank and file. The majority of the leaders of Irgun, including Benjamin, the commander of the *Altalena*, had spent years in British prisons and deportation camps as a result of denunciations by the Jewish Agency. They suspected the Government; and the Government suspected that the arms of the Irgun battalions, despite the latter's formal incorporation into Haganah, might one day be turned against them.

In the end the Government agreed to the first of Irgun's demands — 20 per cent of the arms to Jerusalem — but remained adamant on the surrender of the remaining 80 per cent ; and three days before the actual arrival of the ship the negotiations broke down.

The *Altalena* arrived on the morning of Sunday June 20 at the beach of Kfar Vitkin, 20 miles north of Tel Aviv. This beach, with a small natural harbour, fairly well protected against detection by United Nations Truce Observers, had been designated as the place of unloading by the Israeli Government. To avoid detection, the arms and men had of course to be unloaded at night and immediately transported away by a fleet of trucks. When the negotiations were broken off, the Government had warned Irgun that it would not help with the unloading — assuming that Irgun alone would be unable to carry out the difficult job and be forced to accept the Government's terms. Irgun, however, decided to go ahead with the unloading alone.

When the *Altalena* arrived at Kfar Vitkin on Sunday at 5 A.M. it was too late to start unloading her, so she was sent back to cruise during the day on the high seas outside territorial waters. It is characteristic of the atmosphere surrounding this whole extraordinary intrigue, that when Menachem Beigin, Commander-in-Chief of Irgun, telephoned to the Government's liaison officer, David C., and informed him that " the girl " (this was the code name for the *Altalena*) had been sent back to the high seas, the latter replied : " Well done ". Beigin then asked whether the Government would reconsider its decision and help in the un-loading after all ; and the War Office man replied that " Maybe they would send a few trucks ". In fact, however, the Cabinet had by that time made up its mind to force a showdown with Irgun, and the latter, with considerable naïvety, walked into the trap.

The *Altalena* returned to Kfar Vitkin on Sunday evening after dark, and during the night the 900 volunteers and some of the arms were disembarked. The whole population of the village of Kfar Vitkin, which is a Labour Party stronghold, and some units of the Israeli Army, helped in the unloading. The first mate of the ship, Jack B., veteran of the Eighth Army, described to me the next day how " the people in Kfar Vitkin were throwing flowers at us. Schoolboys were wading through the water carrying cases of ammunition over their heads to keep it dry and crying with joy. We felt that the country needed our anti-tank guns and Spandaus as the desert needs water."

However, with the rise of day the men on the beach discovered that they were surrounded by Government troops including armoured cars, artillery, and everything the Israeli Army could muster. At the same time the Government's two corvettes were closing in on the *Altalena* from the sea. These troop movements, and particularly the movement of the corvettes (usually stationed in Tel Aviv harbour), could not fail to attract the attention of the United Nations Observers, and in the morning a United Nations plane circled over Kfar Vitkin : the landing was discovered. There was no longer any point in sending the *Altalena* back to sea.

The events of the rest of the day are a story of confusion and almost hysterical behaviour, both on the Government's and Irgun's side. Some time during the morning the Commander of the Government troops sent a ten-minute ultimatum to Beigin demanding " unconditional surrender ", but Beigin had meanwhile boarded the *Altalena* and the walkie-talkie communication between the boat and the shore had broken down. The mayor of the neighbouring town of Nathanya, Ben Ami, was called in to mediate ; but his car broke down on the way. When at last he arrived in Kfar Vitkin he found, in his own words, representatives of both parties " discussing the pros and cons of Irgun philosophy versus Mapai [1] philosophy ". In between, sporadic bursts of automatic fire were exchanged on the beach, and the first killed and wounded lay on the sands. Then the delegates turned to discussing the ten-minute ultimatum, whose time-limit had already expired by several hours ; and Irgun's Second-in-Command, Meridor, said to the Commander of the Government troops, Dan Epstein, " You can't address us in this language, not even the British dared to do that ; who are you after all, and where were you when our boys were hanged ? "

Ben Ami, who is a jovial, chubby, Palestine-born town mayor, tried to talk some sense into them, and asked to be taken to see Beigin ; but on the way across the armed camps on the beach he " ran into some old friends among the Irgun people, with whom I had been interned in Latrun, so we engaged in reminiscences and some more time was lost ". All of which goes to show that even at this point nobody believed that the Government troops would really open fire.

About noon Ben Ami returned to Nathanya, where he had a meeting with two leading Government representatives, to whom he submitted Irgun's agreement to all arms being deposited in Government armouries " under joint supervision ". Irgun had also agreed that the Government should have the final say about their distribution. (Obviously, once U.N.O. had spotted the arms, they would have to remain in sealed armouries for the duration of the truce ; but the U.N.O. aspect, as will be seen,

[1] Mapai : Hebrew Labour Party.

was the least of the worries of all parties concerned.) The Government representatives, however, declared that they refused any further negotiation with Irgun, and some time in the afternoon they opened fire without further warning on Irgun's men encircled on the beach. These men surrendered the next morning and were allowed to leave, having each been made to sign a somewhat ridiculous undertaking that, if convoked by the authorities, they would present themselves at the place indicated.

Meanwhile the ship itself had sailed in the afternoon from Kfar Vitkin to Tel Aviv with only the crew, some Irgun leaders and a few soldiers still on board. The idea was that, if they beached themselves in Tel Aviv, the whole population of the capital would run to the seashore to unload the arms — some four-fifths of which were still inside her hull. Incidentally the Government's corvettes also ordered her to proceed to Tel Aviv, as the Government hoped to be able to seize her in the harbour.

The ship arrived in Tel Aviv during the night; the captain beached her in the shallows about a hundred yards from the shore, and, by a further coincidence, just in front of the Kaete Dan Hotel, headquarters of the United Nations Truce Mission in Israel. During the whole following day, until about four o'clock in the afternoon, the *Altalena* served as a sitting target for the machine-gun fire, and later the artillery, of the Government troops on the shore — with the whole U.N.O. staff and all the foreign correspondents watching the show from the terraces of the hotels and cafés. At 4 P.M. she was finally set on fire by several direct mortar hits and burned out, with the arms and ammunition still in her hold. The Prime Minister and Minister of War, Ben Gurion, in reporting the events to the State Council, exclaimed: " Blessed be the gun which set the ship on fire — that gun will have its place in Israel's War Museum ".

About forty people had been killed in the fighting on the beaches, on board ship, or while trying to swim ashore.

It is difficult to decide which party had behaved more foolishly during this whole affair : the Government or Irgun. While the ship was still burning in Tel Aviv harbour, I talked in Nathanya, in Ben Ami's house, with some of the volunteers who had arrived on her. One was an attractive dark girl, a student of mathematics and physics at the Sorbonne. She said : " I gave up my studies to defend the Jewish State. I know nothing about political dissensions, and still don't know the difference between Mapai and

Irgun. As we approached the shores we were received by the fire of Jewish guns, and four of us were killed. This ends all hope."

The feelings of the majority of the population were of a similar kind. While Jewish artillery fired shells into the helpless ship, the mayor of Tel Aviv, Israel Rokakh, heading a delegation of the mayors of Petakh Tikwa, Nathanya and Ramat Gan, pleaded with Ben Gurion to order a cease-fire so as to give Rokakh an opportunity to board the ship and persuade the Commander to hoist the white flag. Rokakh almost went down on his knees, pleading for an act of mercy : " After all they are our children ; they bled yesterday in Jaffa and Jerusalem, and they will bleed to-morrow again that we may live ". Ben Gurion refused, under the pretext that he had no power " to interrupt military operations without a Cabinet decision ".

Meanwhile on the beach mass hysteria had reached its peak. Young Irgun boys were running towards Haganah armoured cars tearing their shirts open and yelling " Shoot at me, but let our brothers on the ship live ". One wounded boy with half his head blown off kept running round in circles on the sand like a decapitated chicken. Irgun men ran up to the U.N.O. observers, who were watching the show from the Kaete Dan terrace, as if sitting in the dress circle, and yelled at them, " Come and help us, you bastards, can't you see that people are being murdered here ? " When the ship was already ablaze and the captain was waving a white sheet from the bridge, artillery continued to pump shells into her, while machine-guns fired at people swimming in the sea from a hundred yards' distance. One of the members of the American Hebrew Committee of National Liberation, Samuel Merlin, who had travelled with us from Paris, was on board. He was wounded in one arm ; when he jumped into the water from the burning ship and clung to a rubber dinghy (he can't swim) they went on machine-gunning him and hit him in the leg. Abraham Stavsky, the man who had been accused and acquitted of the murder of Arlosoroff (cf. p. 305) and had successfully run the British blockade thirteen times, was wounded on board and killed by machine-gun bullets while swimming towards the shore. Beigin was the last man to abandon ship.

The ship continued to burn for twenty-four hours, a hundred yards from the shore — with, in her hold, the luggage of the 900 volunteers, and thousands of rifles, bren guns, Spandaus, anti-tank and anti-aircraft weapons. At that time Tel Aviv still had

not a single ack-ack battery. The captain's request to be permitted to board the ship and extinguish the fire with the help of
the Army, was refused by the Government. Nor did the Tel
Aviv fire-brigade turn up.

The night after the tragedy, Foreign Minister Shertok and
Beigin each held a Press conference. Beigin's was timed to start
after Shertok had finished, but Shertok dragged his conference
out to prevent correspondents going to the rival show. The
same night the Government arrested some two hundred and fifty
people in Tel Aviv, in addition to round one hundred soldiers
who had refused to obey the order to fire. The leaders of Irgun
went into hiding, and for a few hours it looked as if civil war were
at hand. That it was avoided was as much due to the good sense
of the Haganah commanders and rank and file, who treated their
Irgun prisoners as comrades, refusing to pay much heed to Ben
Gurion's rantings, as to Menachem Beigin who, still dripping
from the swim, ran to Irgun's broadcasting station and made a
remarkable one-hour speech, full of bitterness, but culminating
in the order not to shoot or return the fire of Government troops.

After a week or so of internal tension, tempers gradually
calmed down. The renewal of the war, a fortnight later, did
the rest. During the second truce, the dissolution of Irgun and
the induction of its members into the Army was completed. It
was a happy ending, quite out of keeping with Jewish history :
the victory of the new type of Israelis grown on Palestine soil
over the obstinate fanaticism of ghetto-bred politicians.

To-day Irgun is a matter of the past ; certain considerations
which previously imposed silence are no longer valid, and the
way is open for a more correct assessment of its part in Palestine
history. In the summer of 1946, when the world gasped with
horror about the blowing up of the King David Hotel, Jewish
Agency spokesmen treated Irgun as Fascist thugs, though in fact
Irgun had acted in agreement with the Agency's own Haganah.
Yet such is the dilemma of truth and propaganda that, at a moment
when the whole future of Jewish Palestine was touch and go, its
friends had no other choice but to keep silent. A half-truth is a
half-lie ; on the other hand, as Pascal says somewhere, " Truth
without charity is an idol which we must neither love nor worship".

In the midst of the mass hysteria which surrounded the
Altalena incident, the same predicament arose. A number of

people knew of the Government's connivance in the breach of the truce which the smuggling-in of arms and men represented, and that the Government's representatives had themselves selected Kfar Vitkin as the landing-place.   But to denounce Israel's Government for the breach of a farcical truce, which left without any control the numerous Arab ports and vast desert areas, while the tiny area of Israel was teeming with United Nations observers, would have meant sacrificing to the idol of truth without charity. So once more Irgun had to act as the whipping-boy, as the irresponsible truce-breaker, discrediting the goody-goody, law-abiding Government.   That the latter wanted to have it both ways is only human in the circumstances ; but the gesture of Pilate has never commanded much sympathy.

It may be added that in his statement on the *Altalena*, Foreign Secretary Shertok repeatedly emphasized that the Government's action was primarily motivated by Irgun's " defiance of State authority ", while the attempted breach of the truce was in the Government's eyes merely " a secondary consideration at best ". It was a curious statement coming from a Foreign Minister ; a more revealing admission of the purely internal nature of the conflict, with U.N.O. as a welcome pretext, could hardly be imagined.

One closing remark about the ethical aspects of Irgun terrorism. I have always held that the dilemma of Ends and Means is the core of the human predicament. As the problem admits of no final solution, each period has to attempt a temporary solution adapted to its own conditions :

" That attempt has to proceed in two steps. The first is to realize with open eyes that a certain admixture of ruthlessness is inseparable from human progress. Without the rebellion of the Barons, there would be no Magna Carta ; without the storming of the Bastille, no proclamation of the Rights of Man. So the more one cherishes ethical values, the more one should beware of crankishness. The trouble with some well-meaning ethical movements is that they have so many sectarians and cranks in their midst. . . .
" But the second and more important step is to realize that the End only justifies the Means within very narrow limits. A surgeon is justified in inflicting pain because the results of the operation are reasonably predictable ; but drastic large-scale operations on the social body involve many unknown

factors, may lead to unpredictable results, and one does not know at what point the surgeon's lancet turns into the butcher's hatchet. Or, to change the metaphor, ruthlessness is like arsenic ; injected in very small doses it is a stimulant to the social body, in large quantities it is deadly poison. And to-day we are all suffering from moral arsenic poisoning." [1]

Judged by these standards, I believe that by and large Irgun Z'vai Leumi's fight for Israel's survival was morally justified. When the obvious fallacies, like the labelling of a national resistance movement as " Fascist " or " Revolutionary " according to taste, are discarded, Irgun appears as an instance of the historically inevitable, violent reaction which oppressive action never fails to beget. Irgun was neither better nor worse than the Irish, Macedonian, Polish, Indian or French resistance movements ; with the exception of two incidents — the hanging of the sergeants and Deir Yassin — their self-imposed system of warnings, and their rejection of indiscriminate murder, make them appear in a rather more favourable light than most of their predecessors in history. They never accepted the tenet that the End justifies all Means, which is the creed of totalitarian movements, and which was adopted by their rivals of the Stern Group. Between the hypocrisies of Haganah for which they often acted as scapegoats, and the savagery of the Sternists, they succeeded to the very end in maintaining a precarious balance sustained by a complex system of moral reasoning, good discipline and a spirit of quixotic chivalry. They were a small group of men, persecuted both by the Mandatory and their own kin ; to revert to the previous metaphor, their ruthlessness was the arsenic injected into Jewry's social body which made it fight — not the deadly poison which convulses the totalitarian State. This difference, though only a matter of gradations, was demonstrated by Irgun's voluntary self-liquidation after the proclamation of the State and its self-transformation into a *bona fide* democratic party, — as opposed to the Stern Group's persistence in terrorism.

It was a remarkable transformation, the more so as the Government and majority parties did nothing to make it easier for Irgun to submit to their rivals and persecutors of yesterday. The leaders of the Provisional Government were wont to answer all criticism with apologetic references to the youth and inexperience

[1] From a talk delivered in a B.B.C. broadcast series, " The Challenge of Our Time ", in May 1947.

of the administration, and its sudden emergence from semi-illegality ; it would have been only logical to extend this plea for indulgence to their opponents who had lived for years not in the Agency's twilight, but in the shadow of the gallows.   It would have been easy for the Prime Minister or one of his colleagues to make a generous gesture — if only in a speech on the lines that both parties had made mistakes in the past, and that the Government, though disapproving of Irgun's methods, appreciated their courage and honoured their dead.   Never has a gesture of this kind, not even in the midst of battle, been made by any of the leaders of Israel.

The reason for all this is again the long historic gap in Israel's political education.   Her leaders are politicians, not statesmen ; how could it be otherwise since they never carried the responsibilities of statehood ?   For a Churchill, rooted in the nineteenth century, it was a natural gesture to call the Opposition into the Government in the nation's emergency ; even de Gaulle, though rooted in the seventeenth, included all parties in his first Government.   They were statesmen who could draw on precedents and echoes from the past.   Israel's new-baked Government had no precedents and no past ; like a young school teacher facing an unruly class, it was beset with inferiority complexes and obsessed with the urge to assert its authority by draconic means.   The *Altalena* was a critical climax, and probably the gravest test for the young State.   That the crisis was overcome, and the country found its way towards the beginnings of a democratic routine, is the ultimate proof of Israel's growing political maturity.

V

PROPHETS AND PHARISEES

TEL AVIV TRIVIA

Monday, June 7

Second day in Tel Aviv. Air raids and truce rumours. Visitors all day : the usual melancholy procession of girl-friends and cronies of twenty years ago. Wanted a time-bridge to re-establish broken contacts. We have a room on the sea with a balcony; when we close the french windows we suffocate in the khamssin, when we open them we are deafened by the roar of the surf and the café orchestra underneath playing alternately " Carmen " and the new patriotic hit, " The Negev ", amplified by loud-speakers straight into the room. Then the telephone, the air-raid sirens, more visitors, and the first sweat stains appearing on the sticky shirt. The endearing madhouse atmosphere of Tel Aviv has got us already.

At the moment it is a mixture of delirious enthusiasm for the infant state (which is just over three weeks old), of bitterness and suspicion. Everybody is sceptical about the prospects of a truce, and its outcome if there is to be one. People here have thirty years' experience of more than a score of enquiry commissions, round table conferences, mediations and broken promises.

Wednesday

At four Alexis Ladas, of the U.N.O. mission, rang up to say that both Jews and Arabs have accepted the truce. At six Shertok gave a press conference at the Scopus. I cabled :

" Moshe Shertok, Foreign Minister of Israel, announced the Jews' unconditional acceptance before a tense audience of correspondents, to the accompaniment of the wailing of an air raid siren. Shertok spoke with affable informality and answered questions for a whole hour. His easy-going manner expressed more than the actual wording of his statement that Israel accepted the truce for diplomatic and not for military reasons."

Friday

First day of the truce.

This morning we watched from the roof of the Gat-Rimmon Bernadotte's shining white aeroplane circle over Tel Aviv like a motorized dove of peace ; only the olive branch was missing.

On the way to the Scopus we ran into Alexis, who told us that the Stern Group had made a statement to an American journalist, to the effect that they were going to bump off U.N.O.'s military Truce Observers. So I rang up Amikam, editor of the Sternist paper *Mivrak*, whom I had known well in 1945 when he had just finished a four years' prison sentence for participating in a bank robbery on behalf of the Group. He promised to meet us in the evening at Kaete Dan's, where he arrived shortly after 10 P.M.

He is an extremely correct, blond young man with exquisite manners ; a little shy, with a warm, open smile. In other words, the typical terrorist according to the Hitchcock convention that a terrorist should look exactly the opposite of what one expects a terrorist to look like. I can't help liking him — until the fanatic kernel pierces through the gentle flesh. The point in making the date with him was to make him meet Alexis privately and thereby to convince him that the U.N. people are quite human.

Alexis Ladas was just the right person for that — he is a young Greek of the dark, Mediterranean type, frequently mistaken for a Jew, with a spontaneous and informal manner. Besides, like Amikam and myself, he has " done time " : as a member of the Greek resistance movement he was captured by the Italians and spent two years in jail under sentence of death and devoured by lice. He turned up shortly after Amikam, and the three of us adjourned to another table in a dark corner of the terrace, where, to break the ice, we began to compare prison experiences and their psychological effect on one. It is amazing how common certain patterns of experience are, regardless of the difference of country and conditions. The convict-orderlies, gaolers, chief wardens and librarians seem to belong to an international race ; it was almost like talking about the Old School. After a while I left them alone at their table, and when, a quarter of an hour later, M. and I joined them again, they were engaged in a heated debate about the correct pronunciation of ancient Greek words, Amikam maintaining that the Greek he had learnt in college in Poland was the real thing, and Alexis' a corruption. Then we returned to prisons, and the feel of being under sentence of death. We had particularly disliked the idea of being fetched at night, and that the next morning the routine in the prison would go on as if one had never existed. In between Alexis managed to say, quite off-hand, " By the way, I hope you aren't going to bump me off " and Amikam just chuckled in a friendly, polite way. However that may be, this morning the Stern Group issued a communiqué disowning yesterday's interview (" irresponsible misrepresentation ", etc. etc.), and denying any threat.

Before all this happened, Shertok came for dinner. He told us a long story about last-minute negotiations with King Abdullah, who was anxious to come to terms with the Jews provided a way could be found to save his face *vis-à-vis* the other Arab princes. Just before the war Goldie Meyerson (now Israeli ambassadress to Moscow) went to Amman disguised as an Arab woman, but found a changed Abdullah — aged, tired, resigned. He made some discreet hints to the effect that the power of decision did not rest entirely with him — referring of course to Glubb — and said with resignation that events must take their course.

Each time I started on the subject of Israel's attitude to Russia, Shertok side-tracked the conversation. I think that neither he nor Ben Gurion realizes the amount of apprehension, even among well-meaning people abroad, that Israel might topple over to the other side. They are so sure of themselves that they think they must be above suspicion, and that every impartial observer must see at once through the slanderous attempts to brand them as bolshies. Above all, they can't afford to antagonize the Russians by any explicit, pro-Western statement, as without Czech arms Israel would be sunk. But the real trouble is, they think that everybody knows their feelings and appreciates their predicament. With all their shrewdness the Jewish politicians suffer from the naïve belief that everybody sees them as they see themselves.

Saturday

Drinks with Alexis, who was very depressed : the first batch of the U.N.O. military Truce Observers has arrived, among them some young and inexperienced American officers. One of these almost wrecked the precarious truce negotiations in Galilee by assembling six Jewish and six Arab officers on a bridge, and asking them in pidgin English : " Who shoot after truce ? — who

S

break truce ? — who shoot, say — eh ? " Naturally both parties started yelling and accusing each other, and had they not both been covered by machine-guns from the other side, they would have started shooting again there and then.

Sunday

Saw two more old friends, Dr. Hahn and Dr. Eppler. Both have typically Palestinian careers : Hahn is an M.D. who graduated at Vienna University and couldn't obtain a licence to practise under the British ; so, being an amateur painter, he opened a workshop for handpainted dolls. Eppler is an Austrian banker who couldn't find a job either ; so, being an amateur conjuror, he made his living as " Dr. Mabuse the King of Magicians " in a borrowed dinner-jacket in a Haifa music-hall. Now Hahn is back at medicine, and Eppler a high civil servant. Another member of our gang at Vienna University was less lucky. A parliamentary stenographer until the Anschluss, he now has to make his living as a night-watchman, — with ulcers.

Monday

The first Egyptian pilot who was forced down in Israeli territory crash-landed somewhere near Rechovot. A buxom Haganah girl from the village happened to be first on the spot and kept watch over him with a sten-gun. To be the prisoner of a woman, and in particular of a Jewish girl, is about the most deadly humiliation for a Moslem. After a while the young pilot started to cry, and exclaimed, throwing his arms into the air : " Allah ! my father told me never to leave Cairo ".

Tuesday

Abram Weinshall and Peter Bergson [1] for lunch.

Abram has started a campaign for introducing the English electoral system to replace the present proportional representation, which is mainly responsible for the ridiculously high number of splinter parties. At the last election to the representative body of the Jews of Palestine, held in 1944, there were round 250,000 votes cast and not less than twenty-five parties competing for them — including a list of " The Young Men from Aden ", the

[1] Founder and Chairman of the Hebrew Committee for National Liberation in the United States.

" Orthodox Female Workers " and the " Maccabi Sports Club ".
The system of voting for party lists instead of individual candidates furthermore leads to the development of powerful Party
Machines and Party Bureaucracies which play a decisive part in
making or breaking the political and professional career of the
Israeli citizen. The famous " party key system " provides for a
proportional distribution not only of the number of parliamentary
seats, but also of the administrative jobs and the share in the
budget allocated to each party. In fact, each political party in
Israel is a kind of limited company, coterie, life insurance and
masonic lodge, all in one. A Revisionist doctor makes his living
on Revisionist patients, goes to Revisionist cafés and frequents
only Revisionist circles. You can live for years in Tel Aviv
knowing hardly anybody outside your own political clique ; and
to be seen frequently with people of different allegiance soon
brings one into an odour of suspicion. One of the most urgent
needs of Israel is a bar like the one in the House of Commons,
where members of different parties can meet over a drink in
between debates and find out that the other chap is human too.
But then, Israelis don't drink ; and if the future Parliament has
a restaurant, each party will be given a separate table — with the
number of chairs carefully calculated according to the party key.
It is all a consequence of the gap in the past : for the next generation or so, Israel will be feverishly busy making up for two thousand
lost years of political life.

The war is producing the beginnings of an Israeli folklore.
The soldiers from the Negev have taken to growing beards and
drooping moustaches ; those from Galilee grow Guardee moustaches turning up at the ends. There is a new Hebrew army
slang developing. The soldiers all wear different types of headgear : Palmach mostly a kind of little boy's sun-hat, with the
brim turned down all round and pulled over the face, which gives
them a rather dumb yokel look ; others wear knitted caps with
pom-poms on top ; others a sort of baseball player's cap with a
long peak ; others motley Army caps which British Quartermaster
Sergeants sold wholesale to Haganah before leaving. Very few
have rifles — Israel's standard small-arm is the sten-gun. None
have kitbags ; when a unit moves, the soldiers' luggage, consisting
mainly of cardboard suitcases, is dumped on a lorry.

The days of British rule — just one month back — have already
become almost legendary, and another kind of folklore is beginning

to grow : stories and legends about the War of Independence.
Example : Jasha's story about a patient of his, a woman of sixty-
five, who escorted her grandson, an Irgunist wanted by the
police, across Tel Aviv to a safe hiding place — walking three
steps behind the unarmed boy with a revolver in her handbag.
A number of these bourgeois Jewish mothers and grandmothers
have done quite astonishing things — like the women in the
French Resistance.

Friday

In the evening we went to the Hebrew Chamber Theatre's
new play on *kibbutz* life, which is outstanding. It tells the story
of the events which led to the death of Uri, a boy born and reared
in the *kibbutz*. It starts with Uri's arrival back in the *kibbutz*
from an agricultural school. He learns that his parents have
divorced — in other words his mother has moved from the room
which she had shared with his father, Willi, to the room of another
man called Abraham. Uri resents this but soon calms down ;
there is no room for Hamlets in a communal settlement. He meets
Mica, a young refugee girl who came to Palestine a short while
ago from Poland via a Russian forced labour camp, and they
become lovers. All is well until Ginger, Uri's friend from the
agricultural school, turns up. Ginger is a commander in Palmach.
Palmach is busy smuggling illegal immigrants into the country
and fighting guerilla actions against British troops intent on
rounding up the immigrants. Ginger asks Uri to join Palmach ;
Uri agrees at once, but would like a few days' delay because on
this very day his affair with Mica is going to be legalised : they
are to move from their respective tents into one double room
which, according to the customs of the settlement, means that
they are considered as married. But Ginger insists that Uri join
the same night ; almost without hesitation Uri agrees. He breaks
the news to Mica ; she implores Uri to spend just one night
in the room designed for their future married life. " But why ? "
asks Uri. " What's the difference ? One night more or less."
And Mica explains the difference. Once they have taken possession of the room, she can't be chased out of it. It will be legally
her room (for only married couples are entitled to a room ; the
young bachelors sleep in tents). And a room is a home ; and a
home is the one thing she has wanted, more bitterly and stubbornly
than anything else in her wretched ten years of refugee life — she

is nineteen. Of course she is fond of Uri; but the centre of the issue, her craving and obsession, is the room.

Uri is twenty; he was born and brought up in this communistic settlement; he is quite incapable of understanding why a girl should want a room. He slaps her on the back and pushes off.

The next time he sees her, on his way to a new assignment, he is just as affable, non-committal and Tarzan-like as before. He doesn't even give Mica a chance to tell him that she is pregnant. He pushes off again.

A Palmach camp in the mountains. A bunch of illegal immigrants have landed at night somewhere on the beach. British troops are trying to intercept them. To prevent this from happening a bridge has to be blown up. Uri, commander of the Palmach unit, accepts without hesitation Simeon's offer to undertake this dangerous job. Simeon is a middle-aged man with several children whose wife is in hospital on the danger list. All this does not move Uri. But when a friend tells him that instead of sending Simeon, Uri should have undertaken to do the job himself, he decides unhesitatingly that this is right. He pushes off to blow up the bridge as phlegmatically as he pushed off to leave Mica in the lurch, and is promptly killed. End of a young Tarzan — callous, gay, unsentimental, matter-of-fact, brave. He is not an attractive hero; but he is the truest symbol of the native generation which Hebrew literature has as yet produced.

Mica is the counterpoint. She is not a native of the country like Uri; she is a refugee, over-sensitive, tragic, sentimental, with a past full to the brim with Things to Forget — among these a sordid abortion which she underwent in a refugee camp in Teheran. She believes herself unworthy to bear the child of Uri the hero, and decides to commit suicide. But the secretary of the *kibbutz*, the ubiquitous Biebermann, explains to her that all her problems are so much hot air, and that all that matters is that she should produce the child, one more citizen of Israel — finis, curtain.

There is a narrator who sums up the deliberately crude moral of a very subtle play in the simplest possible language. The stage decorations are reduced to a Shakespearean minimum; the scenery is changed by stage-hands while the action goes on. The actors were, until a short time ago, amateurs; and some still are.

Thursday

Drinks with Robert Capa, the photographer. He says that nowhere on his travels, from China to Moscow and from India to the U.S.A., has he found such bad public relations as here : " At least the Jews aren't guilty of mere mediocrity ".

Incredible as it sounds, Israel's Government of thirteen Ministers includes neither a Ministry of Information nor a Ministry of Education, although there are separate Ministries of " Religion and War-Victims ", " Social Welfare ", " Police and Minorities ", " Communications ", " Immigration and Health " and so on. The omission of two of the most important ministries is again a consequence of the fatal party key system. Having forgotten in the first instance to envisage a Minister of Information, the Government could not now co-opt one as this would upset the precarious party balance. As for Education, the socialists, the orthodox, and the neither socialist nor orthodox, each run their own schools ; and for the time being it is quite unthinkable that they should accept the authority of one Minister. The curse of the two thousand missed years. . . . A primitive people will start a primitive community and gradually develop its institutions ; but for a community with ripe and over-ripe political philosophies to learn the ABC of nationhood is a different and unique task.

Lunch with Moshe A. from Field Security — a good-looking, young, blond, alert *sabra*. He said that although he was an anti-Communist, the effect of reading *Darkness at Noon* was to make him less so. We had a long discussion on the stereotyped pattern. The psychological clue to A. and his like is that after what Britain has done and is doing to them, they can't help feeling that anything is better than Anglo-Saxon perfidy, and thus a process of wishful thinking sets in concerning Russia which gives an unconscious twist to all facts and arguments. The nearer one is to Scylla the more harmless appears Charybdis.

But there is another aspect to this dreary tragedy. These people are not attracted by Russia, but pushed towards her. At the bottom of their hearts they know quite well what the M.V.D. has in store for them. To fall for the temptation of sirens and mermaids is in the nature of man ; but the urge to sleep with a crocodile out of sheer despair is a privilege of our time. Mr. Bevin as a pin-up girl of Western democracy makes even the crocodile seem to have some sex-appeal.

Saturday

The heat is getting really bad; the row of sea-front cafés under our windows blare tinned music through their loud-speakers all day, and in the evenings one is forced to sit around on café terraces until after midnight because, owing to the black-out, one can only remain indoors with shutters closed and curtains drawn, which means suffocation. The maintenance of the black-out in the second week of the truce is quite silly. The Egyptians have never made a night raid on Tel Aviv even during the war; to start now during the truce, with Bernadotte's staff sitting in the Kaete Dan, would be suicide on their part. The strange thing is that most Tel Avivians agree that the black-out is logically un-warranted, yet do not seem to mind. " It's better to be careful," they all say, " one never knows." Then they go on by explaining that we have no idea of air raids because during the blitz, as everybody knows, all Londoners stayed day and night in deep shelters.

This low morale of the majority of civilians in Tel Aviv con-trasts strikingly with the self-sacrifice of the people in the settle-ments and in the Army. It is much more pronounced than the usual contrast between front line and hinterland in other wars, for here it reflects the gulf between refugees and pioneers, between the older and younger generations. The majority of the people in Tel Aviv today are middle-aged refugees, whose tragic experi-ences have not always made them more pleasant or public-spirited. Israel will only begin to take shape after the disappearance of this lost generation which, like the green slime floating on a pond, blocks the fresh springs of the nation's vitality.

Unfortunately, most foreigners here only come into touch with the negative aspects of this land of contrasts, and form an accordingly one-sided picture. The Truce Observers who have alternative dealings with Jews and Arabs undergo gradually the same process as the British administrators did before them.

Sunday

Dinner with Nicole de R., French newsreel man Decae and a British deserter who has joined the Israeli Army. He is the mercenary-adventurer type who gave so much trouble in Spain. When he got drunk he confided that he was through with the whole thing and so were two of his buddies, only waiting to get together enough money and push off somehow to Cairo, serve their term, and have done with it.

. . . The eternal overlapping of the tragic and the comic. The bank-robber and Alexis arguing about Greek pronunciation was pure comedy; a turn on the switchboard of fate and Alexis might lie somewhere on the pavement of Tel Aviv with a bullet in his stomach, and Amikam run amok with a gun across the streets.

Monday

Visit to Ein Hashofet, a collective settlement which had served as the main model of the fictitious commune in my Palestine novel. We had an icy reception; in the communal Dining Hall all the familiar characters avoided our table. I had thought that in the novel they were rather idealized; now I began to feel like the murderer revisiting the scene of his crime.

It was a rather painful return. But it's all very well for the out-sider to arrogate to himself the part of the judicious observer; if one lives the hard and single-minded life of a collective settle-ment one is bound to become hypersensitive and intolerant of criticism. And that goes for the whole Israeli community. In the struggle for survival objectivity becomes a luxury, and detachment a crime. This antithesis between action and con-templation is one of the insoluble dilemmas. Projected into the writer's sphere it becomes the dilemma between truth and propaganda. . . . Title for a worst-seller:

" The Antinomies of Truth and Propaganda

or

The Art of Sitting between Two Stools in Twelve Painful Lessons "

Back to Haifa in the colourful dusk. At dinner in the Lev Hacarmel Hotel Mr. W., the proprietor, joined us. He has just lost his elder son, killed ten minutes before the truce began in Jerusalem. His younger son, a pharmacist, told us several stories about British intrigues which sounded somewhat unconvincing. But then, if you know that X. is the devil, the harder you try to prove it the more unconvincing you will sound; in the end, to prove the truth you will resort to the lie.

Thursday

The Egyptians have seen the light : hoping that civil war in Israel is imminent, they have refused to let a Jewish supply convoy pass to Negba and have also attacked Colonel Bonde's white U.N.O. plane. Bonde thereupon notified the Israeli Government that Egypt has broken the truce and that Israel is free to act against the Egyptians. But that of course does not mean the lifting of the arms embargo. If, the Egyptians having officially been branded as truce-breakers, the Jews now imported arms, they would in turn be breaking the truce *vis-à-vis* Syria, Transjordan, Iraq and the Lebanon. Even if Syria, for instance, were convicted of importing arms, the Jews could not do the same without being found guilty of breaking the truce towards the other Arab states. Operation Deluge of diplomatic logic.

In fact, of course, the truce is broken by both parties continually ; and the U.N.O. people know it as well as everybody else. The whole thing is even more farcical than the Spanish nonintervention comedy was.

Friday, June 25 (after the Altalena incident)

Yesterday a Palmach unit broke up Irgun's headquarters, smashed the furniture and tore up the files. On Beigin's orders not to shoot at any price, the Irgun boys stood by white-faced and silent, watching the destruction. Outside, the street was lined with Palmach armoured cars ; although the whole Irgun is convinced that Palmach is out for Beigin's head, Beigin insisted on walking past the cars with deliberate slowness. When they got past, a random shot was fired behind them, and B. had to be restrained by Captain Halpern, who was with him, from walking back and starting an argument. Halpern explained to him, not illogically, that if he wanted to commit suicide he should hire the opera hall and invite the world press ; otherwise it would hardly be worth while.

The number of arrested people is two hundred and fifty in Tel Aviv alone, with at least the same number in the rest of the country. Among them Peter Bergson and Meridor (cf. p. 77). Merlin, who was shot in the leg while hanging onto a rubber dinghy, is in hiding. I had a message asking me to visit him — he was lying in bed in a schoolteacher's flat somewhere in underground Israel, reading Eliot's *Four Quartets*. I took down his story and checked it against the other testimonies collected before.

Then an Irgun courier girl took me to another flat, where I saw Menachem Beigin for the first time in my life. I had actually talked to him before, but without seeing him — in a dark room in Tel Aviv in 1945, when he was the man most wanted by the British Police, with £500 on his head. On that occasion we had argued for about an hour in the pitch darkness which Irgun's conspiratorial precautions prescribed. I had tried to convince him that England was one thing, the Palestine Administration another; that with the end of the war the White Paper would be abolished, and that Israel's future was that of a Dominion in the British Commonwealth. Beigin had said in substance that he didn't believe British policy would change, even if Labour came into power; but that even if I were right, his job was to fight the Palestine Government, and that he couldn't get his boys to risk the gallows by telling them that it was all a temporary misunderstanding and the English ultimately very nice people.

Judging by his voice coming across the table in the dark, I had imagined the owner of the voice as a tall, ascetic-looking man with a fanatic expression. Actually he is rather short, thin, frail, very short-sighted, with a gentle, earnest young schoolmaster's face. Obviously voices, like cigarettes and food, change their flavour in the dark. His manner is that kind of self-assured awkwardness which comes to people who, by achievement, have learned to find a *modus vivendi* with their own shyness. He talks as thoughtfully and unfanatically as his propaganda is bombastic and violent; he wears the loose, ill-fitting clothes of a scholar, and has the scholar's dry charm. We got on much better than at the time when he had been the Invisible Man, and I took down his version of the *Altalena* and counter-checked it again. I have got by now some forty pages of notes on it.

Monday

Last night had a long *tête-à-tête* with Jasha. He seemed rather depressed — it is the anti-climax which comes when one has at last achieved something one wanted very badly — in his case the Jewish State. Before, one always lives in the naïve illusion that once the desired aim has been attained, all problems will automatically solve themselves and the golden age begin. It is the same process whatever the object of one's craving — a motor car, a little house with a garden, a visa to America, or National

Independence. It is always the story of running after a girl — and wondering afterwards what all the excitement was about. *Post victoriam omnes cives tristes sunt.* Jasha and all Israel seem to be living through the hangover of the morning after the nuptials.

After we got home, a pathetic little chap representing the non-Zionist, non-Stalinist true socialist party of Israel came to see me with a suggestion that I should help to call an international round-table conference of Jews and Arabs which is to solve the problem on purely marxist lines. He said, personally he didn't know any Arabs who would come to this conference, but I could find some in Cairo or Beirut. Secondly, he wanted me to start a campaign in defence of Israel's two conscientious objectors, who both belong to his party. He then came out, somewhat reluctantly, with the statement that his party was in favour of the war of defence, but refused to fight under the present Government, which did not represent true socialism. Only under a true socialist government were they prepared to join the army. I asked him what he thought would happen in the interval between leaving the country undefended and the advent of the true socialist government. He said " Yes, it is very difficult, but one has to stick to one's principles ". He might as well have said " Fortunately we can preach our gospel, as nobody takes us seriously ". Another symbol of the irresponsibility of leftist sectarianism, of the no-man's-land politicians of the British I.L.P., the American Wallaceites, the French dialecticians around Sartre. Unconsciously they all know that they can afford to save their purist consciences, because when the Arabs or the Nazis or the Russians invade them they will be defended by their less dialectical compatriots.

Sunday

The only oriental colour in this war comes from the monitored reports of the Arab broadcasting stations. Samples : [1]

" While the Jews are busy smuggling arms, the U.N.O. observers are sleeping with the beauties of Israel " (Beirut Radio).

[1] I made a collection of the juiciest bits of these monitored Arab broadcasts which unfortunately went astray. The above samples are odd cuttings in my files, without dates. Some of the most blustering death-to-the-Jews harangues came from the Near East Arabic Radio in British Cyprus, which, according to a statement by Mr. Bevin in the House of Commons, was run by " an independent group of Arabs and Englishmen ".

" Jewish planes continuously fly over the Iraqi positions in Jerusalem and drop poisoned food to the Moslem warriors " (Damascus Radio).

" We Arabs should refuse to accept Jerusalem as a gift from Bernadotte because we should then be under an obligation to the Western nations — we must win Jerusalem with blood and by fire " (Ramallah Radio).

" The Zionists must be wiped off the face of the earth. The Arabs must choose either the unity of Palestine or death " (Near East Arabic Radio, Cyprus).

Friday

News item from *Yediyoth Hadashot* (New News), one of the two daily papers which are published in Hebrew and German for the benefit of recent immigrants :

" Four cakes of so-called Jew-soap, which were manufactured from the corpses of Jews in German extermination camps, were yesterday ritually buried in a corner of the cemetery of Haifa reserved for martyrs. The four cakes of soap, which had recently been found in Germany and brought to Israel, were clad in shrouds and buried in the earth amid prayers."

News item from the *Palestine Post* a few days before :

" As British policemen were evacuated on board the *Empress of Australia*, one party tore the Jewish flag down from the quay and stamped on it."

Saturday

Drinks (lemon squash) with three former terrorist girls of Irgun. One is a rather pretty Polish student type who fought as an officer in the taking of Jaffa ; the second looks like an Ukrainian peasant-girl, the third is a dark Yemenite. They were rather overwhelming, and did not conceal their contempt for any female who had no experience with gelignite and sten-gun. We discussed literature ; the agreed favourites were *The Count of Monte Cristo* and *Treasure Island*. They reminded me somewhat of the Socialist Woman Sniper Ludmilla Pavlichenko, who toured England during the war on a Soviet goodwill mission, explaining to bewildered English housewives how she had shot single-handed 217 German fascist beasts.

Sunday

That Yemenite Irgun girl yesterday kept conspicuously silent in the discussion about literature. Except those born and educated in Israel, most of the Yemenite Jews are illiterate. Even among the second generation the majority are employed on low menial work — as housemaids, night-watchmen, shoeblacks, dustmen. They don't intermarry with " white Jews "; though no legal or social restrictions exist, there is an unavowed colour-bar operating. To a lesser extent this also applies to relations between Sephardi and Ashkenazi Jews. If all goes well, Israel will have within a generation a colour problem on top of all her other problems.

Tuesday

Went to Rehovot to visit the Sieff Research Institute and the new Weizmann Institute for Physics and Physical Biology. They are doing all sorts of top secret scientific war work there, but David Bergmann, warm and simple as always, showed us around without any fuss about secrecy. He has been for many years Weizmann's chief Research Assistant and private secretary; and had, though he never hinted at it, a greater share in Weizmann's chemical discoveries than is publicly known.

The war research which they are doing is ingenious and fascinating, but is still on the secret list. Among the more peaceful developments, Bergmann's pet idea is to plant castor trees all over the Negev, as they grow anywhere and need no looking after. The end products extracted by new methods from the fruit of the tree include nylon which stands boiling without deformation of the fibres, and can be used for anything from women's stockings to mosquito nets. Also they have found a method of detoxicating the protein in the beans. They have a number of ingenious new contraptions for turning salt water into fresh water, which are in use in a number of Negev settlements and Army camps. Among their more distant future projects are thermo-electric units for residential blocks, which make electricity by exploiting the difference in temperature on the roof and in the cellar.

Unfortunately as it isn't the season, couldn't show M. the curious products of the grafting and hybridisation experiments with citrus plants : grapefruit and oranges as big as footballs, pipless giant tangerines and luscious avocado pears — the magic fruit of Canaan.

The Weizmann Institute for Physics has just been completed and is the most modern of its kind anywhere, including America. It will have three departments : physical chemistry, isotope research for biological purposes ; and a department for applied mathematics within the building — an innovation. They are also building an electronic brain.

The research stations in Rehovot are probably the only first-rate thing in this country by international standards. Certainly Israel's future lies in the direction of pioneer industries based on original methods — fermentation, technical crops, artificial plastics and the like modern magic on an industrial scale. This day with Bergmann was a very heart - warming experience. The good, clean academic atmosphere acted like a disinfectant on our politics-infested minds.

Meeting N. in the garden, it occurred to me that all nuclear physicists seem to have the same mannerisms of a carefully culti-vated awkwardness — a graceful gaucherie, and an oblique academic humour of a somewhat surrealistic tang.

Sunday

The truce ended on Friday, the Arabs having refused to agree to its extension. After all their boisterous radio threats most people here thought that this time things would get really tough, and that Israel would be forced into a desperate back-to-the-wall fight. However, the Arab blitz did not materialize and the first three days of the renewed war brought the same small-scale ding-dong fighting as before.

Tuesday

The greatest military event yet in the whole war : the Israeli Army has captured Lydda, Ramleh and a number of Arab villages around. The Arab Legion has pulled out into the Judaean hills round Latrun, but even Latrun is in danger of being out-flanked by the Israelis.

We visited Ramleh a few hours after it was taken. It has not been seriously defended, and after the Legion withdrew the town immediately hoisted the white flag. The Arabs were hanging about in the streets much as usual, except for a few hundred youths of military age who have been put into a barbed wire cage and were taken off in lorries to an internment camp. Their veiled mothers and wives were carrying food and water to the cage, arguing with the Jewish sentries and pulling their sleeves, obviously quite unafraid. A man in European dress, mistaking my correspondent's badge for officer's insignia, introduced himself as a local chemist and asked for permission to re-open his drug-store, which I granted unhesitatingly. Groups of Arabs came marching down the main street with their arms above their heads, grinning broadly, without any guards, to give themselves up. The one prevailing feeling among all seemed to be that as far as Ramleh was concerned the war was over, and thank God for it. I have rarely felt more intensely not the injustice, but the complete unnecessariness of this war.

Thursday

The air raids have started again; on Tuesday there were twenty people killed by several bad hits, but yesterday nobody.

On Tuesday I gave a talk to the Rotary Club about the cultural problems of the future : the task of creating a new style of life adapted to the new environment, avoiding the traps of provincialism, chauvinism, levantinism. The response was frankly hostile, and when I ended with a plea for less Jewish and more European history in the schools and for the latinization of the alphabet, I thought I was going to be stoned with the cream-buns from the buffet. " If he thinks Western culture so wonderful," wrote an evening paper the next day, " what's he doing in Israel ? "

Friday

Last night we went to a party where I talked to a girl who was brought up in the Herzlia Gymnasium, Israel's leading secondary school. She had to learn long passages of the Bible by heart; some of the questions at her closing exam were : " What did God say to Jeremiah ? " " What is written in the Seventeenth Chapter of the First Book of Moses ? " She also had to learn Talmud, but the only thing she could remember about it was " something about the things you have to do and say if you find tomatoes fallen from a cart in the street ".

Sunday

The Arabs, having taken a frightful beating, have agreed to renew the truce.

The Arab League is rapidly breaking up, with Ministers resigning for reasons of health everywhere from the Euphrates to the Nile. The new truce looks like the beginning of the end.

Friday

A few days ago Irgun soldiers in Jerusalem arrested five Englishmen, alleged to be spies. After some haggling they handed them over to Haganah. Now Ben Gurion has given an interview to Cy Sulzberger of the *New York Times* in which he said in the same breath that the Englishmen had been " kidnapped " by Irgun, and that the Government is going to bring them to trial.

Ben Gurion behaves at times rather like a pocket dictator. The common denominator of these paternal despots of the Left is the conviction that democracy is a good thing in theory, but that they just happen to know what is best for their own people in their particular country. These matey, hectoring trade union bosses — Ebert, Bevin, John Lewis, etc. — are the sergeant-majors of the Labour Movement, who have come to replace the bold knights of the socialist idea.

Saturday

Counterpoint : tea with an old planter family in Petakh Tiqwa. Endless complaints about socialist totalitarianism. But their garden is going to seed because since the war they can't get any more cheap Arab labour, and refuse to employ Jews at trade union rates. That's what Israel would be like without " socialist terror ".

Monday

Week-end in Nazareth and Haifa. I have never liked Nazareth with its monasteries like army barracks, its absence of bazaars, its corrupt Christian Arab population of tourist touts and souvenir pedlars. Since they were conquered by the Israeli Army they seem to have become even lazier, sulking in the cafés over their games of tric-tràc.

In Haifa Abram Weinshall took me to the house of a rich Arab who is more or less the spokesman of the remaining Arab population of about two thousand. We spoke French ; Mr. T., who is a Christian Arab, explained that he had stayed behind because if choose he must, he would rather live in a Jewish than in an Arab state. " You have no idea, Monsieur, what it means to live under

Arab rule : no freedom of expression, no civilized life." He said this attitude was less exceptional among Christian Arabs than it might seem.   This said, he launched into a long list of complaints : that the Arabs in Haifa are not allowed to walk in the Jewish quarters ; that they are debarred entry to the Town Hall ; that they don't get their rations ; that the property of those who have left has been looted ; and that all this was a bad and short-sighted policy on the part of the Jews, who should give an example to the world how to treat minorities.   Most of which is true, though only half the truth.

Then came another torrent of complaints and laments.   Suddenly it struck me that speaking for a minority with a justified grievance, Mr. T. was behaving exactly as the Jews used to behave.   It was the same mixture of sob-talk and casuistry, the same wearying relentlessness in airing complaints, in playing on the other man's bad conscience — until his perfectly good case was lost in the exasperation caused by constant over-emphasis. Jews are created not by race, but by conditions.

Tuesday

Watched the arrival of the Russian diplomatic mission, acclaimed by a crowd of approximately a hundred people, the majority of whom cheered, while a minority booed.   On his arrival in Haifa, the Soviet Minister to Israel, Yershov, made the following laconic statement to the assembled Press, local and foreign :

" We have arrived.   Now we are here.   That is the best news I can give you."   (Applause.)

Saturday ·

Yesterday an old, almost blind man came to see me, feeling his way through the room with a stick.   He is Dr. R., formerly a deputy in the Rumanian Parliament and President of the Rumanian Zionist Organization.   When the Red Army occupied Rumania, he learned that he was high on the list of those marked for deportation.   He also heard that one of the few grounds on which people were exempted from deportation was blindness.   He persuaded a surgeon friend to perform a double iretectomy on him, depriving him of sixty per cent of seeing-power in one eye, seventy per cent in the other.   In spite of this he was taken on a stretcher from the hospital to the deportation train, but unloaded again when he

T

seemed to be dying. He left me the manuscript of a book he has written. . . .

Sunday

Listened to Begin's first public speech in Tel Aviv in an open-air cinema, with thousands thronging in the streets and on the roofs of the houses around. It was a disappointing speech — emotional rhetorics without a constructive programme. There are periods when the cart of history has to be pushed in blind enthusiasm and rage; once the hump is passed the time has come to survey the landscape with open eyes.

The phenomenon of discontinuity in history: if a backward nation has missed certain stages in its development — the rise of capitalism, the ascent of its middle classes, the storming of its Bastilles — can it ever fill the gap? In organic development the embryo has to repeat the story of the race; but in social evolution such nations are made to jump from phase B to phase E by external over-stimulation. Example: the Japanese, the Arabs, in a different way the Jews. Can such nations ever become socially sound and balanced without reverting to the missed phases C and D? Alexis says Karl Polanyi is lecturing on a similar theme, based on Malinovsky.

Parallel: people who miss their childhood by having, through external circumstances, responsibility forced on them too early; infant prodigies who have never played marbles.

Monday

The British are carrying on in the Security Council as before. Water should only be supplied to Jerusalem after Israel has agreed to the return of the Arab refugees (a potential fifth column of some three hundred thousand); the internees of Cyprus are still kept behind barbed wire as hostages. And Russia marches on. Never has the fate of the world been administered by such little men. Never have so few done so much harm to so many.

More crank visitors. Among them a German who cures diseases by soul-waves and *mana*. He has a *mana*-circle in Tel Aviv, and I am to collaborate in making propaganda for Israel abroad on soul-wave lines. Another one wants me to start a campaign to propagate Hebrew morse signals.

The monomaniac taking to a fixed idea is the Jewish equivalent of the Englishman in the tropics taking to drink.

Wednesday

First Israeli-Soviet diplomatic incident. The Soviet Mission went to a concert to which both they and the American envoy, Macdonald, were invited. As Yershov did not turn up, only his staff, the orchestra played the American, but not the Soviet anthem; so in the first interval the Russians walked demonstratively out. Rumours, explanations, apologies, and now all is well again.

Thursday

Dinner with N., one of the old leaders of the Zionist movement in Europe. Now he lives in Jerusalem, but as he does not belong to the inner circle of Mapai, nor even to any of the other parties, he can't get a job, says " I am a forgotten man ". N. would make an excellent ambassador to any western European country; but owing to the closed-shop system of political coteries, most of the diplomatic jobs go to little yes-men who will set the European chancelleries bristling as the old Jewish Agency did.

Friday

Bergson has grown a beard in prison and looks like a gentle little rabbi. Somebody brought him a bottle of brandy in jail which he polished off in three weeks; this earned him the reputation of an alcoholic. He quarrelled with the prison guard, told him rashly that this was worse than a Nazi concentration camp. The guard showed him the Dachau number tattooed into his forearm, and asked to be transferred to another job.

Saturday

M. is back from a week's holiday in Cyprus. In the visitor's book of the English hotel in Famagusta where she spent a night, a lot of people had written in the " Coming from " column: Israel. This was crossed out in each case, with the comment: " does not exist ". So she added in each case " yes it does ".

Our balcony has become a sort of club where all kinds of people drift in and out in the evenings, most of whom are not on speaking terms with each other. There are always tense moments with M.'s voice chiming in : " Now what would you like to drink ? ", followed by the stern rebuff : " Lemonade ".

Among the visitors : a Trotskyite architect from New York,

a Canadian fur dealer, lots of South Africans, all volunteers in the Israeli Army ; and a little French boy of fifteen who came on the *Altalena* and would like to go back home to school but can't raise the money for his ticket — which the French Consul has refused him although his parents were killed in the Resistance and he is a " pupille de la nation ".

Sunday

The last few days I spent mostly in Government offices collecting material. All Government offices are concentrated in Sarona, an eighteenth century colony of German Templars on the outskirts of Tel Aviv. The Templars, who all turned Nazi, have left, and their dusty little houses, each surrounded by a derelict garden, have now been turned into the various Ministries. Bulldozers are working all day to make the cart-tracks into roads, and officials with enormous brief-cases climb in and out of ditches to get from one Ministry to another.

Spent an hour gossiping with Z., who now has a dud job in the Ministry of the Interior — another forgotten man of the Old Guard. He told me how the Israelis discreetly sounded a Russian diplomat in Lake Success about the right type of person to represent them in Moscow. The Russian said : You probably think you should send somebody who speaks Russian to perfection and knows Pushkin by heart. But that is of no importance. You may also think that you should send somebody who knows exactly how many tons of pig-iron are produced under the Five Year Plan and how many inches of rain fall in Galilee. But that is of no importance either. You may further assume that your ambassador should be thoroughly acquainted with the history of the Bolshevik Revolution. But that's least important of all. What I suggest is that you should send somebody who is a member of your ruling party and has the full confidence of the leader of your Government — as is our practice.

They offered the job to Goldie Meyerson, who said : " I speak not a word of Russian, have never read Pushkin, know nothing of pig-iron and rain and have entirely forgotten what Stalin and Trotsky quarrelled about." So Goldie got the job.

Monday

Schaerf, Chief Secretary to the Government, told me some stories about the trivia of state-making.

One of the difficulties was that nobody in the Jewish Agency had the faintest idea about diplomatic protocol, about the procedure of having the National Flag copyrighted or whatever it's called, and the like paraphernalia of statehood. When they had to accredit the first Israeli envoy — the one to Czechoslovakia — they borrowed the Exequatur of the only foreign consul available at the time in Tel Aviv, who happened to be the consul of Guatemala, and cribbed the text of it.

Also, they had a dress-rehearsal for the reception of Yershov, with the Chef du Protocol, Dr. Simon, playing Yershov's part. He started twice addressing Ben Gurion with " Your Excellency " until B. G., waking from his dreams, said : " Mi zeh ? Aniy ? " — " Who's that ? Me ? "

Even earlier, during the civil war, Schaerf and others were preparing long drafts about the administrative structure of the future state, but couldn't quite believe that one day it would really come into being, nor take their own plans quite seriously. When some sub-committee, which they had forgotten ever having appointed, one day produced sketches for the future Israeli postage stamps, they all burst out laughing. From time to time Ben Gurion, who was only interested in matters military, would ask Schaerf : " Is it true that you are preparing a State ? "

Wednesday

The war is over, and the elections have been postponed ; so we probably shan't stay much longer, and to round off the picture I made last week a kind of Grand Tour of the members of the Government.

They are a fairly homogeneous team, and, with few exceptions, share the same Eastern European small town background. Their manners are informal and democratic, and are best characterized by the story about Ben Gurion, who on arriving at a gathering of friends straight from a diplomatic reception in striped trousers and a black coat, apologized for not having had time " to change out of his working clothes ".

There are few exceptions as far as social and cultural background are concerned. One is the Minister of Justice, Dr. Felix Rosenblueth — half hefty Bavarian, half Jewish lawyer. He has assembled around him an excellent staff of German legal experts ; on entering his Ministry one is transferred from Cracow to the Weimar Republic. The opposite extreme is Shitreet, the only

Sephardi Jew in the Government, Minister for Minorities and Police. He used to be a police officer under the British Mandate.

With Ben Gurion I had a two hours' talk yesterday in his flat. He has aged considerably since I last saw him in 1945; short and stocky, his broad, Judeo-Slavonic head is bald in the middle, with tufts of white hair sticking up on both sides — which gives him the look of a temperamental patriarch. He speaks with great warmth and persuasion, if not always with a ring of sincerity. About half the time was taken up with politics, meaning Russia; the other half with cultural questions. On the latter we disagreed entirely. He said for instance something to the effect that " Jewish democracy is older and deeper than so-called Western democracy; we want to build a native Jewish democracy, not to imitate the West ". That's good enough as a sonorous phrase at a meeting, but the fact is that ancient Israel was a theocracy and never a democracy; that since it ceased to exist the Jews have had no democratic experience as a nation; that Israel's Constitution, which is now being drafted, is of course based on Western models; and that Israel, if it is to be a modern nation, must, not imitate, but assimilate Western tradition. To this B. G. answered that I had not the faintest idea what Jewish tradition meant; every Jew was an aristocrat, even if a proletarian; it wasn't true that there was a two thousand years' gap in Jewish history; although during that time Jews couldn't administer themselves politically, they carried the spiritual heritage with them and continued to live with the Prophet Ezekiel while waiting for the Messiah. I answered that this was exactly what I meant : they had lived in the past and in the future, but not in the present; that is what I call the gap in experience and social evolution. Where are Israel's Luthers, Cromwells, Galileos ? At the time when Shakespeare wrote his tragedies, the only event in Hebrew literature was Rabbi Lurie of Safed's cabbalistic exercises.

Ben Gurion repeated paternally that I knew nothing of Jewish tradition; nor, he added, did a number of his colleagues in the Government — he mentioned the names of several, all of German or Western European origin. Besides, I need not worry about losing touch with Western civilization, as within ten years everything ever written worth reading will have been translated into Hebrew.

All this would not be serious if Ben Gurion could be dismissed as a narrow-minded bigot. But in fact he is a Socialist, and more-

over a Greek scholar specializing in Plato. Israel's first Prime
Minister is a strong man of action with intellectual leanings, not
an ignoramus. His attitude is the result of that deep-rooted
complex — cultural claustrophilia. It is perhaps the most general
common denominator of the population of Israel, however much
they may otherwise differ by their country of origin, their cultural
of social standards. No party, group or individual is entirely
immune from it — from the orthodox rabbis to the extreme left.

Friday

Bernadotte has been murdered.

The P.I.O. was like a disturbed ant-heap; several girl secretaries crying, the press officers and censors looking panicky, the
correspondents in the euphoria of once more living through
historic events. In the streets and cafés the reaction was one of
unmitigated horror. Everyone seemed to feel that the bullets
that riddled the Mediator's body had torn into the State's own
precarious texture. As the news spread along the sea-shore
among the festive Shabbath-eve crowds, a cloud of dismay seemed
suddenly to descend. Low-voiced groups gathered at the street-
corners; it was startling to see women crying at the death of
a man who was a stranger in Israel and politically detested by
almost everybody. But they understood that the United Nations'
Mediator was a symbol in the world's eyes; and the old inherited
knowledge of the Jew, the Negro in the Southern States and of
all hunted minorities told them that, however united they are in
condemning the deed, its blood will be on their heads.

We went to a café on the beach which is frequented mainly by
Sternists and is used by them as a kind of soldiers' club. This
place usually closes about 11 P.M., but tonight, though it was
much later, there was a revelling crowd there dancing Horra and
Cracowiak. They are a queer, picturesque and ambiguous lot of
fierce-looking Yemenite gun-molls, Sephardi beauties and young
men of dashing countenance. Some of them wear long side-
whiskers; others the Negev type of moustache and beard. Particularly remarkable was a young man in navy blue tight trousers
and a green shirt, with a black patch over one eye and a dagger
flapping on his buttocks, dancing last-century Montmartre
apache style. Then a Sternist girl came in who once made international news by engaging in some wild and pointless terrorist
activities in Western Europe. She is a little chit of a girl of great

vivacity, and entirely infantile. What she needs is a good talking-to by a nice, reasonable Jewish mamma, but as it happens her nice Jewish mamma was killed by the Gestapo, and that started her on her career as a pocket-heroine

It was all pretty disgusting, but the one thing which had unmistakably emerged was that the murder had taken the Sternists themselves completely by surprise. Behind their knowing airs and awkward jokes, they were hiding their uncertainty as to which line to take. It is a fundamental tradition of Palestine terrorism to assume immediate responsibility for each act committed ; but in this case the Stern Group has not done so, and the members of the Group have obviously received no inside directives whether to approve of the murder or decline responsibility for it. In fact they were as disconcerted by the news as everybody else, though their automatic reaction to it was of course a different one.

At the P.I.O. by that time everybody was more or less drunk. We went home and I wrote an article which, after an account of public reactions, went on :

" To the outside observer the assassination of Count Bernadotte may appear as belonging to the same category as the former terrorist actions. But both objectively and in the public's psychological reaction this is essentially a new development. The underground struggle against the hostile mandatory Power conformed, whatever one's opinion about the rights and wrongs of the case, to a classic and recurrent historic pattern. Hence the murderers of Lord Moyne, the gaolbreakers of Acre, the operators of secret radio stations, enjoyed the passive sympathy of a considerable section of the population, even among those opposed to violence in principle. Public opinion was equally divided when Irgun smuggled much-needed defence arms and clashed with the Government. At that time I pointed out that both sides had an arguable case. But this time such considerations do not apply. There is historical logic in violence versus oppression, in the illegal rescue of the homeless, in gun-running for the defence of a small country invaded by several big ones ; there is no logic and no conceivable justification to the sane mind for Sten-gunning the representative of an international body, even if his policy were regarded as objectionable. Hence this time opinion is undivided against the handful of runners-amok who perpetrated this crime. It is characteristic that Irgun Z'vai Leumi, by far the larger and more responsible of the so-called dissidents, has officially and categorically denied

any responsibility for the deed. This is the first time Irgun
has taken such a step, which completes the transformation of
the former underground body into a political party. This
significant development means that terrorism is dying out in
Israel except for a small body, numbering approximately 2,000
men, who are deprived of public support."

Friday

All evidence confirms that the Sternist leaders knew nothing
of the Bernadotte murder. But instead of condemning the act
outright they have issued ambiguous statements and pamphlets
which are neither here nor there and which implicitly condone it
by phrases like " Am I my brother's keeper ? " This seals their
fate. Some three hundred of them have been arrested, including
Friedman-Yellin; the Government has issued an emergency
decree against terrorism which enables it to outlaw the Group.

I am sorry for a few individuals among them; David Yellin,
with whom I had a moving encounter in 1945 ; Amikam, the
gentleman bank-robber; Scheib, whom I have never met but
who always reminded me of Nardi in *The Magic Mountain*. The
marxian dictum that man is a product of his environment has
never been more fitting than when applied to this group of young
fanatics. Stern's ideology was the ultima ratio of a tortured
people. Now once more history is repeating its dreary pattern
according to which the regicides must share the fate of their
victims. For, as Machiavelli drily remarked, " he who founds a
republic and does not kill the sons of Brutus, will only reign a
short time ".

The last Irgun units which had enjoyed special status in
Jerusalem have peacefully disbanded and joined the regular Army.

As for the actual assassins of Bernadotte, my hunch is that they
will never be found, and that they are protected by a power outside
the reach of Israel's police.

Sunday

C. of the American Delegation told me that some Sternist
has explained to him that I am an agent of British Intelligence.
That rather fits the pattern. Had tea, and drinks on the next day,
with Macdonald, the American Envoy. He is a nice, donnish type,
but I wonder whether an American don is the right match for
the propaganda and infiltration experts of the Soviet Mission.

For a while, before proper accommodation was prepared for them, both the American and the Soviet delegations lived in the Gat-Rimmon — Yershov actually occupied our former room. The stars and stripes and the hammer and sickle floating side by side over the hotel façade were the delight of all press photographers. But it was less encouraging to know that one delegation would immediately settle down to silent termite work, while the other would carry on with its happy routine. Why can't they get over a few bright young publicists from the *New Leader* or *Partisan Review* crowd, to counteract the Russian propaganda which is blowing in from all sides in this draughty corner of the world?

Monday

On Thursday had a long talk with the head of the Education Department, and on Friday with the Director of the Herzlia school. Education in Israeli schools is at present based on quite shocking principles. No doubt this is a transitional phenomenon, but frank criticism is essential to hasten the end of this state of affairs and minimize the damage to the young generation.

There are three officially recognized types of school, or " educational trends " as they call it. Firstly, orthodox religious schools, secondly " general " schools, and thirdly socialist schools run by the cultural department of Histadruth.[1] Thus from the kindergarten onwards children are systematically conditioned on political or religious lines, and have a bias instilled into them which affects their whole outlook on life according to their parents' choice; moreover the three competing " trends " tend to perpetuate class divisions and make adherence to a political party hereditary as it were.

The religious schools which, according to the Education Department's figures, are attended by twenty-three per cent of all children between the ages of four and eighteen, make their pupils quite unfit for twentieth century life. Unlike some Catholic lay schools in Western Europe, which provided a solid all-round education and were sometimes quite outstanding, the Orthodox seminaries stuff their pupils' heads with mediaeval scholastic exegesis almost to the exclusion of any other branch of knowledge.

The socialist schools are attended by twenty-seven per cent of all children of the primary school age, mainly in the collective settlements and big towns. Their level varies from place to place

[1] Histadruth : the Hebrew Federation of Labour

according to local conditions, and their methods are experimental, with much *avant-garde* dilettantism and some promising aspects. They aim at some form of synthesis between Biblical tradition and a superficial, simplified marxist philosophy.

Secondary education, from fourteen or earlier to eighteen, is to an extent of eighty per cent carried out by the "general" schools. In the average general secondary school, children at the age of fifteen have to devote, out of a total of 35 school hours per week, 4 hours to studying the Bible, $1\frac{1}{2}$ hours to studying Talmud, 5 hours to studying Hebrew literature; but only $1\frac{1}{2}$ hours to the study of history, which means mainly Jewish history.

The director of the Herzlia Gymnasium explained to me the method of teaching political geography. The first difficulty, he said, is to convince Palestine-born children that there are Jews in other parts of the world who are their kin. This is done by explaining to the children that the work of rebuilding Israel depends economically on those alien Jews, through their donations to the Keren Kayemeth — the Jewish National Fund. "Chile does not mean anything to a little Israeli child — until he learns that so and so many pounds have been collected by the Keren Kayemeth in Chile. Then suddenly Chile becomes a reality."

History is taught by an equally egocentric system. For the study of antiquity the Bible serves as the main source, and Israel as the hub of the ancient world. The confused events of the Dark and Middle Ages are summed up as a series of migrations by barbarian tribes anti-clockwise round the Mediterranean, while the Jews in the same period migrated clockwise in the opposite direction. And so on.

All this reminds me of the first school I went to in Budapest. The Hungarians too, as a small nation wedged precariously between the Slavonic and Germanic worlds, were inclined towards this kind of mystical ultra-chauvinism. One of the first poems I had to learn by heart was Petöfy's classic:

> If the globe is the cap of God
> Hungary is the feather in the cap. . . .

Not all teachers in Israel take an equally centripetal view of the world at large; but the majority do, particularly of the older generation, who themselves have been brought up in religious seminaries, and who occupy most of the responsible posts. Among the younger teachers I met some good modern types who one day will break the power of the old fogies.

One shouldn't be too hard in passing judgment on what is no doubt a transitory and inevitable phenomenon. Israel can't become a nation without passing through a phase of intense nationalism. It is part of the process of filling in the gap. In ten to fifteen years' time the young people of the next generation will get fed up with all this provincial chauvinistic stuff, with the prophets and pharisees around them, and start flinging open the windows to the great world outside. The sooner it happens the better.

Tuesday

Another curious feature of the native generation is their retarded maturity, a mild form of psycho-sexual infantilism. It may have something to do with the change in climate or diet, but nobody knows. The children of my old friends give at twenty-five the impression of being eighteen. Characteristic is Mala's story of a married girl of twenty-four, who kept on playing with dolls, although she was pregnant.

Wednesday

Went with Mala to visit Jaffa jail where most of the Sternists are kept. At the gates we found a disorderly scrum of female relatives fighting to get in first, the inexperienced guards trying in vain to get them into an orderly queue. All the frames, window-panes and doors have been smashed up by the detainees, who rule the prison in a kind of perpetual pandemonium. Boys and girls sit together on the window-sills ; this is the first coeducational — or rather cohabitational — prison in the world. Saw Stanley and Amikam — the latter as quixotic as ever : " We are not imprisoned — we are besieged. Yesterday I exceptionally permitted the prison governor to enter our living quarters for some plumbing inspection, but that was the only time." The young fanatics are having the time of their lives ; the middle-aged are tired and fed up with the pointlessness of the whole thing. The Government is at a loss what to do with them as there is not a shred of evidence to implicate anybody in the Bernadotte murder.

Monday

Jewish New Year's Day — the first in Israel. Everything closed ; no cars, buses, cinemas, restaurants.

The Jerusalem Truce Commission and the Israeli Military Governor (who is technically responsible for the lack of security-measures to protect Bernadotte) are exchanging diplomatic notes with accusations and counter-accusations that read like the Fish-wives' Morning Gazette.

Sunday

The Sternists in Jaffa have staged a bloodless jail-break. Yesterday was visiting day, but as the prisoners had beaten up a police officer, the visits were cancelled as a punishment. The women at the gate started protesting, and at that the prisoners threw mattresses through the windows and jumped out. After a short scrap the police on guard surrendered their arms into the safe custody of the prisoners " to avoid ", as they said, " a second *Altalena* ", and in exchange for a promise that the arms would be returned to them in the evening. The prisoners then more or less took possession of Jaffa, crowded into cafés or went for a swim in the sea. A police sergeant served everybody with free beer from the canteen, and Stanley gave a press conference in his cell. In the evening they all flocked back to the prison except those who had hitch-hiked to Tel Aviv, and whom the military check-posts would not allow to return as they had no passes. Some of them thereupon went back to Jaffa in a rowing-boat. To-day everything is quiet again ; all the prisoners except two have gone back to jail. The arms were returned to the police ; there were no casualties.

All this is pure Alice in Wonderland to the stranger to Israel. In fact it is a postscript to the old complicated game between Haganah and Sternists. The only aim of the Sternists' jail-break was to cover the Government with ridicule, in which they fully succeeded. The Army and Police preferred ridicule to bloodshed, remembering how narrowly the country had bye-passed the danger of civil war at the time of the *Altalena* ; and also because they all have an uneasy conscience towards the terrorists who, hardly out of British prisons, are now in Israeli prisons. Everybody condemns the Bernadotte murder and the Stern Group in general, but at the same time feels that the latter were never given a fair chance to return to the fold and become normal citizens again.

Tuesday

Went to Haifa to get my return visa at the British Consulate which, it having moved to new premises, I couldn't find for about an hour, as no taxi-driver or policeman knows where it is. This is a rather fantastic state of affairs in a country where six months ago

all public offices were British. At last I found it on the top floor
of an unfinished building. Marriot the Consul has gone to
London; his deputy sat with a resigned expression behind a
desk, holding the fort. I was probably the only customer the
Consulate had seen for days.

There are rumours in the papers that " opposition in the
Cabinet and among Labour M.P.s against Mr. Bevin's Palestine
policy is growing ". For the last three years not a month has passed
without the same rumours reported in almost identical words.

Wednesday

Preparing to leave.

To-day is Atonement Day and the town is as dark and dead
as a town can be

I wonder what Israel will be like the next time. I have seen it
change, since my first stay in 1926, with the rapid, jerky movements of a growing plant in one of those quick-motion films which
telescope weeks into seconds. Already I hear myself explaining
to fellow-tourists in 1953 : " You should have seen the state this
country was in five years ago. . . ."

I have been looking for a fitting end for this diary. The other
night Professor Marcus, the surgeon, provided me with one over
the best bottle of Moselle I have had for years. It is the story of
how the Lord got thoroughly fed up with mankind and decided
to arrange for a second Flood ; but this time it was to be a
thorough job with thirty fathoms of water everywhere, and there
would be no Ark and no Dove. The Lord despatched the Archangel Gabriel to make the decision known to all concerned.
When Gabriel had delivered his message to the leader of the
Moslems, all Moslems turned towards Mecca and started praying
for a cushy corner in Paradise, with houris and wine. Gabriel
went on to the leader of all the Christians, and the Christians all
over the earth fell to their knees and prayed for forgiveness of
their sins at the Last Judgment. Finally the Archangel broke
the news to the leader of the Jewish community, who began to
scratch his beard and gave a great sigh.

" Lord," he said, " what a difficult life it will be under thirty
fathoms of water."

BOOK THREE
PERSPECTIVE

" The Jews are like other people, only more so. . . "
Anon.

I

THE POLITICAL STRUCTURE OF ISRAEL

I. *The Trade Union Empire*

The State of Israel may be defined as an anachronistic ideal realized by ultra - modern means. A powerful international organization works for the transformation of the most cosmopolitan people of the world into citizens of a miniature State. A race of born linguists turns back to a language which has been dead for two thousand years. The children of the pioneers of international trade take pride in living in collective settlements where the use of money is abolished. Israel's clock is turning back full circle — but it is an electric clock on a functional façade.

This paradox permeates the whole cultural, economic and political life of the new State. As a result, Israel's social structure has developed into a unique phenomenon, whose study will fascinate sociologists for some years to come.

According to the figures submitted by the Jewish Agency to the Anglo-American Committee of Enquiry in 1946, 24 per cent of the workers in Israel are engaged in agriculture, but among the European fathers of these workers only 4 per cent worked in agriculture. 40 per cent of the workers in Israel are engaged in building, transport and factory work, but among their fathers abroad the corresponding figure was only 18 per cent.

Generally speaking, out of 100 workers in Palestine the fathers of 50 were traders abroad, and the fathers of 13 had " undefined occupations ". These figures contain in a nutshell the formula of the social transformation which Jewry undergoes in Israel. Practically everywhere else in the world the trend of social migrations is a " horizontal " drift from village and agriculture to town and industry, and a " vertical " drift from working-class to middle-class occupations.

In Palestine, as our statistics show, this tendency was reversed. The children of urban-middle- and lower-middle-class parents migrated into farming and into the industrial proletariat. And just as, in other countries, the ablest and most ambitious are the first to move from village to town, from a proletarian to a bourgeois

U

status, so here it was also a selected vanguard which led the movement " back to the land " and " back to manual work ", according to the tenets of Zionist ideology.

This ideology has already been discussed in an earlier chapter. Until the French Revolution, the Jews in Europe lived mostly segregated in ghettoes, divided from the soil and from socially creative work ; they became, by force of circumstance, a nation whose bulk was composed of middlemen, petty traders and social parasites, with a crust of intellectuals. If the Jews were to make a new start as an independent nation in Palestine, this lop-sided social structure had to be righted and replaced by a normal social pyramid with a broad, healthy base of farmers and manual workers. But while in other countries the worker and peasant classes have organically grown through centuries, in Palestine they had to be artificially created ; the social pyramid here was built from the top downward.

No wonder that this " artificial " working class, these voluntary proletarians, became the socially and economically dominant element in the country. No revolution and no social struggle was needed to bring them into power ; it fell to them automatically from the beginning of modern Zionist colonization. The body in which this power is vested is the *Histadruth*, the General Federation of Labour in Israel.

Although affiliated to the World Federation of Trade Unions, the Histadruth cannot be compared with the Western type of Trade Union any more than, say, a Hebrew prophet with a teacher at the London School of Economics. Histadruth is a creed and cult ; its bureaucrats regard themselves as priests of the new temple ; it is politically a State within the State and economically a monopolistic trust. In other countries Trade Unions are supposed to represent the interests of the workers towards the employers ; Histadruth is both a Trade Union and the greatest single capitalist employer in Israel. Its members embrace 75 per cent of all wage-earners who, with their dependents, represent more than half the country's total population, and the absolute majority of the electorate.

This half of the population not only wields complete political control over the country, but also forms an economically autarchic and self-sufficient body. This is made possible by the numerous cooperative and holding companies controlled by Histadruth, which act as agricultural producers, marketing cooperatives, transport companies, bankers, factory owners, builders and retail cooperatives, book and newspaper publishers — and thus create a practically closed market with a closed circulation of money and goods. The most important of these economic enterprises directly or indirectly controlled by the Histadruth include : agricultural cooperatives embracing some hundred and fifty collective settlements and some fifty smallholders' settlements ; the marketing cooperative *Tnuva* which has the monopoly of buying the total agricultural produce of the former, selling it through its own chain stores and restaurants in the towns and canning the fruit and vegetables in its own factories ; transport cooperatives which have the monopoly of public transport in Tel Aviv and Jerusalem, and a near-monopoly of cross-country bus services ; the retail cooperative *Hamashbir*, which supplies half the total population with goods and industrial commodities and runs its own factories for shoes, textiles, rubber products ; and finally, the building company *Solel Boneh*, which is the biggest enterprise of its kind in the Middle East. Solel Boneh is a trust within the trust, which owns a number of subsidiary industries such as glass-works, foundries, brick factories and a shipyard. It is at the same time the main shareholder of the country's biggest factories — cement and soap.

The financial enterprises of the Histadruth include banks for agricultural credits, workers' credit and saving societies and a life insurance company. The Histadruth's Sick Fund provides medical care for half the population ; it runs 135 schools and 207 kindergartens of its own ; it has its own theatres, publishing houses, sports clubs and so on. In short, half the population has all its physical and cultural needs, from the cradle to the grave, provided by the General Federation of Labour. Israel is not a Socialist State ; but half of Israel forms a Workers' State within the State.

The other half — individual farmers, tradesmen, shopkeepers and artisans — are economically and politically atomized. The traditional opponent of Labour is Capital ; but in Israel the one big capitalist trust is the Labour Union itself ; compared to the Histadruth, all private employers are small fry. Consequently, there is no class struggle in the traditional sense. Instead of it, we have the unique phenomenon of the Labour Trust systematic-ally knocking out of business its private industrial competitors and then buying them up, by methods familiar from the history of the American steel and railroad companies, and prohibited to-day by anti-trust laws in most capitalist countries.

In this economic battle no violence and not even threats are needed ; no private employer can risk the fight, knowing that his own workers have a vested interest in his competitor's victory. The private industrialist can only survive in the long run by coming to terms with the Histadruth. He may do this by selling a controlling part of his shares to the Histadruth, as the country's two biggest factories did. Or he may sell his factory altogether and retain the post of managing director. Finally, he may go into partnership with a cooperative formed by his own workers, and indirectly controlled by Histadruth. It is a kind of aseptic social operation, and as wages are pegged to the cost-of-living index, there is no occasion even for local strikes. For a young country this is certainly a promising social start ; the only question is in what direction the road leads.

Is it a new, bloodless approach to Socialism ? As long as the Jews lived under the British Mandate the autarchic organization of Histadruth could be regarded as a nucleus of the future State. But since the State has come into existence, the Labour Party, which has a controlling majority both in the Histadruth and in the Government, has shown no sign of any intention of putting the Trade Unions' key enterprises under national control. There are, on the other hand, numerous indications of the Trade Unions' desire to remain a State within the State, to watch over their vested interests, and to exclude the " marginal " half of the population from the benefits of what they justly regard as their own exclusive creation.

A characteristic example of this tendency is the development of the bus cooperatives which, as already mentioned, have the monopoly of public transport in the big towns and on the overland roads. Before the war the members of these cooperatives earned in shared profits up to £P200 per month ; a new immigrant wanting a job as a driver or bus conductor could only get it by becoming a member of the cooperative through buying a share in it for the fantastic sum of two thousand pounds. This, of course, hardly any newcomer could afford, and transport cooperatives consequently developed into a kind of exclusive workers' aristocracy.

This is an extreme example ; but similar tendencies can be found in many realms of the Histadruth kingdom. It is certainly not a Socialist tendency in any accepted sense of the word

Socialism. It is not Capitalism either, nor Communism, nor Syndicalism. It is a paradoxical product of a country which came into existence under paradoxical conditions, without any traditional class structure, without a bourgeoisie ; — and with an artificially created working class which took over the functions of the former. This is one of the fascinating aspects of this society of modern Europeans transplanted into an oriental environment ; a society which has not grown organically but was created in the laboratory of some idealistic Frankenstein. It is a tiny laboratory, but the results which it produces may assume a vast significance, as happened once before in this country's history.

II. *The Hebrew Labour Party* [1]

Political Parties are the product of organic development in a nation's history. The history of Israel as a nation contains a gap from the destruction of the Temple in A.D. 71 to the reconstitution of the State in May 1948. During those two thousand years the nations of Europe underwent their slow social evolution towards parliamentary life, civil liberties and security before the law ; while the greater part of the Jews, during the greater part of this period, lived outside the law or on the margin of the law, and were excluded from the stream of social evolution. They only maintained their separate identity by their stubborn clinging to a petrified doctrine and to archaic rites — a stagnant enclave in a world in flux.

No race could have remained unaffected by such warping

[1] To facilitate orientation among the various Parties in Israel which are discussed in the following sections, the results of the elections to Israel's Constituent Assembly on January 25, 1949, are given below. The list comprises only the more important Parties and electoral blocks.

Party	No of Votes (in round figures)	Percentage of Total	Seats obtained
Labour Party (MAPAI)	155,500	34·70	46
United Workers' Party (MAPAM)	64,000	14·54	19
United Religious Front	53,000	12·03	16
Freedom Party (formerly Irgun)	50,000	11·30	14
General Zionists (liberal)	22,500	5·14	7
Progressives (liberal splinter group)	18,000	4·04	5
Communists	15,000	3·44	4
Stern Group	5,500	1·22	1
Revisionists	3,000	0·65	..
Others	53,500	12·94	8
Total	440,000	100·00	120

influences. All the courage, self-sacrifice and initiative of the Jewish pioneers in Palestine could not replace their lack of political maturity and the lack of statesmanship of their leaders, — a direct consequence of that two thousand years' gap in political tradition. As a Jewish witness put it in his statement before the Royal Commission : " We are not an easy people to deal with. . . . To a Jew who comes from the East of Europe an official is a Tchinovnik (a Civil Servant under the Tsarist regime). He must be corrupt. He must be hostile. He is the enemy of the public. . . ." [1]

This deeply ingrained attitude played, as we saw, a considerable part in poisoning relations between the British Administration and the Jews. The same ghetto-heritage of suspicion, intolerance and self-righteousness is making itself felt in the internal politics of Israel in this period of teething. This is equally true of the Parties within the Government coalition and of those in opposition. The common denominator of all of them is their emergence from a historic vacuum, their absence of a civic tradition. Civic virtue is not acquired through opting for a political theory ; it is unconsciously absorbed by the individual growing up in a civilized community. But the majority of the politicians of Israel spent their formative years under regimes where the condition of survival was circumventing the law. The birth-pangs of Zionist colonization were the pogroms in Tsarist Russia at the beginning of the century ; the midwives of Israel were the drunken Russian soldiery, the German S.S., the terror-gangs of the Mufti. It was a Caesarean birth in the sign of knife and forceps ; the gods of justice, tolerance and humanism were absent from Israel's cradle.

Under these auspices the social psychologist might have predicted the development of an anarchic community based on ruthless individualistic competition, without scruples or social morality. Instead of which Palestine became the laboratory of Utopian social experiments — agricultural communes with common property, industries based on cooperative enterprise, an economy dominated by the workers' Trade Unions. The explanation of this paradox is simple. Between 1880 and the beginning of the First World War about three million Jews fled from Eastern Europe, the majority of them to the U.S.A. ; but of these only fifty thousand went to Palestine. Those who did so were naturally a selected élite. Instead of the fleshpots of America, they chose the desert.

[1] Royal Commission Report, p. 119.

Instead of individual escape, they chose the collective ideal. Instead of middle-class careers, they chose to become peasants and manual workers, and thus created that voluntary proletariat out of which eventually grew the Hebrew Trade Union Histadruth and the Hebrew Labour Party, *Mapai*.

The ideal which animated these young men had a distinctly messianic and somewhat confused character. Palestine was not only to be the stage of a Jewish national renaissance, but also a Socialist Utopia, an example to the world at large of how to solve all its social problems. The biblical Essenes, Rousseau and Tolstoi, Herzl and Marx, were the main sources of this messianic Socialism. This heterogeneous ideological mixture was bound to lead in the long run to internal conflicts and explosions. But those early pioneers, in their creative enthusiasm, did not care much about logical consistency.

The social achievements of the Hebrew Labour Movement have been admired by all unbiassed observers. The imposing structure of Histadruth's economic and financial enterprises has already been described ; the communal farming settlements are a fascinating experiment ; the social services of the Labour organizations may serve as a model for many an older and richer nation. Without the hard, intransigent fight of the Socialists against the exploitation of cheap Arab labour, and for the principle that every tenant on nationally owned land has to cultivate it with his own hands, Palestine would have become just another colonial country of rich planters and native underdogs. That it has become instead what it is, and indeed the very existence of Israel as a modern State, is to a large extent due to Mapai and Histadruth.

Against these admirable achievements must be set the negative aspects of Mapai politics : intolerance of opposition, self-righteousness, a budding dictatorial tendency. Historically, these are direct consequences of that absence of political tradition already referred to ; of the political vacuum from which the movement sprang. It is true that its founders were a selected élite ; they were nevertheless a product of their social environment. Israel's first Prime Minister, the Minister of Finance, and many of the other political leaders, started their education in the *Yeshivot*, the religious schools of Russian Jewry. Whatever universities they attended later, the sing-song of Talmudic recitations, scholastic casuistry and the zealotry which the jealous god of the ghettoes exacted from its pupils had left their mark on them during their formative years. Messianic Socialism cannot replace the organic growth of democratic institutions and civic tradition ; fervent idealism is no substitute for habeas corpus ; there is no short-cut from the ghetto to Utopia.

It might have been hoped that thirty years of British Mandate would fill in the historic gap and produce a new generation of Jewish leaders imbued with the traditions of Europe's oldest democracy. Unfortunately for all concerned just the opposite happened. Although the Jews in Palestine lived in a state of physical insecurity, their self-defence organization was never legalized, and from the beginning to the end of the British Mandate had to work underground. Similarly, the rescue of Jews from the European massacre was made an illegal act. Once again the Jews could only protect their lives and save some of their kin by circumventing the law. British rule, instead of being a school for democracy, became a school for conspiracy.

When Israel was born the Jewish nation emerged from an underground existence which in the narrower sense had lasted a decade, and in the broader sense for many centuries. A people living underground must be single-minded, fanatic and intolerant if it is to survive ; but these qualities, when carried over into open-air politics, become a grave handicap. In the first few months of the new State's existence they manifested themselves in the Government's scantily disguised flaunting of democratic procedure and its indifference to legal form — which led to such paradoxes as the launching of a " voluntary " war loan that in fact was compulsory, and the raising of public funds by methods incompatible with the dignity of a sovereign State. There were also some cases of arbitrary arrest and detention, justified *post factum* by British war-time Emergency Regulations — the same regulations which the members of the new Government had unceasingly denounced in the past. Within the Labour Party and the Trade Unions the one-time pioneers have, as so often happens, developed into a somewhat nepotistic coterie of the ancients, with Prime Minister Ben Gurion exercising a kind of paternal despotism over Government, Party, Army and country. To qualify for a responsible position, and in some professions even to make a bare living, the citizen in Israel must be on the right side of the angels — which, broadly speaking, means that he must be a member of Histadruth, by preference a member of Mapai, and by preference of Russo-Polish descent. And as Histadruth has direct control over the economic existence of half the population, while Mapai dominates the Government coalition, to oppose them means courting exclusion from a political or administrative career, social ostracism and sometimes also the risk of economic ruin.

These symptoms are certainly not unique ; similar developments can be found in our time in a number of other nations with a long democratic past and with none of the excuses which the young State of Israel can claim. They should therefore not be overestimated ; but it is nevertheless true that these tendencies, if allowed to continue unchecked, might have a warping influence on the political life of the nation.

III. *The Extreme Left*

The Labour Party, Mapai, occupies the central position both in the Government and in the rainbow of political parties in Israel. The only important group to the Left of Mapai is the United Workers' Party (U.W.P.), formed in 1947 by the fusion of two Socialist splinter groups.[1]

For a better understanding of the position of the U.W.P. it is necessary to go back for a moment to the ideological roots of the Palestine Labour Movement. I have mentioned earlier that the ideals of this movement were somewhat confused and bound to lead to internal conflicts. The principal contradiction in this ideology was that between Socialism and Zionist Nationalism. The proletarian, according to Marx, has no fatherland ; but the Marxist-Zionists, instead of rejoicing that Jewry had got rid of the burden of a fatherland, were turning the clock back to make one. A number of brilliant theoreticians of the movement have tried to resolve this contradiction with the magic wand of dialectics. They never completely succeeded, and the history of the Palestine Labour Movement consists of a series of schisms, reconciliations and new splits, all hinging on the central problem : whether National interest or Socialist doctrine should have the upper hand in determining Labour policy in Israel.

The Mapai never arrived at a clear-cut theoretical decision ; their practical policy, as the dominant Party in Jewish Palestine,

[1] It is known by its Hebrew initials as *Mapam* ; to avoid confusion with Mapai, I shall refer to it by its English initials.

was empirical and opportunistic. The Left Wing groups, on the
other hand, which were eventually to constitute the U.W.P.,
were doctrinaire revolutionary Socialists. The strongest of these
groups, *Hashomer Hatzair*, even opposed until the autumn of
1947 the idea of a Jewish State as a chauvinistic and imperialistic
aim, and advocated instead an Arab-Jewish binational State in
which the " toiling masses " of the two races were to unite against
the Arab effendis and the Jewish capitalists. Like most attempts
to apply Marxist tenets to backward native populations, it was a
programme utterly remote from reality — the reality of the gulf
between twentieth-century Jewish civilization and fifteenth-
century Arab traditionalism. A hundred years or so of patient
effort might have narrowed down the gulf; but it was obvious
that political events were moving at a quicker pace. In fact, the
young idealists of the Zionist Left never made any serious effort
to make themselves understood by the Arab workers, shopkeepers
and fellaheen. And when, on November 29, 1947, the United
Nations Assembly at last decided on Partition, they dropped all
binationalist pretences with an audible sigh of relief, and rallied
with enthusiasm to the Jewish National State. By that irony of
history which is so much in evidence in Palestine, the military
cadres of the extreme Left, *Palmach*, became the best and most
ferocious shock troops in Israel's national war against the Arabs.

Socialist internationalism having thus been defeated here as
elsewhere by the cold realities of our political ice age, there
remained the differences in internal policy between the Israeli
Labour Party and the U.W.P. The U.W.P. presses for a programme not very different from that of the Left Wing of the
British Labour Party : the nationalization of key industries ; the
tightening of price and rent control ; a capital levy ; progressive
indirect taxation ; a State monopoly of foreign trade ; the transfer
of the Histadruth's economic enterprises and social services to
the nation. Regardless of the merits or otherwise of Socialist
planning in the world at large, it must be said that under the
specific conditions of Palestine the programme of the U.W.P. is
undeniably logical, as most of its points merely aim at the legaliza-
tion of a *de facto* state of affairs.

The constructive achievements of the groups united in the
U.W.P., and particularly their collective agricultural settlements,
are wholly admirable ; their social programme is radical, but not
unreasonable. In the field of international politics, however, their

attitude is as amateurish and divorced from reality as it was in the days when they advocated a Judeo-Moslem class struggle against the capitalist world. Their Socialist phraseology has remained unchanged since 1917; absorbed as they were in their unique experiment of creating a Lilliput Utopia at the cost of Brobding-nagian effort in a country remote from Europe, the political changes in the world have passed them by almost unnoticed. Thus in this year of grace 1948 they were still at the stage of passing resolutions with " greetings to the battle-hardened workers of the Soviet Union, which is marching along the road of socialist con-struction that casts its light over the workers of the world " — and so on. To put it bluntly, they are fellow-travellers of the naïvest sort, with touching illusions and an exasperating ignorance of the facts of Soviet reality.

Thus of the two Socialist parties, Mapai, which is by far the stronger, with 46 seats in the Constituent Assembly, pursues an internal policy of opportunistic compromise. Its international attitude is resentful towards Britain, officially neutral between Russia and America, in fact pro-American. The U.W.P., with 19 seats, stands in internal affairs for a consistent Socialist programme, and in foreign politics for collaboration with Russia, but of a rather platonic nature.

For it should be made clear that this Party of somewhat back-woodish pioneer romantics is neither a Communist Party nor directly or. indirectly controlled by Moscow or the Cominform. The whole history and psychological background of the U.W.P. makes it unfit to become a satellite Party. It is more likely that the first attempts at infiltration by what one might call the S.S.S., the Silent Soviet Services, will be met with a howl of protest by the rustic pioneers of the collective settlements and will be followed by a process of disillusionment. The ultimate development of the U W.P. will probably follow the pattern of the anti-Stalinite Left, like the British Independent Labour Party, the Spanish Syndicalists and the Trotskyites — but distinguished from these by an impressive record of positive social achievements.

Nevertheless the growth of popular sympathy towards the Soviet Union, both in the U.W P. and in the country at large, should not be underestimated. The Russians were the first to extend *de jure* recognition to Israel ; and when, in July 1948, the Soviet Ambassador Yershov and his staff arrived in Tel Aviv, they found the ground admirably prepared for them by the Western powers. No diplomatic casuistry could hide the fact from the people of Israel that an army under British command was waging war against them. The almost weekly oscillations of American policy, and the paradox that America recognized Israel but by maintaining the arms embargo deprived it of its means of defence, increased the general feeling of bitterness and disgust with the West. Most important of all, when Operation Deluge left the Jews with practically no arms to face the Arab invasion, Russian-controlled Czechoslovakia was the only country which delivered substantial quantities of arms to Israel and thus made possible its physical survival.

The political sophistication of the Jews in general and of the Labour Party in particular helped them to realize that Russia's gesture was exclusively designed to serve her own political aims. They remembered well that for thirty years Russia had persecuted Zionism as a Fascist movement. The sudden and total reversal of Soviet policy in October 1947 was too obvious a manœuvre to take them in.[1]

They also remembered that until October 1947 the Jewish Communist Party in Palestine had denounced Mapai and the U.W.P. as " tools of Fascist imperialism ", had fought immigration and colonization, and that its policy could be summed up in the motto : " Let's kick ourselves out from here ". Forever discredited with the Jewish working class, they were and remain an insignificant sect which polled at the elections on January 25, 1949, only 15,148 votes, that is 3·4 per cent of the total votes cast. The U.W.P. itself only obtained 14·5 per cent of the votes — as compared to 24 per cent in the elections of 1944, — a defeat which must be regarded as a direct result of having advocated a pro-Russian orientation.

In short, the majority of the Jews understood that Russia was backing them, as a potential winning horse, for the same reasons, though with a much shrewder perception of the realities of the situation, for which the Foreign Office had backed the Mufti. But such critical considerations could not prevent a spontaneous surge of sympathy and gratitude among the politically more naïve layers of the population towards the only Great Power which sent them arms and unwaveringly supported them in Lake Success in the period of greatest danger. Hence the paradox that while the

[1] Since the end of 1948 Russian policy has once more reverted to a violently anti-Zionist line.

majority of Israel's working class remained immune from the Stalinite lure, middle-class families in the Tel Aviv cafés applauded over their cream buns the Russian marches played by salon orchestras in the Viennese style.

It should be repeated that this attitude had nothing to do with Marxism or any political doctrine, and was entirely a spontaneous expression of an emotional leaning towards the only outside country which they felt to be on their side.

" This correspondent ", I wrote in an article dated June 1948, " is hardly susceptible to Stalinite leanings, and yet, had he suffered what people here have suffered in the past six months, while one leading Western democracy waged an almost undisguised war on them and a second looked on, the psychological pressure of circumstances might have turned even him into a fellow traveller. Prime Minister Ben Gurion's speech at the departure of the last British troops from Haifa left the door open for a reconciliation with Britain and was a remarkable proof that the leaders of the country have kept a cool head, despite the burning pressure. But time is running short and the time for mincing words is past. . . . This war of aggression against a small state founded on a United Nations resolution is waged by an army under British control. The remaining Arab forces being strategically negligible, it depends on Britain and on Britain alone whether and when this war will be stopped. Some wars may be the result of historical fatality or inevitable clashes of doctrine or power dynamics. This war is entirely unnecessary and gratuitous. It is not caused by any incurable antagonism between Palestine Arabs and Jews, but has been artificially initiated and artificially prolonged by outside influence against the laws of morality and expediency. The only party to derive profit from it is the totalitarian pretender waiting to step in when the floods recede. It is a tiny country and a tiny war, but a symbolic one. It looks as if Western civilization were determined to commit suicide at the very place of its birth."

The result of the first Israeli elections on January 25, 1949, have proved that the great majority of Israel's working class has remained true to its social-democratic and anti-totalitarian tradition, despite Mr. Bevin's obsessions, Mr. Gromyko's lures, the sickening jolts of American policy and the dismal blundering of the pseudo-machiavellians in Whitehall. But there is a point where emotion threatens to get the upper hand over reason, and in this respect Israel shares the predicament of Greece, Spain and other peoples on the border-line between the two World Powers. Their great majority, like the majority of the " third forces " in the political no-man's-land, incline to Western tradition — if not by profound conviction, at least by leaning towards the lesser evil. And Israel, as always in its history, is a pointed and symbolic example of a global pattern : of millions of war-worn, strife-weary people longing to find peace in the camp which promised them freedom from fear, — and finding themselves repulsed and pushed towards the counsel of despair.

IV. *Jabotinsky and the Revisionist Movement*

The Right Wing opposition movements in Israel — Revisionists and Freedom Party — are the partly legitimate, partly illegitimate spiritual descendants of a remarkable and much misunderstood figure in Jewish history, Vladimir Jabotinsky.

Jabotinsky was a National Liberal in the great nineteenth-century tradition, a revolutionary of the 1848 brand, successor to Garibaldi and Mazzini. He was one of the most colourful figures that modern Jewry has produced. He wrote prose in eight languages, poetry in four, translated Dante and Poe into Hebrew, Hebrew poetry into Russian ; his publications, under the pen-name " Altalena ", range from novels to studies in comparative phonetics. He was idolized by the young, endowed with exceptional personal charm and a brilliant public speaker — on one occasion I saw him keep an open-air audience of several thousands spellbound for five solid hours.

Jabotinsky created the first Jewish fighting force in modern times : the so-called Judean Regiment which fought under British command in Palestine in the 1914–18 war. When the Arabs rioted in 1920 he organized the Jewish self-defence and was sentenced for it by the British Military Administration to fifteen years' hard labour, but amnestied after a few months. He was elected a member of the Zionist Executive in 1921, came almost from the beginning into conflict with his colleagues, resigned, and created in 1925 the Party of Zionist-Revisionists and the para-military youth organization Betar, out of which, through a process of fissure and budding, the terrorist organizations were to develop.

The conflict between Revisionism and official Zionism was mainly one of character and temperament ; it found its dramatic expression in the long and bitter Trotsky-Stalin struggle between their respective leaders. Coming from a race with a long history but without a political background, neither of them had the true political temperament. Dr. Weizmann is a distinguished chemist ; his approach to politics is the scientist's empirical, cautiously hesitant, step-by-step method, tinged with a certain self-righteousness and a deep distrust of the imaginative and unorthodox. Jabotinsky was a littérateur, with the artist's broad imaginative sweep, his intuition, impatience and emotionalism. Dr. Weizmann's background is that of the Eastern Jewish masses ; he was born in the small provincial town of Motl near Pinsk, was brought up on traditionalist lines, and speaks the language to which the Jews of Pinsk are prepared to listen. Jabotinsky came from the intellectual centre of Odessa, was brought up in a cosmopolitan environment, hated everything connected with Pinsk, and spoke all his eight languages with the accent of an Italian opera baritone, which is anathema to Jewish ears. He fought for the latinization of the Hebrew alphabet, for the Westernization of Israel, which was to become the seventh dominion of the British Commonwealth, for a change in the spirit of Jewish education from the Talmudic seminary to the British public school. In short, while the psychology of official Zionism represented a continuation of Eastern Jewish tradition, Jabotinsky and his Revisionists represented a complete break with it.

Jabotinsky was doomed to defeat, for reasons not unlike those which led to the defeat of that other cosmopolitan Jewish littérateur from Odessa, Leon Trotsky. The working classes were not ripe for the International Revolution, and the Jews were not ripe for their Garibaldian March revolution. Jabotinsky's insistence on a Jewish State as the ultimate aim of Zionism was a mortal heresy in the official Zionist Movement of fifteen years ago, and led to the Revisionists' secession from it. Similarly, his demand for a Jewish Army was branded as Militarism and Fascism, and his plan for a mass evacuation of the doomed Jews of Central Europe to Palestine immediately before the war was decried as Utopian and irresponsible.

Jabotinsky died in 1940, at the age of 60, while engaged in organizing a new international Jewish force to fight with the Allied armies. In the light of present events, with the Jewish State an established reality, almost every point of Jabotinsky's programme has either been implemented by official Zionism, or vindicated by the trend of events — except his stubborn fight against the Partition scheme. But though Israel was not ripe for its Garibaldi, who was born a couple of decades too early and had to pay the usual price which history exacts from her precocious children, he is beginning to reap the posthumous rewards which she bestows in such cases. In Israel's deficient Pantheon, where whole centuries are represented by empty rows, he will fill the place of the nineteenth-century liberal patriot — that missing link in the abrupt transition of Eastern Jewry from the Tsarist ghetto to the advanced social experiment in Palestine.

Jabotinsky's is a spiritual heritage; in Party politics he was significantly unsuccessful. The Revisionist Party's development was unfortunate from its beginnings. The gap in Jewish social history to which I have repeatedly referred, the telescoping of centuries of social evolution into a few decades, left no room for a true national-liberal Party : it was crushed between ghetto and Utopia. On the one hand, its national-revolutionary tenets and Western orientation went against the traditionalist instincts of the Eastern Jew. It is characteristic that Jabotinsky the nationalist fought for the latinization of the Hebrew alphabet to break down the barrier between Judaism and Western civilization, while the internationalists of the Zionist Left rejected it as contrary to Jewish tradition.

On the social front Revisionism tried to remain neutral, but without success. The Revisionists' economic liberalism was reactionary in the eyes of the Hebrew Labour Movement. In nineteenth-century Europe social neutrality was possible within limits for a patriotic reform Party; in Palestine, whose history reopens with the twentieth, it was not. If the Jewish State was to become a reality, a Jewish mass immigration was needed regardless of the social quality of the human material ; accordingly, the Revisionists demanded a policy designed to attract small capitalists and middle-class elements to Palestine, and turned with vehemence against Labour's social experiments in agricultural colonization as too costly and restrictive. Nothing could have more provoked the Socialists, who justly regarded their collective farms and cooperative industries as an outstanding social achievement and the very foundation of modern Palestine. And if a Labourite gets angry the word Fascist comes as easily to him as the word Communist to his opponent, and as some more rustic invectives came to our forebears who did not yet swear in " isms ". In truth, Palestine Labour was no more Communist than Léon

lum, and the Revisionists were no more Fascists than Garibaldi.
ut in the incomplete social spectrum of a country without
·istocracy, gentry and big capitalists, and without a Conservative
arty, it was inevitable that a Party of the Right Centre should
eputize in the public eye for an ultra-reactionary Fascist wing.
'hus history itself seemed to conspire to make T. E. Lawrence's
umous dictum about the Semites having no half-shades in their
egister of vision, and being only at ease when they think in
xtremes, come true again in the political life of Israel.

The bitter hostility between Revisionists and the Parties of the
.eft who dominated the official Zionist Movement came to its
limax in the famous Arlosoroff murder case. Dr. Chaim Arlo-
oroff, the popular leader of Palestine Labour, was shot dead one
ummer night in 1933 on the beach between Tel Aviv and Jaffa.
'he Revisionists had been conducting a violent political campaign
gainst Arlosoroff, and two members of the Revisionist Party were
rrested under suspicion of political murder. One was acquitted
traight away ; the second, a certain Abraham Stavsky, was
ondemned to hang in the first instance, but acquitted by the
ourt of appeal. His trial became one of the most fascinating
nurder cases on record, in which Arab footprint-trackers, British
ntelligence agents, political fanatics and hysterical women per-
'ormed a forensic phantasia and whipped the country into a
assion, echoes of which are still audible to-day after fifteen years.
The trial was Israel's Dreyfus Case ; though innocent of the
:harge, the Revisionists were now definitely branded as Fascist
nurderers in the opinion of the majority. A short time after,
hey left the official Zionist Organization and founded the so-
alled New Zionist Organization, which existed until 1947, and
atronized the Irgun and the Hebrew Committee of National
Liberation (Bergson Group) in the United States. Abraham
Stavsky's further career reads like a footnote by destiny to this
urid affair : after his acquittal he became an organizer of illegal
mmigration, successfully ran the British blockade thirteen times
and was killed on his fourteenth mission, the first to the new
Jewish State, when his ancient opponents of the Left, now transformed into the Israeli Government, ordered the destruction of
the *Altalena* on the beach of Tel Aviv.

Thus, by force of historical circumstances, the political record
of the only strong non-Socialist opposition Party in Israel is one
of frustration and sterility. In its early days the Revisionist

x

Party comprised a good selection of young men of middle-class origin, with as much initiative as their opposite numbers of the Left. But for more than twenty years the members of the Party have been barred from participating in the construction of the National Home, and suffered virtual excommunication. Frustration and a chronic sense of grievance have turned them gradually acid and sectarian, and made their ranks swell with a remarkable number of cranks and monomaniacs. In matters of social policy their opposition had originally been directed against certain costly methods of colonization ; now, under the effect of the vitriolic attacks of the Left, they took a frankly reactionary turn and attacked with equal venom all that Labour had created — agricultural settlements, cooperative industries, social services, — in other words, the whole economic and social frame of modern Palestine. In comparison to these imposing accomplishments of the Left, the Revisionist opposition has hardly anything to show in the field of constructive achievement ; and this, historically, is their decisive weakness. In questions of foreign policy their warnings have generally proved right, and most of their demands, after being denounced as Fascist heresies, became gradually incorporated into the official Zionist programme. But to repeat " I told you so " does not make for popularity any more than to seek remedy for an historical injustice by constant denigration of the opponent's positive achievements. And, after all, this injustice was due not so much to subjective causes as to the basic anachronism in Israel's development, which was our starting-point and which permeates all its political life ; to the fact that Western Liberalism of the nineteenth-century brand came both too early and too late for this country, and was passed over in its breathless leap from ghetto to Utopia.[1]

V. *The Freedom Party*

The Freedom Party, which polled at the elections 11·3 per cent of the votes, is the political successor of the former Irgun Z'vai Leumi, which shortly after the State of Israel came into being transformed itself into a political movement, led by Irgun's leader, Menachem Beigin.

Jewish terrorism has, as we have seen, a general and a specific

[1] In the elections to the Constituent Assembly the Revisionists polled less than 1 per cent of the total votes.

aspect. The general aspect is simple enough, and conforms to an eternal pattern in history. Oppression begets resistance, and each resistance movement produces its rainbow-spectrum from opportunists through moderates to extremists. It is also inevitable that the extremists should be condemned as madmen and thugs, or hailed as patriots and martyrs, according to the observer's standpoint. Their deeds, like all deeds of violence, are always repulsive when seen in the close-up of contemporaneity ; in the perspective of later times the lurid detail fades and only the historic consequences of the act remain.

Jewish terrorism originated when the Mandatory regime turned into a regime of oppression. The main facts will be remembered : by preventing the immigration of Jews from outside Palestine, and barring the Jews already inside from the purchase of arable land, the regime cut off the former from their last chance of escape, and condemned the latter to live in one more precarious oriental ghetto. Incidents less tragic than the drowning of the *Struma* refugees, and regimes less overtly hostile than Mr. Bevin's in Palestine, have generated violent revolutions in history ; had the Jews in Palestine not reacted in the same violent and ugly way as other nations have in their hour of destiny, history would have passed them by with a shrug, leaving it to the Mufti and the Arab League to complete Hitler's work.

If, then, in their general aspect as resistance movements, Irgun and Stern Group were legitimate children of history, in their specific ideology they were an illegitimate offspring of Jabotinsky's national liberalism. They treated. him as their patron saint, as the Russians treat Karl Marx, and with about as much justification. They have inherited the Revisionists' maximalist programme, their contempt for the official Zionist leadership, their sense of grievance and hatred of the Parties of the Left ; but nothing of Jabotinsky's liberalism, Western orientation, European spirit. Their ideology was primitive chauvinism, their language a stream of emotional bombast accompanied by biblical thunderings. They were not Fascists, however, unless we call the Maccabeans and the prophet Samuel Fascists too. After all, it was this gentle prophet who ordered King Saul to go and smite Amalek, and not to spare the women and aged ones nor the suckling at its mother's breast. The Old Testament, taken as a practical guide to twentieth-century politics, is a more pernicious influence than Hitler's *Mein Kampf*.

After the proclamation of Israel's independence and the departure of the British troops, the terrorists, emerging from their underground hide-outs, had to face the problem of their political future. Exposed to the sharp daylight of their newly-gained legality, the difference in philosophy and method of action between the two groups became increasingly apparent and led soon to a complete parting of the ways.

The Irgun had, even at the height of the struggle in its underground days, rigidly observed its self-imposed " code of terrorist honour ", and rejected the methods of indiscriminate assassination and total violence which the Stern Group practised. As soon as the chance offered itself, and in spite of the unabated hostility of their former opponents of the Jewish Agency, now transformed into the Provisional Government, Irgun achieved in a relatively short time its remarkable transformation from a conspiratorial underground group into a respectable " above-board " opposition Party. Its military units were disbanded and incorporated into the official Haganah — at first in the territory of Israel proper and, when the Government announced its official claim to modern Jerusalem, in Jerusalem too. At the same time the Hebrew National Committee of Liberation, Irgun's financial and political sponsor in America, voluntarily liquidated itself to demonstrate the complete break with the past and the new Party's unconditional acceptance of the authority of the Israeli Government.

As Irgun had been the military offspring of the Revisionists, its transformation into a legal political Party immediately raised the question whether Revisionism still had any separate *raison d'être*. The question led to a split amongst the Revisionists, whose majority went over to Beigin. In the elections to the Constituent Assembly the Freedom Party obtained 11·3 per cent of the votes (14 seats), as compared to the Revisionist's 0·6 per cent and no seats.

The programme of the Freedom Party is vaguely progressive, eclectic and colourless. Its one specific feature is the rather rhetorical demand for a Jewish State " both sides of the Jordan ". Its social programme, from the nationalization of the basic industries to the reaffirmation of the Rights of Man, contains hardly a point which would be in principle objectionable to the Left. It is the programme of an as yet amorphous movement in transition. If it can consolidate its initial success and rid itself of its chauvinistic bombast, it may gradually rally around itself the bulk of the atomized non-Socialist half of the country, and develop into the liberal reform Party of the middle classes. Mapai in the Centre, U.W.P. on the Left and the Freedom Party on the Right could thus lead within a few years to a healthy three-party system and replace the present chaos of some twenty political Parties bickering for the meagre crumbs of power in the tiny country.

The Stern Group has, since the proclamation of the State, gone, or rather drifted, in a different direction. Its rank and file, much less numerous than Irgun's, had been indoctrinated with the maxims of total terror, without the restrictions imposed by the latter. They are a fanatic brand of young men without any constructive ideas, politically illiterate, who could only have been rehabilitated to the conditions of normal life through the joint efforts of the Government and their own leaders. Neither of the two proved capable of this. The new-baked Government, as so often happens, were more concerned with settling old scores and asserting their authority by draconic measures than with long-term preoccupations of national unity; their problem was not how to reintegrate the former terrorist groups, but how to liquidate them on the first suitable occasion. The leaders of Irgun avoided traps and provocations with considerable restraint; the leaders of the Stern Group lacked both the restraint and the will to carry their activities into the full daylight of democratic politics. Without any political programme of their own they sought to exploit the tide of the popular mood, and at the same time to give vent to their hatred of Britain by adopting an extreme pro-Russian attitude. There is nothing new in this either; the ultra-chauvinistic Croatian Ustachi and German Freikorps after both World Wars have gone the same way.

Apart from the insignificant Communist Party, the Stern Group thus became the only channel through which Soviet influence could infiltrate into the Israeli scene. This should not be interpreted as meaning that any of the official leaders of the group took orders from the Russians. But there is some circumstantial evidence for the assumption that the Silent Soviet Services have succeeded in creating a caucus within the group which, unknown to its leaders, acted as a probably unconscious tool of the former.

At the elections on January 25, 1949, the group received 1·2 per cent of the votes. Its future prospects are no better, and there is little doubt that it will continue for a while as an insignificant sect and vanish with increasing political stability in the new State.

VI. *The Liberals and Clericals*

The remaining Parties of the Government coalition can be
treated briefly.   The so-called " General Zionists " and the
" Progressive Party ", a break-away group of the former, corre-
spond to the liberal Parties in Europe — and are sharing their
fate by gradually vanishing from the political scene.   Together
the two Parties polled 9 2 per cent of the votes.

The " Religious Bloc " is a force composed of not less than
five different religious Parties, including the " Partyless Orthodox
Women's Party ".   It has assembled 12 per cent of the total vote,
but the influence of its somewhat machiavellian rabbis is considerably stronger than these figures indicate.   The Orthodox in
Israel in fact form a religious pressure-group which will trade its
support for the Government in exchange for such concessions as
the interdiction of public transpoit on the Shabbath, or for higher
subventions for the rabbinical schools, and thus introduces an
element of sacred corruption into the political life of the young
country.   The problem of the relations of Church and State,
which is one of the characteristic issues in Israel, will be discussed
in a later chapter.

II

THE REBIRTH OF THE HEBREW LANGUAGE

THEODORE HERZL, the founder of modern Zionism, suffered from the blind spots which mar the vision of the single-minded genius in matters outside the sharp beam of his endeavour. When he was asked what language the Jews, forgathered from the four corners of the earth, would speak in their own State, he said naively that each Jew would of course speak his own language, and somehow they would manage to get along. The idea that they should revert to ancient Hebrew seemed to him absurd : " Why, who of us knows enough Hebrew to ask even for a railway ticket ? "

Yet obviously a unitary State required a single language. In other pioneer countries with a heterogeneous population the strongest ethnic group of immigrants has imposed its language on the others. According to this rule, the language of Palestine should have become Yiddish, the lingua franca of the Eastern Jewish masses. But Yiddish is a strange vernacular, a mixture of mediaeval German, rabbinical Hebrew and half a dozen modern languages, without a fixed grammar, syntax or vocabulary. It is a typical product of exile, which mirrors the physical and cultural homelessness of the wandering Jew. The Zionist masses felt that if they were to be re-formed into a nation this refugee jargon would not do ; that the return to their original home entailed the return to their original language, biblical Hebrew. If the clock of history was to be turned back, it had to be done whole-heartedly. Like Zionism itself, the Hebraistic movement was a blend of mystic and utilitarian motives. A common language of the immigrants was a practical necessity ; the choice of Hebrew followed as an act of mystical logic or logical mysticism.

The movement was started in Palestine in the 1880s by a fanatical little school teacher named Eliezer ben Yehuda ; by the end of the First World War it had triumphed. Hebrew became, together with Arabic and English, the third official language of Palestine under the British Mandate, and in 1948 the sole official language of Israel. The older generation, if they are recent immigrants, speak Hebrew in public, and German or Polish or

Sephardic at home; but the native generation, regardless of their parents' country 'of origin, are brought up in Hebrew schools and speak no other language, except some Berlitz-English which is taught in secondary schools. Biblical Hebrew is the language of Government and Parliament, of schools and courts, of Press and radio, of taxi-drivers and poets. And that means that the cultural life of the country is confined to a medium which has been practically dead for two thousand years.

In previous chapters I have attempted to show how, in the political field, the Jews in Israel are struggling to reconquer the forgotten art of being a nation, to fill in the long gap in their social development. In the cultural field this gap makes itself felt even more. For Hebrew as a spoken language had ceased to develop long before the beginnings of the Christian era. In the time of Jesus the Jews in Palestine spoke Aramaic, and only the learned discoursed in so-called " Rabbinical Hebrew ", a kind of equivalent of Church Latin. After the completion of the Talmud (*circa* A.D. 500) not even the scholars wrote in Hebrew any longer; the language had become too fossilized to be of any use to mediaeval thought and philosophy. The Jewish scholars of the eleventh and twelfth centuries — Moses ben Maimon, Ibn Ezra, Ibn Gabirol — wrote in Arabic, as their descendants wrote in German, English and French. Probably the last literary works of any merit written in the ancient language are the poems of Juda Halevy (*c.* 1085–*c.* 1140); but Halevy, too, wrote his philosophical works in Arabic, as Hebrew had become totally unsuitable for the treatment of abstract subjects and for a precise expression of thought.

Thus the unfortunate Hebrew translator of to-day is faced with the herculean task of rendering Kant and Marx, Freud and Bergson, Whitehead and Ogden in an idiom which even twelfth-century scholars abandoned as obsolete and unfit for their purpose. This is not merely a matter of vocabulary, modern scientific terms can be borrowed from European languages, and this, of course, is constantly done; the difficulty lies in the archaic structure of the language. Metaphorically speaking, the task amounts to the transformation of a Phoenician chariot, by fitting it out with borrowed spare parts, into a racing motor-car.

Fiction and belles-lettres face an even graver handicap. The small and archaic vocabulary of the Hebrew language, its paucity of adverbs and adjectives, are the consequence of arrested development and make for an inflexibility of style which causes translations of Hemingway to be practically indistinguishable from translations of Proust, and Malraux to read like Walter Scott. The modern Hebrew novelist or poet has no linguistic roots in the classics, for there are no Hebrew classics since the Bible, no literary traditions, no idiomatic developments. The instrument on which he has to express the nuances of his twentieth-century emotions and psychology has no half-tones or modulations of key and timbre. It is admirably suited for producing prophetic thunder; but you cannot play a scherzo on a ram's-horn. More precisely, the modern Hebrew writer's predicament may be compared to the imaginary case of a contemporary English author condemned to express himself in the language of Beowulf.

The fact that Hebrew through all these centuries, though dead as a mundane language, remained in use for prayer and biblical exegesis, has increased rather than diminished the handicap of its adaptation to modern use. Church Latin is the dead branch on a living tree which produced the main idioms of Western civilization; on the Hebrew stem only the dead branch was preserved. This is now being artificially revived by the grafting of new shoots; but the mentality of sterile scholasticism and turgid mysticism clings to the language and is only slowly being exorcised. Thus the attempted renaissance of Hebrew culture labours under a twofold difficulty: the archaic texture of the language and its rabbinical aura.

This may explain why modern Hebrew drama and fiction have so far failed to come to grips with the problems of contemporary life. The repertories of the famous Habima, and even of the workers' theatre " Ohel ", are mainly devoted to the past — to plays based either on biblical subjects or on the life of the Polish ghettoes. There are, of course, notable exceptions, like Shamir's excellent play about collective settlements, recently produced by the experimental Chamber Theatre,[1] or Maltze's novel *Maagalot* on the same subject. But though Israel is a pioneer country bursting with vitality and obsessed with its topical problems, by and large modern Hebrew literature is singularly lacking in modernity and " Zeitgeist ". Its general keynote is a somewhat stale romanticism, a sentimental tendency to linger on the sufferings of the past, tinged with the ironical self-pity traditional in Yiddish literature. On Hebrew poetry I do not feel qualified to express an opinion.

[1] See pp. 260-61.

A further major obstacle on the path towards a renaissance of Hebrew culture is the Hebrew alphabet, which consists of consonants only, to the exclusion of vowels. A system of vowels written underneath the row of consonants was devised in the sixth and seventh centuries A.D., but is practically never used either in handwriting or in print. This two-storey alphabet is, in fact, impracticable, as it would require linotype machines with about a dozen different keys for each consonant according to the vowel by which it is followed, and which has to appear underneath it. The result is that the pronunciation and meaning of a written word can only be determined after the reader has guessed the approximate meaning of the whole phrase — a fascinating field of study for the Gestalt psychologist. Thus, for example, the word composed of the three printed signs *Daleth, Vav, Daleth* will mean either " the beloved one " or " uncle " or " boiler " or " David ", according to the context in which it appears.

Written Hebrew not only lacks that unequivocal precision which alone makes the expression of complicated thought possible, it also paralyses the creative writer, prevents him from playing and experimenting with words, prevents innovation and linguistic development.

For, since the meaning of the written word has to be deduced by the reader from the context, unorthodox turns of phrase are simply not understood. It need not be emphasized how much such a system, whose difficulties rank somewhere half-way between those of the Latin and Chinese scripts, impedes the learning of the language, both for the child and the foreigner. I have spent on and off altogether some four years in Palestine and speak Hebrew fairly fluently, but am still incapable of reading a newspaper, to say nothing of books. The majority of new immigrants are in the same position ; they are prevented from fully participating in the cultural life of the country, and are condemned to intellectual sterility. A number of German-Jewish writers of European fame have shared this sad fate ; an even greater number of leading scholars and scientists abroad are prevented by the same reason from lecturing at the Hebrew University. And as the future development of this small and isolated community depends on a steady flow of immigration from, and cultural interchange with, the Western world, the gravity of the problem should not be underestimated.

The only way to avoid the dangers of cultural isolation and

stagnation seems to be the latinization of the obsolete and cumbersome alphabet. If this revolutionary measure could be carried out in backward Turkey, one would have expected it to meet with little resistance in this predominantly European community. But though latinization was proposed some twenty-five years ago by Jabotinsky, and advocated by the son of Ben Yehuda, who published for a short time a Hebrew newspaper printed in Latin characters, the resistance of the traditionalists was too strong, and the experiment failed.

As has already been mentioned, this cultural conservatism is not confined to the clerical Party but is shared by the Socialist Left. Their rejection of latinization is symbolic: though rationalized by arguments about technical difficulties, its real source is a deeply ingrained, instinctive resistance against the final breakdown of the cultural barriers between Jew and Gentile. Such vestiges of cultural isolationism can be found in many walks of life here; they are signs that the harsh daylight of Israel has not yet completely effaced the shadows of the ghetto, whose walls not only segregated from, but also offered protection against, a hostile environment.

For the ghetto was both prison and nest, where generations of Jews, huddled together in the warm twilight of the Shabbath-candles, developed that peculiar feature of Jewish communities which one might be tempted to name " claustrophilia ". It is an awful word; but it comes nearer to the psychological reality of Israel than terms like " chauvinism " or " isolationism ". Its dangers to the cultural future of the young State should not be ignored.

III

BACK TO THE BRONZE AGE?

THESE lines are written on the 15th of Tamuz of the year 5708 since the creation of the world. I have just checked it by looking at the date-line of the morning paper. Day after day the newspapers in Israel appear under similar date-lines, and the corresponding date according to the Christian calendar is only indicated in coy brackets. Even the Socialist and Communist dailies follow the same custom. At the same time, of course, the whole country, with the exception of a few religious cranks, lives according to the Gregorian calendar. Why, then, do the newspapers pretend to count time from the day when God divided the Heavens from the Earth?

This paradox typifies one of the more startling phenomena in Israeli life. While the orthodox religious element represents only a small minority of the population — 12·03 per cent to be exact, according to the last election results — and while the Socialist Parties, with their materialist and anti-clerical doctrine, occupy all political and economic key positions, life in Israel is nevertheless under the sway of clericalism to a degree unequalled in any other country of our contemporary world.

In my collection of curiosities there is a recent menu card of one of Tel Aviv's leading hotels, written in English and Hebrew, which reads :

SPECIAL DINNER

Chopped Chicken Liver

Consommé

Roast Pork (for U.N.O. and the Press)

or

Roast Turkey

Potatoes, Vegetables, Salad

Ice Cream

Thus U.N.O. and the foreign Press may indulge in roast pork, but not the citizen of Israel, as pork is forbidden by Mosaic Law. That doesn't mean that eating pork is strictly speaking illegal, for as yet the State of Israel has no Constitution and no definite Code of Laws. It only means that the proprietor of the hotel in question does not wish to risk a row with the Rabbinate. And the Socialist-dominated Government are adopting exactly the same attitude. They not only abstain from importing pork, ham or bacon (except in small quantities, for U.N.O. and the Press), but only permit the importation of kosher meat — that is of meat slaughtered according to Mosaic ritual under the supervision of the Chief Rabbi in the country of origin. And as kosher meat is both expensive and difficult to obtain on the world market, there has been, since the end of the British Mandate, practically no meat in Israel.[1]

Kosherness, however, is only one of the relatively minor rabbinical plagues in the young State. A major one is the prohibition of all public traffic from sunset on Friday to the end of the Shabbath. This means that the citizen of Tel Aviv, Haifa or Jerusalem is unable, on his only free day in the week, to take a bus-ride to the sea, visit friends, or go for an excursion in the country. Taxis and private cars, however, may, for the time being, circulate ; which means, as is the case with all retrograde legislation, that the masses are victimized while the rich can comfortably circumvent the law.

Israel's University, on Mount Scopus in Jerusalem, has been in existence for over twenty years, but only recently have plans been announced for a medical faculty. The reason has been mainly because dissecting corpses is contrary to Mosaic Law, and the Board of the University has been understandably hesitant. Instances of the orthodox stranglehold on this young and exuberant country can

---

[1] On January 20, 1949, the following news item was issued by *Palcor*, the official information bulletin of the Israeli Government :

" The crisis in the Cabinet caused by the question of the type of meat to be imported has now come to an end. As will be remembered, the three members of the Cabinet who belong to the religious parties — Mr. Moshe Shapiro, Minister of Immigration, Rabbi J. M. Levin, Minister of Social Welfare, and Rabbi J. L. Fishman, Minister for Religion and War Victims — had, during three months, abstained from the deliberations of the Cabinet because of their disagreement with the Government's views on this question. By a majority of 6 votes to 3 the Cabinet has now adopted the suggestion of the religious bloc according to which the importation of meat will in future be jointly controlled by the Ministry of Commerce and Industry and the Ministry for Religion."

In plain words, the Cabinet has capitulated to the rabbis and no non-kosher meat will be imported into Israel.

be multiplied, from the grave danger that marriage, divorce and inheritance may temporarily fall under the exclusive and mediaeval jurisdiction of rabbinical courts, to such grotesque incidents as the Orthodox Party's solemn request that each Israeli Legation abroad should have a " religious attaché " on its staff — or that men and women should be forced to bathe from separate beaches. There is even a Talmudic seminary in Jerusalem where the rites of animal sacrifice are studied in great earnest and secrecy, in the hope that Solomon's Temple will soon be rebuilt on its ancient site. If the Orthodox Party had its way, the State of Israel would regress to the conditions of life before the fall of Jerusalem in the first century A.D.

To the outside observer all this may appear romantic and picturesque, but from the point of view of the new State clericalism is one of the most serious problems to be solved. Two main questions arise : firstly, how was it possible for the old rabbis to get such a hold on this modern pioneer country ; and secondly, the outlook for the future.

The answer to the first question is partly political, partly psychological. The Labour Party, Mapai, commands roughly one-third of the total votes, and can only rule by coalition. It can form a coalition with the United Workers' Party on the extreme Left, whom it dislikes, or with the Freedom Party and other Right-Wing groups, whom it dislikes even more. The only remaining solution is to form a majority with the splinter groups of the Centre ; and among these the most important are the Orthodox Party and the Orthodox Workers' Party — the latter being clerically-minded but socially progressive, like many of the Christian Trade Unions of Europe. Hence, according to the laws of parliamentary arithmetic, if Mapai wants to rule independently of the extreme Right and Left, it has to make concessions to the clergy. For a number of years the Labour Party has lived, at Zionist Congresses, in the Municipal Councils and other autonomous bodies, under the holy terror of the rabbis. Now, as the dominant Party in the State, it is faced with the same problem in a more acute form.

This situation has some analogy with that of the French Third Force coalition. But in France the division of Church and State is the firmly established result of a long historical development, and the M.R.P. would never dream of asking its Socialist partners to abolish, say, civil marriage. In Israel, on the other hand, this division has never been carried out, for the simple reason that there was no State, and that the survival of the Jews as a separate entity was solely and exclusively due to their religious allegiance.   In the segregated Jewish communities behind the ghetto walls, the rabbis were priests and judges, spiritual and secular authority all in one.   Hence the deeply ingrained and mostly unconscious reluctance of the Jews in Israel to defy openly the power of the rabbis, or even to engage in a clean fight for the liberalization of religious observance, however fossilized its rites have become.   Whoever has watched, for instance, a ritual slaughter must be appalled by the preservation of this archaic and cruel procedure ; yet there is hardly a voice in Israel raised against it.   The following excerpt from my diary may illustrate the mentality of the Orthodox leaders, and what would become of Israel if it failed to break their stranglehold.

Tel Aviv, October 7

To-day went to see Rabbi Fishman, Minister for Religion and member of the Cabinet.

The Ministry is a small two-storey house in the former Templar colony at Sarona, now transformed into a Government compound.   It is teeming with little bearded men in skull-caps huddled behind deal tables, and more bearded men in black silk kaftans waiting in the corridors.   Rabbi Fishman is seventy-two, has a white moustache and goatee and a pleasant twinkle in his eye which becomes less pleasant whenever the mildest heresy is uttered.   We started the conversation in Hebrew, but as I was unable to understand his synagogal ashkenazi pronunciation with the strong yiddish lilt, a secretary was called in to translate.   This secretary, a young man with skull-cap and side-locks, lapped up the Rabbi's words like honey, underlined the Rabbi's arguments with a gentle swaying of his head, smacking his lips like a con-noisseur of rare wines, and accompanied their translation with rhythmic gestures of his hands.   (He reminded me of the old Jewish story of the young man telling his friend of his splendid new job : " I have become a Tsetserer to our Rabbi ".   " And what has a Tsetserer to do ? "   " The Tsetserer has to sit at the Rabbi's feet, and when the Rabbi performs a miracle he goes ' Ts—ts—ts ! ' ")

My first question was : What does the Rabbi think of the various movements to reform and liberalize religious observance ?

The Rabbi answered : Israel will live according to the Law as laid down by Moses, which needs not the slightest reform. I asked : What about the Shabbath prohibition of traffic ? Surely this is not based on the Law of Moses, but on a late mediaeval codification (the Shulkhan Arukh, written by a man called Joseph Caro) ? The Rabbi said : No, it is already in the Bible, in the Book of Nehemiah, where it says, "On the Shabbath neither king nor servant shall carry a weight". He leaned back comfortably, and expounded : " Now what does it mean; ' the king shall not carry a weight ' ? What weight would a king carry ? A handkerchief maybe, or a golden ring. So what does the prohibition really mean ? It means that on the Shabbath the king shouldn't ride out. Neither the king nor the servant, neither on a horse nor in a bus."

Triumphant smile of the Rabbi ; translator smacks his lips. I said I couldn't follow his interpretation, and had a different one : " Thou shalt carry no weight " means you mustn't make an effort. For instance a person may be very fat, and to carry his own weight on a hot Shabbath day from Herzl Street to the beach would mean a great effort for him, and the sweat on his brow would be an unpleasant sight in the eyes of the Lord and a breach of the Shabbath. That's why we need buses on the Shabbath.

The secretary translated this with a treacherously appreciative " Ts—ts ", and now the Rabbi said something very revealing. The logical retort would of course have been : " And what about the bus-driver's Shabbath ? " Instead of which he said : " You see, if we had in Tel Aviv a system of electric trams it would perhaps be all right. But a motor car needs *igniting*. And to make fire on the Shabbath is not permitted."

The explanation of this absurdity is to be found in the curiously twisted, labyrinthine logic of the Orthodox Jew. He cares little about the bus-driver, for it was a habit among the Orthodox in Eastern Europe to employ a " Shabbath goy " — a gentile paid to carry out on the Shabbath the menial tasks which are forbidden to the true believer. One of the Shabbath goy's tasks was to light the candles or oil lamps, for the making of fire on the Shabbath was regarded as a major sin. But the matter did not end there. For the Bible says that the servant who is a stranger in Israel's tents should obey the same law as his masters. Hence the Orthodox could not explicitly order the Shabbath goy or the gentile housemaid to break the law. He had to arrange matters by expressing his wishes indirectly within earshot of the servant, say by sighing non-committally : " Now wouldn't it be nice if we had the light on ! " It was an echo of this long-standing tradition which made the Rabbi come out with the theory that the Lord makes a sharp distinction between Shabbath traffic by electric trams and by internal-combustion engines.

I asked : What about electric switches ? He must have expected the question, for he explained at once that he has an electric clock-device installed in his house which switches the light automatically on at the proper hour on Friday evening, switches it off at midnight, and on again on the Shabbath evening. I complimented him on his ingenuity, but the secretary said with a smile, pitying my ignorance, that he too, and every Orthodox household, had a similar contraption installed. I found out later that all synagogues, most schools and a number of apartment houses in Israel have been using this automatic clock-switch for years.

To complete his victory, the Rabbi pulled out the Book of Nehemiah from his shelf and showed me the passage about carrying weights (xiii, 17-19).

More about the Shabbath. Not only is the use of any vehicle prohibited, but even visiting friends on foot is a ticklish question, for the Bible says " Al yi'tseh mi maqomeh'kha " — Thou shalt not leave thy place on the Shabbath. This, the Minister explained, means that nobody is allowed to walk further than a mile and a quarter from his house. Why just a mile and a quarter ? Because in ancient Israel the " place " of a family within the tribe embraced a space of about a mile and a quarter in radius. In some Orthodox settlements there are actually wire fences put up, marking the limit of a Shabbath walk. However, Tel Aviv has a suburb, B'ne Barak, mainly inhabited by Orthodox believers, who, the Rabbi explained, like a Shabbath stroll on the beach. A satisfactory way to make this possible was found by the following arrangement. The burghers of B'ne Barak walk in the direction of the beach, carrying a plate of food. This they put down on the ground when they reach the mile and a quarter limit. The spot on which the food is put down is considered to have become their new " place ", and they can proceed for a further mile and a quarter ; and so on.

" You see," concluded the Minister, " that we need no tikunim — no reforms. All these devices by which we adapt the Mosaic Law to our modern days are merely tikunot — interpretations. *Tikunim* are forbidden, but *tikunot* are permitted and are a proof of scholarly learning and ingenuity."

His way of referring to past events was to say : " Seven hundred and fifty years ago ", or " Three hundred years ago ", to avoid having to say " At the end of the twelfth century ", or " In the seventeenth century ", which would imply acceptance of the Christian calendar. As counting from the creation of the world would involve too much cumbersome arithmetic, they count backwards — which about sums up the way their minds work. To my question whether he would agree that the teaching of secular history in the schools was desirable, the Rabbi answered : " I have never studied history, but I am told by experts that I am an expert in history ". At which I thought it was about time to take my leave. The experience would have been merely amusing as a journey to Wonderland ; but as it happened it was an interview with a Minister in the Government. It was a journey to Wonderland nevertheless, into the petrified forests of a ghetto religion which for many centuries has ceased to be a living system of worship. Long generations of rabbis and scholars had devoted their lives to the sterile brain-acrobatics of mediaeval scholasticism, to commenting on each other's commentaries, to pondering on the hidden meaning of words (as each Hebrew letter stands also for a figure, each word has a number-value which lends itself to endless numerological games) ; and above all to devious *tikunot* or interpretations of the law. Through these " interpretations " one generation after another learned the art of cheating the Lord and their own consciences. They were a technique which became a conditioned mental reflex, so that the first approach to a law or prohibition was how to " interpret " it, never taking no for an answer. How far this mental corruption in matters divine was the product of social pressure which forced the Jew to live on the margin of the law, and how far the Talmudistic mentality reacted on his pattern of social behaviour, is a moot point. The outcome at any rate was a vicious circle, a perpetuum mobile for generating anti-semitism, which linked persecution and evasion in a monotonously alternating tidal rhythm.

One of the main *raisons d'être* of Israel is to break this vicious cycle. Already the Orthodox are in a minority, and the native generation, grown up under hard pioneering conditions, show signs of developing a mentality which conforms to the advice given to their ancestors by one who wished them well : to answer Yea or Nay, for whatsoever is more cometh of evil. But the ghetto is putting up a tenacious rearguard action. And behind the political arguments for appeasing the rabbis, there lurks, as we saw, a deeper psychological reason for the uneasy acquiescence, even of the extreme Left, to the holy blackmail exerted by the Orthodox Parties. For almost twenty centuries Israel had no political and social history, and was cemented together solely by religious tradition. If this tradition goes, if Mosaic Law is recognized as an anachronism, what spiritual foundations will remain ? For unlike other nations, Israel has no Cromwell and no Joan of Arc, no Voltaire, Goethe or Lincoln ; its heroes are the Prophets, its only classic the Bible. Once again we find that a paradox in present-day Israel — a Socialist country under clerical sway — is explained by the gap in its past history.

We have also seen, however, in previous chapters, how quickly this vacuum is being filled in the political field, how centuries of European evolution are telescoped into a few years under the tropical conditions of Israel's mental climate. Hence the next developments in the relations between State and Church are relatively easy to foresee. During the first few years of the internal consolidation of the new State, while the Parties are manœuvring for power, the Orthodox will retain their political key-position and benefit from the rivalry of the others. In all likelihood the first Constitution will place marriage, divorce and other matters of personal status under the exclusive jurisdiction of religious courts. This will mean, among other things, that there will be no civil marriages in Israel ; that women will be unable to obtain divorce ; that there will be no travel on the Shabbath ; that restaurants will not serve cheese after meat, this being also against Mosaic Law ; and that generally speaking Israel will be a very picturesque country for romantically-minded travellers, but from this particular point of view a rather tiresome country to live in.

This state of affairs, one can confidently predict, will last some five or, at most, ten years. Then the young native generation, which has no memory of ghettoes and is developing a national tradition of its own, will carry out a vociferous but bloodless secular revolution and achieve a clean division between Church and State.

IV

THE CULTURE OF THE NEW STATE —
A SUMMING-UP

I

An English foreign correspondent,[1] who had spent two months in Tel Aviv, said with a sigh: "When I arrived here I was pro-Jewish and anti-Zionist. Now I am becoming pro-Zionist and anti-Jewish."

This is a fairly precise summing-up of an experience which a great number of well-meaning strangers undergo in Israel — newspaper men, diplomatic staff, U.N.O. personnel. They become converted to Zionism not by arguments but by the hard facts of Zionist pioneer achievement. The modern villages in the desert, the drained marshes and reclaimed dunes, the schools, hospitals, factories and social services, the bustling bee-hive activity of the whole country, the tough and healthy native generation born of soft and sickly parents — all this makes an irresistible impact on any open-minded observer from abroad. He is forced to admire what he sees — and almost as forcibly tempted to dislike it. The older the civilization of his native country, the stronger the temptation to dislike, and the more guilty he feels when aesthetic revulsion gains the upper hand over his objective judgment.

For to the aesthete this pioneer country has as yet nothing to offer. Life in Israel is lacking in tradition and style, form and colour, humour and grace. Tel Aviv's architecture is the drab functionalism of the early 'twenties at its worst. The streets have no skyline; the cheap, peeling stucco on the concrete blocks makes the whole town look as if it had the measles; the sea-front is hemmed in by a row of sordid little cafés with blaring loudspeakers. The Army has as yet no uniforms, but the dominant colour in the streets is khaki, even in peace-time: workers, clerks, bus-drivers, schoolboys, flapper-girls and servants of the State mostly wear

---

[1] Michael Davidson of *The Observer*, whose feature articles were among the best written on the early days of Israel.

khaki shorts and shirts. This imparts to the dreadfully over-crowded streets the powerful but shapeless dynamism of a muddy stream. The cinemas, restaurants and cafés offer no privacy and relaxation; they are swirling eddies in the stream, which suck you in and spit you out an hour later, feeling even more limp and sweaty than before. The boiling air is saturated with the noise of radios, café orchestras and children yelling from the street up to their mammas on the second floor. But all this pandemonium lacks the local colour, and hence the specific charm, of an oriental bazaar or an old Italian port. It is the colourless, shapeless bustle of Jewish suburbs all over the world, of Whitechapel or Nalewki, Orchard Street or the Faubourg du Temple. The stranger, after a fortnight or so in Tel Aviv, begins to feel like a fresh-water fish thrown into a salt-water pond; he gasps for air and develops acute symptoms of claustrophobia.

Aesthetically, Tel Aviv is the worst feature of Israel, the architect's Sodom and Gomorrah. But the new Jewish residential quarters in Haifa or Tiberias are much in the same style. As for the countryside, no greater contrast is imaginable than that be-tween the picturesque squalor of the Arab villages, now mostly dead and deserted, and the sober purposefulness of the Jewish settlements. These pioneer villages do not fit the landscape, the houses do not fit the climate, rural life is devoid of folklore and tradition. The oldest villages, like Petakh Tikwa or Rekhowoth, founded at the turn of the century, look like Ukrainian or Polish townlets transplanted to the Judean plain; others, like Naharia, are German Kurorts grafted on by plastic landscape surgery, complete with Biergarten and Familien Pension. The tourist, who came to admire, feels at the same time both moved and repelled. And this is not a matter of aesthetic snobbery, but of a kind of vitamin-starvation of the senses.

This absence of a native tradition, of an organically grown pattern of life, makes itself felt in every sphere. The Orthodox Jews who used to spend their days in prayer at the Wailing Wall are the most traditionalist element in Israel; yet they strut in the scorching heat wearing fur caps, waistcoats, caftans and knee-boots, apparently believing that this seventeenth-century Polish costume, the uniform of the ghetto, was worn by the Hebrew tribes in the desert. The national dance of the Hebrew youth is the Ukrainian Horra; the national anthem of Israel is a melody by the Czech composer Smetana; the popular song of the day, the " Negeb " is the song of the Russian partisans fitted with Hebrew words. The food is Viennese or Polish, rich and heavy, as unsuitable for the climate as are the fur caps of the devout. There are no native arts and no native crafts (except that of the Yemenite silversmiths imported by Jews from Aden, and now rapidly becoming commercialized) ; painting and sculpture are unoriginal and eclectic.

By and large, the Jews in Palestine have remained untouched by the native mode of life ; they have not learnt from the Arabs how to build houses that are cool, spacious and cheap, nor to make succulent *kebab* on a charcoal fire. They have imposed upon the country their own immigrants' pattern ; but unlike other pioneers, who had roots in the national traditions of their mother country out of which the branch of their colonial civilization developed, the Jewish colonists had no particular mother country and no specific cultural roots of their own. They came from the Diaspora, from the ghettoes and suburbs and D.P. camps of the world, and brought with them bits of alien civilizations picked up in transit. That is perhaps why life in Israel's capital has such a shapeless, nondescript quality about it, and why Tel Aviv gives the impression of being the large Jewish suburb of a non-existent city.

This suburban character of cultural life is further accentuated by the absence of distinct social classes. Israel has no aristocracy, no gentry, no patrician bourgeoisie, no real proletariat. Its population has a uniform social background : that of the *petite bourgeoisie*, the lower middle classes of Eastern European Jewish small towns. There are of course rich and poor, but in their tradition and culture they all belong to the same social stratum. The greengrocer's wife and the Cabinet Minister's wife speak with the same accent, use the same vocabulary, share the same tastes, values and outlook on life.

Most of these remarks apply equally to any other young and raw pioneer country. Life in the Middle West is hardly more inspiring in its cultural aspect than life in Tel Aviv. And the visitor to New Zealand does not expect to find there the atmosphere of Florence. Nothing could be more unfair than to judge this country of pioneers and refugees by the standards of mellower civilizations. Years spent in concentration camps or in draining the Hule marshes are no equivalent for an English public school education. All this is so obvious that it would hardly need stressing if any other country were concerned ; but in the peculiar case of Jewish Palestine, expectations are quite out of keeping with reality, and here cultural factors play a sometimes decisive part in shaping political destiny.

This, indeed, is the core of the problem of Israel's relations with the outside world. The tourist who embarks for New Zealand or the American Middle West knows more or less what to expect and risks no shock of disappointment. But the stranger to Israel, whether diplomat or journalist, has, partly through the fault of an over-zealous Zionist propaganda, a completely wrong picture in his mind. He expects something in the vein of picturesque Maccabeans fighting under palm trees in a kind of Max Reinhardt production, while prospective Freuds and Einsteins play chess in the café round the corner. The fact is that there are few palm trees in Israel, for eucalyptus and citrus plants pay quicker and better returns ; that the scenery is more Polish than oriental ; that it is both a hard pioneer country and a bitter refugee country, disillusioned by experience, stubbornly fighting for life, with an aching void in its past and an interrogation mark for its future. The muses and the social graces are still under embargo ; most of the things which make life attractive and worth living are for to-morrow.

2

Each war or revolution produces its lost generation. Israel's lost generation are the middle-aged, those who came here at a time of their life which still allows them to remember Europe. Not the fleshpots of Europe : for most of them lived in penury. Not the safety of Europe : for they were persecuted. They do not plan or even yearn to go back, for their bridges have been burnt — either by their own free will, or by the torches of their persecutors. They know that for them, as for the whole nation, there is no turning back. The very word " homesickness " is blasphemy, for their home is here, and they have denied Europe as Europe denied them.

Nevertheless they are a lost generation. They finger lovingly their Israeli passports, but they cannot get accustomed to the climate. They are proud of living in Israel's capital, but its provincial atmosphere oppresses them. They Hebraise their names, Steinberg into Har-Even, Wolfson into Ben-Dov, but Hebrew remains an acquired language to them. The children in school take to the biblical language like ducks to the pond, but the parents speak it haltingly and read it with even greater difficulty ; after years of effort they manage to get through a newspaper, but Hebrew books are beyond their ken and they feel left out, condemned to intellectual sterility.

There also exists a lost generation in a different sense of the word, though the two overlap to some extent. They are the people who have spent years — sometimes as many as ten — in concentration and D.P. camps, and who only survived by becoming conditioned to circumventing the law — for the law for the Jew on the continent of Europe was deportation and death. Few can sustain such pressure without some deformation of character, and a large number of the immigrants of recent years are psychological problem-cases, some of them with a marked asocial tendency. This trend will of necessity continue until the last D.P. camp is empty and the last survivors of the European disaster are transferred.

The other main sources of immigration, present and future, are the Sephardi Jews from Syria, Egypt, Iraq, the Yemen and North Africa, whose economic and physical existence is becoming increasingly precarious. They are orientals both in character and appearance; their colour varies from olive to dark brown; their main language is Arabic. The socially most useful elements among them are probably the Yemenites, from the southernmost tip of the Arabian peninsula; they are short, dark, wiry men who look and speak like Arabs, are extremely devout, straight-thinking and primitive. At the opposite end of the scale are the youngsters from the slums of Cairo, Salonika and Beirut, with a Levantine mentality, emotionally unstable, an easy prey both to the lures of the black market and to terrorist romantics.

Already some 25 to 30 per cent of Israel's population are oriental Jews; and by virtue both of their higher birth-rate and of the increasing pressure in the neighbouring countries, they will, in all probability, outnumber the European element in the not too distant future. This fact makes the cultural problem of Israel appear in a new light, which as yet few of the political and intellectual leaders of the country are prepared to face.

To summarize these overlapping trends: at the beginning of modern Zionist colonization, the dominant element among the immigrants were pioneers who came out of their own free will, drawn by the twofold ideal of a national renaissance and a Socialist Utopia. Since then, successive waves of persecution, starting in Pilsudski's Poland and ending with the recent pogroms in Egypt, have diminished the importance of the idealistic volunteer element and proportionally increased the flood of refugees, both from Europe and the Arab countries, who came out of sheer necessity, without any idea or ideal in their heads. This process has led to a considerable deterioration in the human material out of which the new State is being built. Some of them are unwilling or unable to assimilate themselves to the language and ways of the country and are condemned to vegetate for the rest of their lives in intellectual sterility; others have, through the tragic circumstances of their past, become socially deformed. In their ensemble, these form the lost generation of Israel; a transitory and amorphous mass which as yet lacks the character of a nation. Only in the native youth, born and reared in the country, does the first intimation of the future profile of Israel begin to outline itself.

The Palestine-born young Jew's nickname, " sabra ", is derived, as already mentioned, from the prickly, wild-growing, somewhat tasteless fruit of the cactus plant. In physical appearance he is almost invariably taller than his parents, robustly built, mostly blond or brown-haired, frequently snub-nosed and blue-eyed. The young male's most striking feature is that he looks entirely un-Jewish; even his movements are angular and abrupt, in contrast to the characteristic curvy roundedness of Jewish gestures. The girls, on the other hand, seem as yet to remain physically closer to the European Jewish type. They are somewhat heavy in hip and bosom and mostly darker than the boys. On the whole, there can be little doubt that the race is undergoing some curious biological alteration, probably induced by the abrupt change in climate, diet and the mineral balance of the soil. It also seems that the female is slower in undergoing this transformation, more inert or stable in constitutional type. The whole phenomenon is a striking confirmation of the theory that environment has a greater formative influence than heredity, and that what we commonly regard as Jewish characteristics are not racial features, but a product of sustained social pressure and a specific way of life, a psycho-somatic response to what Toynbee calls " the stimulus of penalizations ".

In his mental make-up the average young *sabra* is fearless to the point of recklessness, bold, extroverted and little inclined towards, if not openly contemptuous of, intellectual pursuits. The children are particularly good-looking; after puberty, however, their features and voices coarsen and seem never quite to reach the balance of maturity. The typical *sabra*'s face has something unfinished about it ; the still undetermined character of a race in transition. His diction is abrupt and unmodulated, which sometimes gives the impression of rudeness. The relations between young people of different sexes are of a comradely, back-slapping kind ; romantic passion and erotic flirtation are both absent. They mature late, marry early, and start a family at once.

The *sabra*'s outlook on the world is rather provincial and hyperchauvinistic. This could hardly be otherwise in a small and exposed pioneer community which had to defend its physical existence and build its State against almost impossible odds. One cannot, it must be repeated, create a nation without nationalism ; and only young fanatics could perform the near-miraculous feat of defending isolated frontier settlements with small-arms and home-made explosives against tanks. Thirty years of an unsympathetic British Administration, the oscillations of American policy, the glaring impotence of the U.N. organization, have made words like Western Civilization and Humanistic Values sound rather like mockery in the young *sabra*'s ears.

This, of course, is a transitory phenomenon. In a decade or two, with Israel's position safely established in the Middle East, the cessation of outward pressure will no doubt produce a corresponding change in the mentality of the young generation. But a change in what direction ? What kind of a civilization will Israel's be ? Will it be a continuation of Western thought and art and values ? Or the superficial veneer of Levantinism ? Or will it go back to its ancient roots and develop out of them a modern but specifically Hebrew culture ?

For the time being the leaders of Israel seem determined to choose the third alternative. The whole educational system is based on it. The Old Testament is taught in the schools not as a religious subject, but as the main source of History, Literature, Ethics and Philosophy, to the marked neglect of other sources of human progress. In the average curriculum of secondary schools, the senior classes are given, as we saw, eleven hours per week of Bible and Hebrew classics, but only an hour and a half of history, half of which time is again devoted to Jewish history. Among the unavoidable teething troubles of Israel this egocentric tendency in education is probably the most dangerous.

No doubt this " cultural claustrophilia " is also merely a passing

phase. It will vanish with increasing security and self-assurance.
What kind of civilization will take its place one cannot foretell,
but one thing seems fairly certain : *within a generation or two
Israel will have become an entirely "un-Jewish" country.* Already
the native generation shows a marked difference in physical appearance and general outlook from Jews in Europe or America,
and with each generation this contrast is bound to increase. The
possible repercussion of this process on the future of the Jewish
communities outside Israel will be discussed in the Epilogue.

EPILOGUE

In the Proclamation of Independence of the new State, on May 14, there is a paragraph which says :

"Exiled from the Land of Israel, the Jewish people remained faithful to it in all the countries of their dispersion, never ceasing to pray and hope for their return and the restoration of their national freedom."

It is the kind of phrase which has been so often said before that one hardly realizes what momentous implications it carried on that specific occasion for the seven or eight million Jews outside Palestine. For it was the occasion on which their prayer had been fulfilled ; and the logical consequence of the fulfilment of a prayer is that one ceases to repeat it. But if prayers of this kind are no longer repeated, if the mystic yearning for the return to Palestine is eliminated from the Jewish faith, its very foundations and essence will have gone.

Towards the end of the Passover meal which commemorates the Exodus from Egypt, Jews all over the world lift their glasses and exclaim : " To next year in Jerusalem ". For nearly twenty centuries this was a moving ritual symbol. Now that no obstacles bar any longer the fulfilment of the wish, the alternative before the faithful is either to be next year in Jerusalem, or to cease repeating a vow which has become mere lip-service.

In fact, the greater part of the formulae and vocabulary of Jewish ritual has become meaningless since May 15, 1948. The Proclamation of Independence affirms that " the State of Israel will be open to Jews from all the countries of their dispersion ". In future, Jews can no longer refer to themselves with the ritual stock phrase of living in the Diaspora, or in Exile — unless they mean a self-imposed exile which has nothing to do with religion or tradition.

The existence of the Hebrew State — that is, a State whose language and culture are Hebrew, not Yiddish, Polish or American — puts every Jew outside Israel before a dilemma which will become increasingly acute. It is the choice between becoming a citizen of the Hebrew nation and renouncing any conscious or implicit claim to separate nationhood.

This dilemma is not derived from abstract speculation, nor from the claims of logical consistency ; it is imposed by hard historical circumstances. Anti-Semitism is once more on the increase. In his address to the Anglo-American Committee of Enquiry, the aged leader of Zionism, Dr. Weizmann, summed up a lifetime of experience :

" I am worried, but I don't see how I can stop it or what can be done. [Anti-Semitism] is a sort of disease that spreads apparently according to its own laws. I only hope that it will never reach the terrible dimensions which it reached in Europe. In fact, I somehow think that the Anglo-Saxon countries may be immune from it. But that is a hope, a pious wish — and when I look at Canada, South Africa, even Great Britain, even America, I sometimes lose my freedom from fear . . . I believe the only fundamental cause of anti-Semitism — it may seem tautological — is that the Jew exists. We seem to carry anti-Semitism in our knapsacks wherever we go. . . ."

It is the twenty-first instalment of a twenty-century-old story. To expect that it will come to a spontaneous end is to go against historical and psychological evidence. It can only be brought to an end by Jewry itself.

Before the prayer was fulfilled by the rebirth of Israel this was difficult if not impossible. To renounce being a Jew meant in most cases to deny solidarity with the persecuted, and seemed a cowardly capitulation. Apart from pride, there was the consciousness of an old heritage which one had no right to discard, of a mission uncompleted, a promise unfulfilled. Jewry could not vanish from the scene of history in an anti-climax.

Now the climax is reached, the circle closed. It is no longer a question of capitulation, but of a free choice. The proclamation of the Hebrew State is a signal to Jewry to pause on its long journey, review its situation with sincerity towards itself, and face facts which some time ago it was excusable and even honourable to shun.

The dilemma would not arise if being a Jew were merely a matter of religion like being a Protestant, or merely a matter of racial descent like being a French-Canadian. But both these comparisons are fallacious. The Jewish religion is not merely a system of faith and worship, but implies membership of a definite race and potential nation. The greater part of the sacred texts is national history. To be a good Catholic or Protestant it is enough to accept certain doctrines and moral values which transcend frontiers and nations ; to be a good Jew one must profess to belong to a chosen race, which was promised Canaan, suffered various exiles and will return one day to its true home. The " Englishman of Jewish faith " is a contradiction in terms. His faith compels him to regard himself as one with a different past and future from the Gentile. He sets himself apart and invites being set apart. His subjective conviction creates the objective fact that he is not an English Jew, but a Jew living in England.

Nor is the condition of the American Jew comparable to that of, say, the American of Irish descent. The latter's relation to the " old country " is a cultural tie to a recent past of one or two generations ago. The American Jew's " old country ", taken in the same sense, is not the Jewish State, but Poland or Lithuania. Whether his distant ancestors ever lived in Palestine, or rather how many of them did, and how many were Romans, Crusaders, Levantines, Slavs and Germans, is a moot point for the historian and anthropologist. All one can say is that with the exception of the " race-theorists " nearly all modern authorities hold that Jewish characteristics are a product of sustained environmental pressure, and not of racial heredity. An excellent summary of the evidence can be found in Toynbee's *Study of History* ; and a striking example in the native generation of Israel itself, which, as we saw, is rapidly changing in appearance and character in an entirely un-Jewish direction.

The conclusion is that since the foundation of the Hebrew State the attitude of Jews who are unwilling to go there, yet insist on remaining a community in some way apart from their fellow-citizens, has become an untenable anachronism. This attitude is as a rule defended by two types of argument. The first is some explicit or implied theory of a separate Jewish race — which, apart from being historically untenable, the Jews are the first to denounce when it is propounded by their enemies. The second is religious tradition, with all its implied nationalism and Chosen Race ideology. Like all acts of faith, this must be accepted or rejected *in toto*. The true orthodox believer must draw the consequences, now that the opportunity is offered to him, other- wise his creed will become lip-service. But orthodox Jewry is a vanishing minority. It is the well-meaning but confused majority which, through inertia, perpetuates the anachronism by clinging to a tradition in which it no longer really believes, to a mission which is fulfilled, a pride which may become inverted cowardice. Such honest sentimentalists should stop to think whether they have the right to place the burden of the ominous knapsack, now void of contents, on their children who have not asked for it.

To break the vicious circle of being persecuted for being " different ", and being " different " by force of persecution, they must arrive at a clear decision, however difficult this may be. They must either follow the imperative of their religion, the return to the Promised Land — or recognize that that faith is no longer theirs. To renounce the Jewish faith does not mean to jettison the perennial values of Judaic tradition. Its essential teachings have passed long ago into the main-stream of the Judeo-Christian heritage. If a Judaic religion is to survive outside Israel, without inflicting the stigma of separateness on its followers and laying them open to the charge of divided loyalty, it would have to be a system of faith and cosmopolitan ethics freed from all racial presumption and national exclusivity. But a Jewish religion thus reformed would be stripped of all its specifically Jewish content.

These conclusions, reached by one who has been a supporter of the Zionist Movement for a quarter-century, while his cultural allegiance belonged to Western Europe, are mainly addressed to the many others in a similar situation. They have done what they could to help to secure a haven for the homeless in the teeth of prejudice, violence and political treachery. Now that the State of Israel is firmly established, they are at last free to do what they could not do before : to wish it good luck and go their own way, with an occasional friendly glance back and a helpful gesture. But, nevertheless, to go their own way, with the nation whose life and culture they share, without reservations or split loyalties.

Now that the mission of the Wandering Jew is completed, he must discard the knapsack and cease to be an accomplice in his own destruction. If not for his own sake, then for that of his children and his children's children. The fumes of the death chambers still linger over Europe ; there must be an end to every calvary.

THE END

Lightning Source UK Ltd.
Milton Keynes UK
UKOW06f1935141217
314497UK00005B/384/P